Imagining Cleopatra

ARDEN STUDIES IN EARLY MODERN DRAMA

Series editors:
Lisa Hopkins, Sheffield Hallam University, UK
Douglas Bruster, University of Texas at Austin, USA

Published titles
Early Modern Theatre and the Figure of Disability
by Genevieve Love
ISBN 978-1-350-01720-7

Staging Britain's Past: Pre-Roman Britain in Early Modern Drama
by Kim Gilchrist
ISBN 978-1-3501-6334-8

Imagining Cleopatra

Performing Gender and Power in Early Modern England

Yasmin Arshad

THE ARDEN SHAKESPEARE
LONDON • NEW YORK • OXFORD • NEW DELHI • SYDNEY

THE ARDEN SHAKESPEARE
Bloomsbury Publishing Plc
50 Bedford Square, London, WC1B 3DP, UK
1385 Broadway, New York, NY 10018, USA
29 Earlsfort Terrace, Dublin 2, Ireland

BLOOMSBURY, THE ARDEN SHAKESPEARE and the Arden
Shakespeare logo are trademarks of Bloomsbury Publishing Plc

First published in Great Britain 2019
This paperback edition published 2021

Copyright © Yasmin Arshad, 2019, 2021

Yasmin Arshad has asserted her right under the Copyright, Designs and Patents Act, 1988, to be identified as the author of this work.

For legal purposes the Acknowledgements on pp. xi–xiii constitute an extension of this copyright page.

Series design by Irene Martinez Costa
Cover image: *The Death of Cleopatra* (oil on canvas) by Pierre Mignard
(© Private Collection/Bridgeman Images)

All rights reserved. No part of this publication may be reproduced or transmitted in any form or by any means, electronic or mechanical, including photocopying, recording, or any information storage or retrieval system, without prior permission in writing from the publishers.

Bloomsbury Publishing Plc does not have any control over, or responsibility for, any third-party websites referred to or in this book. All internet addresses given in this book were correct at the time of going to press. The author and publisher regret any inconvenience caused if addresses have changed or sites have ceased to exist, but can accept no responsibility for any such changes.

A catalogue record for this book is available from the British Library.

A catalog record for this book is available from the Library of Congress.

ISBN:	HB:	978-1-3500-5896-5
	PB:	978-1-350-24887-8
	ePDF:	978-1-3500-5898-9
	eBook:	978-1-3500-5897-2

Series: Arden Studies in Early Modern Drama

Typeset by Integra Software Services Pvt. Ltd.

To find out more about our authors and books visit www.bloomsbury.com and sign up for our newsletters.

For my parents
and
Arshi,
Farhan, Nabeel and Saara

CONTENTS

List of illustrations ix
Acknowledgements xi
Note on spelling and list of abbreviations xiv

Introduction 1

1 'Sight of that Face': Passion and politics in Mary Sidney's *Antonius* 35

2 'Twixt majestie confuz'd and miserie': Samuel Daniel's *Tragedie of Cleopatra* 69

3 'Will Yet this Womans Stubborne Heart be Woone?': Lady Anne Clifford and Daniel's *Cleopatra* 105

4 'Then thus we have beheld': Staging Daniel's *Cleopatra* 145

5 'She did make defect perfection': The paradox and variety of Shakespeare's Cleopatra 177

Epilogue and conclusion: Cleopatra after Shakespeare 213

Appendix: The *Cleopatra* statue and the poems at
   the Vatican 225

Notes 246
Select bibliography 293
Index 313

LIST OF ILLUSTRATIONS

Cover Image: *Death of Cleopatra* by Pierre Mignard (1612–95), Knole. It is not known when this painting came to Knole, but it was first recorded at the house in the 1799 inventory

1 *The Cleopatra*, flanked by the poems of Castiglione and Favoriti in the Galleria della Statue, Vatican Museums, Vatican City 9
2 Rosso Fiorentino, *The Death of Cleopatra* (c.1525) 10
3 *Sardonyx cameo: the suicide of Cleopatra* (late sixteenth century), Italy 14
4 Martial Ydeux, *The Death of Cleopatra* (c.1550–75), ceramic, Limoges, France 15
5 Bess of Hardwick, *Penelope flanked by Perseverance and Paciens* (c.1573), Hardwick Hall, Derbyshire 17
6 Michelangelo Buonarroti, *Cleopatra* (c.1535), Casa Buonarroti, Florence 19
7 Guido Reni, *Cleopatra with the Asp* (c.1628), Picture Gallery, Buckingham Palace 20
8 Hans Sebold Beham, *Cleopatra, Sitting*, engraving (c.1530–50), Germany 21
9 Gaspard Isaac, *Helen, Cleopatre, Lucrece*, caricature (c. sixteenth century) 22
10 'Lady Ralegh as Cleopatra', here identified as Lady Anne Clifford as Cleopatra, by an unknown artist 106
11 Detail of painting illustrated in Fig. 10 showing the inscription 108

LIST OF ILLUSTRATIONS

12 *Portrait of Lady Raleigh (née Elizabeth Throckmorton 1565–1647)*, artist unknown, 1603 117
13 *Sir Walter Ralegh*, attributed to 'H' monogrammist, 1588 118
14 Detail of painting illustrated in Fig. 10 showing miniature worn by the sitter 119
15 *Anne, Countess of Pembroke*. Engraving by Robert White, mid-to-late seventeenth century 125
16 *Richard Sackville, 3rd Earl of Dorset*, by William Larkin (1613) 126
17 Masque design, *Lady Anne Clifford as Berenice, Queen of Egypt*, by Inigo Jones, 1609 128
18 Charlotte Gallagher as Daniel's Cleopatra, recreating the pose in the Cleopatra portrait 147

ACKNOWLEDGEMENTS

This book has been many years in the making, across two continents and over numerous plane journeys. I began this project at University College London under the supervision of Helen Hackett. Without her unstinting encouragement and support this book would not be possible. Her wisdom and guidance infuse this work. I was also fortunate to have had Henry Woudhuysen, Chris Laoutaris and Chris Stamatakis as my advisors. They have each helped shape my research and challenged me to think deeply and in different ways. It has been a privilege to work under such distinguished mentors, and I am especially grateful for their generous ongoing support and friendship.

The examiners of my thesis, Bridget Escolme and René Weis, were kind and generous in their advice and notes. I am deeply appreciative of Bridget Escolme's help with this publication, and René Weis' continued guidance.

During this process, I got to know a wonderful community of scholars. Many of them generously supported my work. I owe a special debt of gratitude to John Pitcher for his guidance, and for co-organizing a conference on Samuel Daniel in 2015. Duane Roller graciously agreed to be interviewed at his home in Santa Fe. Jaime Goodrich, Jason Lawrence and Selene Scarsi generously translated the Vatican Cleopatra poems in the Appendix. Particular thanks are also due to: Edward Chaney, Alison Findlay, Margaret Hannay, Karen Hearn, Farah Karim-Cooper, Paulina Kewes, Eleanor Lowe, Alexander Samson, Robin Simon, Crosby Stevens, Jenny Tiramani, Marion Wynne-Davies and Martin Wiggins. In addition, Robert Harding at Maggs Bros. kindly sent information about a destroyed dedication to Lady Anne Clifford and an image of Cleopatra used in the book.

The Staging Daniel's *Cleopatra* project would not have been possible without the support of colleagues, students and friends. I would like to thank the cast and crew who made this project such a memorable experience, especially Emma Whipday who came on board to direct the play. I owe many thanks to Stephen Cadywold of the UCL English Department for handling the financial side of things, and to Anita Garfoot for her help. Philip Bird provided perceptive feedback on the production. Beth Eyre, Charlotte Gallagher, Elspeth North, Emily Stiff and Mike Waters happily agreed to be interviewed about their experience performing in the play, and Sam Brown about the music. Many friendships have grown out of this project. We will always miss Emily and her loveliness.

I am grateful to Michael Dobson, Martin Wiggins, Chris Laoutaris and the Shakespeare Institute Players, for inviting us to present 'The Staging of Daniel's *Cleopatra*' at the Shakespeare Institute in Stratford-upon-Avon. I am also grateful to Lord Robert Sackville, the Sackville-West family and the National Trust at Knole in Kent for making possible the event, 'Lady Anne Clifford and Cleopatra at Knole: Talk and Performance'.

The librarians and archivists at the Bodleian Library, British Library, Cambridge University, Christie's Archive, the Heinz Archive and Library of the National Portrait Gallery, the National Trust, the Newberry Library, Tate Library and Archive, Senate House Library, UCL Library and the Warburg Institute helped me locate material and images. Marijke Booth at Christie's showed me how to read their records.

It has been a pleasure to work with the team at Arden Shakespeare. I would like to thank Margaret Bartley for believing in this project, and Mark Dudgeon and Lara Bateman for their gracious guidance. Tanya Pollard and Lisa Hopkins, the series editors, provided valuable insight. On the production side, warm thanks are due to Ian Buck, to Cheryl Merritt and Rebecca Willford at Integra, and copy-editor Jennifer Darby, for their careful and excellent help.

My family and friends have been my strength and sustenance throughout this process. Although my parents are not here today, their love and support are the foundation of everything I am. My mother, Nuzhat, who saw me embark on this journey, and my father, Saeed, instilled in me an early love of literature and learning. Their wisdom and courage are always with me. My sister and brothers and their families, Zainab and Kaleem, Kamran and Regina, and Rehan and Asma looked after my every need in London. I owe them much.

May Maxwood, Hatice Husnu, Anita Patel and Jagruti Oza were there for me in more ways than I can say. Ashley Mansour, Yi Ling Huang, Hardeep Kaur, Georgina Cammalleri, Liz O'Dwyer and Rathika Muthukumaran were treasured cheerleaders. My friends in New Mexico spurred me on at every stage. Josephine Billingham has been a wonderful fellow traveller.

My biggest thanks are to my three men, Arshi, Farhan and Nabeel, and a dear daughter, Saara, gained along the way. Their love, sacrifice, encouragement and laughter made this an exciting and enduring journey. My husband Arshi took care of everyone and everything with joy. He patiently read my chapter drafts with insight and inspiration.

Some parts of Chapters 3 and 4 were published as 'The Enigma of a Portrait: Lady Anne Clifford and Daniel's *Cleopatra*', in *The British Art Journal* 11, no. 3 (2011), 30–6. Some parts of Chapters 3 and 4 were also published as 'Daniel's Cleopatra and Lady Anne Clifford: From a Jacobean Portrait to Modern Performance', *Early Theatre* 18, no. 2 (2015), 167–86, with Helen Hackett and Emma Whipday. I am very grateful to the editors for the kind permission to reproduce these. It is difficult to put into words the incredible gratitude I owe Chris Laoutaris for generously reading some chapters in this book, for his thoughtful comments and guidance, and for the Renaissance adventures.

So many people helped me in this endeavour, any deficiencies in this book are my own.

NOTE ON SPELLING AND LIST OF ABBREVIATIONS

In quotations and early modern titles, the use of i/j, u/v and the long *s* (ʃ) has been brought into line with modern practice. I have otherwise retained original spellings. References to classical texts are mainly to editions in the Loeb Classical Library. All citations from Shakespeare are from Arden 3 editions or the most recent Arden edition, unless otherwise stated.

The following abbreviations are used for frequently cited primary and secondary sources:

Bullough	Geoffrey Bullough, ed., *Narrative and Dramatic Sources of Shakespeare*, *Vol. V* (London: Routledge and Kegan Paul, 1964)
Escolme	Bridget Escolme, *Antony and Cleopatra*, Shakespeare Handbooks (Basingstoke: Palgrave Macmillan, 2006)
Garnier	Robert Garnier, *Two Tragedies: Hippolyte and Marc Antoine,* ed. Christine M. Hill and Mary G. Morrison (London: Athlone Press, 1975)
Greville	*The Prose Works of Sir Fulke Greville, Lord Brooke*, ed. John Gouws (Oxford: Clarendon, 1986)
Hackett	Helen Hackett, *Virgin Mother, Maiden Queen: Elizabeth I and the Cult of the Virgin Mary* (Basingstoke: Macmillan, 1996)

Hannay	Margaret P. Hannay, *Philip's Phoenix: Mary Sidney, Countess of Pembroke* (Oxford: OUP, 1990)
Jondorf	Gillian Jondorf, *Robert Garnier and the Themes of Political Tragedy in the Sixteenth Century* (Cambridge: CUP, 1969)
New Critical Essays	*Antony and Cleopatra: New Critical Essays*, ed. Sara Munson Deats (New York: Routledge, 2005)
Norbrook	David Norbrook, *Poetry and Politics in the English Renaissance*, revised edition 2002 (1984; rpt., Oxford: OUP, 2009)
Pettegree	Jane Pettegree, *Foreign and Native on the English Stage, 1588–1611: Metaphor and National Identity* (Basingstoke: Palgrave, 2011)
Plutarch	Plutarch, *Lives of the Noble Grecians and Romans*, trans. Sir Thomas North in *Narrative and Dramatic Sources of Shakespeare: Vol. V*, ed. Geoffrey Bullough (London: Routledge and Kegan Paul, 1964)
Spence	Richard T. Spence, *Lady Anne Clifford: Countess of Pembroke, Dorset and Montgomery (1590–1676)* (Stroud: Sutton, 1997)
Worden	Blair Worden, *The Sound of Virtue: Philip Sidney's 'Arcadia' and Elizabethan Politics* (New Haven: Yale University Press, 1996)
Works	*The Collected Works of Mary Sidney Herbert, Countess of Pembroke, 2 vols.*, ed. Margaret P. Hannay, Noel J. Kinnamon and Michael G. Brennan (Oxford: Clarendon, 1998), here *Vol. 1: Poems, Translations, and Correspondence*

Other abbreviations

CSP	Calendar of State Papers
CUP	Cambridge University Press
EEBO	*Early English Books Online*
ELR	*English Literary Renaissance*
HLQ	*Huntington Library Quarterly*
MaRDiE	*Medieval and Renaissance Drama in England*
N&Q	*Notes and Queries*
OED	*Oxford English Dictionary* online: http://www.oed.com
ODNB	*Oxford Dictionary of National Biography*, OUP, 2004; online edn. Sept. 2014: http://www.oxforddnb.com
OUP	Oxford University Press
PRO	Public Records Office
RES	*Review of English Studies*
SPO	State Papers Online: http://go.galegroup.com.libproxy.ucl.ac.uk/mss/start.do?p=SPOL&u=ucl_ttda&authCount=1

Editions of Shakespeare

Bevington	*Antony and Cleopatra*, ed. David Bevington (1990; rpt., Cambridge: CUP, 2007)
Case	*Antony and Cleopatra*, ed. M. R. Ridley based on the 1906 Arden Shakespeare edition

	of R. H. Case (Cambridge, MA: Harvard University Press, 1954)
Neill	*Antony and Cleopatra*, ed. Michael Neill (1994; rpt., Oxford: OUP, 2008)
Spevack	*Antony and Cleopatra, A New Variorum Edition*, ed. Marvin Spevack (New York: MLA, 1990)
Weis	*Antony and Cleopatra*, ed. Emrys Jones, intro. René Weis (London: Penguin, 2005)
Wilders	*Antony and Cleopatra*, ed. John Wilders (London: Arden Shakespeare, 2006)

For, some the world must have, on whom to lay
The heavie burthen of reproche and blame;
Against whose deedes, th'afflicted may invay,
As th'onely Authors, whence destruction came:
When yet, perhaps, 'twas not in them to stay
The current of that streame, nor help the same;
But, living in the eye of Action so,
Not hindring it, are thought to draw-on wo.

So much unhappie do the Mightie stand ...
That if by weakenesse, folly, negligence,
They do not coming miserie withstand,
They shall be deemed th'authors of th'offence,
And to call in, that which they kept not out;
And curst, as they who brought those plagues about.

And so remaine for ever rigistred
In that eternall booke of Infamie;
When yet how many other causes led
As well to that, as their iniquitie?
                    (Samuel Daniel, *Civil Wars*, 1609, V.65–7)

Introduction

> Besides her beawtie, the good grace she had to talke and discourse, her curteous nature that tempered her words and dedes, was a spurre that pricked to the quick.
>
> (Plutarch, 275)

Cleopatra VII (69–30 BC), Queen of Egypt, is one of the most renowned and enduring figures from classical antiquity, yet remains one of its most elusive. Her story moved into poetry immediately after her death, becoming primarily the domain of the artist rather than remaining that of the historian.[1] The narrative of Octavius's victory over Cleopatra, of a feminized Eastern otherness and of the Augustan age as being propitious in ushering in the Christian era, became part of a founding myth of Western culture.[2] The image that dominates popular culture now derives mainly from Shakespeare and is that of the sultry siren of the East lounging on a burnished golden barge. His subtly complex description of Cleopatra's 'infinite variety' has become a phrase so well known, and emptied of meaning, that it was even used to describe the marketing war between the two soft-drinks giants, Coca-Cola and Pepsi. *The Economist* wrote of Coke: 'She is the world's best-known brand, a venerable star beginning to fret that age might be withering, and custom staling, her infinite variety.'[3] Although it is Shakespeare's Cleopatra who permeates our consciousness today, this is often in a very simplified and debased form, lacking in the nuance with which this most controversial of history's queens was invested since she captured the literary Renaissance imagination. There is a need to look back beyond Shakespeare's Cleopatra to understand the sources and cultural contexts that produced her. In doing so, we discover that there was already a strong interest in the Egyptian queen and her story in the sixteenth century, well before Shakespeare wrote his play, and views towards her were deeply conflicted and multi-faceted. We also find that Shakespeare's creation does not stand alone – as is all too often thought in the history of Cleopatra representations. It is, in fact, part of a continuum, a cornucopia, of Cleopatras which turn Shakespeare's version into a work that is part of a dialogue, rather than an isolated monolith.

Early modern conceptions of Cleopatra offer a rich, complex and variable set of models for understanding the period's responses to race, female sovereignty and classical antiquity. They are also pertinent in understanding our own responses today. Cleopatra is still used as a powerful emblematic figure in the divisive politics of our time. In the conflicted response to female leadership in the 2016 US Presidential election, she appeared in a *Tatler* article as an example of strong female leaders Hillary Clinton should emulate. Later, a *Washington Post* cartoonist depicted President Trump as Shakespeare's Cleopatra, so hyper-decadent, so gluttonous that even the asp slithers away repulsed.[4] This book provides a new literary and cultural history of one of the world's most contested and politically charged iconic female figures. It investigates images of Cleopatra in the early modern period and examines how her story was mediated and used in different circumstances – from drawing lessons found in classical history to being a model of female heroism. It combines a close reading of literary and dramatic works with historical and political contexts, and asks: why did Cleopatra matter to those who wrote about her? What were the topical resonances and implications of writing about the Egyptian queen in the period? It analyses the innovative elite neo-Senecan closet dramas of Mary Sidney Herbert, the Countess of Pembroke, and of Samuel Daniel, which preceded Shakespeare, and explores how their Cleopatras inflected Shakespeare's – the first dramatization of the story in non-elite circles in England. Ranging between differing media, this interdisciplinary investigation draws on early historiographical works, political and philosophical treatises, coterie dramatic productions, and gender, race and performance studies, as well as evidence from material culture, to consider what was known and thought about Cleopatra.

The study breaks new ground by looking at how material artefacts intersect with the history of Cleopatra and considers how performance is a potent adjunct of that material culture. It investigates a remarkable and mysterious portrait of a young Jacobean woman, depicted as Cleopatra holding the asp in the dramatic moment of her suicide. I identify its inscription as coming from Daniel's *Tragedie of Cleopatra*, and its sitter as plausibly being Lady Anne Clifford. The painting highlights the intersections between portraiture, performance and politics in the period. The choice of lines from the play used in the painting speak to ideas of resistance and the politicization of gender, and may tell us something about the female response to the Egyptian queen in the period.

The portrait is the only known survival from the period based on a scene from a contemporary play, and the only known visual image of a seventeenth-century costumed imagining of Cleopatra. It inspired a University College London (UCL) performance-based project of staging Daniel's *Cleopatra* in 2013. The production, testing the performability of Daniel's closet drama, was the first known staging of the play in at least 400 years. Insights gained from the staging help to gauge the infinite variety of Cleopatras that emerged from centuries of myth-making about the Egyptian queen. The performance experiment also helps situate the widely varying versions of Cleopatras within a process that both includes and decentres Shakespeare, while at the same time adding richness to his portrayal by revealing the literary and cultural influences which underpinned it and with which it entered into dialogue. It underscores how Daniel might have influenced Shakespeare and facilitated the move from coterie narrative to the public stage. The book devotes three chapters to Daniel, highlighting the wide currency of his play in the period, the significance of the portrait, and the performance-project.

The Introduction begins by providing a context for views about Cleopatra, by looking at Greco-Roman and medieval sources and examining shifts in attitudes towards more positive constructions in the sixteenth century. It then gives a more detailed description of the book's methodology, structure and purpose.

Rome's enemy: Contexts and early reception

Cleopatra VII committed suicide on 10 August 30 BC, ten days after Antony, and almost a year after the naval catastrophe at Actium. According to the Greek historian Plutarch, she was thirty-eight years old at her death; of these, she had reigned as queen for twenty-two years and been Mark Antony's partner for fourteen.[5]

In his biography of Cleopatra, Duane W. Roller points out that she was the only woman in all of classical antiquity to rule independently (not succeeding through a dead husband), and she tried to save her kingdom from an ever-encroaching Roman war machine.[6] Much has been written about her life, her suicide and her relationships with two of Rome's most powerful generals, Julius Caesar and Mark Antony, in the two millennia since her death. In the twinned ancient discourses of race and gender, Maria Wyke notes in her study that she was 'doubly marked as the other – both Egyptian and Woman – and, therefore, doubly deserving of defeat'.[7] In her self-representation, she portrayed herself as goddess, and as actual, royal and divine mother; in Rome's representation, she was a drunken disgrace to her dynasty, and a sexual predator who enticed Antony away from his duty. Her purported ambition was to rule Rome. Stories abounded about her wealth and extravagance – both coveted and condemned as Eastern decadence. As part of Octavius's agitation for war, and since Antony still had powerful connections in Rome, the campaign of vicious rhetoric concentrated on the Egyptian queen rather than on his co-triumvir.[8]

Augustan poetry written soon after Actium and Cleopatra's death employed many of the same motifs and rhetoric used against her in the build-up to the battle.[9] For Horace, Antony is 'a Roman soldier, / bought and sold' who 'beares stakes and arms for a woman', but Cleopatra is a *fatale monstrum*, a deadly monster, a drunken destructive threat to Rome, successfully vanquished.[10] Although Horace acknowledges the boldness of her death, to avoid being humiliated in a triumph, her elimination is naturally celebrated in the language of the victor. In his elegy, Propertius places Cleopatra in a catalogue of dominating women from myth and history, such as Semiramis and Omphale. Attacking her enslavement of Antony and her desire to rule Rome, Propertius refers to her as the *meretrix regina*, the whore queen (3.11.39). For Virgil, in *The Aeneid*, she is nothing more than the 'Egyptian mate' (8.688), unworthy of even her name and title.[11] This narrative strategy was nurtured in the later histories, especially in Dio Cassius and Lucan, who positioned her as a malicious schemer and a painted and bejewelled temptress. This strategy and the categorization of Cleopatra with supposed unruly women became the markers and signifiers of the negative tradition against her, which continued into the early modern period and beyond. In *Women and Power*, Mary Beard details the ways the classical world employed to cast women as illegitimate users and abusers of power.[12] Many of the same ways, I would argue, were used to demonize Cleopatra, including her depiction as a monstrous hybrid.

Although writing late in the first century AD, Plutarch provided a detailed and more balanced account of Cleopatra in his 'Life of Marcus Antonius' that was distinctively different from the Augustan attitude, imbuing her with a vivid personality. He used contemporary and close personal sources, including his great-grandfather who was in Athens when Alexandria fell; a family friend, Philotas, an acquaintance of Antony's palace staff; Quintus Dellius, a confidant of Antony's and Cleopatra's; and Olympos, Cleopatra's personal physician.[13] Plutarch's method of comparing the virtues and vices of his subjects – with his ability to wonder at the lovers, even as his rational tone condemned them – provided complexity and paradox to the Cleopatra story. However, although Plutarch could marvel at Cleopatra, his view as discussed in this book, of seeing her as 'the last and extreamest mischiefe' for Antony, was in the end essentially Roman.[14]

What the persuasive Augustan discourse of race and gender sought to erase was that Cleopatra VII, a Ptolemy, and the descendant of a companion of Alexander the Great, was the living representative of two of the longest surviving Greek dynasties. To the ancient world, her Greek lineage afforded her a much higher status than that of the Romans. A contemporary Sibylline Oracle, most likely about her and from the 30s BC, foresees an age of harmony in which the arrogance and aggression of Rome are contained by a woman. It suggests that in her own time she was viewed by some in the Greek world as a figure of resistance.[15] Al-Masudi, the tenth-century Arab historian, describes her as scholar and architect and 'the last of the wise ones of Greece'.[16] Although a symbol of the feminized East, she was referred to in the Egyptian records in the masculine, perhaps in recognition of the quality of her rule.[17]

Rome and her successors promoted the view of their righteous defeat of a decadent queen. In the Middle Ages, Cleopatra became a medieval exemplum. Dante, in the *Inferno*, placed Cleopatra in the second circle of hell with the lustful, where she could be seen swirling with Dido, Semiramis and Helen of Troy.[18] Boccaccio, writing in the fourteenth century, castigated her in Augustan terms: 'Cleopatra was an Egyptian woman who became an object of gossip for the whole world ... She came to her rule through crime. She gained glory for almost nothing else than her beauty, while on the other hand she became known throughout the world for her greed, cruelty, and lustfulness.'[19] There was, however, also an alternative version which developed in the medieval era, with Cleopatra's story becoming one of courtly love as in Jehan de Tuim's *Li hystoire de Julius Cesar* (*c.* 1240), and in the fourteenth-century *I Fatti de Cesare*.[20]

In *The Legend of Good Women*, written some thirty years after Boccaccio, Chaucer placed Cleopatra as first among the good women in his collection.[21] She is Antony's wife and 'Was nevere unto hire love a trewer quene' (l. 694) for dying after her 'knyght' (l. 684). Chaucer's Cleopatra is 'fayr as is the rose in May' (l. 613). Although 'Fayr' is, of course, an ambiguous term, meaning beautiful or fair-skinned, and a rose could be dark or light-coloured, Chaucer seems to be describing Cleopatra very much like a conventional pale-skinned courtly love heroine. A sense of ambivalence, however, complicates his representation of the Egyptian queen. In the opening section to the *Legend*, Chaucer presents himself as commanded to write the work by Queen Alceste, as penance for his representation of women's inconstancy in *Troilus and Criseyde*.[22] That he is perhaps writing his praises of women reluctantly is suggested by the way Chaucer rushes over many of the stories, with Cleopatra's being the shortest of the accounts. In this context, his praise of Cleopatra could be read as ironic. Although she is portrayed as blameless for Antony leaving his wife and for the events at Actium, Chaucer also plays up Cleopatra's exoticism and sensuality by having her strip and jump naked into a pit of serpents (l. 697).

Sixteenth-century emerging Cleopatras: From statue to the literary and decorative arts

In her study of the Antony and Cleopatra tradition, Marilyn Williamson notes that during the Middle Ages, the Greek sources, such as Plutarch and Dio, dropped out of sight, while the Latin ones dominated.[23] The sixteenth century, however, was a watershed period in shifting attitudes away from the misogyny and ethnic suspicion prevalent in past representations towards an emerging sympathy for Cleopatra. By the end of the century, Cleopatra had captured the European literary and artistic imagination in an unprecedented way, as a figure noteworthy for her courage and nobility in death. Two major factors contributed to this shift: the first was the discovery in 1512 in Rome of a beautiful ancient statue believed to be of Cleopatra, reclining in a near-death pose, with the asp entwined around her upper arm (Figure 1).[24] The second was the rediscovery and translation of Plutarch into vernacular languages, including into the French by Jacques Amyot in 1559, and into English by Sir Thomas North in 1579.

The *Cleopatra* statue (identified as Cleopatra because of a snake armlet entwined around its left arm, thought to be the asp, and now known as Ariadne sleeping) was first installed in the Vatican's Belvedere courtyard in 1513, by Pope Julius II, and placed in a privileged position next to the *Laocoon*. Later, in the 1550s, it was moved to an elaborately decorated room called the 'Stanza della Cleopatra'. Renaissance scholars, writers and artists were greatly intrigued by the statue, and some believed it was the actual replica of Cleopatra carried in Augustus's triumph in the autumn of 29 BC, 'staging the moment of her death'.[25] Plutarch alluded to such a replica, saying of Augustus: 'in his triumphe he carried Cleopatraes image, with an Aspicke byting of her arme'.[26] Propertius stated that 'I saw her arms bitten by the sacred snakes and her body drawing in the hidden poison that brought oblivion' (3.11.52–6). Dio described the triumphal celebrations:

> the Egyptian celebration surpassed them all in costliness and magnificence. Among other features, an effigy of the dead Cleopatra upon a couch was carried by, so that in a way she, too, together with the other captives and with her children, Alexander, also called Helios, and Cleopatra, called also Selene, was a part of the spectacle and a trophy in the procession. (*Roman History* 51.21)

Cleopatra, in spite of her death, featured as a trophy in Augustus's triumph.

The statue had an immediate influence on the literary and visual sphere, inspiring many paintings and engravings. It became the accepted model in Europe for portraying the Egyptian queen's suicide, often showing her death erotically.[27] It also inspired many poems in the sixteenth and seventeenth centuries, including ones by Baldassare Castiglione (1478–1539), Bernadino Baldi (1553–1617) and Agonisto Favoriti (1642–82).[28] These were so admired that they were inscribed on pilasters framing it.[29] Castiglione's poem, composed during the papacy of Leo X (1513–21), is noteworthy for highlighting the horror and pity of Cleopatra's situation, and for its influence on the later poems. Cleopatra is given a voice through her statue, in the rhetorical device of *prosopopeia*. Speaking of her sorrows, she begs for tears to mourn Antony, saying 'I lived without crime if / You

FIGURE 1 The Cleopatra, *flanked by the poems of Castiglione and Favoriti in the Galleria della Statue, Vatican Museums, Vatican City. Iconographic Database of the Warburg Institute.*

think it a crime to love' (ll. 49–50). I believe the poem, which was printed and widely circulated from 1530, represents a defining shift from the narrative deployed by the Augustan poets. Writing about the poem, Brian Curran notes the influence of Plutarch's characterization of Cleopatra's grief after Antony's death.[30]

The pose of the Vatican *Cleopatra*, with the raised arm and the snake entwined around the upper arm, is strikingly responded to in the panel in Figure 2.

FIGURE 2 *Rosso Fiorentino*, The Death of Cleopatra *(c.1525). Courtesy of Herzog Anton Ulrich-Museum, Braunschweig, Germany.*

In the painting, Cleopatra's pallor and her closed eyes signify the sleep of death, while her maid-servant, shown standing to the left, heightens the dramatic potency of the image. The maid-servant's healthy skin tones and the rich dark colours of the draped fabrics and furnishings contrast with Cleopatra's paleness, accentuating the Egyptian queen's fair skin. The statue inspired many other paintings from as early as 1515, often reflecting Cleopatra's sorrow and anguish.[31]

Although scholars have noted the sympathetic interest inspired in European paintings by the discovery of the statue, the Vatican poems remain relatively unknown. Mary Morrison sees the influence of the statue on the increased production of Cleopatra paintings in the middle of the sixteenth century as inspiring the publication of nine tragedies in the latter part – three each in Italy, France and England.[32] It is highly likely that the poems would have also been a significant influence on the Italian plays, and on those who had access to Italian sources. The Italian works were the first to be produced and include Giambattista Giraldi Cinthio's *Cleopatra tragedia* (written 1541, performed for the court of Ercole II d'Este in 1555; published 1583), Cesare de' Cesari's *Cleopatra* (Venice, 1552) and Celso Pistorelli, *Marc' Antonio e Cleopatra* (Verona, 1576). In addition to these plays, an important biography, *La Vita di Cleopatra Reina d'Egitto* (1551), was written by Count Giulio Landi. In France, Etienne Jodelle's *Cléopâtre Captive* (staged before King Henri II in 1552/3, published 1574) was enormously influential as the first tragedy in French. It was followed by Robert Garnier's prequel *Marc Antoine* (Paris, 1578), and Nicolas de Montreux's *Cleopatre* (performed 1594; published 1595). In England, Mary Sidney completed *Antonius* (1590; published 1592), a translation from the French of Robert Garnier, and commissioned a play by Samuel Daniel, *The Tragedie of Cleopatra* (1594). A lost play should be added to the aforementioned list: Fulke Greville's *Antony and Cleopatra*, which Greville destroyed as discussed later. Samuel Brandon's *The Tragicomoedi of the vertuous Octavia* (1598), which presented the story from Octavia's point of view, was also written on the theme.[33] Apart from these tragedies, Daniel's verse epistle, *Letter from Octavia to Marcus Antonius* (1599), imagined what Octavia might have said to Antony, giving her a voice.[34] Greville's unpublished *Letter to an Honorouble Lady* also belongs to this period and alludes to Octavia.[35]

The above-mentioned Cleopatra tragedies, written in the neo-Senecan style and for elite circles, focus on the final part in Plutarch. This gives a moving account of Cleopatra's death after Antony and the fate of her dynasty, allowing her to be seen as a figure of tragic heroism. Landi's *Vita*, though following Plutarch, shows more sympathy and emotion than Plutarch for the Egyptian queen's situation, and was an influence on Cesari.[36] The Vatican *Cleopatra* presents an important example of the intersections and confluences between archaeology, history, literature and art. Morrison observes that, while following Plutarch closely, when Cesari describes the dead Cleopatra, lying 'nobly and beautifully on her bed with the snake wrapped around her arm', he is 'using another historical authority – that of archaeology'. He is describing the statue in the Belvedere.[37] The influence and interconnectivity can be seen to go further: Cesari is regarded as a source for Jodelle,[38] who in turn was a source for Garnier, who was translated into English by Mary Sidney. Cleopatra's grief after Antony's death is an important focus of Mary Sidney's *Antonius*, and her sorrow and her nobility in death of Daniel's *Cleopatra*. It can be argued, therefore, that there is a kind of genealogy at work here, and that the history of representations of Cleopatra is partly one in which there are clear lines of succession.

The late sixteenth to early seventeenth centuries were a time of shifting perspectives: humanism and the revival of classical philosophy, and interest in the *ars moriendi* tradition (the art of dying well) shifted views on death and suicide. Seneca, whose philosophical writings pervaded Renaissance commonplace books and influenced thinkers like Montaigne, stated that 'fortune is powerless over one who knows how to die'.[39] Under Stoicism, death liberated the soul and suicide was an honourable practice, when committed with calm and composure. Bridget

Escolme points out that although Antony's suicide could hardly be viewed in these terms, Cleopatra's forethought and courage in death could be seen as stoic virtue and constancy.[40] A different reading of Antony's and Cleopatra's suicides was also made possible with the publication of Montaigne's *Essais* in French beginning in 1580. Although John Florio's translation did not appear in English until 1603, many educated people would have been able to read them in the original. Even though religious law forbade suicide, Montaigne saw it as a possibly glorious act in cognitive, metaphysical terms.[41] While he viewed Antony as an example of 'great public figures ... whose lust made them forget the conduct of affairs of state',[42] he also asks: 'Might we not even make death luxurious like Antony and Cleopatra, those fellows in death? I leave aside as harsh the efforts devised by philosophy, and as ideal those devised by religion.'[43] This view allowed sympathy and admiration for the lovers' suicide, while condemning their privileging of private passion over public duty. This inherent duality, or opposition, in the Antony and Cleopatra story, and the resulting threat of civil tumult caused by a monarch's neglect of duty, underpins the dramas of Mary Sidney and Daniel, allowing for the use of topical political commentary.

Translations into English of the complete works of Tacitus in the 1590s, with its negative accounts of the Roman emperors and court corruption, shifted perspectives about Rome and Octavius.[44] René Weis persuasively questions whether the Augustan view of Octavius's victory, and the view that the resulting *Pax Romana* created the conditions necessary for the birth of Christ, would have held sway with writers and thinkers in Protestant Elizabethan England. Weis notes that the idea of Rome's world domination prophesied in *The Aeneid* was adopted in the ensuing Christian centuries by Catholic Rome, whose seat was St Peter's Basilica in Rome. It therefore seems likely that perspectives on an idealized classical Rome would also have shifted, especially among those who did not acknowledge papal supremacy.[45]

Just as a sympathetic interest in Cleopatra emerged in literature and painting, it also developed in other areas, such as in sculpture, decorative objects, tapestry, jewellery and in historical exposition in the period. These reflected the increased interest in the Egyptian queen's story and moved her away from medieval exemplum. A late sixteenth-century cameo (Figure 3, for example), designed for a jewelled pendant,

FIGURE 3 Sardonyx cameo: the suicide of Cleopatra *(late sixteenth century), Italy.* © *The Trustees of the British Museum.*

presents 'Cleopatra as both ancient heroine and fashionable contemporary woman'. Dressed in a filmy draped material, designed to reveal her breasts, she is shown with a snake around her arm biting her breast. Her hair is finely arranged in an *all'antica* style (in the manner of the ancients), and she is wearing contemporary pearl drop earrings.[46]

The death of Cleopatra can also be seen depicted in decorative bowls, as in the Limoges piece (Figure 4), which shows a blonde fair-skinned Cleopatra committing suicide as her maid looks on in horror. The piece is striking for the theatrical composition of the scene. Both the cameo and the

FIGURE 4 *Martial Ydeux*, The Death of Cleopatra *(c.1550–75), ceramic, Limoges, France. Courtesy of the Wallace Collection, London.*

bowl, as we also see in Chapter 3, form part of a narrative which link the English and continental tradition surrounding representations of Cleopatra.

In addition to these images, the appearance of Antony and Cleopatra in a wide breadth of objects and different media in art is also underlined by a sixteenth-century Italian marble wall plaque, now at the National Gallery of Victoria, Melbourne, Australia. Created as a decorative panel for a private home, it treats Antony and Cleopatra as significant figures, grouping them with reliefs of eight classical heroes and heroines from antiquity.[47]

The story of Antony and Cleopatra, illustrated in tapestries in the medieval and post-medieval era in Europe, often focused on Cleopatra's banquet for Antony when she first received him. However, a fascinating collection of five original large appliquéd tapestries was hung at Hardwick Hall (built in the 1590s) by Elizabeth, Dowager Countess of Shrewsbury (Bess of Hardwick), portraying an alternative perspective of Cleopatra.[48] The collection, showing the noble women of the ancient world, is recorded in the inventory of 1601 as 'pictures of the virtues' dating from *c.*1573. Four of the five listed panels survive, but, unfortunately, the one of Cleopatra has been lost. The surviving panels depict the central commanding female, flanked on either side by two smaller figures of the virtues which personify her. These are: Penelope with Perseverance and Patience; Zenobia with Magnanimity and Prudence; Artemisia with Constancy and Pietas; Cleopatra with Fortitude and Justice; Lucretia with Chastity and Liberality.[49] The tapestries were originally produced at Chatsworth (possibly for the State Apartments), and after Bess's move decorated the Withdrawing Chamber at Hardwick Hall. They were produced at a time when Mary Queen of Scots, known for her needlework and whose household included tapissiers (and who as discussed in this book was also associated with Cleopatra in anti-Catholic polemics), stayed at Chatsworth in the 1570s. In her project of improving Chatsworth, Susan Frye notes that Bess of Hardwick created 'the most ambitious known artwork produced by an English woman in the early modern period'.[50] The wall-hanging for Penelope (Figure 5) gives some indication of what the hanging for Cleopatra might have looked like.

The Cleopatra tapestry effectively links the culture of the English Renaissance. Although the inclusion of Cleopatra among these noble women may be seen as problematic,[51] the wall-hanging fits within the shifting categorization of the Egyptian queen taking shape in written works of the period. Cleopatra, as I discuss below, was contemporaneously appearing in some instances in catalogues of women known as good wives, such as Penelope, Artemesia and Lucrece, and great queens such as Zenobia. The Hardwick Hall embroideries of the noble women of the ancient world show that she was also being seen as such by women in the period. Fortitude and Justice were appropriate virtues for emerging Cleopatras.

FIGURE 5 *Bess of Hardwick*, Penelope flanked by Perseverance and Paciens *(c.1573), Hardwick Hall.* © *National Trust Images/Brenda Norrish.*

From history to myth-making

The conflicted responses towards Cleopatra meant that she was imagined in widely varying versions in sixteenth-century sources in England. She appears not only in catalogues of women from myth and history who were known for their wanton wickedness, such as Helen of Troy and Delilah, but also alongside women who have immortal praise, such as Penelope and Lucrece. She is seen as not inferior to Portia and Artemesia in following her husband in death.[52] She is mentioned in a catalogue of great queens who created cities and buildings, such as Artemesia and Zenobia, but she is also grouped with Semiramis for satisfying her lust and pleasure.[53] She is an example of intemperance, known for the richness of her banquets.[54] She also appears in a book of herbs for her patronage of the physician Dioscorides and in a book of remedies that mentions a 'booke of Cleopatra' which has a remedy (a wolf's left foot) for a wife's loss of interest in her husband.[55]

Thus, she is both a destroyer of cities and a builder of cities. She is a fickle beauty who never loved, and one of the greats who fell for love. She is an example of lust and luxury; she is worthy of note for her courage and nobility.[56] She is a malicious whore, a harpy and a loyal wife. She is both dark and fair-skinned: she is a 'blacke Egyptian'; a 'browne' or 'nutbrowne lady', so dark that her skin acted as a foil for her teeth; and she curled her fair 'golde haire' with her bodkin (dagger).[57] She is also still the doubly other – Egyptian and Woman – 'the Egyptian Epicure, the verie miraculous monster of all her sexe'.[58]

The images in Figures 6–9 depict a variety of Cleopatras from the sixteenth and seventeenth centuries: a dark-skinned and a fair-skinned Cleopatra; a gluttonous Cleopatra; and a Cleopatra envisioned as an ugly hag (in a caricature playing on her categorization with Helen of Troy and Lucrece and on their reputed beauty causing the downfall of men).

FIGURE 6 *Michelangelo Buonarroti,* Cleopatra *(c.1535).* Casa Buonarroti, Florence, Italy/Bridgeman Images.

FIGURE 7 *Guido Reni,* Cleopatra with the Asp *(c.1628). Picture Gallery, Buckingham Palace, Royal Collection Trust/© Her Majesty Queen Elizabeth II 2018.*

FIGURE 8 *Hans Sebold Beham*, Cleopatra, Sitting, *engraving (c.1530–50), Germany. Courtesy Maggs Bros., London.*

FIGURE 9 *Gaspard Isaac*, Helen, Cleopatre, Lucrece, *caricature (c. sixteenth century). Warburg Institute, London. The caption reads: 'Rome would not have suffered the scourge of Tarquin / Nor Egypt buried Antony and his empire / Nor Priam watched the flames reduce Troy to ashes / If, in your youth, you had had such ugly mugs.'*

While these works indicate how divergent and multi-layered views were of Cleopatra in the period, it is also worthwhile to look at sixteenth-century dictionaries, such as Thomas Elyot's *Bibliotheca Eliotæ Eliotis librarie* (1542) and Thomas Cooper's *Thesaurus Lingua Romanae et Britannicae* (first published in 1565). Scholars and writers in the Renaissance would turn to such works for reference. Elyot's *Bibliotheca* underlines the fascination for Cleopatra in the period. In a list of historical names, the entry for Cleopatra is given eighteen lines, whereas the entries under Octavius and Augustus barely merit more than two-and-a-half lines, and there is no separate entry for Antony. She is described as 'excellyinge in pleasantness and sharpnes of wyt' with mentions of her sumptuous gluttony, the pearl story (discussed below), seductiveness, the allurement of Julius Caesar and the destruction of Antony, and suicide by asp.[59] The entry for Cleopatra in Cooper's *Thesaurus* is reproduced below:

> *Cleopâtra*, The name of divers great Ladyes speciallye Queenes of Æypyt. Of whome one excelling in pleasantness and sharpenesse of witte, first allured unto hir Julius Caesar, afterwarde Marcus Antonius, companion in the Empyre with Augustus, whome shee brought into suche dotage, that in following hir appetite, he spyred unto the whole of Empyre: wherefore he was afterworde destroyed by Augustus. This woman so exceeded in sumptuous gluttonie, that she putting an excellent pearle, into tarte vinegar (wherein being resovled) receyved it into hir bodie, being esteemed at *Cénties*, HS, which is of our money 50000. li. This Lady after the death of Antonie, inclosed hir selfe in a tombe, and having two serpentes sucking at hir pappes so dyed.[60]

Interestingly, in both works, it is Cleopatra's wit rather than her beauty or sensuality that seduces Julius Caesar and Antony. The brief sketch in Cooper provides two details which became part of the tradition surrounding Cleopatra in the period.

The first is the suggestion that she died by applying two asps to her breasts. The classical sources, such as Plutarch, mention that the report of Cleopatra's suicide was by a snake bite to the arm, while also allowing for the possibility of poison since no asp was found. Octavius seems to have believed (or promoted) the idea of the asp, based on descriptions of Cleopatra's effigy carried in his triumph as discussed above. Quite early on, however, another tradition also developed about her death with the asp being applied to the breast. The earliest surviving poem which speaks of this is a Latin work preserved in the *Codex Salamasianus* (second half of the eighth century). Although Chaucer depicted Cleopatra as jumping naked into a pit of serpents, and some sixteenth-century sources speak of her stabbing herself in the heart with her bodkin,[61] the idea of the asps to the breast was more prevalent. This depiction was especially so in the visual sphere and seems to have really taken off in sixteenth-century depictions of Cleopatra's suicide, emphasizing the passion and eroticism of her death. Where images in the Middle Ages often portray the asp applied to both breasts, in Renaissance paintings the asp is often applied to the left breast. This idea was perhaps reinforced by the discovery of the *Cleopatra* statue, which has the left breast exposed. Shakespeare combines both the traditions surrounding Cleopatra's death – to the arm and breast. Domitius Calderinus mentions this combined method in his commentary on Martial (last quarter of fourteenth century).[62]

The second detail describes Cleopatra's sumptuous gluttony and her 'putting an excellent pearle, into tarte vinegar' and drinking it when dissolved to impress Antony. Sixteenth-century sources reveal a significant interest in the story of Cleopatra's pearl and its value. Pliny's account of the story in Book IX of his *Natural History* was well known in the period. He effectively conflates Roman distaste for women's extravagance with a condemnation of Cleopatra: 'Women glory in hanging these on their fingers and using two or three for a single earring, and foreign names for this luxury occur, names invented by abandoned extravagance ... There have been two pearls that were the largest in the whole of history; both were owned by Cleopatra'. Pliny then launches into the pearl story, comparing Cleopatra's destruction of the greatest pearl with her destruction of one of Rome's greatest generals.[63]

The fascination with Cleopatra's pearls is of particular interest because of their contradictory connotations in the sixteenth and early seventeenth century. In her study of gemstones, Marcia Pointon observes that pearls, unlike other gems, cannot be cut and improved, and therefore stand for purity and natural perfection.[64] The idea of their purity and beauty is emphasized in the Middle English poem *Pearl* (*c*.1400), mourning the death of a virginal daughter.[65] They were also connected with Christ's selection of the pearl to convey the kingdom of heaven, and they were especially associated with Elizabeth I in the period.[66] The above-mentioned connotations are present in sixteenth-century sources; for example, Thomas Stapleton writes of Cleopatra's 'excellent pearl' and its value, and then says 'But it is another maner of dishe, and of a much higher price that Christ hath left us'.[67] In a section on the phoenix, Sebastian Münster cites Pliny as saying the bird flew over Egypt and is found mainly in Arabia. He then links the phoenix's love of pearls to Cleopatra's and the valuable pearl she owned.[68] The phoenix was associated with Egypt by Herodotus, Ovid and others, and in medieval bestiaries with Arabia. Thus two of the emblems employed by the English queen as part of her iconography – pearls and the phoenix – also had a close connection to the Egyptian queen in the period. This discourse had a topical relevance to Elizabeth, and it may perhaps be linked to the time of Nicholas Hilliard's *Phoenix Portrait* (c.1575), which shows her in pearls with a striking phoenix pendant at her breast.[69]

There were other affinities between Cleopatra and Elizabeth which would have been apparent to writers at the time. Both were known as linguistically accomplished queens; were aware of the importance of their self-presentation and were represented as goddesses (Cleopatra as Isis, and Elizabeth as Diana); faced a powerful imperial enemy; and, most importantly, they were the last of their powerful dynasties – the Ptolemies and the Tudors. While Cleopatra and Elizabeth might not have been seen as exactly the same, the Egyptian queen's story could be used for topical resonance by emphasizing those aspects which had an immediate application to current affairs. Although there was an interest in other oriental queens, and in warrior queens such as Boudica, in the period, the interest in Cleopatra remained unrivalled.[70] Between 1590 and 1606–7, five plays were written on the story of Cleopatra in England – by Mary Sidney, Daniel, Samuel Brandon and Shakespeare, and the lost play by Greville which was destroyed by its author after Essex's fall.[71] Cleopatra and her story clearly spoke to late Elizabethan and early Jacobean England, which was experiencing its own complicated response to a queen and her passing.

Important work has been done on Cleopatra by Janet Adelman in her seminal book on Shakespeare's *Antony and Cleopatra*, and in the recent editions and handbook of the play by David Bevington, Michael Neill, René Weis, John Wilders, and Bridget Escolme.[72] These works have established the themes and issues which surround the study of Cleopatra today. Their primary focus has, however, necessarily been Shakespeare's representation. Although authoritative books have been written about Cleopatra, such as those by Lucy Hughes-Hallett and Mary Hamer, they concentrate on Cleopatra's historical and cultural impact. Marilyn Williamson's study looked at the literary tradition, but it was more of a survey with only two pages devoted to Mary Sidney.[73] Written before critical methodologies included readings of historical context, gender and race, it was grounded mostly on secondary sources.

New Historicist readings have been useful in opening up possibilities for topical readings. They have shown that Elizabethan literature relies on allegory which does not necessarily depend on a one-to-one identification between a fictional character and a figure in the real world, but instead can represent selected aspects of such a figure.[74] This use of allegory is seen, for example, in the many Elizabeth-figures, such as Gloriana, Una and Belphoebe, in Spenser's *The Faerie Queene*, or manifestations of Elizabeth, such as Helen of Corinth, in Sir Philip Sidney's *Arcadia*. Each of these figures represents a different aspect of Elizabeth, and none of her represents them completely. In her influential study of the Renaissance response to female authority, Katherine Eggert finds that if these New Historicist 'studies of early modern literature have taught us anything, it is that England's literature from 1558–1603 was preoccupied with the anomalous gender of the country's monarch'.[75] While England had experienced female rule under Mary Tudor, her brutal persecution of Protestants and marriage to Philip II of Spain only served to complicate the conflicted response and difficulties sixteenth-century writers had with the concept of queenship.

The political nature of the 1590s Cleopatra plays has been considered by many scholars. Although closet drama was private, it was as Marta Straznicky notes, a recognized vehicle for political resistance to Elizabeth's increasingly autocratic and 'inactive' rule.[76] Margaret Hannay pioneered a compelling topical political reading of *Antonius* and its use of classical history, underscoring the concerns and anxieties of the forward Protestant cause, which advocated a more militant foreign and domestic policy.[77] We see these concerns furthered in Daniel's *Cleopatra*, with shifting political concerns in his early (1594–1605) editions and the much-revised 1607 version. Danielle Clarke observes that closet drama was used as a critique of the Elizabethan government in the 1590s and was associated with Tacitean political thought and resistance to increasingly autocratic rule. In her analysis of closet drama, Wendy Piatt emphasizes the ambivalence towards Augustus that developed in the period. Paulina Kewes' work has furthered the political approach, finding affinities between Cleopatra and Elizabeth I as well as between Egypt and England. Jane Pettegree usefully looks at Cleopatra in representations of the foreign and native on the English stage.[78] In her recent study, Julie Crawford employs the term *Mediatrix* to investigate the political influence of women's literary interventions.[79] Crawford is thinking along the same lines as I do in this book about women's diverse roles in literary production, and the political nature of what was previously thought of as 'private' cultural activity by women, looking at many of the same elite networks. However, where I focus on the figure of Cleopatra and the politics of the appropriation and influence of her story, Crawford examines the role of women's cultural production.

My book contributes to the above political studies by looking at the use of Taciteanism in the 1590s Cleopatra plays, and the use of artefacts and other material remains to understand Cleopatra, altering our perception of the Egyptian queen in the period. It makes a significant contribution to our study of neo-Senecan closet drama by testing the hypothesis that closet plays can be performed. In so doing, it sheds new light on women's participation in elite drama in Shakespeare's time, showing that the portrait of the Jacobean lady, plausibly Anne Clifford in guise as Daniel's Cleopatra, might be evidence of a private performance.

The works of Tacitus were frequently reprinted in the sixteenth century on the continent, and both Sir Philip Sidney and Robert Devereux, 2nd Earl of Essex, were known for their enthusiasm for the Roman historian. With his negative accounts of Roman emperors and their corrupt courts, Tacitus provided English courtiers with a guide on how to negotiate the often duplicitous and dangerous corridors of power. In examining the use of Roman historians, Malcolm Smuts demonstrates how Taciteanism worked both to reinforce cynicism about courtiers and politicians, and to advocate military preparedness.[80] Essex's patronage included Henry Savile and Richard Greenway, early English translators of Tacitus. It also included Antonio Pérez, a leading European scholar of Tacitus, double-agent and former secretary of Philip II of Spain. To some extent, Essex's secretariat operated like a modern-day cabinet office with its talking points on various political issues. The use of similar phrases, *sententiae* and Tacitean aphorisms can be seen in a close reading of many of Essex and his circle's writings, with an accompanying interest in an obscurity of style as a literary strategy (discussed in Chapter 2).[81] Tacitus was especially taken up after the fall of Essex by his followers. A Tacitean view, with its emphasis on the role of deception, reinforced opinions of Spain's intrigue and untrustworthiness as a partner in peace. That there was a topical reading associated with Cleopatra in the period is also supported by Pietro Martire d' Anghiera's *The decades of the new worlde* (1555), which compares Spain's imperial greed with Cleopatra's 'wanton appetite' for sumptuous pearls.[82]

My methodology in this book seeks to recuperate allegorical representation and its originary political contexts. For this, I draw on scholars who practise such a flexible topical reading without necessarily aligning themselves with New Historicists. Important models are provided in the political reading developed by David Norbrook, which attempts to unite literary and historical studies; by Annabel Patterson who explores the use of coded criticism and signals when making political statements or drawing topical allusions; and by Blair Worden's examination of the use of public allusion in Philip Sidney's writing.[83] In gender and closet drama, and performance-based research, I have looked to the work of Marion Wynne-Davies and Alison Findlay. I also draw from Marta Straznicky's reading that closet plays were not opposed to theatricality, as they form part of the same dramatic sub-genre as academic drama, which was performed at universities.[84] Helen Hackett's work as part of a movement in interest in Elizabeth I and her literary/allegorical associations and manifestations has shaped my thinking.[85] Chris Laoutaris' innovative interdisciplinary readings have provided me with a deeper understanding of elite women and the significance of their memorializing practices in patriarchal societies.[86]

The image patterns and models for Cleopatra discussed in the Introduction show the rich iconographical history and variety of her representation, and continue to speak to the succeeding chapters. They draw on my examination of ninety-two sources that mention Cleopatra in some way, to show what was being thought and written about the Egyptian queen in the fifty-year period preceding the first dramatization of her story in England.[87]

Ways of imagining: Structure and purpose

The book is divided into five main chapters, plus this Introduction and a brief epilogue. As the subject of Cleopatra is so wide, I focus in this book on the three major extant plays written by Mary Sidney, Daniel, and Shakespeare, within a seventeen-year span of each other in the late Elizabethan and early Jacobean periods. Each work as discussed below is innovative in its own way.

Chapter 1 begins by discussing the *Antonius* (1590) of Mary Sidney, a translation of Robert Garnier's *Marc Antoine*, as the first dramatization of the Cleopatra story in English.

It explores why Mary Sidney chose to translate Garnier and provide dramatic currency to the Egyptian queen and her story, and argues that by situating *Antonius* in a personal and political context we can locate its contemporary significance. The chapter provides some background to the Sidney and Essex circles and their uses of history. It engages with the idea of women's translation in the period, arguing that Mary Sidney was appropriating Garnier's political allegory to new and changing circumstances for topical commentary. In so doing, she was making a statement about the consequences of monarchial neglect of domestic and foreign affairs, giving voice to the anxieties and concerns of the Dudley-Sidney alliance and the forward Protestants.

Chapter 2 analyses Samuel Daniel's *Tragedie of Cleopatra* (1594), which is significant as the first original drama in English about Cleopatra and important in evoking her suffering in defeat. Particular attention is paid in this chapter to the topical political uses of classical history, the conflict between the private and public selves of a monarch, and the idea of what happens when majesty is confused and wavers from its essential role as ruler. It emphasizes the splendour Daniel saw in the Egyptian queen, and the sensitivity and elegance he brought to portraying her tragedy. It also explores the use of Taciteanism and how Daniel deployed the concept of *obscura verba* (an obscure manner of speaking) in the play. The chapter is an expansive one, looking at Daniel's early *Cleopatra* and then at his revised 1607 edition, arguing that his alterations may be due to the emerging nostalgia for Elizabeth that set in early in the rule of James I, and to circumstances in his own life.

The third chapter investigates a fascinating portrait of a Jacobean lady, depicted as Cleopatra, holding the asp. The painting has remained relatively unknown in the art and literary worlds, and in the few cases where it has been discussed, it has been misidentified. This chapter includes detective work about the portrait's provenance and the mystery surrounding it, identifying the portrait's inscription as coming from Daniel's 1607 edition, and its sitter as plausibly Lady Anne Clifford. Might the picture be evidence of an elite private performance of a closet drama, or might it be connected to Clifford's inheritance battle and be a coded message to her husband? The painting, a British literary portrait of some significance, is the only survival from the period based on the scene of a contemporary play. It remarkably represents a young aristocratic lady imagining herself as Daniel's Cleopatra, with lines of resistance to Caesar's tyranny at a time when James I identified himself with Augustus. The portrait alters our perceptions of Cleopatra in the period, demonstrating that elite women found affinities with the Egyptian queen and identified with the powerful female sovereignty she represents.

Chapter 4 examines insights gained from a UCL staging of *The Tragedie of Cleopatra* at Goodenough College, London in 2013, undertaken to test the feasibility of an elite performance of Daniel's closet drama, as possibly recorded in the portrait discussed in the previous chapter. Although it was thought that these types of plays were only written to be read and not performed, recent scholarship is increasingly questioning this assumption. Our production shows that Daniel's closet drama is highly performable. The chapter highlights themes and new emotional cores that became apparent during the staging and rehearsal process, including the idea of Cleopatra as a figure of female complaint. It also underscores the idea of Shakespeare visualizing the implicit scenography built into Daniel's play. The final part of the chapter briefly discusses the performance of selected scenes of the play at the Shakespeare Institute in Stratford-upon-Avon, and in the Great Hall at Knole House in Kent, where Anne Clifford might have performed the part.

Chapter 5 discusses Shakespeare's *Antony and Cleopatra* (1606–7), which was the first dramatization of the story in non-elite circles in England. This chapter resituates Shakespeare's version on a spectrum, which also includes its precursors in a new and exciting way. I suggest that, although different in many ways, Shakespeare's play is more like the closet dramas that preceded it than has been previously considered. The chapter looks at how Shakespeare's Cleopatra was influenced by Mary Sidney's and Daniel's Cleopatras, and how he departed from them. It explores how Shakespeare drew on the infinite variety of Cleopatras that were available to him to create his Egyptian queen, including divergent views of her race and beauty. It also examines the play's unusual publication history and investigates its significance in its own time, and looks at connections between *Antony and Cleopatra* and Daniel's 1607 *Cleopatra*. By resituating Shakespeare's Cleopatra and his play in its Jacobean context, the chapter underscores the historical-political contextualization of his tragedy.

Finally, the epilogue and conclusion includes a brief survey of works written in the seventeenth century after Shakespeare, and looks at the influence of Daniel on Dryden. The adaptability within Cleopatra's story meant that just as she could be depicted in proto-republican plays as a symbol of decadence, she could also re-emerge in Royalist plays as a figure of resistance. The discussion of the Cavendish sisters' *Concealed Fancies*, which positions Cleopatra as a figure of virtuous resistance, links back to their great-grandmother Bess of Hardwick's interest in the Egyptian queen. The chapter examines the enduring fascination with Cleopatra and her literary afterlife, including a rare Egyptian portrayal of Cleopatra in drama.

An appendix, 'The *Cleopatra* statue and the poems at the Vatican', provides a more detailed discussion of the statue and English translations of the three poems by Castiglione, Favoriti and Baldi (the latter two are translated here for the first time).

Each element of the book's title, *Imagining Cleopatra: Performing Gender and Power in Early Modern England*, can be examined as separate issues. The role of 'Imagining' is important because of the many attempts to imagine Cleopatra in art and literature through the centuries, and the young Jacobean lady's self-imagining as Cleopatra in the portrait. It is also significant because 'imagining' itself was politically charged and dangerous at this time (the Treason Acts are discussed in Chapter 1). The concept of 'Performance' forms part of the sub-title because Cleopatra, especially in the careful and regal staging of her own death, was known for her theatricality, and because womanliness itself was seen as a form of performance, played by boy-actors. Shakespeare's Cleopatra is particularly aware of this counterfeiting of roles, both in the cross-dressing episode with Antony, and in her fear that she shall see 'Some squeaking Cleopatra boy her greatness / I'th' posture of a whore' (5.2.218–19). Questions of gender as performance are explored in many other plays in the period, especially in plays with cross-dressing elements, such as Shakespeare's *Twelfth Night, As You Like It* and *The Merchant of Venice*. The book itself offers an account of a performance-project and therefore engages in performance in its many senses.[88] The role of 'gender' is significant because in the categorization of women in debates over their worthiness, Cleopatra became the symbol on which each generation projected their notions of the structures of patriarchy and the place of women.[89] The ancient twin discourse of gender and race became more pronounced into the early modern period, particularly in the construction of unruly foreign women, and in the myth of the Amazon.[90] In the powerfully persuasive Augustan narrative of Cleopatra's enticement of Antony as a scheming and tyrannical foreign queen, we see the beginnings of the discourse of gender and race and of the dichotomy between East and West.[91] The final element of the title, 'Power', is important, since the political story of Cleopatra is about female sovereignty and power politics on an epic scale: the fall of a great queen; the end of a major dynasty; Rome's defeat of Egypt; and the institution of Rome's first emperor Augustus. Her story also spoke to views about queenship and imperial power in the late Elizabethan and early Jacobean periods.

This book decentres Shakespeare. It makes an original contribution to the study of early modern Cleopatras by offering a new and interdisciplinary approach to the subject. It ranges beyond secondary sources, emphasizing primary research, and attention to performance. In this book, I argue that there is a need to look back beyond Shakespeare's Cleopatra to understand the sources and cultural contexts that produced her. In doing so, we find that sixteenth-century writers were already avidly interested in Cleopatra, and produced widely divergent and even contradictory depictions of her, influenced by alternative traditions and shaped by different rhetorical and political purposes. Out of these competing discourses arose the closet dramas of Mary Sidney and Daniel, which are more complex than has sometimes been recognized. In particular, I explore new approaches to Daniel's play via its connections with a portrait and a performance-based project. These fresh explorations of Mary Sidney's and Daniel's Cleopatras enable us to look at Shakespeare's Cleopatra in a new light. This book is not only about Cleopatra; it is also about those who attempted to represent her in some way. As such, it offers an original approach to the study of how Elizabethan and Jacobean political, social and dramatic cultures overlapped, by tracing the representation and reception of a single, catalytic figure.

1

'Sight of that Face': Passion and politics in Mary Sidney's *Antonius*

> [D]ay and night,
> In watch, in sleepe, her Image follow'd thee:
> Not dreaming but of her, repenting still
> That thou for warre hadst such a Goddes left.
> (*Antonius*, 1.104–7)[1]

The dramatization of the story of Antony and Cleopatra began in England in the late Elizabethan period with the work of a woman writer-translator, Mary Sidney Herbert, Countess of Pembroke. Her *Antonius*, a translation from the French of Robert Garnier's *Marc Antoine* (1578), is dated at its end as having been completed 'At Ramsburie. 26. November. 1590'.[2] Earlier that year on 'The 13. of May 1590. At Wilton', Mary Sidney also completed work on another secular French text: *Excellent discours de la vie et la mort* (1576) by the prominent Huguenot theologian, political theorist, and diplomat Philippe de Mornay.[3] He had been a close friend and political ally of her brother, the renowned courtier and poet Sir Philip Sidney. Both her translations, *Antonius, A Tragœdie* and *A Discourse on Life and Death*, were published together in 1592.[4]

Garnier's neo-Senecan tragedy, based on Plutarch and Dio Cassius, focuses on the final day of Antony's life. Set in the aftermath of Actium, and ultimately centring on Cleopatra, it covers Antony's suicide and ends before hers. In a departure from the scheming seductress of the Augustan sources, Garnier's Cleopatra is portrayed as a complex character – she is a queen, a wife and a mother, and loves Antony completely. For her, he is 'My life, my soule, my Sunne' (2.395), and she would rather 'to deepest mischiefe fall' (2.401) than betray him to Caesar. The neo-Senecan mode allowed playwrights to address difficult moral and political issues from a variety of perspectives. In a period when writers were exploring neo-Stoicism and its possibilities, Garnier presented his Cleopatra as constant and courageous, a heroic figure. He did this while still upholding the ideals of personal responsibility and self-reliance in the face of an uncertain and unjust world.[5] However, although Garnier emphasizes Antony's and Cleopatra's suffering and love for each other, his enduring concern is the threat of civil unrest and tyranny caused by a ruler's private passion.[6]

Garnier's literary career spanned the French Wars of Religion and the periods of uneasy peace. He was a political dramatist, known in France for using his tragedies to criticize the state. Although Garnier was a Catholic, and the Sidneys supported the Protestant cause, his plays spoke against the violence in France. If Mary Sidney translated Garnier's 1585 revised edition of *Marc Antoine*, as scholars agree, then this was the version printed in his collected works.[7] She would be keenly aware of Garnier's view that ancient Roman history offered political lessons to contemporary France, during its bloody civil wars. His dedications and prefaces to his plays in the collection tell us as much.[8] *Porcie* (1568) appeared with the sub-title: *tragedie Françoise, representant la cruelle et slanglante saison des guerres civiles de Rome: propre et convenable pour y voir depeincte la calamité de ce temps* (a tragedy in French representing the cruel and bloody season of the civil wars of Rome: proper and fitting for the depiction of the catastrophe of our times). The dedication to *Cornelie* (1574) describes the tragedy as 'propre aux malheurs de nostre siècle' (appropriate to the misfortunes of our age). This connection is established in Garnier's dedication to *Marc Antoine*. He writes: 'les representations Tragiques des guerres civiles des Rome' (the representations of the tragic civil wars of Rome) is applicable to 'les malheureux troubles de ce Royaume aujourd'huy' despouillé de son ancienne splendeur et de la reverable majesté de nos Rois' (the unfortunate troubles of this kingdom, stripped today of its ancient splendour and the reverent majesty of our kings). The Countess's decision to translate Garnier must have been informed by an understanding of, and an interest in, this intensely political application and use of Roman history.[9]

Mary Sidney's translation is significant in adapting continental tragedy, and its use of ancient Roman history for political commentary, to drama in England, and for encouraging the development of late sixteenth-century English Senecan closet drama.[10] Her *Antonius* was an influence in the literary production of other plays on the theme of Antony and Cleopatra. These include Samuel Daniel's *Tragedie of Cleopatra* (1594), which she commissioned as a companion piece to her work; Samuel Brandon's *The Tragicomoedi of the vertuous Octavia* (1598), which attached aspects of her Cleopatra to his Octavia instead; and Shakespeare's *Antony and Cleopatra* (1606–7), for which she was a source.[11] As mentioned previously, Fulke Greville's lost play *Antony and Cleopatra* was also written in the period. Greville, the friend and biographer of Philip Sidney, destroyed his play (sometime after 1601) in the aftermath of the Earl of Essex's fall, fearing the authorities might see it as politically subversive.[12]

Antonius is important not only as the first drama about Cleopatra in English but also as the first drama published in English by a woman. Mary Sidney's work is bold on a number of fronts: in its representation of the Egyptian queen as constant and seeking 'vertue' (2.651); in its interrogation of queenship and female sexual identity; and in its exploration of the consequences of monarchical neglect of domestic and foreign affairs. The political themes inherent in the play, especially those of the duties of a monarch and the end of a dynasty, held particular relevance to England in the late 1580s and early 1590s. During this period, criticism of Elizabeth I's 'inactive' foreign policy and her failure to attend to national security and secure the succession was widespread.[13] The play's political story thus spoke both to the Protestant politics of the Dudley-Sidney alliance and to the anxiety prevalent at this time. Mary Sidney's highly influential family – with its affiliation to the militant or forward Protestant cause and its assessment of the malaise in mid-late Elizabethan policy – added a politicized dimension to any such translational endeavour of hers.[14] The careful subscription of her work as completed at the great country houses of Wilton and Ramsbury signalled the Pembroke origins and politics of her translations. Her husband Henry Herbert, the 2nd Earl of Pembroke, was one of the great Protestant earls. Their Wiltshire estates and Baynard's Castle, their London house, were politically significant meeting places associated with the alliance and the French Protestant or Huguenot cause. Philip Sidney's widely circulated 'A Letter to Queen Elizabeth Touching her Marriage with Monsieur', objecting to the Anjou match in 1579, was probably commissioned at a meeting at Baynard's Castle, with the Sidneys' uncle Robert Dudley, the Earl of Leicester, present. Henri of Navarre's agent is known to have visited Wilton with Philip in 1583.[15] By 1590, Mary Sidney had established Wilton as a centre for Protestant intellectuals, and in August 1592, the court stayed at Ramsbury on its northern progress.[16]

With her exceptional education and interest in French and Italian literature, Mary Sidney is likely to have been familiar with the treatment of Cleopatra on the continent as a subject suitable for elite tragedy.[17] The Egyptian queen was, in fact, the subject of the first neo-Senecan tragedy in French, Etienne Jodelle's *Cléopâtre Captive*. Staged before King Henri II in 1552/3 (published 1574), as a private courtly occasion, it was enormously influential and a source for Garnier.[18] As discussed in the Introduction, the discovery of the *Cleopatra* statue in Rome in 1512, staging the moment of Cleopatra's death, inspired great interest and sympathy in her story in poets and writers. They moved the Egyptian queen away from the purely Augustan narrative and gave her a voice. Mary Morrison stresses that the continental dramatists idealized Cleopatra, making 'her appear noble and virtuous, in spite of what the choral odes may say about her lust and ambition'.[19] Thus, although Garnier's declared sources were Greco-Roman, there were precedents for his divergence from these sources and his presentation of Cleopatra as not just a seducer and destroyer. Like other dramatists of the period, he used classical or classically influenced sources, while also portraying Cleopatra as a figure of heroic constancy both in relation to Antony and Octavius. Garnier's play, written as a prequel to the events dramatized in Jodelle, also captured something different in continental representations, showing Antony's anguish, remorse and suspicions in defeat,[20] as he realizes now 'nought remains, (so destitute am I)' (1.24). The potential of a duality of perspectives in Cleopatra's tragedy, and of looking at the lovers' mental and emotional states in Garnier, was taken up by Mary Sidney. It was then enhanced by Daniel in his sequel to her work.

In looking at the sixteenth-century European fascination with the Egyptian queen, Geoffrey Bullough observes that 'with the *Cléopâtre Captive* of Etienne Jodelle the dramatic cult of Cleopatra reached France'.[21] With her *Antonius*, Mary Sidney introduced the story of Cleopatra from translation to coterie drama in England, which in turn exerted an influence on the public stage. By translating and reshaping Garnier's play, and by commissioning Daniel to write the first original drama about Cleopatra in English, Mary Sidney established the foundations for Shakespeare's more famous depiction of Cleopatra. These plays encode a complex set of political and intellectual backdrops not only on the Egyptian queen, but on Elizabeth I and female sovereignty. This chapter investigates why Mary Sidney chose to translate *Marc Antoine* and provide dramatic currency to the Egyptian queen and her story in England. I argue that by situating *Antonius* and the

Garnier-Sidney Cleopatra in a personal, cultural and political context, we can locate its contemporary significance and see that her decision was a complex, deliberate and multi-layered one. I begin this chapter by looking at the reasons for Mary Sidney's translation, the Elizabethan culture of translation, and then at the Garnier-Sidney Cleopatra. In the sections that follow, I explore the concepts of sympathy, passion and regret, and virtue in the play in relation to their political significance and the ways in which Mary Sidney uses *Antonius* as Protestant political allegory. The chapter provides contextual material on the Sidney and Essex circles, their use of history, and on the anxieties and concerns of the forward Protestants. It emphasizes the importance of connections to women in both Garnier's and Mornay's works.

Contexts and culture

Mary Sidney completed her translations of *Antonius* and the *Discourse* two years after her return to society from mourning the deaths of her father, Henry Sidney; mother, Mary Dudley Sidney; and older brother, Philip. They had died tragically in 1586, within six months of each other at a time when she too was seriously unwell.[22] Her parents died of natural causes, while her brother succumbed to an infectious wound sustained at the battle of Zutphen, fighting Catholic Spain in the Netherlands. He was regarded as the ideal Renaissance man – 'one of the very diamonds of her majesty's court'[23] – and he was one of the few Elizabethan noblemen to die in the war. A state funeral was held for him in St Paul's Cathedral where he was celebrated as a Protestant martyr. Many of the poets eulogized Sidney, and the English and Dutch universities published books honouring him. For Mary Sidney, who could not traditionally take part in the public mourning because of her gender, her loss was private and profound.[24] She was not just a mourning sister; she was the mourning sister of a hero.

When she re-entered court life in November 1588, it was with a magnificent procession resplendent in the Sidney blue and gold for the Accession Day celebrations, following the defeat of the Spanish Armada.[25] Her entry can be seen as a statement of the resurgence of the Dudley-Sidney Protestant alliance, and as a declaration of her roles as Philip's self-appointed editor and literary executor, and as author and patron in her own right. The Earl of Leicester had died in September 1588, and with her brother Robert's imminent posting to Flushing, and an ailing older generation, she now suddenly became her family's most potent representative.[26] According to Margaret Hannay, there is no evidence that before this time she had been viewed as 'the heir of Sidney's muse, as writer or as patron'.[27] Her literary career thus began with remarkable determination, and with a strikingly performative gesture, in support of her family's political stance.

She might have undertaken her translations as a way of honouring her family, choosing works that her brother would have approved in support of the Protestant cause. In the Second Part of *The Countess of Pembroke's Ivy Church* (1591), Abraham Fraunce portrays Pembrokiana (the Countess) celebrating Amyntas's memory, who 'commaunded yearely for ever' (sig. L1v) that the Nymphs and Shepherds meet and 'With new found tytles remember him' (sig. L2r). Scholars think that this ritual of storytelling 'probably had a basis in a real gathering', with Ivychurch being Mary Sidney's favourite Wiltshire haunt. As a former protégé of Philip Sidney's now under the Countess's patronage, Fraunce is likely to have had some insight into her life in this period.[28] We can only speculate whether his lines about the commemorations at Ivychurch were literal or symbolic descriptions of Mary Sidney's enterprise. It is intriguing, however, to wonder whether some portion of *Antonius* formed part of the memorial rites for the fourth anniversary of Philip Sidney's death. The full work is dated as completed about six weeks after the anniversary on 17 October, and four days before Sidney's birthday on 30 November. The danger to the state of the ruler's private passions might have resonated with Mary Sidney as a theme both on a political and a personal front. The conflict of private and public issues is the focus of *Gorboduc* (1561), the only English play praised by Sidney in his *Defence of Poetry* for its Senecan style, and for its 'notable morality, which it doth most delightfully teach, and so obtain the very end of Poesy'.[29] Both *Antonius* and *Gorboduc* share concerns about the end of a dynasty and succession, as does Daniel's *Cleopatra*. For Mary Sidney, this might perhaps also have had a resonance not only with the national problem of Elizabeth's childlessness, but also with the question of who was the true successor to Philip, and how could his legacy – political and literary – best be handed on.[30]

She might have felt sympathy for Cleopatra, who is advised by her hand-maiden Charmion to memorialize Antony:

> builde for him a tombe
> Whose statelinesse a wonder new may make.
> Let him, let him have sumtuouse funeralles ...
> Make all his combats, and couragiouse acts:
> And yearly plaies to his praise institute:
> Honor his memorie: with doubled care.
> Breed and bring up your children of you both
> In *Cæsars* grace: who as a noble Prince
> Will leave them Lords of this most gloriouse realme.
>   (2.612–14, 620–5)

In spite of the magnificence of Sidney's funeral, no permanent memorial had been erected to him, due to financial concerns.[31] Some elements of Charmion's advice, such as the instituting of 'yearly plaies to his praise' to 'Honor his memorie' (2.621–2), might have appealed to Mary Sidney as she focused on extending her brother's literary and political legacy. She was, as Chris Laoutaris points out, like other elite women of her period actively involved in 'expanding the limits of women's engagement in the public demonstrations of grieving' and in memorializing her dynastic legacy.[32] Cleopatra, however, is here being advised to save herself, her realm and her dynasty, by separating her fate from Antony's and appeasing a rapacious tyrant. Although Mary Sidney's work might have come out of a time of grief, her decision to translate *Antonius* four years after her loss was a careful and appropriate one; to publish this work two years later has to be seen as a deliberate and political choice.

Mary Sidney's translations allowed her to create a space for herself as an author. During the early modern period, translation was deemed a suitable activity for educated elite women, as it conformed more to ideas of feminine virtue and modesty than original writing, especially when confined to the private sphere.[33] However, recent scholarship on early women's writing challenges the assumption that translation was a passive or secondary exercise. It establishes that elite women who translated religious or secular works were active and passionate proponents of their particular familial causes.[34] Recent studies, for example, explore the use of political allegory in Lady Jane Lumley's *Iphigenia*, and the religio-political significance of translations in the *Common Book of Prayer* possibly contributed by Katherine Parr and Elizabeth I.[35] Developments in translation theory, especially in the notion of translation in the period, show that early modern translators 'viewed themselves as co-authors of the work, with the right to modify the original text'.[36] Brenda M. Hosington defines translation as the process of appropriating and mediating works from the source culture to new and, at times, urgent cultural contexts.[37] The Countess of Pembroke's identity as her brother's memorializer and her revision and expansion of the Sidney Psalms afforded her a unique position of authority, piety and prestige. She used this position not simply to mourn her brother, but, as Jaime Goodrich observes, to develop 'her political credibility by building on contemporary perceptions of Philip Sidney's own translations'.[38] In translating and publishing the *Discourse*, Mary Sidney was aiding in the dissemination of Protestant works of her brother's continental connections – a process he had begun when translating parts of Mornay's *Of the Truth of the Christian Religion*, and the

Divine Weeks and Works of the Huguenot poet Guillaume de Salluste Du Bartas.[39] In *Antonius*, she was allowing her name to be publicly attached as co-author to Garnier and the Cleopatra story, appropriating the play for the Protestant cause and its new urgent contexts.

In certain circumstances, translation also provided what Annabel Patterson has appropriately called 'functional ambiguity'. In the tense atmosphere of the 1580s and 1590s, writers began to use coded criticism and signals when making political statements or drawing topical allusions. This criticism was implicitly understood and looked for by readers, but it was veiled enough to provide deniability with the authorities to avoid official censure. The Treason Act of 1571 and the 1581 'Act against Seditious Words and Rumours Uttered against the Queen's Most Excellent Majesty', supplemented in 1585 by the Act of Surety of the Queen's Person, made even the realms of fantasy and 'imagining' the Queen's demise (and therefore any allusion to the succession) highly fraught and dangerous. Translation, especially when close to its source, provided the cover of a foreign original.[40]

Antonius, a close translation, significantly appeared without Garnier's dedication, as then did Thomas Kyd's translation of Garnier's *Cornelie* in 1594. The Sidneys had learnt in 1579, when the Puritan writer John Stubbs lost his right hand as punishment for making many of the same objections as Philip Sidney had against the Anjou match, to use 'privileged genres' when lobbying the Queen.[41] Hannay sees the use of Roman historical allusion for topical comment as 'parallel to the use of the Psalms as a privileged genre for political statement'.[42] As an elite neo-classical play not intended for the commercial playhouse, *Antonius* avoided the censorship of the Revels Office and afforded more potential for political comment. As a translation of a play about ancient times past, it hedged against the risk of dramatizing contemporary events by leaving it to the reader 'to see the parallel in the present'.[43] These, then, were the contexts and culture, and the bounds of privilege and restriction, in which Mary Sidney introduced Garnier and the story of Cleopatra to English drama. Imagining the Egyptian queen in the age of an English queen, whose own dynasty was coming to an end like the Ptolemies, took extraordinary skill and a remarkable balancing act.[44]

Despite its importance, literary scholars paid little attention to *Antonius*, except as a source for Shakespeare, until the explosion of interest in women's writing in the 1980s and 1990s. Early feminist scholars, in their valuable effort to rediscover women's texts, sought to find proto-feminism in works by early modern women writers. They read Mary Sidney's Cleopatra as 'subversive in context to sixteenth-century ideology' and 'revisionary' in relation to Garnier.[45] However, views towards the Egyptian queen were widely divergent in the period, as demonstrated in the Introduction, and both Garnier and Mary Sidney were working with these conventions. In light of these treatments, the Garnier-Sidney Cleopatra seems somewhat less subversive. Although some writers viewed her as an example of lust and luxury, and as a destroyer of men and cities, Cleopatra also appeared in works grouped with other noble and courageous wives from antiquity known for their constancy, such as Portia, Penelope and Lucrece. Both these negative and positive images of Cleopatra are present in Garnier, with the play voicing both ambivalence and sympathy. Mary Sidney might have found an appeal in Garnier's rendering of Cleopatra, with its different perspectives on the Egyptian queen as both seductress and wife.

While scholars now generally recognize the Sidney Psalms for their political intent and support of the Protestant cause, there is still a debate about *Antonius* and its contemporary significance.[46] Recent scholarship has increasingly moved away from seeing Mary Sidney's translation as simply a refuge for grief. Though critics continue to differ in detail and emphasis, they have developed more of a consensus on the importance of a political reading in her work.[47] As discussed in the Introduction, Hannay's work has pioneered a persuasive political reading of the Countess's play, underscoring the concerns of the forward Protestant cause. Developing this approach, Victor Skretkowicz sees *Antonius* as topical commentary on the war in France and a plea for help for the Huguenot cause. For Danielle Clarke, Mary Sidney's choice of Garnier constitutes a critique of Elizabethan government in the 1590s. Paulina Kewes furthers this reading, finding affinities not only between Cleopatra and Elizabeth I, but also between Octavius and Philip II of Spain. Julie Crawford looks at Cleopatra as a figure of constancy, with constancy a key term for political integrity.[48] This chapter contributes to these studies. It examines the significance of Mary Sidney's *Antonius* and the Garnier-Sidney Cleopatra, by setting her decision to translate and publish Garnier and Mornay together in the context of personal and political circumstances in her own life.[49] For Mary Sidney, these were not writers from some distant era, but contemporary authors and Mornay a family friend. She would have been aware of many of the political (and some personal) resonances in their works when she selected them. In all likelihood, she hosted Mornay at Wilton or Baynard's Castle, during his diplomatic missions to England in the late 1570s and in 1580, when Philip stayed with the Pembrokes for extended periods. It is also likely that Mornay visited the Sidneys in 1592 when he returned to England after Philip's death.[50]

That Mary Sidney had a particular interest in Cleopatra is evidenced by her translation of one play about the Egyptian queen and her commissioning of another. She might also have discussed Cleopatra in some way with her brother. The scholar Gabriel Harvey, under whom Philip Sidney studied Roman history, noted Sidney's enthusiasm for Julius Caesar as a man of action and resoluteness. He recounts that Sidney admired Julius Caesar 'above all others' for his 'singular life and actions'.[51] It is not improbable to think that in this enthusiasm he and his sister might have discussed the Egyptian queen, linked so famously with Caesar. Like Queen Helen of Corinth in the *New Arcadia*, Cleopatra too was a love-lorn queen, and in Philip's *Arcadia*, the love of princes that is ruled by passion always brings about private and public disorder.[52]

By the time Mary Sidney translated Garnier in 1590, he was an acclaimed writer at the forefront of French Senecan theatre. In *Marc Antoine*, she was selecting a work that her brother would have approved, both for its neo-Senecan genre and for its use of classical history to draw moral lessons.[53] Garnier's play would have appealed to her as a Sidney and as a woman.

Fashioning the Garnier-Sidney Cleopatra: Sympathy and topical allusion

Among the poems that Mary Sidney would have seen prefixed to Garnier's *Marc Antoine* is a quatrain by the poet Françoise Hubert:

Malagré du Temps les perdurable cours,
Ton nom cache dedans l'onde oubliese
Reflorira, Cleopatre amoureuse,
Ayant GARNIER chanter de tes amours.[54]

[Despite the perpetual course of time,
Your name, hidden within the wave of forgetfulness,
Will flower again, loving Cleopatra,
Having Garnier to sing your loves.]

Hubert, who had married Garnier in 1575, was here not simply praising her husband's work and the resurrection of Cleopatra's story some twenty-five years after Jodelle's dramatization. She was recognizing that Garnier had found sympathetic qualities in the Egyptian queen and given her a feminine voice which reflected her circumstances. Hubert is speaking directly to Cleopatra – a woman to another woman – and it is her female voice that raises the idea of Garnier's work as the remedy for 'forgetfulness'. In prefixing Hubert's poem to his play, Garnier was giving his wife a voice in his printed edition, while also creating a context of wifely devotion and eloquence for his depiction of Cleopatra. By rendering Garnier's text into English, Mary Sidney added her voice as co-author to the representation of Cleopatra. She was in the unusual position of appropriating and articulating a male voice ventriloquizing a female voice – adding a poignant quality to these overlapping memorial voices so interwoven in the feminine. The term 'ventriloquized' is usually used in looking at non-dramatic appropriations of the feminine voice by male poets, most specifically at female lament. The work of some poets, though, can seem potentially exploitative, such as in Nicholas Breton's fashioning of Mary Sidney's grieving voice in his poem 'The Countess of Penbrooke's Love' (1592).[55] Here as Garnier's translator, it is Mary Sidney who fashions both Garnier's voice and Cleopatra's, with her own voice emerging.

The Garnier-Sidney Cleopatra is not the Cleopatra of the Augustan sources. Rather than depicting her as ambitiously calculating, she is portrayed as essentially noble and is seen as such by others. For her, Antony is 'More deare than Scepter, children, freedome, light' (2.417), and it is this complete submission to passion that has been so calamitous; yet it is this which is also simultaneously epic, and almost superhuman in its absolute dominating single-mindedness. She blames herself completely for their defeat, 'I am sole cause: I did it, only I' (2.455), and thinks her 'ev'lls' so 'wholy unsupportable' that 'No humain force can them withstand, but death' (2.432–3). Cleopatra knows that the loss at Actium 'was not his offence, but mine' (2.459) and wishes she had never insisted on joining Antony in battle. She realizes that in the end it is she who has brought about their defeat and deprived him 'of Empire, honor, life' (5.1834). It is, in fact, the Roman Lucilius who defends Cleopatra against Antony's fear that she might 'Practize with Cæsar' (3.891), a charge also later expressed in Shakespeare, saying 'Beleeve it not: Too high a heart she beares / Too Princelie thoughts' (3.893–4). In *Marc Antoine*, Garnier evoked the anguish of a woman who has lost everything and is preparing to die. Cleopatra is as much a queen here as a woman, who has lost her realm and 'the love of him / Who while he was, was all hir woes support' (4.1595–6). In *Antonius*, Mary Sidney furthered Garnier's sympathetic representation of Cleopatra, while also emphasizing those aspects of Antony's and Cleopatra's tragedy that held an application to contemporary politics. She thus subtly shaped a reading of the play that was both Garnier's and her own.

Although *Antonius* is usually regarded as an exceptionally close translation, it was also a creative literary act in which Mary Sidney's authorial voice was not absent from the text.[56] The Countess rendered Garnier's alexandrines into blank verse, except for putting the Choruses into rhyme, in the same year as Christopher Marlowe's *Tamburlaine* (published in 1590, first performed in 1587), showing the freedom and flexibility of this form.[57] Mary Sidney's careful alterations to the text afforded her the cover of a foreign original, while allowing her to signal her vision and political intent in her translation. By centring her changes mainly in the Argument, which is not a translation, she was able to maintain this cover and still crucially frame the text, create expectations, and direct interpretations. The modifications and additions she made here (apart from adding in necessary historical background) seem specifically designed to develop and highlight those aspects in Garnier that were important to her, as discussed below.

Among her changes, she suppressed mention of Antony's first wife, Fulvia, and reduced details of his marriage to Octavia, effectively concentrating on Cleopatra and diminishing the image of the Egyptian queen as a seductress. To focus dramatic attention on Antony's situation and his mental state, Mary Sidney reordered the narrative sequence, restoring it to the original chronology in Plutarch. She also added a sentence describing the motivation behind Antony's return to Egypt after his marriage to Octavia. According to her, it was while he was on a military campaign that coming 'into Siria, the places renewed in his remembrance the long intermitted love of *Cleopatra* Queene of Aegipt' (ll. 8–9) and 'the exquisite delightes and sumptuous pleasures, which a great Prince and a voluptuous Lover could to the uttermost desire' (ll. 10–12). She similarly provided a motive to Cleopatra for having the fatally injured Antony hoisted up through her monument's window, explaining that Cleopatra did not open the door 'least she should be made a prisoner to the *Romaines*, and carried in *Cæsars* triumph' (ll. 31–2). The Countess also emphasized the battle at Actium (even as she cut some of Garnier's details), by adding the phrase that, in following Cleopatra, Antony delivered to '*Octavius* the greatest victorye which in any Sea Battell hath beene heard off' (ll. 21–2). At the end of the Argument she included the detail of 'The Stage supposed Alexandria: the Chorus, first Egiptians, and after Romane Souldiors' (ll. 35–6); and of the two sources Garnier mentions, she included Plutarch (ll. 36), and omitted Dio Cassius, cutting Garnier's final words 'et au 51. livre de Dion'.[58]

Echoes in Mary Sidney's phrasing suggest she carefully went back to original sources, consulting both Sir Thomas North's 1579 translation of Plutarch, as well as Jacques Amyot's 1559 one in the French. The suppression of Dio, however, could be due to two factors. First, as her editors suggest, Dio was less familiar to her English readers. Second, it is likely that to Mary Sidney he represented one of antiquity's harshest critics of the Egyptian queen.[59] He was influential in forming Cleopatra's image as a calculating schemer, believing that she acted with deliberate malice in sending a false report of her suicide to Antony. According to Dio, Cleopatra hoped that Antony 'would not wish to survive her, but would die at once', leaving her free to seduce Octavius and ensure her own survival (*Roman History*, L.1.10). Mary Sidney would have wanted distance from this representation of Cleopatra in shaping her own more sympathetic one.

The above changes in her adaptation of the Argument yield suggestive clues as to what Mary Sidney's objectives were in her translation: to increase the focus on Cleopatra, to heighten sympathy for the lovers by looking at their mental and emotional states, to highlight the battle of Actium and to specify to English readers the setting and the shifts in Choric identity in the play. The idea of the power of passion and its devastating consequences is emphasized throughout *Antonius*. Mary Sidney stresses the impact of Cleopatra's memory on Antony's mind as he is pulled away from his campaigns and duty, advancing the notion that the Egyptian queen's image 'haunts' (3.922) him. Her provision of a motive for Cleopatra's not opening the monument door, and her focus on this in the Argument draws attention to Dircetus's moving account of these events in Act 4. The scene is a transformative moment in the play, as through resolute action and sheer physical strength Cleopatra struggles to raise the wounded Antony with 'hir womens helpe' and by her 'strong armes into hir windowe' (4.1648–50). Eve Rachelle Sanders notes that by including this moment in the Argument as well, Mary Sidney enhances Garnier's portrayal of Cleopatra as a heroic figure.[60] Throughout the play Mary Sidney works to enhance this stature, changing Garnier's blunt final line 'mon ame vomissant' (5.1999), my soul spewing forth, to the more poetic and philosophical 'fourth my soule may flowe' (5.2022), thus adding to the Stoic idea of death as a powerful form of independence and resistance to tyranny.[61]

For English readers, any allusion to the greatest 'Sea Battell' and the naval catastrophe at Actium in the Argument would naturally evoke the Spanish Armada – the sea battle England had recently faced and the possible catastrophe it had narrowly averted. This parallel would perhaps encourage them to root for Cleopatra and to see her as a figure of resistance to imperial expansionism. Although the Armada was defeated in 1588, there were active and viable threats of future Armadas.[62] The mention of Cleopatra's sixty galleys in the Argument would have a political resonance with the reporting style of Renaissance news dispatches and recall the Armada's sixty-five galleons. Ships and galleys are mentioned, in fact, throughout the tragedy. By highlighting these links in the Argument, Mary Sidney was signalling the focus on Actium in the play, and the topical inferences that could be drawn between Egypt and England. Had the Armada succeeded, Britain would have faced an assault from the Spanish ships and land forces, with a coordinated attack by the Duke of Parma's troops, leading to a probable military occupation of South-East England. Once established in Kent, the Spanish would have been able to dictate terms to Elizabeth, just as Octavius was imposing conditions on Cleopatra.[63] England might have been overrun 'With Souldiors, strangers, horrible in armes' (2.265). Mary Sidney also emphasizes that the Chorus's identity shifts in *Antonius*, as does its perspective, and that it is unstable. The Chorus is Egyptian in Acts 1–3, made up of Roman soldiers in Act 4 and absent in Act 5. At this point in the play, as Jane Pettegree comments, 'Roman victory silences the communal Egyptian voice, accentuating Cleopatra's isolation.'[64]

When Mary Sidney decided to translate Garnier, she was making a statement about the consequences of monarchical neglect in foreign and domestic affairs. The Dudley-Sidney alliance had seen many of its aims of promoting the cause of international Protestantism thwarted in the mid-to-late 1580s, and Elizabeth was seen as dangerously neglectful in her refusal to name a successor. The Queen's thrifty approach to foreign policy made her reluctant to devote resources to the war in the Netherlands and the French Huguenots. Forward Protestants saw her policies as those of hesitancy and vacillation in some matters and dangerous obstinacy in others. In 1585–6, Elizabeth's support for the Netherlands campaign was seen as being too little and coming too late. In 1587, after urging from Sir Francis Walsingham and Lord Burghley to intervene in France, Elizabeth promised additional resources to the German prince John Casimir to raise an army to support Henry of Navarre, but quickly changed her mind. Burghley, who usually advocated a cautious approach in foreign policy, was moved to write to Walsingham that 'thus you see how her Majesty can find means at small holes to stop her own light. And so must I tell her today'.[65] Within the next year, the vehemently belligerent Catholic Guise faction had taken Paris, and Henry III had formed a pact with the pro-Spanish Catholic League.[66] The Protestants were increasingly weakened on the continent, and England, like Egypt, was in danger of isolation and attack by an expansionist imperial power. Antony's comments about women's mutability, that 'by nature women wav'ring are, / Each moment changing and rechanging mindes' (1.146–7) would have resonated with Elizabethan readers, as would Cleopatra's own acceptance of her 'errour and obstinancie' (2.475).

Garnier's political allegory of the Roman civil wars had an application to English Protestant anxieties, readily lending itself to new cultural constructs and topical resonances in late sixteenth-century England. Skretkowicz notes that Mary Sidney emphasized the horrors of war by using the technique of repetition. In the First Chorus, she added two sets of doublings to the first and fourth line below:

Warre and warres bitter cheare
  Now long time with us staie,
And feare of the hated foe
  Still still encreaseth sore.

(1.231–4)

This repetition, and her rewriting of Garnier's final line in the above quotation: 'Augmente en nos cours nuict et jour' (1.232), increases in our heart night and day, to 'Still still encreaseth sore' (1.234), underscores the ugliness of war.[67] As with France, the possible foreign and civil wars in England could be devastatingly long and horrifically drawn out.

Mary Sidney accentuated resemblances between Elizabeth I and Cleopatra in *Antonius*, so enhancing its topicality. Antony's description of Cleopatra as the 'Idoll of my heart' (1.7.78) echoes the rhetoric of courtship and adoration that had emerged around Elizabeth in the last decades of her reign.[68] Diomede's blazon of Cleopatra's Petrarchan beauty mirrors the visual iconography of Elizabeth in her portraiture:

The Allablaster covering of hir face,
The corall coullor hir two lipps engraines,

Her beamie eies, two Sunnes of this our world,
Of hir faire haire the fine and flaming golde.

(2.721–4)

Although this was the conventional Petrarchan way to describe any mistress, it was frequently applied in encomia to Elizabeth, as in Edmund Spenser's blazon of Belphoebe/Elizabeth in the *Faerie Queene*. Spenser describes his queen in very similar terms: 'Her face so faire as flesh it seemed not ... In her faire eyes two living lamps did flame ... Her yellow lockes crisped, like golden wyre.'[69] For Mary Sidney, Cleopatra's race might not have been an issue with the easy comparisons to Elizabeth and other topical resonances possible in Garnier. An alabaster Cleopatra depicted in all her Petrarchan beauty was less threatening and less foreign. As we have seen in the Introduction, there was already a tradition for fair-skinned Cleopatras and notions about her race were conflicted. Lisa Hopkins points out that informed Renaissance readers would know that Cleopatra was 'not of indigenous Egyptian origin', but a Ptolemy, descended from Alexander's Greek general.[70]

In translating *Marc Antoine*, Mary Sidney went further to English Garnier's French Cleopatra. Pascale Aebischer notes that she erased references to the saintliness of Cleopatra's love and beauty, her 'saintes amour' and her 'visage saints' (2.658), changing this to simply 'face' in Diomede's blazon (2.721).[71] She also erased explicit references in the description to Cleopatra's painted lips and whiteness (a sign of regal power and wealth in France). Garnier's depiction might have been too dangerous when Elizabeth was known for her own cosmetic practice and 'red and white painted beauty'.[72] Rather than cosmetically whitened, the Garnier-Sidney Cleopatra is, as Joyce Green MacDonald describes, 'emphatically, white-skinned'.[73]

Mary Sidney emphasized Cleopatra's eloquence and knowledge of languages in her translation of Diomede's description further highlighting resemblances with Elizabeth:

> Yet this is nothing the enchaunting skilles
> Of her cælestiall Sprite, hir training speache,
> Her grace, hir Majestie, and forcing voice,
> Wither she it with fingers speach consorte,
> Or hearing sceptred kings embassadors,
> Answer to eache in his owne language make.
>
> (2.727–32)

For Garnier's 'des artifices / De son spirit divin, ses mignardes blandices' (2.719–20), describing Cleopatra more as a coquette with cunning 'blandices' or 'flatteries', Mary Sidney gives us 'the enchaunting skilles / of her cælestiall Sprite, hir training speache'.[74] Elizabeth was also known for her knowledge of languages. John Florio's praise for the Queen's linguistic skills in the second preface 'To the Reader' in *Worlde of Wordes* (1598), his Italian-to-English dictionary, seems to echo the Plutarchian description of the Egyptian queen's linguistic skills on which the Sidney-Garnier Cleopatra is based. He observes 'that no embassador or stranger hath audience of hir Majestie, but in his native toong'.[75] That both queens were known for their linguistic powers, and that this was recognized in the period by contemporaries, is evidenced by Gabriel Harvey's note in his copy of Hoby's translation of Castiglione's *Courtier* (1561). In the section on 'The Chief Qualities Required in a Gentilwoman', Harvey notes '*Cleopatra. The Queen.*' by the line 'To be seene in the most neccessarie languages'.[76]

Mary Sidney's changes in the play served to heighten topical allusions in new contexts. Just as Cleopatra is not presented from the Roman point of view, neither is Octavius. As I noted previously, the popularity of Tacitus in the late sixteenth century led to a shift in perspective about the Augustan age as a propitious age directly linked to the birth of Christ. This allowed for more sympathy for Cleopatra and Antony.[77] Mary Sidney rendered Garnier's already negative portrayal of Octavius Caesar even more unfavourable, making him appear coarser, crueler and more arrogant where possible. For example, she added an unequivocally anti-Elizabethan resonance to Octavius's exchange with Agrippa advocating rule through repression rather than clemency, using Elizabeth's assertion that she ruled by 'the people's love'.[78] Mary Sidney also altered Caesar's reference to Antony's and Cleopatra's children as 'jumeaux d'adulterie' (4.1420), the twins of adultery, to '*Cleopatras* bratts' (4.1437).[79] In doing so, she emphasized the cold cruelty of Caesar's plans as he instructs Agrippa that 'Murther we must, untill not one we leave' (4.1515). Kewes has tried to recover Mary Sidney's political vision in accentuating Garnier's anti-Octavian construction, by highlighting the link that forward Protestants saw between Philip II's design for a universal monarchy and Octavius's similarly insatiable quest for imperial power.[80] The Sidneys had more reason than most to be interested in Philip II since Philip Sidney was named after him as Queen Mary's husband.[81] Like Philip II and his aggressive ambitions, Octavius relishes that 'As Monarch I both world and *Rome* commaund' (4.1377). As the son of the last Holy Roman Emperor, Charles V, Philip II exulted in Spain's imperial triumphalism, promoting his connection to imperial Rome and to the iconography of its Emperors in his own self-presentation, as evidenced by his Pompeii Leoni statue.[82]

That the Sidney circle were also seeing affinities between the Spanish king and Octavius is indicated by Fulke Greville, who cites Philip Sidney as referring to Philip II as 'Augustus-like', saying,

> the undertaking of this Antony single – I mean France – would prove a begetting of brave occasions jointly to disturb this Spanish Octavian in all his ways of crafty or forcible conquests, especially since Queen Elizabeth, the standard of this conjunction, would infallibly incline to unite with the better part.[83]

Although it is impossible to determine whether these were Sidney's comparisons or Greville's – and Greville is known for his deliberate obscurity – the words clearly suggest the application of Cleopatra's story to contemporary events. They express the forward Protestants' anxieties about 'this Spanish Octavian' and the situation in France, echoing Cleopatra's view of Octavius's war tactics: '*Cæsar* makes conspiring warre' (2.571).

Mary Sidney appropriated Garnier's political allegory to new and changing political circumstances for topical commentary. She sharpened comparisons between Egypt and England, Cleopatra and Elizabeth, and Octavius and Philip II. She used allegory not to assert direct one-to-one comparisons, but as the *Oxford English Dictionary* and *Spenser Encyclopedia* define the use of allegory at the time: 'in such a way as to indicate, by "aptly suggestive resemblances"' meanings that the reader could then recover.[84] This tallies closely with her brother's mode of reading history under the auspices of Gabriel Harvey (promoting an interpretation of classical history which was pragmatically oriented for application to the present political climate). Thus, in so doing, she was participating in the prevalent literary practice of her day, as exemplified by her brother Philip in his *Arcadia*, and Spenser in the *Faerie Queene* and *The Shepheardes Calender* (1579).[85] In the allegorical structures of Book V of the *Faerie Queene*, first published in 1596, Spenser obliquely comments on the Spanish Armada (V.8.24–30), and the trial of Mary Queen of Scots (V.9), guiding us to recover this meaning in the Proem to Book V with the insight provided by 'Ægyptian Wisards old'.[86] The allegorical aspects of Mary Sidney's *Antonius* were, therefore, part of an ongoing trend in the 1590s. At the beginning of Canto 8, referring specifically to Cleopatra, Spenser also writes of the power of women's beauty in making men forget their public duty: 'so did warlike *Antony* neglect / The worlds whole rule for *Cleopatras* sight' (V.8.2). In this respect, Spenser echoes the Garnier-Sidney interpretation of the impact of Cleopatra's image on Antony (discussed below).

For forward Protestants, Philip II and his imperial ambitions represented the greatest threat to England, France and the Netherlands on the international front, while a possible succession crisis and attack from an enemy within dominated domestic concerns. When Mary Sidney published her *Antonius*, it had been just three years since the execution of Mary Queen of Scots, and fears of a Catholic insurgency remained. While in the context of the 1590s and the Protestant rhetoric of the day, Mary Queen of Scots could also be seen as a queen who, like Cleopatra, had submitted to passion, the most urgent context in *Antonius* was the end of the dynasty and the Armada. Many Protestants feared that after Elizabeth's death they would face an interregnum that would be decided by a bloody civil and foreign war.[87]

For Mary Sidney, Garnier's tragedy was a means of memorializing her brother. It was a remedy for monarchical neglect and 'forgetfulness', providing coded advice to the Queen to secure the succession and not repeat the mistakes of the past. The lack of support for the cause of international Protestantism had led to the formation of a Franco-Spanish alliance in the first place, and, subsequently, the Armada. *Antonius* looked back as much to the Sidney Protestant politics of the 1580s as to the new anxieties and looming concerns of the 1590s.

Passion and regret

Antonius, foregrounding the danger of privileging private passion over public duty, explores the fall of great princes and warns of civil turmoil. Set on the final day of Antony's life, on the day Octavius enters Alexandria, sorrow and remorse permeate the play, as grief turns to acceptance of a grim new reality. A fire motif running through the play adds to the image of burning devastation, emphasizing both the destructive force of Antony's and Cleopatra's passion and Egypt's subjugation by Rome.[88] Philostratus' words underline the effect of this all-consuming passion, as 'Love, love ... / Hath lost this Realme inflamed with his fire' (2.283–4) and 'ashes made our townes' (2.286). Antony and Cleopatra know they have no option but to commit suicide or be led in the Roman triumph, while the Egyptian people know they face imminent foreign occupation. The use of the words 'since', 'still' and 'yet' evokes a sense of misfortune and helpless suffering. Antony realizes that in his end he is ultimately powerless since all forces are now aligned against him: 'Since cruell Heav'ns against me obstinate', and 'since men, since powers divine, / Aire, earth, and Sea are all injurious' (1.2, 4–5). The First Chorus, representing the Egyptian people, stoically meditates on the word 'still', knowing that 'still as long as we / In this low world remaine' (1.167–8) then 'Mishappes' will be 'our dayly mates' (1.169). For Cleopatra, no other loss, 'Loosing my Realme, loosing my liberty / My tender of-spring' (2.412–13), compares to losing Antony's love: 'yet, yet loosing more / Thee *Antony* my care' (2.414–15). For Cleopatra, Antony 'is my selfe' (2.595), but a distraught Antony addressing himself, feels he is 'scarse maister of thy selfe, / Late maister of so many nations' (1.130–1).

A sense of deep pathos is captured in the Egyptian queen as she attempts to deal with the devastation of defeat and the anguish that Antony now regards her as disloyal to him. Her very first lines in the play position her as a figure of constancy, as she wonders in disbelief that he should think 'That I would breake my vowed faith to thee?' (2.397) and 'yeelde thee to the rage / Of mightie foe?' (2.398–9). Rather than listening to advice to save her realm and herself, Cleopatra would rather die than live without Antony, stating quite simply that 'Without this love I should be inhumaine' (2.559). Along with profound pathos, there is a strong critique here – this is an astonishing admission of dependency by a monarch on another. In privileging her role as a lover, Cleopatra has lost sight of her queenship.

Passion has led to a loss of state on both a national and personal level, and a sense of inner division permeates the play. Loss of statehood is often coterminous with loss of self-hood in this period.[89] For Antony, it is the persistence of Cleopatra's 'Image' and the way that it haunts him that has ensured his downfall:

> Thy only care is sight of *Nilus* streames,
> Sight of that face whose guilefull semblant doth
> (Wandering in thee) infect thy tainted hart.
> Her absence thee besottes: each hower, each hower
> Of staie, to thee impatient seemes an age.
>
> (1.111–15)

His later repetition of this sentiment in the play, 'Each day, each night her Image haunts my minde, / Her selfe my dreames: and still I tired am' (3.922–3), suggests, as Sanders observes, how fully Cleopatra has become the subject of Antony's mind. He thinks and speaks of 'her Image', 'Her selfe', before he speaks of 'I'.[90] It is only after Actium that Antony realizes he has been careless of virtue, and so lost himself.

For Cleopatra, it is her 'Image', the 'sight of her face' and its impact on Antony, which in the end is the cause of their downfall:

> My face too lovely caus'd my wretched case.
> My face hath so entrap'd, so cast us downe,
> That for this conquest *Cæsar* may it thanke,
> Causing that *Antony* one army lost
> The other wholy did to *Cæsar* yeld.
>
> (2.437–41)

Cleopatra sees her beauty as a burden, a separate entity working against her and Antony. It is her 'too lovely face' which has caused her 'wretched case' (2.437) and been their undoing. Cleopatra's self-division and disenchantment with beauty is developed in Daniel, and places her with other women who have suffered because of their great beauty.

The sense of sorrow and remorse in the play is heightened by the use and idea of lament. Plaint is built into its very structure, in soliloquy, in choral lament, and in reported speech, as Antony, the people and Cleopatra all lament their circumstances. Philostratus's description of the Roman pillage of 'terror here and horror' (2.267) is the Egyptian people's lament as they mourn not only their condition but also the predicament of their queen: 'harts faile us, hopes are dead: / Our Queene laments' (2.270–1). The poems by Castiglione, Baldi and later by Favoriti on the Vatican *Cleopatra* gave the Egyptian queen a voice, expressing her sorrow and subjectivity.[91] French tragedy was in a state of experimentation in this period, and Garnier, who was at the forefront of this movement, followed Jodelle in giving Cleopatra a voice, while also fully incorporating the idea of plaint into his play. In Garnier's hands, the Roman civil wars became a lament for the French religious wars.

Garnier wrote his tragedy in a period that saw increasing outbreaks of civil war in France, including, in 1572, the St Bartholomew's Day massacre of Protestants. He saw war as punishment for individual or national transgression of moral law. Garnier's drama spoke of the threat of civil war ignited by private passion and interests. A loyal royalist, and a member of the King's Council, Garnier adopted a Tacitean view of the dangers to the state of a weak or corrupt monarch. His French readers would have found some parallels between Henri III and Antony as a pleasure-loving ruler.[92] Garnier's topical allegory of war also spoke to English fears of what might happen after Elizabeth's reign. France, like England, had a monarch in Henri III who was childless. With Henri III's death and the succession of the Protestant Henri IV in 1589, hardline religious views in France became more entrenched as the country faced full-scale civil war and a Spanish invasion.[93] In Mary Sidney's hands, Garnier's topical allegory became a warning of what England might also endure.

Mornay's *Discourse,* Garnier's *Antoine* and connections to women

Philip Sidney and Mornay were both in Paris during the St Bartholomew's Day massacre. They became friends when they sought refuge from the horror and carnage at the house of Sir

Francis Walsingham (Elizabeth's ambassador at the time and Sidney's future father-in-law). Mornay, a French aristocrat, was an influential political and philosophical theorist of the Huguenots. His *Excellent discours de la vie et de la mort* was written in 1575, three years after the massacre, and published the following year. Mornay's *Discourse* emphasizes Stoic virtue, the need to promote reason over passion, the fickleness of Fortune, the dangers of tyranny, and in discussing death and suicide, argues that 'to cast ourselves out of this world is in no sort permitted'.[94] Garnier's tragedy published in 1578 shares similar concerns with the conflict between reason and passion, tyranny and suicide. Garnier's *Antoine* and Mornay's *Discourse* were thus contemporaneous works – a product of a time of terror and war – and, like Garnier's tragedy, Mornay's essay does not advance any partisan interest.

For Mary Sidney, the events in France and the cause of international Protestantism were not some distant happening. The war in the Netherlands took her brother's life. With the backing of Walsingham and Philip Sidney, Mornay had visited England on diplomatic missions seeking support for the Huguenot cause. They had been bitterly disappointed at the Queen's meagre support. As Elizabeth Pentland observes, Mary Sidney knew four eyewitnesses to the massacre, all of whom could have been killed: Sidney, Walsingham, Mornay and his wife, Charlotte Arbaleste.[95] She would have heard the chilling details from her brother and been familiar with the stories of the others. Much of the Huguenot leadership which assembled in Paris for the royal wedding of Marguerite de Valois to Henri of Navarre was slaughtered at the time, and more than a thousand mutilated bodies of French Protestants were thrown into the blood-reddened Seine. The Mornays each went through harrowing ordeals in the quest to survive.[96] Mary Sidney's thinking about the dangers of civil war and the cause of international Protestantism would have been further informed by these events.

The ties of shared politics and a seminal friendship are well documented between Philip Sidney and Mornay.[97]

However, what some scholars have overlooked in Mary Sidney's decision to translate Garnier and Mornay together is that the *Discourse* is also a work connected to a woman. It was written by Mornay at the request of his wife, with translated excerpts from Seneca, and dedicated to her as Mademoiselle Du Plessis, as 'en faveur de vous' (a compliment to you).[98] Since Mary Sidney did not translate the prefatory dedication, this biographical subtext has remained relatively unnoticed. In translating the *Discourse*, she selected the work of her brother's friend and political ally, and also a work that, like Sidney's *Arcadia* to her, was inspired by and dedicated to a female family member. Where Hubert's female voice suggested Garnier's tragedy as a remedy for 'forgetfulness', Arbaleste requested Mornay's essay as a comfort to women. Both works were deeply rooted in the suffering of civil war, and both were closely connected to female family members. In Garnier, just as the Egyptian people know 'Our harmes worse dayly growe' (1.235), so the Roman Chorus worries 'Shall ever civile bate / gnaw and devour our state?' (4.1731–2). In the *Discourse*, Mornay blends classical and Christian ideals, without specifically referring to the massacre. Mornay passionately advocates an active public life and, calling imperial ambition a 'greedinesse of honour', he criticizes avaricious emperors, notably singling out Augustus, along with Alexander the Great and Charles V.[99] In this respect Mornay's piece can be read as a philosophical/political commentary on the Garnier play. In her biography of her husband, written for their only son in 1594, Arbaleste writes with pride of the *Discourse* being 'very well received by those of both religions'.[100]

Mary Sidney's decision to publish her work in 1592 might have had something to do with the dismay forward Protestants felt at Elizabeth's decision to recall the Earl of Essex from Rouen in France. She had finally agreed to send him there in August 1591, three years after the Armada, to assist Henri IV.[101] Mornay had arrived in England from Rouen on New Year's Day 1592 as Henri's agent and was intimately involved in these events. Arbaleste's biography provides rare insight into how Elizabeth's decision was perceived by Mornay and most probably by members of the alliance:

> But the negotiations proved inconceivably difficult although the chief nobles owned that his requests were most reasonable, necessary, dangerous to refuse and if they were refused would bring ruin on the King of France and imperil themselves. But no arguments could move the Queen from her determination that no more soldiers should go to France for she feared that their dispatch would furnish the Earl of Essex, Commander of the English troops, with an excuse for staying abroad. She, on the contrary was trying, at any cost, to get him back, by bribes, by persuasion, by threats of disgrace, all because he was the person she loved best in the whole world and for whom she most dreaded danger ... In short M. du. Plessis ... persuaded the King to apply the only possible remedy, to wit, pacifying her by sending the Earl home to England. Once this was done reinforcements were at once embarked though it is very true that they would have been of much greater use if they had been sent sooner.[102]

Elizabeth's decision to recall Essex could be viewed as uncomfortably close to Cleopatra's monarchical dependency and passion for another, as well as analogous to the Egyptian queen's decision to abandon the battle at Actium. Mary Sidney's publication of her translations in 1592 (the date entered in the Stationers' Register is 3 May 1592) appears connected to these events, and by the court's impending northern progress via Ramsbury in August, in a bid to lobby for the forward Protestant cause.[103]

Virtue in action

Blair Worden points out that for members of the Sidney circle, and later the Essex circle, who had done much to introduce

Tacitus to England, Protestantism became combined with humanism. This type of humanism was associated with the translation of classical history or philosophy and its application to the present political moment. It was especially centred in Cicero's dictum that 'virtue consists in action', when undertaken with foresight, prevention, resoluteness and personal responsibility.[104] Philip Sidney had encouraged his brother, Robert, to read Tacitus and his heavily annotated leather-bound copy survives (in the British Library), with his notes marking the section on 'vertu'.[105] The type of reading of history that Sidney is espousing – for Robert, or when he read Livy with Harvey – is one indebted in some ways to Machiavelli's redefining of 'virtù' and to his reading of the history of classical antiquity. As I discuss further in Chapter 2, that reading of classical history privileges a kind of ruthless pragmatism to do things at the opportune moment that is self-serving. Elizabeth was seen as vacillating, not acting with foresight, and not listening to 'uncorrupt counsel'.[106] Cleopatra seeks virtue in death, resolving that 'My only ende my onely dutie is' (2.649). For her, virtue is defined in a particularly Tacitean way, as 'That which us beseemes' (2.652) and she 'neither gaine, nor profit seke[s] therein' (2.645).

Although Antony is still in shock that 'one disordred act at *Actium* / The earth subdu'de, my glorie hath obscur'd' (3.1125–6), he knows that as a ruler 'Who heares nought, sees nought, doth nought of a king' (3.1199) he has left their subjects prey to the yoke of 'greedie Tyrannie' (3.1202). Just as a fire motif runs through the play so does sea imagery, and sometimes this is fused, as in the 'boyling tempest' (1.152) of the First Chorus's opening lines, doubly underscoring the destructive force of passion. This motif runs through all the acts, until Act 4, when with Antony's death Actium recedes, and Cleopatra's suicide and the certain end of her dynasty become just a matter of time. The people are left with a 'thousand thousand woes' (1.227), and Cleopatra is left with 'A thousand sobbes' and 'thousand plaints' (5.1999–2000), as she weeps over Antony adorning his mouth with 'A thousand kisses, thousand thousand more' (5.2019).

It is only in her end, with her anguished goodbye to her children in which she exhorts them 'your birth and high estate / Forget, my babes' (5.1885–6), that she sorrowfully accepts full responsibility for her neglect of duty and its impact on her monarchy, her state and her dynasty:

> Alas! Of mine the plague and poison I
> The crowne have lost my ancestors me left,
> This Realme I have to straungers subject made,
> And robd my children of their heritage.
>
> (5.1825–8)

Even here, for her, the loss of Antony ranks above all else, and the thought of joining him in death is imbued with sexual longing:

> To die with thee, and dieng thee embrace:
> My bodie joynde with thine, my mouth with thine,
> My mouth, whose moisture burning sighes have dried:
> To be in one selfe tombe, and one selfe chest,
> And wrapt with thee in one selfe sheete to rest.
>
> (5.1986–90)

There is a natural ambivalence and duality in Cleopatra's tragedy: just as Mary Sidney found sympathetic qualities in the Egyptian queen, she would also have seen shades of John Lydgate's charge that neglect and division are the chief cause of the destruction of regions and cities.[107] Although in the play, Cleopatra is courageous and portrayed as very much a queen, *Antonius* warns that even an essentially noble monarch can make disastrous mistakes when swayed by passion.

Mary Sidney's *Antonius* was at the forefront of a movement excavating Roman history for topical commentary and drawing lessons of political theory through drama.[108] In 1591, Philip and Robert Sidney's friend, Henry Savile, translated Tacitus's *Historiae* and *Agricola* into English and combined this with his own sketch, *The Ende of Nero and the Beginning of Galba.* Although interest in Tacitus, as Kewes notes, is often associated with the Jacobean era, Savile's translation, like *Antonius*, looks back to Protestant politics of the previous decade as well as to the 1590s and the end of Elizabeth's reign. It voices parallel concerns about the unsettled succession, the spectre of civil war and Spanish imperialism.[109] History was the preoccupation of Philip Sidney's friends and relatives, including Leicester. Worden aptly describes the importance of history to Sidney and his circle, stating that while 'ethical Humanism [which shows how men ought to be] was inherited by his generation, political history [which shows how men are] was discovered by it'.[110] For members of the circle, history was of use because it repeated itself. Mary Sidney was thus participating in the accepted literary practice and tradition of her close circle, using Roman history to extend her brother's legacy and support her family's political cause. Daniel paid her the highest compliment by dedicating his *Civil Wars* to her in 1609, a work he began when under her patronage at Wilton in the early 1590s. Pointing to the concerns with the succession and civil and foreign wars, and perhaps to the basis of their shared project, Daniel writes that 'it was a time which was not so well secur'd of the future'.[111]

Mary Sidney's decision to translate Garnier was a deeply complicated one. In Garnier, she found a work that was a means of memorializing her brother and a remedy for political inaction, reminding Elizabeth to not repeat past mistakes. There was much in Garnier that was already proto-feminist and had a topical relevance to England. Mary Sidney appropriated this, exploring political and intellectual issues related not only to the Egyptian queen but to Elizabeth I and female sovereignty at large. In this chapter, we have seen that she introduced a Cleopatra who was a figure of tragic female heroism to drama in England. We have thus already seen that Cleopatra held an interest for two of the most powerful aristocratic women of the period, Bess of Hardwick (discussed in the Introduction) and Mary Sidney. They both saw her as a figure of virtuous resistance, moving her beyond the seductress and destroyer of the Augustan narratives.

In selecting Daniel to continue his *Cleopatra* after her *Antonius*, Mary Sidney chose a poet eminently well suited in his ability to give Cleopatra an original English female voice. His *Rosamond* had already asked him to move his mind to 'a wofull womans case'.[112] In the next chapter, we will see how Daniel followed his patron's use of Roman history and developed the sorrow and pathos in the Egyptian queen's tragedy.

2

'Twixt majestie confuz'd and miserie': Samuel Daniel's *Tragedie of Cleopatra*

> With that (as all amaz'd) she held her still,
> Twixt majestie confuz'd and miserie.
> Her proud griev'd eyes, held sorow and disdaine,
> State and distresse warring within her soule.
>
> (*Cleopatra*, sig. D1r)[1]

Samuel Daniel's neo-Senecan closet drama, *The Tragedie of Cleopatra*, was entered in the Stationers' Register on 19 October 1593, and first published in 1594 in the third edition of *Delia and Rosamond augmented*. Written as a companion piece to the *Antonius* of his patron, Mary Sidney, Daniel's play, based on North's Plutarch, focuses on the final hours of Cleopatra's life. Beginning after Antony's death, with the Egyptian queen only staying alive to negotiate Octavius's clemency for her children, it ends with her suicide to die 'uncaptiv'd, and unwon' (sig. B3v). Daniel's work is important as an influence on Shakespeare and for evoking something new in English representations of Cleopatra, showing the grace, hesitancies and suffering of a great queen in defeat.[2] His rendering, centring on

Cleopatra's motherhood, and her guilt and sorrow, powerfully imagines the mental and emotional state of the Egyptian queen as her dynasty falls. Daniel thus added a more humane and penetrating dimension to Cleopatra's personal tragedy, while using the prose Argument prefaced to the play, and the all-Egyptian Chorus, to emphasize the national tragedy caused by her failure as ruler. This dualistic approach afforded Daniel the opportunity to explore the ambivalence inherent in the story of Cleopatra. He highlighted the splendour and pathos he saw in her, while using the play's political story to draw lessons from ancient history, as is more generally a feature of closet drama, and for topical commentary.

Cleopatra was a product of the intellectual and political influences of Wilton, and can be seen as a collaborative effort with Mary Sidney. Written at her behest and under her patronage, it was a continuation of her work. Peter Davidson and Jane Stevenson have introduced to the study of early modern women's cultural production the idea of elite women as 'devisers' of works. They argue that 'there is a case for expanding our ideas of what constitutes a cultural intervention to consider works that communicate a woman's intentions without necessarily being created by her own hand'.[3] These works, executed by others, were nevertheless expressions of the female patron's interests and views. Mary Sidney can be seen as a deviser in relation to Daniel's play.[4] Daniel confirms this in his dedication to the Countess in the 1594 edition of *Cleopatra*, saying he was 'contented with an humble song' – that is, his sonnet sequence *Delia*, on which he was working – but her 'well grac'd *Anthony*' required 'his *Cleopatras* company'.[5] He was being encouraged to turn to the higher genre of tragic drama, not just by Mary Sidney, but by other members of her circle, including Spenser.[6] In 'Colin Clouts Come Home Againe' (1595), written sometime after *Delia* and before *Cleopatra*, Spenser famously praised Daniel as 'a new shepheard late up sprong, / The which doth all afore him far surpasse', advising him to 'rouze his feathers quickly' to 'Tragick plaints and passionate mischance'.[7] Daniel says that Mary Sidney inspired him further to raise his spirits 'from out their low repose, / To sing of state, and tragick notes to frame'.[8] As we saw in *Antonius*, passion led to a loss of state on a national and personal level, with a sense of inner division permeating the play. In *Cleopatra*, while being roused to write about nationhood and high statecraft, Daniel explores the word 'state' as signifying both the body politic and an individual person's condition of existence.[9]

As a powerful author-patron, the Countess of Pembroke influenced what was being written. In Daniel, she found someone who shared the belief of the Sidney and Essex circles that history was for use since it was cyclical in nature and repeated itself. This group, Worden observes, saw history as providing 'important parallels with, and practical lessons for, the present', supplying 'the data on which political judgments can be based'.[10] Rather than conflicting with the Christian view of history which is linear and purposeful – from Genesis to Apocalypse – the classical view of history could be seen as occurring cyclically within this long linear framework.[11] *Cleopatra* responds to and enlarges on the themes and preoccupations of *Antonius*. These were imaginative works connecting to real history, to think about England and female sovereignty in the early modern period through another country. It is noteworthy that the Countess's translation was first published in 1592 as *Antonius, A Tragœdie*, along with *A Discourse of Life and Death*, and then published singly in 1595 as *The Tragedie of Antonie*. This change in title demonstrates that the two plays were intended to be viewed as companion pieces. That Mary Sidney's second edition was published in 1595 (a year after Daniel) might be due to the interest generated in Daniel's *Cleopatra* and in their tragedies as collaborative works.

Daniel's closet drama was a publishing success, quickly going through seven editions between 1594 and 1607. He was a habitual reviser of his work and although the 1594 text was reprinted almost identically in the 1595 and 1598 editions of *Delia and Rosamond augmented*, the 1599 *Cleopatra* appeared in *The Poeticall Essayes* with a revised first act. This strengthened the poetic tone and philosophical thought of Cleopatra's long opening soliloquy and included other minor changes throughout the play.[12] This text was reprinted with more minor revisions in the *Workes* of 1601/2, and published with additional alterations in the *Certaine Small Poems* of 1605. Daniel's 1607 *Certaine Small Workes*, reprinted in 1611, marked his final reshaping of *Cleopatra*. It offered a much revised and expanded version of the play, with a softening in his portrayal of the Egyptian queen (the 1607 edition is discussed below and in Chapter 5 in relation to Shakespeare). A posthumous edition of his *Whole Workes*, using the 1601/2 text, was brought out in 1623 by his brother, John Danyel. *Cleopatra* thus went through a total of nine editions, with five sets of alterations. As such, it is unique in the representations of Cleopatra in literature, in that Daniel's revisions and changes to his editions express a sustained authorial interest and an evolving engagement in her characterization over at least a thirteen-year period.[13] In this chapter, I look at Daniel's early Cleopatra and then at his final reworking of the Egyptian queen. I examine the possible reasons for his major 1607 revision, and seek to locate this in the context of circumstances in Daniel's own life, especially the impact of his most controversial work, *Philotas* (1605), and the trouble its apparent allusions to the Earl of Essex caused two years earlier.

Daniel's *Cleopatra* responds to prevailing topical concerns, which for forward Protestants became centred on the possibility of a succession crisis caused by an ageing Elizabeth's refusal to name an heir. They feared that in such an event, a weakened England would face a two-pronged attack – both from Catholic Spain and from the Catholic threat within. Kewes persuasively argues that the end of the Ptolemaic dynasty, which hit a raw nerve with the impending end of England's own Tudor dynasty, is given significance in *Cleopatra* in the Argument itself: 'And so, hereby came the race of the Ptolomies to bee wholie extinct, and the flourishing rich kingdome of Egypt utterlie over-throwne and subdued' (sig. B2r). The Chorus in turn blames Cleopatra for not taking heed of the lessons of history: 'And thus she hath her state, herselfe and us undonne' (sig. C3v). The queen's actions have brought about not only her own downfall, but also the ruination of her kingdom, her dynasty and her people.[14]

For Daniel, however, there was something more in Cleopatra – there was the aesthetic as well. He found a complexity and substance in her, which made his rendering of her as a woman in crisis much more than a political vehicle. Daniel imbued Cleopatra with pathos and grace, highlighting her hesitations and vulnerability. This is depicted in her reaction to Dolabella's message, with her realization that there is no more temporizing with Caesar and that her suicide is now upon her:

> She turns her backe, and with her, takes me in,
> Reades in thy lines thy strange unlookt for tale:
> And reades, and smiles, and staies, and doth begin
> Againe to reade, then blusht, and then was pale.
> And having ended with a sigh, refoldes
> Thy Letter up: and with a fixed eye,
> (Which stedfast her imagination holds)
> She mus'd a while, standing confusedly.
>
> (sig. H3v–H4r)

That Daniel was able to create something distinctive and sympathetic, while following the Countess's use of ancient Roman history, is a testament to his sensibility and poetic imagination. His Cleopatra's blushing and turning pale in the above lines is in the same tradition of whiteness as his patron's fair alabaster Cleopatra (2.426). However, while Diomede's blazon in *Antonius* lists Cleopatra's physical attributes in Petrarchan terms (coral lips, fine gold hair), Daniel emphasizes Cleopatra's beauty but provides no physical description to indicate her racial identity.[15] Issues of Cleopatra's race disappear in Daniel as he introduces similarities with an ageing Elizabeth (discussed further below).

Although Daniel's neo-Senecan drama is little known now, its wide currency and circulation in its own time have been pointed out by Peter Blayney in his study of early English plays. Looking at the number of editions these plays went through inside a twenty-five-year period to form a best-seller list, Blayney notes that if he had included closet and academic plays, *Cleopatra* would have ranked second in the number of editions published. It reached its eighth edition seven years more quickly than did *Doctor Faustus* (1604), and it did better than any of Shakespeare's plays. Although this account is complicated by the fact that *Cleopatra* was never issued singly, and was always published in a collection of Daniel's poems, it still shows the high profile of his work.[16] In this chapter, I use the 1599 edition of *Cleopatra* published in *Poeticall Essayes*, and the 1607 *Cleopatra* in *Certaine Smalle Workes*.[17] The 1599 *Cleopatra* is chosen when looking at Daniel's early representation, since this is the edition in which he made his first careful revision, strengthening Cleopatra's philosophical thought and expression. Coming some five years after his play was first composed, it is that much deeper into the impending succession crisis with an ageing Elizabeth on the throne. It is also the edition in which he chose to introduce his *Letter from Octavia* and include the first five books of the *Civil Wars*, and the edition printed in Bullough as a probable source for Shakespeare's *Antony and Cleopatra* (1606–7).[18]

The Queen's two bodies

Daniel's play, foregrounding the conflict between the public and private selves of a monarch, explores what happens when majesty is confused. Daniel's Cleopatra sorrowfully realizes 'I was not I' (sig. B3v) and wishes 'were I not I' (sig. B4v), in what may be seen as a deliberate echo of Philip Sidney's 'I am not I' from Sonnet 45 in *Astrophil and Stella*.[19] For her this self-referential echo is a rejection of her own subjectivity and sense of self as queen.[20] She is here both disappointed in and rejecting her sense of self as ruler, and has no single essence, no single 'I', being divided between 'I' as woman and 'I' as ruler. With Antony already dead, she is only delaying her suicide to save her children's lives:

> That's it alas detaines me from my tombe,
> Whiles Nature brings to contradict my soule
> The argument of mine unhappy wombe ...
> Bloud, Children, Nature, all must pardon me.
> My soule yeelds honor up the victory,
> And I must be a Queene, forget a mother,
> Though mother would I be, were I not I;
> And Queene would not be now, could I be other.
>
> (sig. B4v)

The conflict between the role of a mother and a queen touched on in *Antonius* – with the Egyptian queen's wrenching goodbye to her children before her suicide – is made central in *Cleopatra*. In Daniel, the focus shifts more specifically to her son, Caesario, allowing for a more sympathetic and detailed treatment, with Cleopatra actively trying to save him. Cleopatra is facing a decidedly unnatural choice here: to be noble in her end she must quell her maternal instinct to stay alive and protect her son.[21] She knows that her 'dissolution is become / The grave of *Ægypt*, and the wracke of all' (sig. B3v), and wonders in desperation 'O my devided soule, what shall I do? / Whereon shall now my resolution rest?' (sig. G1r). Struggling to decide on a best course, she asks, 'When both are bad, how shall I know the best?' (sig. G1v).

For Daniel and his readers, the division between the private and public selves of a monarch held an immediate resonance with a queen regnant. Marie Axton has shown that Elizabeth I's own strategy of self-empowerment involved a delicate balancing of the feminine frailty of the body natural and the masculine strength of the body politic.[22] Daniel's informed readers would have found affinities between Cleopatra's desire of 'could I be other' (sig. B4v) and Elizabeth's own speeches, which had, at times, obliquely hinted at a wistfulness about the special burden that a female monarch faced. In these she wished that she were also someone else and not a queen.[23] Daniel may have drawn on this to invoke sympathy for his Cleopatra. This sense of wistfulness is more deeply expressed in the voice of a poem 'On Monsieur's Departure' (c.1582), presumed to be written by a grieving Elizabeth on the failure of the Anjou match. Although no manuscripts of the poem are known to exist from Elizabeth's lifetime, and so its circulation remains unknown, a line from her work – 'since from myself another self I turned' (l. 6) – also exists in another variant form: 'since from myself my other self I turned'. The poem survives in a late seventeenth-century copy in the hand of an amanuensis of Archbishop William Sancroft's (1617–93), and is believed copied from an early seventeenth-century manuscript which includes the variant.[24] Although the 'other self' has usually been read as referring to Anjou, the words bear striking affinities to the theme captured in *Cleopatra* of the conflict between a monarch's divided selves. They may perhaps reflect Elizabeth's own recognition of a moment of self-reflective isolation as she realized she would have to shut down the body natural part of herself and any desire she may have had for children of her own.[25] As such, her words 'from myself my other self I turned' can be read as her acknowledgement that she was turning away from not just Anjou, but also her feminine self, her younger fertile self and her potential child.

When Daniel was writing in 1599, forward Protestant fears of Elizabeth's submission to passion and a Catholic match were, of course, long averted. She had chosen to remain unmarried, positioning herself, instead, as the nation's Virgin Queen and symbolic mother, but Protestant memories of that traumatic time still existed and were now revived in relation to succession anxiety. They were also rekindled in context with Elizabeth's relationship with Essex and other favourites, amid concerns that her passions might unduly govern her reason in political matters. There was thus continuing tension between her private and public selves.

The dichotomy between the public and private was also a personal and important one for Daniel. John Pitcher observes that 'the division between public and private audiences is everywhere in his work'.[26] In *Cleopatra*, Daniel was able to locate and explore the division between public and private states in the Egyptian queen's story itself, since these types of states are directly connected with the dilemma of the monarch.[27] Majesty cannot waver from its essential role as ruler. Cleopatra blames herself for being 'made the meanes of miserie' (sig. C1r) for her nation and sees herself as an example to future princes, saying:

> And let me write in letters of my bloud
> A fit memoriall for the times to come,
> To be example to such Princes good
> As please themselves, and care not what becom.
>
> (sig. C1r)

In the politically fraught atmosphere of the 1590s, Elizabeth was also seen as a prince who pleased herself. As the nation's mother, she was viewed as careless of her charge by not naming a designated Protestant heir, leaving England open to the danger of civil war and a Spanish invasion. The Queen's positioning of herself as the nation's mother was readily used against Elizabeth to show her as a negligent mother and, as Helen Hackett points out, was 'deployed to depict the unhealthy state of the body politic'.[28] The Puritan parliamentarian, Peter Wentworth, used this maternal imagery in his pamphlet, *A Pithie Exhortation* (1598), comparing Elizabeth to 'a nursing mother', urging her to look after the nation's welfare by appointing an heir as 'wee your children cry upon you' not to 'unaturallie leave us ... spoile of the mercilesse bloodie sword'.[29] Daniel's emphasis on Cleopatra's motherhood would find resonance in this climate with Elizabeth's own symbolic role and perceived neglect of England.

The sense of frustration and impatience among forward Protestants with her refusal to name an heir and rejection of a more aggressive policy towards Spain is reported by André Hurault, Sieur de Maisse, the French ambassador to the Elizabethan court. In his contemporaneous *Journal* of 1597, Maisse records the Earl of Essex telling him in a private conversation that 'they laboured under two things in this Court, delay and inconstancy, which proceeded mainly from the sex of the Queen'.[30] That a general sense of neglect and delay was being felt is confirmed by Henry Percy, 9th Earl of Northumberland, who was connected to the Essex circle by marriage to the Earl's sister, Dorothy Devereux. In his correspondence with James VI of Scotland, whom the English nobility were beginning to court as the possible heir, he complains: 'The nobility are unsatisfied ... That offices are not given them as they were wont; that her majesty is parsimonious and slow to relieve their wants'.[31] Forward Protestants feared England would soon be facing the serious consequences of what they perceived to be female monarchical hesitations.

In Daniel's *Cleopatra*, the Egyptian Chorus questions the impact of monarchical decisions on the common man:

> But is it Justice that all we
>   The innocent poore multitude,
>   For great mens faults should punisht be ...
> O why should th'heavens us include,
>   Within the compasse of their fall
>   Who of themselves procured all?

(sig. F2v)

The Chorus stresses that it is the innocent people who suffer devastating consequences for the actions, inactions and failings of their ruler. In the *Civil Wars*, the work on which must have begun during his Wilton years, Daniel expressed his particular brand of historiography and perspective of the ambiguous nature of the public view:[32]

> For, some the world must have, on whom to lay
> The heavie burthen of reproche and blame;

Against whose deedes, th'afflicted may invay,
As th'onely Authors, whence destruction came.
(*Civil Wars* V, stanza 65)

This raises the question of whether we should see the Chorus in Daniel as impartial observers of history, or as those who jump to a quick moralizing condemnation of Cleopatra as the sole author of their destruction.

One queen who had been unable to negotiate the divide between the two selves of a monarch successfully was Mary, Queen of Scots. She had confided in Thomas Randolph, the English ambassador to Scotland, on 8 March 1564, that 'Princes at all times have not their wills, but my heart being my own is immutable'. To John Guy, her words were an honest and revelatory response to Elizabeth's pressure to try and marry her off, implying she 'intended to keep something of her own in her heart'.[33] Her unwise alliances, however, left her open to charges of lustfulness from her enemies and to pointed comparisons with the Whore of Babylon. Anti-Catholic English Protestant works, such as those by William Fulke (1573), compared the Whore of Babylon with Cleopatra in 'riot', an implicit identification with Mary.[34] As Pettegree notes, the available analogues in the 1590s between Cleopatra and Mary Stuart – modified with her execution in 1587, to show her more as a tragic figure contained 'within a moral tale of political folly' – provided a useful cover for Mary Sidney's and Daniel's works.[35]

Motherhood compared and majesty confused

Daniel extensively explored the dualism he located in *Cleopatra*, using the Egyptian queen and her fate for topical commentary and lessons of political theory, while emphasizing the suffering and grace in her personal tragedy. He created a Cleopatra who was very different from his patron Mary Sidney's characterization of her as a faultless Petrarchan beauty. His portrayal is of a sorrowful Cleopatra, a 'wofull mother' (sig. B4v) and a 'wofull Queene' (sig. G3v), worried after her death for her 'distressed seede', who 'Kings design'd, must subjects live to other; / Or else, I feare, scarse live, when I am dead' (sig. B4v). Although Daniel's references to Cleopatra's maternity would find resonance with Elizabeth's role as the nation's metaphorical mother, it is in his rendering of her as a literal mother that he also captured the pathos and tragedy in her situation. As she says:

> No other crowne I seeke, no other good.
> Yet wish that *Cæsar* would vouchsafe this grace,
> To favour the poore ofspring of my blood.
>
> (sig. D2r)

Daniel imagines a Cleopatra in her final days whose only focus is to save her children. She is depicted throughout the play as a mother, struggling to part with her son, knowing she has no choice but to send him far away to India if she is to have any chance of saving him. Realizing that this 'may be tis the last / That ever I shall speake to thee my Sonne', she asks in anguish, 'What, must I end when I have scarce begun?' (sig. G1v). All her hesitancy and division in the play are about her son; there is no doubt in her mind about Caesar's plans for her as his 'greatest Trophey' (sig. F1v), or about her impending suicide.

The portrayal of Cleopatra's actual motherhood produced a silent contrast with, and a criticism of, Elizabeth's metaphorical motherhood. Against the Egyptian queen's heartache and tenderness for her children, England's queen could be construed as appearing heartless, unfeminine and unnatural. Daniel was thus able to create a close integration between his use of political commentary and his sympathetic characterization. In this he adopted a strategy similar to the use of political commentary in other literary productions of the period, such as Spenser's *Faerie Queene*, which resisted any dogmatic position, instead exploring the implications of a multiplicity of viewpoints.[36] This would have held an appeal to Daniel's natural scepticism and his ability to see both sides, refined further by the influence of Montaigne on the dangers of certainty.[37]

Daniel's tragedy echoes the Garnier-Sidney view of war as punishment for individual or national transgression. The metaphor of fire in *Antonius*, representing the destructive force of Antony's and Cleopatra's passion, shifts in *Cleopatra* to one of confusion in the aftermath of Antony's suicide and Octavius's 'easie entrance' (sig. H3r) into Alexandria. There is a sexual resonance here, of a political rape, as Caesar takes advantage of Egypt and its monarch's 'confus'd weakenesse' (sig. H3r). Cleopatra blames herself for bringing 'confusion to my state' (sig. C1r), as she wonders:

> Yet do I live, and yet doth breath extend
> My life beyond my life? nor can my grave
> Shut up my griefes, to make my end my end?
> Will yet confusion have more then I have?
>
> (sig. B3r)

Confusion is personified here, with it being positioned as an adversary in the opening lines of the play itself, extending the idea of a political rape. Confusion is everywhere, as Daniel contrasts the Egyptian queen's personal confusion and suffering with the war and foreign occupation bearing down on her people. The word 'confusion' and its cognates occur at least eleven times in the play, and the motif of confusion, further underscored by riot and disorder, runs through all five acts of *Cleopatra*. As Cleopatra's world is falling apart, so is 'Egypt servile rendred / to the insolent destroyer' (sig. H3r). This is a marked departure from the Augustan narrative which constructed Cleopatra as seducer and destroyer.

The Fourth Chorus's criticism of Cleopatra's monarchical neglect seems to reflect the forward Protestant view of Elizabeth's neglect of England's future well-being:

> For all (respecting private pleasure,)
>   universally consenting
> To abuse their time, their treasure,
>   in their owne delights contenting:
> And future dangers nought respecting, ...
> Made this so generall neglecting.
>
> (sig. H3r)

The Chorus emphasizes that even 'Kings small faults, be great offences', leaving the way open to 'licence, lust, and riot' (sig. H2v). Cleopatra's 'confus'd weakenesse' has caused 'confus'd Disorder' (sig. H2r), resulting in the subjugation of her realm, the end of her dynasty and her suicide. The Final Chorus's closing lines sums up the reason for the rise and fall of empires: 'Doth Order order so / Disorders overthro?' (sig. K4v). However, by this point in the play we experience the triumph of Order as oppressive and as a loss, and we strangely regret the overthrow of the Disorder personified by Cleopatra, as conventional values are turned on their heads.

The idea of *Cleopatra* as complaint

In looking at how Daniel shaped his Egyptian queen, scholars have examined the influence of Daniel's sources, especially Garnier's *Marc Antoine* (1579) and Jodelle's *Cléopâtre Captive* (1552).[38] Both these French neo-Senecan dramas were major influences: Mary Sidney's *Antonius*, the work which led to Daniel's commission to write a companion piece, was a translation of Garnier, while Jodelle's *Cléopâtre Captive* was influential as the first French tragedy to revive classical traditions. Like Jodelle, Daniel's tragedy is set after Antony's death. However, while these plays have been discussed as sources, what scholars have missed is the possible influence on Daniel of the *Cleopatra* statue in the Vatican's Belvedere Courtyard and the many poems it inspired in the sixteenth and seventeenth centuries, including Castiglione's.[39] The statue was an influence on the Italian and French neo-Senecan Cleopatra tragedies, and was described in influential works, such as William Thomas's *Historie of Italie* (1549), as 'the sorowful Cleopatra, liyng by the river side'.[40] It seems plausible to think that Daniel, with his connections to Florio, and his knowledge of Italian, would have been aware of these poems and the statue. He may also have heard of them while travelling in Northern Italy during 1590 and 1591, shortly before he came under Mary Sidney's patronage.[41] Castiglione's poem, in particular, speaks sorrowfully in Cleopatra's voice foregrounding her grief, and might well have influenced Daniel's own view of the grace and pathos in her tragedy.

Daniel recognized that in 1594, at Wilton, he had captured something new in his shaping of Cleopatra, showing her suffering, vacillation and confusion in defeat.[42] While the neo-Senecan form is known for drawing on Stoic influences and themes, Daniel also emphasized a close scrutiny and attention to Cleopatra's emotions, thus adopting a sceptical and self-reflective stance, in the manner of Montaigne. Daniel's choice of title, *The Poeticall Essayes*, for his first collected edition, can be seen to reflect his enthusiasm for Montaigne's *Essayes*.[43] In his dedication to Mary Sidney in the 1611 edition, Daniel explained his approach, saying he had attempted to imagine Cleopatra's tragedy:

In th'habit I conceiv'd became her care
Which if to her it be not fitted right
Yet in the sute of nature sure it is
And is the language that affliction might
Perhaps deliver when it spake distresse.[44]

He is trying to give expression to the inner story of what it would have been like for Cleopatra when her dynasty fell. In his portrayal, Daniel creates a great queen with a sophisticated mind who recognizes all is lost. Drawing on Plutarch, Mary Sidney highlighted Cleopatra's eloquence and linguistic skill in her translation. Daniel's Cleopatra knows that all she has left are her words and that there is no way out. Her language is thus elaborate and inventive.[45] This is not the only form of mediation. Daniel also captured this language of 'affliction' and 'distresse' in his Cleopatra's expression and inner being: 'Her proud griev'd eyes, held sorow and disdaine' with 'State and distresse warring within her soule' (sig. D1r). She is shown wrestling with her devastatingly altered circumstances, both in her own eyes – 'Now who would thinke that I were she who late / With all the ornaments on earth inrich'd' (sig. B3v) – and in the eyes of others, such as in this moving description by Proculeius:

> Like as a burning Lampe, whose liquor spent
> With intermitted flames, when dead you deeme it,
> Sends forth a dying flash, as discontent ...
> Th'imperious tongue unused to beseech,
> Authoritie confounds with prayers, so
> Words of comand conjoin'd with humble speech.
>
> (sig. D1v)

Daniel's emphasis here is very much on contradictions in the Montaignian mode, which later underpins Shakespeare's own appropriation of Montaigne in *Antony and Cleopatra*. As I argued in the Introduction, Shakespeare's Cleopatra is far more complex than the simplified image of her as a sultry siren that dominates popular perceptions today, and we see here that this complexity derives from sources and precedents – including Mary Sidney and Daniel – which already offered sophisticated and subtle versions of Cleopatra.

In England, Daniel's poem *The Complaint of Rosamond* (1592) can in many ways be seen to inaugurate the complaint genre, or to at least prompt the flurry of female complaints written between 1592 and 1594 which were also inspired by Ovid's *Heroides*.[46] The poems on the Vatican *Cleopatra* by Castiglione, Baldi and later Favoriti gave the Egyptian queen a voice expressing her sorrow and subjectivity, showing that her story was suitable for the genre of female complaint.[47] Writing *Rosamond* prepared Daniel for writing about Cleopatra. His poem, a complaint in the voice of the ghost of Rosamond Clifford who was seduced by Henry IV and poisoned by his queen, explored tragic femininity and the vulnerable situation of elite women. Daniel's *Cleopatra* was first published with *Delia* and *The Complaint of Rosamond*, two femino-centric texts. Kewes has seen this placement, particularly that of *Rosamond* and *Cleopatra*, as inducing 'the reader to compare the repercussions of the monarch's sexual incontinence in terms of gender and historical setting'.[48] I would argue that this spatial proximity also serves to emphasize Cleopatra's tragedy, placing her in the tradition of female complaint. While Garnier experimented with the idea of complaint from the perspectives of all those mourning their condition after Octavius's victory, the tragedy of Cleopatra was clearly ready to be explored in greater depth from the female perspective.

Daniel's commission to write such a play brings Cleopatra into direct contact with the genre and idea of plaint. The opening soliloquy of Daniel's Cleopatra mirrors Antony's long opening speech and complaint in the Garnier-Sidney interpretation. Her soliloquy can in effect be described as a lament for her loss of self, for Antony's downfall, for her children's fate, and for the Egyptian state, as she accepts responsibility for her 'unforseeing weakenesse' (sig. B3v), which has brought devastation to all. Cleopatra places herself within this tradition, referring to herself as a 'wofull woman' (sig. D1v), left to 'this horror, to lamenting' (sig. D2r). Spenser seems to have recognized in Daniel that 'most, me seemes, thy accent will excell / In tragick plaints and passionate mischance'.[49]

John Kerrigan has drawn attention to the fashion for female complaint in the sixteenth and seventeenth centuries in England and discussed the concept of 'Complaint Enlarged', as writers explored complaints in Renaissance tragedy, epistles and plaints in music.[50] Daniel, I would argue, seems to have taken an interest in exploring and experimenting with the genre of female complaint in both non-dramatic and dramatic forms. We thus have his *Complaint of Rosamond* (1592), a complaint in the form of a narrative poem; *The Tragedie of Cleopatra* (1594), a complaint in dramatic form; and *The Letter from Octavia to Marcus Antonius* (1599), an epistolary complaint.[51] In *Cleopatra*, Daniel takes us through the various stages of grief and complaint – bereavement, the loss of state, the idea of living beyond the moment when life has ended, anger, self-blame and regret, betrayal, and a sense of isolation.[52] Elizabeth Harvey points out that 'there is a profound affinity between the representations of the abandoned woman and male constructions of the feminine voice'.[53] Daniel seems to have gone even further and found a personal affinity with the women in crisis about whom he wrote.

Daniel's portrayal of Cleopatra is distinctive in drama in English for the voice he gave to her suffering, imagining her distress in her final days. In 1599, Daniel also introduced his *Letter from Octavia*, written as an epistolary complaint to Antony who was in Egypt with Cleopatra. It was dedicated to Margaret Clifford (née Russell), Countess of Cumberland, whose own husband, George Clifford, 3rd Earl of Cumberland, was well known for his philandering. *Octavia* was published with Daniel's first revision of *Cleopatra*, which, as Russell E. Leavenworth notes, resulted in a softening of some of the Egyptian queen's self-accusatory statements.[54] It is remarkable that Daniel produced and published works in the same collection that were written sympathetically from both Cleopatra's and Octavia's points of view, giving both a voice. It is also noteworthy that in both these works Antony's voice is absent; they are purely focused on the women, emphasizing the perspective of each. Writing about Daniel's sympathy for women in distress, Joan Rees comments that he was well able to 'enter into Octavia's grief' and still see the splendour and suffering in Cleopatra.[55]

If we accept that *Cleopatra* is a complaint in dramatic form, then what becomes apparent is that Daniel is exploring female complaints in different forms in order of historical occurrence.

Cleopatra was first published in 1594 with *Delia* and *Rosamond*, and it is only in this edition that the works appear in the order in which they were composed (*Delia*, followed by *Rosamond* and then *Cleopatra*). However, a survey of Daniel's editions from 1599 to 1611 finds the complaints are in the order of historical occurrence, suggesting a deliberate placement of works in this particular sequence in all seven editions: *The Letter from Octavia, Cleopatra* and *Rosamond*.[56] Each of these works reflects Daniel's deep sympathy towards the vulnerable situation of elite women.

Some feminist scholars, however, have not viewed Daniel's Cleopatra in the same way. They see his portrayal, especially his early rendering, as a deliberately regressive and conservative departure from Mary Sidney's constant Cleopatra. Mimi Dixon, for example, sees Daniel's Cleopatra as a 'stereotypical femme fatal', who is 'too dark, seductive, and exotic – for empathy'. Eve Sanders finds Daniel's play to be a 'condemnation of Cleopatra as an example of lust, vanity, and inconstancy'.[57] This is a very different reading to the one I argue here. In the light of more recent political readings of *Cleopatra*, Daniel can be seen as furthering his patron's vision and sympathetic in his treatment. It is apparent if we look back at the publication history of the Countess's play (discussed earlier in this chapter) that she viewed Daniel's representation as such and saw both works as companion pieces. Daniel de-emphasized Cleopatra's race and sexuality, giving prominence to her motherhood, suffering and vulnerability. He is exploring the different possibilities for female heroism in his work. His transformation of Cleopatra, as shown through this chapter, is significant in its construction of female subjectivity in literature.[58] Daniel brought a sensitivity and elegance to the Egyptian queen's tragedy, giving her an original English female voice. As we will see in the following chapter, a young Jacobean aristocratic woman specifically identified with Daniel's Cleopatra and wanted to speak through his lines.

Age, disenchantment with beauty, and grace

In a departure from both Plutarch and the Countess, Daniel aged his Egyptian queen, portraying her in her 'beauties waine' with 'new appearing wrinkles of declining' (sig. C2r). Plutarch tells us that when 'Cæsar and Pompey knew her she was but a young thing, and knew not what the worlde ment: but nowe she went to Antonius at the age when a womans beawtie is at the prime, and she also of best judgement'.[59] With an ageing Elizabeth on the throne, and fears of a succession crisis after her death, Daniel's deliberate ageing of his Cleopatra heightened the topicality of his play, reflecting the preoccupation with transience and mutability in this period. The unease felt in the 1590s about the Queen's mutability reached a peak as her subjects were forced to contemplate the possibility of her death. While Spenser expressed this political anxiety in the *Mutabilitie Cantos* in his portrayal of the Cynthia/Diana figure, they were not published until 1609, perhaps because they were regarded as too critical. This anxiety was also expressed in other works, including Ralegh's *The 21th: and last booke of the Ocean to Scinthia* (1592), Chapman's *Hymnus in Cynthiam* (1593), and Henry Cuffe's 'A Poem made on the Earle of Essex (being in disgrace with Queene Elizabeth)', which abounds in images of sickness and decay.[60]

By the 1590s, Elizabeth's age and beauty had become a political matter, and even imagining a declining Elizabeth could be seen as treacherous under the severe Treason Acts of 1571 and 1581. Although Elizabeth's royal iconography depicted her as ageless, wearing what Roy Strong describes as 'the mask of youth', she was already sixty in 1594 when Daniel first wrote his play, and there was an acute interest in the Queen's ageing body.[61] For Elizabeth, facing the unique burdens of a female monarch, her beauty, or the fading of it, was not just about looks; it was also a power issue. Lacking Mary Sidney's 'protective screen of a foreign original', Kewes emphasizes that 'Daniel's manipulation of the story was by far the more provocative.'[62]

Perhaps one of the most interesting themes in Daniel's *Cleopatra* is the Egyptian queen's response to her own beauty and to what that incredible face, 'the wonder of her life' (sig. K2v), has brought her. Although she admits that in her youth at the height of her beauty she 'thought all men must love me of dutie; / And I love none' (sig. C2r), Cleopatra is now weary of men falling in love with her. This is shown in her reaction to Dolabella's falling for her and to his warning that she is to be led in Caesar's triumph:

> What, hath my face yet powre to win a Lover?
> Can this torne remnant serve to grace me so,
> That it can *Cæsars* secrete plots discover
> What he intends with me and mine to do?
> Why then poore Beautie thou hast done thy last,
> And best good service thou could'st do unto mee.
> For now the time of death reveal'd thou hast,
> Which in my life didst serve but to undoe mee.
>
> (sig. G4r)

There is a disenchantment with beauty: for the Garnier-Sidney Cleopatra it is a burden; for Daniel's Cleopatra, her beauty is 'poore Beautie'. The theme of self-division is further developed as she separates her beauty from herself, addressing it as a separate entity. Her beauty is a victim of itself, bringing about her fate and undoing – her liaisons with Rome which 'Have had mine age a spoile, my youth a pray' (sig. H4r). This is a very different characterization from Shakespeare's Cleopatra.

In Daniel, Cleopatra sees herself as a debtor to the men who care and have cared for her. There is something deeply vulnerable and humanizing in this sense of indebtedness, revealing insecurity in spite of her great beauty and power. She feels this way both towards Antony for loving her in 'This Autumne of my beauty bought so dearely / For which in more then death, I stand thy debter' (sig. C2v), and to Dolabella for showing her grace in her defeat, saying: 'I must die his debter, / For *Cleopatra* now can love no more' (sig. G4r). She is now a 'wofull wife' (sig. H1r), focused on joining Antony in death so 'That both our soules, and all the world shall find / All recknings cleer'd, betwixt my love and thine' (sig. C2v). This image system and discourse of 'debt' and 'reckning' is a significant transformation of Cleopatra from the Augustan narrative which portrayed the Egyptian queen as deeply calculating and planning to seduce Octavius to save herself.

Just as the word 'confusion' runs through the play, so does the word 'grace'. It occurs at least fifteen times in the play (though used in a variety of senses), and carries here the force of both its political and religious meanings. Cleopatra is seeking grace for her children from Octavius, wishing 'that *Cæsar* would vouchsafe this grace, / To favour the poore ofspring of my blood' (sig. D2r). She is repeatedly advised to 'come / And to sue for grace' (sig. C4r), and to rely on Caesar's mercy when he has none to give. Octavius's meeting with Cleopatra, and the particular tensions within the scene, became apparent in staging the play. The dramatic tensions in this pivotal scene in Daniel, and the idea of Shakespeare visualizing the implicit scenography built into Daniel's play, are discussed in Chapters 4 and 5. Later paintings depicting Caesar's meeting with Cleopatra and his signalling to her to 'rise', suggest an enduring iconographic legacy from Daniel's representation of this scene.[63]

Knowing that Caesar is seeking 'but t'entertaine / In her some feeding hope to draw her forth' (sig. F1v), Cleopatra resolves on her suicide. The Nuntius describes the pathos in her suicide, 'The doubtfull combate try'd twixt Life and Honor' (sig. K1r), as she struggles in her last moments between her instinct to live as a mother, but chooses instead to die as a queen. The grace that she has been seeking from Caesar, and of which she gets a glimpse from Dolabella, is hers in death, as she dies nobly and free:

> Yet loe that face the wonder of her life,
> Retaines in death, a grace that graceth death,
> Colour so lively, cheere so lovelie rife,
> That none would thinke such beauty could want breath.
>
> (sig. K2v)

Her beauty, which has proven a burden for her in her lifetime, is seen by others as heavenly, and in death as having 'a grace that graceth death'. The use of 'grace' here points ahead to the 'strong toil of grace' (5.2.347) in *Antony and Cleopatra*, supporting the view that Daniel did leave his mark on Shakespeare. In Daniel, although the private hesitations and distress of a queen are full of pathos, their public consequence creates endless suffering. *Cleopatra* shows that when majesty is confused, it becomes 'the meanes of miserie' (sig. C1r) for the queen and for the state, bringing destruction to both.

The 1607 *Cleopatra* and nostalgia

Daniel published his final version of *Cleopatra* in the 1607 *Certaine Small Workes* (reprinted in 1611). This was a much revised and expanded edition of the play and marked a further softening in his sympathetic characterization of the Egyptian queen. This section examines why Daniel undertook such a major reworking in 1607, looking in detail at circumstances in his own life, especially the disaster over *Philotas*, and argues that the impetus for the changes between the early *Cleopatra* and the final version came from these contexts.

Among the changes in 1607, Daniel moved away from narration towards more dramatic action and added characters such as Caesario, Charmion, Eras and Diomedes to the list of speaking parts, while eliminating the neo-classical Nuntius (or Messenger). His most significant change was a restructuring of the play, with the inclusion of a whole new opening scene. Rodon's account of Cleopatra's emotional parting with her son, delayed in previous editions until Act IV, now became part of the very opening. Daniel was thus able to make Cleopatra's desperation to save Caesario and her struggle to part with him the immediate focus of the play. The addition of Caesario also allowed for a moving scene later in the play when he is led to his death, having been betrayed by his tutor. As a result, the Egyptian queen's motherhood and suffering are foregrounded more deeply in the 1607 *Cleopatra* than in any of the earlier editions. Cleopatra's poignant words to Caesario, 'That blood within thy vaines came out of mine, / Parting from thee, I part from part of me' (sig. G6v), further heightened the pathos of her situation. Daniel's informed readers would have been well aware of the fate that awaited Caesario.

In his prefatory poem, 'To The Reader', newly added to the 1607 *Certaine Small Workes*, Daniel expressed what his works and his revisions meant to him,

> As if the thing in doing were more deere
> Then being done, & nothing likes thats past ...
>   I may pull downe, raise, and reedifie
> It is the building of my life the fee
> Of Nature, all th'inheritance that I
> Shal leave to those which must come after me.
>
> (sig. ¶3v)

Daniel clearly saw revision as the thing to do and in the prefatory poem there is a sense that he is putting things in order: these works are 'all th'inheritance' he shall leave. He altered all his works in varying degrees: among them the sonnet sequence *Delia* was altered five times, *Rosamond* six times and *Musophilus* three times.[64]

Daniel's attitude towards revision might also owe something to the culture and tradition of the Sidney circle.[65] Both Philip and Mary Sidney tinkered with and revised their works, which circulated as manuscripts, never quite being able to leave them alone because they never really finished them. Mary Sidney constantly revised the Sidney Psalms, and although a beautiful leather-bound 'final' presentation copy was prepared for Elizabeth I, variants of the Psalms continued to be transcribed and circulated among contemporaries.[66] Philip had similarly kept revising his *Arcadia*. H. R. Woudhuysen points out that while modern readers tend to view works in print as being in their final form, for some Renaissance writers, including Daniel, a first printing was 'only an intermediate stage in the creation of a work', after which the process of 'revising, rewriting, and restructuring could properly begin'.[67] Although it is important to take the different media of print and manuscripts into consideration, this predilection for revision was to do with viewing texts as malleable, subject to change. It seems Daniel followed his aristocratic patrons and the culture of manuscripts in this tradition with his printed texts. If works were seen as not for one time but for different times and changed accordingly within this circle, then we can logically conclude that topical allusions and their application also shifted and changed over time.

While critics have examined the 1607 changes because of the connections to Shakespeare, it can be argued that Daniel's most important revisions and restructuring in *Cleopatra* are to elements of the story that do not appear in Shakespeare.[68] Whereas Shakespeare accentuates Cleopatra's sensuality, Daniel depicts Cleopatra as a mother and a queen in defeat, and these characteristics are more prominently underlined in 1607. Indeed, Daniel's emphasis on Cleopatra's anguished parting with Caesario, and later, on Caesario's execution scene, owes little to Shakespeare, and little even to Plutarch.[69] The relationship of the 1607 edition and Shakespeare's *Antony and Cleopatra* is discussed further in Chapter 5. In critical examinations of the influence of Shakespeare on these revisions, scholars have often overlooked the circumstances in Daniel's own life that might have influenced this reshaping, especially the impact of *Philotas*, and his patron Mountjoy's death.

Philotas was performed at the indoor Blackfriars Theatre by the company of boy actors, the Children of the Queen's

Revels, sometime during the winter season of 1604–5. This neo-Senecan play charts the fall of Alexander the Great's favourite, Philotas, and the manipulation of events by the devious counsellor, Craterus. It incurred Robert Cecil's wrath, and its apparently sympathetic allusions to the Earl of Essex led to Daniel being summoned before the Privy Council. As a result, Daniel went through one of the most difficult years of his life. He denied any deliberate connection to Essex in his *Philotas*, stating that having written the first three acts of the play in 1600, he then set it aside (presumably around the time of Essex's fall), completing it in 1604. However, Laurence Michel points out that even in its original sources, in Curtius and Plutarch, Daniel must have noted a great many similarities in personal characteristics between Philotas and Essex. Both men were widely perceived as ambitious, valiant, magnanimous and headstrong.[70] Defending himself in the 1605 Dedication to Prince Henry attached to the play, Daniel says: 'These ancient representments of times past; / Tell us that men have, doo, and always runne / The selfe same line of action'.[71] There are many similarities in themes between *Philotas* and *Cleopatra* relating to the cyclical nature of history, the fall of the great, and the hubris of emperors. *Philotas* was obviously seen by the authorities as commenting on the Essex affair. Daniel was humiliated and wrote letters of apology to Robert Cecil, then Lord Cranborne, and to Charles Blount, Lord Mountjoy.

In spite of Daniel's claim to the contrary, most recent scholars accept that Daniel was involved in a politically dangerous exercise.[72] In the previous decade, Daniel came under new patrons, Fulke Greville and Lord Mountjoy, who were connected to Essex and his circle. Daniel's patronage by Greville developed into a close friendship. He also had a long-standing association with Mountjoy, who was involved in an open affair with the already married Lady Penelope Rich, Essex's sister and the thinly veiled Stella of Sidney's sonnets. There is little doubt that Daniel was affiliated in the 1590s with the Essex circle. His 1595 *Civil Wars* included high praise of Mountjoy and Essex, implicitly comparing the Earl to

Henry Bolingbroke. With Essex's execution, these lines were prudently removed from the 1601/2 *Workes*. Spenser may have been referring to Daniel in *Prothalamion* (1596), when he praised 'some brave muse' who would sing of Essex's virtues.[73] Daniel also addressed verse epistles to members of the circle, including Sir Thomas Egerton and Henry Wriothesley, Earl of Southampton, who was arrested with Essex for his part in the conspiracy.

The Essex circle and its supporters held the most hope for the future in the accession of James VI of Scotland. They envisaged with James's reign the possible removal of Cecil, the implementation of forward Protestant policies towards Spain, and less of the inaction they felt plagued Elizabeth's female rule, particularly in her last decade.[74] The Earl of Essex and Penelope Rich both communicated with James in Scotland, via secret encrypted correspondence, in an effort to establish favour. Norbrook points out that James had paid tribute to Philip Sidney in an elegy printed in the volume produced by Cambridge University to coincide with Sidney's funeral. As a result, there was hope that his accession might 'usher in a new age in which those who admired Sidney's political ideals and poetic achievement would be patronized by an enlightened king'.[75] The death of Elizabeth, when it came in 1603, was received with some relief, as her last years had been marked by corruption, a general sense of delay and political unrest.[76] For Essexians, it must have seemed that she had lived just long enough to order the execution of her favourite.

However, disillusionment with James set in fairly quickly, with a resulting nostalgia for Elizabeth as unpopular opinions about her were radically revised.[77] The Hampton Court Conference of 1604 was a clear statement of James's desire for peace with Spain and a turning point in public opinion. Worden notes that the 'cult of nostalgia for Elizabeth' was greatest among those who had advocated a militantly anti-Spanish policy and saw James's pacifist diplomacy towards Spain as a failure.[78] The King's *Basilikon Doron* (published in 1603) also caused anxiety, as the divine right of monarchs enshrined in it could be contrasted with Elizabeth's more moderate sovereignty.[79] Many saw the King's tolerance of Catholics and his desire to make peace with Catholic nations as a sign of Stuart crypto-Catholicism. This fear was especially emphasized because of his mother Mary Stuart's Catholicism. James's court was viewed as rife with favouritism (Robert Carr had become a favourite in 1606) and anxieties about national identity and sovereignty were heightened by the influence and, to English eyes, shocking familiarity of Scottish nobles with the King. With the union of the two crowns there was now a foreign king on the English throne, and many looked back nostalgically to the Tudor dynasty.[80] Lady Anne Clifford, who was tutored by Daniel, bears testimony in her *Diary* to this change in court culture, noting that 'we all saw a great change between the fashion of the Court as it is now and of that in the Queen's time'.[81] In 1606, James's entertainment for his brother-in-law, King Christian of Denmark, degenerated into a notoriously drunken rout, as reported by Sir John Harington. Reflecting his own sense of nostalgia, Harington commented that in all his time at the Elizabethan court 'I never did see such lack of good order, discretion, and sobriety as I have now done'.[82]

Nostalgia for Elizabeth was sometimes used as a medium for criticism of James. Greville's 'Dedication to Sir Philip Sidney' may be viewed as a pioneering work in the strategy of criticizing the King by praising his predecessor.[83] Greville had been forced to resign by Cecil from his post as treasurer of the navy in 1603, a post obtained under Elizabeth's reign with the support of Greville's friend Essex. As further punishment, he was denied access to state papers that would have allowed him to write a biography of Elizabeth. Although his 'Dedication' was mainly written around 1610–12, and completed in 1614, some parts were started as early as 1604.[84] Daniel might have been employing a similar strategy to that of Greville, his friend and patron, in his 1607 *Cleopatra*. In the 1605 Dedication to Prince Henry attached to *Philotas*, Daniel voiced his own present humiliation and the feeling of nostalgia, describing himself as a 'remnant of another time', while looking back to 'late Elizas raigne' (sig. A5r):

> And therefore since I have out livd the date
> Of former grace, acceptance, and delight,
> I would my lines late-borne beyond the fate
> Of her spent line, had never come to light.
> So had I not bene tax'd for wishing well
> Nor now mistaken by the censuring Stage
> Nor, in my fame and reputation fell,
> Which I esteeme more than what
> Or th'earth can give. But yeares hath don this wrong.
> To make me write too much, and live too long.[85]

Daniel's words echo Cleopatra's lines, 'Yet do I live, and yet doth breath extend My life beyond my life?' (sig. B3r). Shaken over *Philotas*, Daniel might have felt an increasing nostalgia for Elizabeth. The above lines are omitted from the 1607 dedication to Prince Henry, as perhaps being too self-revelatory.

In the year following *Philotas*, Daniel's difficulties mounted. Appointed as Licenser of the newly established company the Children of the Queen's Revels in 1603/4, he approved the performance of three controversial plays, which landed the company in trouble: John Marston's *The Dutch Courtesan*, *Eastward Ho!* by George Chapman, Ben Jonson and John Marston, and his own *Philotas*. As a result, he lost this position, adding to his humiliation. Hugh Gazzard argues that Daniel did not let these plays through because of carelessness or stupidity, but through 'a concentrated effort to smuggle more or less outspoken criticism of the dominant political grouping into its very stronghold'.[86] John Pitcher notes that Daniel might have misjudged what could be said freely about Essex in the early days of Jacobean rule, and mistaken the protection he would receive from his patrons who were trying to realign themselves in the new order.[87]

Although Daniel was able to re-establish himself with Mountjoy, now the Earl of Devonshire, the Earl died suddenly in 1606, catching a respiratory infection while undertaking a journey to London to see Cecil. This was in an effort to restore his reputation after his secret marriage to Penelope Rich. Lord Rich had divorced his wife soon after Essex's fall, and although Mountjoy had wanted to legitimize their union and the children from their long-standing affair, their marriage was ecclesiastically forbidden.[88] In 1606, Daniel commemorated Mountjoy in a *Funeral Poem*. While working on his revised *Cleopatra*, Daniel must still have been deeply affected by the traumatic events of 1605 and 1606. Along with his own circumstances, he might also have been thinking of his beloved patron. Perhaps the mental anguish for Daniel from his own loss of reputation, coupled with Mountjoy's death, made him think of putting his works in order, as evidenced by the 1607 preface 'To the Reader'. Of his patron's noble and brave death, Daniel wrote in the *Funeral Poem*: 'This action of our death especially / Shewes all a man. Here onely is he found' (sig. B4v). Might Daniel have felt a deeper sympathy for Cleopatra who had also shown nobility in death?

Significantly omitted from Daniel's 1607 *Cleopatra* are the lines about the queen's divided self, which are so striking and important in his early version:

> Bloud, children, Nature all must pardon me.
> My soule yeelds honor up the victory.
> And I must be a Queen, forget a mother,
> Though mother would I be, were I not I;
> And Queen would not be, could I be other.
> (1599 *Cleopatra*, sig. B4v)

With Elizabeth's death, the conflict between being a queen and a mother was no longer an issue for English elite culture. The concerns and anxieties about the end of a dynasty and an ensuing succession crisis had also passed; what remained now was a loss of hope in the present and nostalgia for the era gone by. Daniel's revised *Cleopatra* still retains a sense of loss of self, as in the lines: 'That flatterie could perswade I was not

I?' (sig. H3r) and 'I must not be, unlesse I be mine owne' (sig. H3v). Perhaps in 1607 these lines also spoke to the flattery of counsellors, such as Cecil and Northampton, who had ingratiated themselves with the King, and to English anxieties about a loss of national identity.

It is also interesting to note some changes in other lines that serve to soften further Cleopatra's characterization. In previous editions, Cleopatra admits that she has only learnt to love Antony with his death, saying 'Which *Antony*, I must confesse my fault / I never did sincerely untill now' (1599 *Cleopatra*, sig. C2r). Daniel omits these lines in 1607, as well as the lines about Cleopatra thinking that 'all men must love me out of dutie; / And I love none' (1599 *Cleopatra*, sig. C2r). However, in both the early and the revised *Cleopatra*, the Egyptian queen speaks movingly of how 'affliction' makes her truly love Antony. Through Eras, Daniel also adds lines about Cleopatra's constancy, following his patron Mary Sidney's Cleopatra. His Cleopatra refuses to respond to Eras's suggestion that she 'might have articuled / With *Cæsar*' (sig. H4r) to hold her state. By making Cleopatra more sympathetic, Daniel is able to make Caesar appear more cold and ambitious. In some ways, this seems to be a similar technique to Greville's of praising (with Daniel here softening the image of) the queen to criticize the new ruler. James had made this topical allusion easy by associating his own image with Augustus. At his coronation, he had proclaimed himself 'Caesar Augustus' of Britain, wanting to base his *Pax Britannica* on Augustus's *Pax Romana*.[89]

In the early and the revised *Cleopatra*, Arius and Philostratus, the Egyptian philosophers, bemoan the conditions of their fallen state, and place the downfall of the Ptolemies in the context of the cyclical rise and fall of empires. The decline came when, 'with lust, and ease made feeble', Cleopatra and the Egyptians laid themselves open to a Roman conquest, made easy by an 'unwary peace, with fat-fed pleasure'.[90] In the 1590s the idea of 'unwary peace' had resonance for forward Protestants who were frustrated by Elizabeth's policy towards

Spain. As topical allusions and their application shifted and changed over time, Daniel's 'unwary peace' could have a contemporary political application to the Jacobean peace, which after 1604 became widely associated with court luxury and vice. As discussed in the Introduction, a Tacitean view, with its emphasis on the role of deception, further reinforced views of Spain's general untrustworthiness as a partner in peace. Tacitus and other Roman historians also associated a prolonged peace with luxury and decline,[91] both views found in Daniel. Pitcher has shown that in the Brotherton Manuscript, a manuscript of Daniel's previously unpublished verse written sometime during the years 1609–18, Daniel continues to be preoccupied with concerns about the long Jacobean peace. Daniel states that 'an unactive peace, disarmes our mynds' and makes similar associations of this peace with 'lust', 'wantonness' and 'gluttony', as in the exchange between Arius and Philostratus.[92] For Daniel, as for the surviving members of the Essex circle, there was much to be pessimistic about and nostalgic for in 1607.

A virtue out of confusion

The literary culture of the Essex circle further refined Daniel's interest in neo-Tacitean discourse. Essex was known for his enthusiasm for Tacitus and neo-Senecan drama, and Greville and Mountjoy were both supporters of Senecan drama. In his heavily annotated copy of Tacitus (now in the British Library), Robert Sidney, a member of the Essex inner circle, marked a passage on Tiberius's 'obscura verba', highlighting this as an 'obscure manner of speaking'. He also annotated and marked sections on 'vertu'.[93] Both these Tacitean concepts of an obscurity of style and the importance of virtue, especially personal and martial virtue, were a preoccupation of the Essex circle. As I mentioned in Chapter 1, this related to the Machiavellian concept of 'virtù', which emphasized virtue in civil and military affairs. Quentin Skinner notes that this concept underscored 'the dangers of political decisions being made in a slow or hesitant way'.[94] Robert Sidney was following in the tradition of reading Tacitus that his brother Philip had encouraged, and which the Essex circle had now fully taken up.

In *Cleopatra*, Daniel also follows this obscurity of style. This can be seen in the lines quoted earlier in this chapter, and which are worth revisiting below, depicting Cleopatra's vulnerability and hesitation in her response to the warning in Dolabella's letter. Daniel is here making a virtue out of her confusion:

> Shee turnes her backe, and with her takes me in,
> Reades in thy lines thy strange unlookt for tale,
> And reades, and smiles, and staies, and doth begin
> Againe to reade, then blusht, and then was pale.
> And having ended with a sigh, refolds
> Thy Letter up; and with a fixed eye,
> (Which stedfast her imagination holds)
> Shee mus'd a while, standing confusedly.
>
> (1607 *Cleopatra*, sig. K4v)

Confusion and contradictory terms describe Cleopatra in moments when she seems to have most emotional depth: 'stedfast her imagination holds' as 'Shee mus'd a while, standing confusedly' (sig. K4v). Daniel describes Cleopatra as blushing and going pale and then sighing. These are physiological markers that have great significance in the period: sighing was believed to cool an over-heated heart, and expresses an unconscious response to the strength of emotion experienced. As sighing and blushing are automatic biological reactions, they are considered signs of a person's honest response and lack of duplicity. Therefore, reading and the physiological response become intertwined and powerfully politicized. Something similar can be seen in *Lear*, in Cordelia's response to the letter from Kent, in which she heaves and pants at news of her father, as she goes through a range of conflicting emotions, as if the letter 'pressed her heart' (4.3.17–33). This inner contention is deliberately contrasted by Shakespeare to Goneril's cold response to a letter in an immediately preceding scene, which signifies her duplicitous nature. In both Daniel and Shakespeare, we see a similar interest in the physiological responses to reading letters as signs of virtue or sympathy which have an impact on the state. Although it may seem strange to compare Cleopatra and Cordelia, Daniel's sympathetic Cleopatra exhibits virtue in the reception of letters, as does Cordelia. This fits in with the paradox about Daniel's Cleopatra: she is most steadfast and also most believable when she exists in this confusion. Daniel seems to be making a virtue out of confusion in the Tacitean tradition of deliberate evasion or semi-concealment.[95]

In a fascinating manuscript entitled 'Instructions to a Secret Agent in France, circa 1595, Etc.', with advice to Robert Naunton, Essex stressed that all 'rules and patternes of pollecy are as well learned out of olde Greeke and Romayne storyes, as out of states which are at thys day'.[96] Essex scrutinized ancient history for lessons of politics and war, and it is thought that he and his inner circle had read Daniel's 1595 *Civil Wars*, given their interest in history and its high praise for the Earl. *Cleopatra* and the *Civil Wars* were actually the first works in which Daniel theorized on history.[97] It is interesting to speculate if the Essex circle had also taken up *Cleopatra* in some way.

There is little doubt that the Antony and Cleopatra story was seen to have topical political applications. Greville's account of this, as discussed previously, provides insight into contemporary perceptions. In his 'Dedication', Greville describes how he had originally written three tragedies:

> whereof *Antony and Cleopatra*, according to their irregular passions in forsaking empire to follow sensuality, were sacrificed in the fire; the executioner, the author himself, not that he conceived it to be a contemptible younger

> brother to the rest, but lest ... [it] be construed or strained to a personating of vices in the present governors and government.[98]

He goes on to explain that he feared his work would be seen 'not poetically, but really, fashioned in the Earl of Essex then falling', that is as unmistakably offering a topical reading and no longer providing the cover of deniability.[99] Greville must have burnt his tragedy sometime after the trouble over *Philotas*. Perhaps the pressure Cecil exerted on Daniel by summoning him in front of the Privy Council was also intended to pressurize Greville, to keep him in check. Whether Daniel's *Cleopatra* was taken up by the Essex circle will always remain speculative, although the story of Cleopatra clearly had a political utility for those in the Sidney and Essex circles – as evidenced by the work of Mary Sidney, Daniel, and Greville.

In this chapter we have seen, however, that for Daniel the tragedy of Cleopatra held something personal. A sustained authorial engagement in her characterization over a thirteen-year period is to do with more than drawing political lessons. He saw the splendour in her and saw how moving her story really was, showing her vulnerability, confusion, and grace in defeat. Daniel contributed a complexity and sophistication to Cleopatra's tragedy by imagining what it must have been like for her as her dynasty fell. The events of 1605–6 are the sort that affect one for a lifetime, and perhaps in his revised *Cleopatra* Daniel could feel an even deeper level of sympathy for the loss of reputation and suffering of the queen 'that hath lost all this all / To whom is nothing left, except a mind' (sig. H5v). As we will see in the next chapter, Daniel's Cleopatra emerged as a figure that elite women could look to for agency and resistance.

3

'Will Yet this Womans Stubborne Heart be Woone?': Lady Anne Clifford and Daniel's *Cleopatra*

The previous chapters have emphasized the shared topical project of Mary Sidney's *Antonius* and Daniel's *Cleopatra*, and their representation of Cleopatra as a figure of sympathy and resistance. But how might Cleopatra have been perceived by women in aristocratic circles in the period? A rich and fascinating portrait of a Jacobean lady, depicted as Cleopatra holding the asp in the dramatic moment before her suicide, is of exceptional interest for what it reveals about elite English women's response to the Egyptian queen (see Figure 10). It is also significant as the only known example to survive from the period based on a scene from a contemporary play (as identified and discussed below). Inscribed with lines of poetry that end with the defiant declaration 'Witnes my soule parts free to Anthony / And now prowd tyrant Cæsar doe thy worst', the painting may add something new to our knowledge and understanding of early modern women's performance, their subjectivity and ideas of female heroism.[1]

FIGURE 10 *'Lady Ralegh as Cleopatra', here identified as Lady Anne Clifford as Cleopatra, by an unknown artist. Christie's 23 July 1948 (77). Photograph © National Portrait Gallery, London. Present whereabouts unknown.*

This carefully staged painting, by an unknown artist, is of a young woman standing by a basket of figs, wearing a curved jewelled headdress from which her long, dark, curled hair falls loose over her left shoulder. In her raised right arm – perhaps an influence of the pose of the Vatican *Cleopatra*[2] – she holds the asp, and in the left, down by her side, a sceptre. She is draped in an ermine-lined velvet robe, her costume accentuated by a heavily beaded and jewelled dress, with the bodice strikingly designed to reveal her breasts through the fine translucent smock worn below. Around her neck is a string of pearls, identifying her with Cleopatra, who was traditionally associated with these jewels.[3] Adding to the interest of this portrait are an open jewelled miniature pinned to the woman's dress as a locket and an inscription in the right-hand corner of the painting. The miniature is of a young man, depicted *all' antica*, in the manner of the ancients, wearing a Jacobean version of classical Roman dress, suggesting that he is her Antony. The inscription, painted as a handwritten note on a torn and folded piece of paper, might be intended to resemble an early modern letter or, perhaps, a thumbed copy of a player's lines. The distinctive 'clubbing' of the ascenders and descenders in the script suggests that the portrait was painted in the early seventeenth century (see Figure 11).[4] Art specialists from Christie's, the National Portrait Gallery, Tate Britain and UCL have also confirmed that the painting is from this period and that it appears to be English.[5]

That this is a portrait of a particular woman in role as Cleopatra rather than simply an allegorical painting is suggested by the sitter's distinctive features, and by the fact that the latter type of work is usually inscribed with a classical motto or brief quotation, not lines from a contemporary play. It is remarkable that a Jacobean lady chose to be depicted in this guise. Although, as I have argued, there was a more complicated and multi-layered view of Cleopatra in this period than previously thought, she was still portrayed in many works as a symbol of 'women's evil inclination'.[6] While there are many examples of English women choosing to be depicted as

FIGURE 11 *Detail of painting illustrated in Fig. 10 showing the inscription. Photograph © National Portrait Gallery, London.*

the Egyptian queen in the eighteenth and nineteenth centuries,[7] this early Stuart painting is a strikingly rare and bold example. In their study of Restoration portraits of women, Catherine MacLeod and Julia Marciari Alexander point out that 'the iconography of Cleopatra, while frequently invoked in the literature of the period, was rarely used in role portraits' at this time; this was even less so in the Jacobean era.[8]

The painting, which has been discussed by scholars in only isolated instances, has remained relatively unknown in the art and literary worlds. In the rare cases where it has been discussed, it has been misdated and misidentified, with its true import missed. In this chapter, I examine this remarkable portrait, tracing its pedigree and its journey through the London auction houses, and the tantalizing mystery surrounding it. I argue, instead, for a new and compelling identification, and for what this may tell us about its sitter and the fascination with Cleopatra in the period.

Investigating the portrait's provenance

The painting has been reproduced and discussed in three works in recent years: Kim F. Hall's *Things of Darkness* (1995); Anna Beer's *Bess Ralegh* (2003); and Pamela Allen Brown's essay 'A New Fable of the Belly' (2007).[9] In each of these cases, the authors discuss the portrait as depicting Lady Ralegh, Elizabeth Throckmorton, wife of Sir Walter Ralegh, even though the sitter here does not resemble her known portraits. Although these scholars shed important light on the portrait, by basing their work on the identification found in the National Portrait Gallery archive, which in turn relied on auction-catalogue entries, they misinterpret it. Hall and Brown seem to have accepted its identification unquestioningly, and, although Beer recognizes this as doubtful, she still reflects that in it 'Bess's wantonness and her wit, her very femaleness, echo through representations of her power'.[10]

The portrait raises several significant questions about early modern closet drama, and sheds new light on the different modes of self-representation aristocratic English women might attempt in this period, whether in private stagings or in settings where coded messages might be sent. It is therefore important to establish the picture's provenance and to locate it. Over the last century, the portrait has been sold twice at Christie's. It appeared first on 20 November 1931, when Muriel Dixwell-Oxenden, Lady Capel Cure, held a large sale of works from the Broome Park estate in Barham, Kent.[11] It might have been part of the Oxenden Collection, which she inherited on the death of her father, Sir Percy Dixwell-Oxenden, 10th and last Baronet, in 1924. The painting might also have passed through descent from her maternal line. Lady Capel Cure's maternal grandfather was the Earl of Winchilsea, and her grandmother was Lady Louisa Greville, in a direct line from Robert Greville, the adopted heir and cousin of Fulke Greville, Daniel's patron and friend.[12] Christie's catalogue listed the portrait (lot 4) as: 'Portrait of Lady Raleigh, as "Cleopatra", Elizabeth, daughter of Sir Nicholas Throckmorton, Maid-of-honour to Queen Elizabeth. In jewelled dress, wearing a miniature of Sir Walter Raleigh. *With inscription*. On panel – 43in. by 32 ½ in.'. The portrait was sold for six guineas to an 'F Howard' of Dorking Surrey, who, after seventeen years of ownership, re-sold it at Christie's on 23 July 1948. Francis Howard was a client of Christie's and had eight lots for sale on this date. Listed as lot 77 and described as 'Lady Raleigh as Cleopatra Holding the Asp – *with inscription* – on panel – 43 in. by 32 in.', the portrait was purchased by 'Dent' for eight guineas.[13]

Christie's was directly hit by incendiary bombs in 1941 during the Blitz, and with its King Street premises destroyed, lost many of its records. The 1948 sale was held at Spencer House, in St James's, where the auction house had temporarily relocated. As a result, little is known of Dent, but the use of his last name only in Christie's files suggests he must have been a known client or dealer. The *Art Sales Index* has no record of the painting being sold again at auction after 1948, and since then it has disappeared. Its only visual record is the photograph the National Portrait Gallery had taken at the 1948 auction.[14]

Searching for Dent

In an effort to locate the painting, it was important to identify Dent, the last known owner of the painting. There apparently was a dealer called Dent at this time.[15] Another possible candidate appeared to be Major Leonard Dent (1888–1987). He was an influential collector of Rowlandsons since 1935, and might have had an interest in attending the auction, as it included eleven Rowlandsons. However, none of the Rowlandsons at the 1948 sale were bought by Dent, and Major Dent's son, Gerard Dent, is not familiar with the picture, which is not the usual type of painting his father collected.[16] According to Gerard Dent, his father only collected Rowlandsons that were rural, not caricature, and was very particular as to what kind he liked. He thought it unlikely, though, that his father would have missed such an auction and did not think it impossible that his father might have bought and sold paintings not intended for display. Leonard Dent was a regular client of Christie's, and a sale of his collection on 10 July 1984 was listed under his last name only, as 'Christie's Dent Collection Pictures Thomas Rowlandson'.

In 1972, Leonard Dent catalogued his collection at Hillfields, his home in Burghley Common in Berkshire. He stated that some of the items were inherited from his uncle Percy Macquoid (1852–1925), the co-editor of the *Dictionary of English Furniture* (1924–7).[17] Macquoid, a noted theatrical designer and artist, designed the sets and costumes for Herbert Beerbohm Tree's production of *Antony and Cleopatra*, which opened on 27 December 1906 in London. It is tempting to speculate that Leonard Dent might have developed an interest in Cleopatra because of his uncle's work and purchased the portrait either as a gift or on behalf of someone else.

The trail with Dent, however, ends here. I also looked at Dent as possibly being one of the Dent-Brocklehursts, of Sudeley Castle, who were still collecting pictures after the War. The Sudeley archivist has, however, confirmed that the painting was not bought by a Dent-Brocklehurst in 1948 and does not form part of their collection.[18] At present, therefore, all that can be confirmed about the portrait's provenance is the chain of three owners from the sales at Christie's.

The inscription

With the whereabouts of the painting unknown, interpretations, including my own, must rely on the photograph taken by the National Portrait Gallery. Even so, this can yield a good deal more information than has hitherto been recognized, and indeed there has been some active misinterpretation of it. In her study of race, Hall links the portrait to her discussion of 'female inquiry into male fascination with the "foreign other"', and in particular, to Sir Walter Ralegh's *Discoverie of Guiana* (1596).[19] However, by not examining the origin of the inscription itself, she misinterprets it. Hall describes the inscription as a poem that floats above Lady Ralegh's head, in which by 'reenacting the moment of Cleopatra's suicide', she 'fashions herself both as object of desire *and* as loyal wife'.[20]

The words in the inscription are in fact from Daniel's *Tragedie of Cleopatra* (first published in 1594), and can be identified as coming from his much-revised 1607 edition (or perhaps the 1611 reprint). The sixteen-line inscription is unusual in being so long, in being from a recent work and in being painted on a *trompe-l'œil* image of a piece of paper. The lines seem to be deliberately excerpted from different parts of Cleopatra's final speech.[21] Ending with 'And now prowd tyrant Cæsar doe thy worst', they serve to sharpen the message of Caesar's tyranny by portraying Cleopatra more sympathetically. In the inscription, only one line, the fourth from the end, differs from the 1607 version. In Daniel, this reads as: 'And Egypt now the Theater where I'. In the inscription, the line flows better and reads, 'And Egipt now where Cleopatra I'. This may suggest compositor error in the edition, which is known to have been poorly printed.[22] The line could alternatively have been adapted for the purposes of the portrait to clearly identify the sitter's role. Apart from this, the only other difference between the inscription and the printed edition occurs in the sixth line from the bottom, where the word 'last' in 'Last of Breath' is capitalized in the inscription, but not in the play text. This emphasis on Cleopatra's last breath heightens the impact of her dying words.

Since the lines are from Daniel's 1607 *Cleopatra* (or the 1611 reprint), the portrait must have been painted in or after that year.[23] It seems implausible then that Lady Ralegh, with her husband in the Tower since 1603 on treason charges, would have an interest in responding to her husband's 'rhetoric of foreign travel',[24] by being painted as Cleopatra eleven years after the publication of the *Discoverie*. She came and stayed with Ralegh in the Tower, bringing their son with her, only later taking a house on Tower Hill to be close to her husband. This was a time when according to Ralegh's biographers, Mark Nicholls and Penry Williams, Lady Ralegh was desperately marshalling support for continuing appeals for fair financial treatment. By the end of 1609, the Raleghs' beloved home, Sherborne, was forfeited to James I and passed to his favourite, Robert Carr.[25] When the terms of Ralegh's imprisonment were tightened in 1611, his wife's continual presence had become so important to him that he begged the Chamberlain of the Exchequer, Sir Walter Cope, to 'move my Lord Treasurer in my behalf that by his grace my wife might agayne be made a prisoner with me, as she hath bine for six yeeres last past'.[26] The Lord Treasurer was Robert Cecil, now Lord Salisbury, who had turned against the Raleghs. If Lady Ralegh had wanted to use *Cleopatra* to respond to her husband's *Discoverie* she would presumably have done so earlier, at a less dire time.

Like Hall, Brown does not examine the inscription. In exploring the issues surrounding the identity of the sitter of the Persian Lady portrait, Brown also briefly discusses the 'stunning portrait of Elizabeth Throckmorton, Lady Ralegh, playing Cleopatra's final scene'. She finds it to be an example of the genre of European paintings in which 'the great beauty is dressed up as a woman famous in myth, literature, or history' and is 'daring us to divine her role, as if in a parlor game' in which 'sonnets and poems are often incorporated'.[27] As examples, she cites Artemisia Gentileschi's portrait of herself as Judith slaying Holofernes and portraits of other beauties depicted as Salome and Lucretia. The concept, however, of trying to divine the sitter's role does not hold in the case of this painting since the inscription itself contains the identifying words revealing the sitter as 'Cleopatra I'.

Although in her discussion Beer states that 'there is a scroll with a quotation from a popular play of the time, Samuel Daniel's *Cleopatra*', she does not go further and date the excerpt.[28] Daniel, as discussed previously, was a habitual reviser of his work, and his play, a closet drama rather than a work for the commercial playhouses, was a publishing success, going through six reprints between 1594 and 1607. Reading what the inscription may be trying to convey is difficult without dating the edition of *Cleopatra* from which the lines are actually drawn. As such, Beer's speculation, that the Raleghs might have been 'perceived as the Antony and Cleopatra of the London world' with 'Cleopatra/Bess challenging the "proud tyrant" Caesar/Elizabeth', does not work.[29] Elizabeth had died in 1603 and so if anyone could be identified as the tyrant in this scenario it would have to be James I.

Daniel and the Raleghs

There are well-documented connections between Daniel and Sir Walter Ralegh, as well as between the Raleghs and Daniel's patron, Mary Sidney. So, in theory, it is possible that Lady

Ralegh could have drawn on Daniel's work. Sir Walter and Lady Ralegh had family and political connections with the Sidneys and Herberts, and strongly shared the anti-Spanish stance of Mary Sidney's literary circle. In 1603, the Countess tried to exert her son Philip Herbert's influence with James, to save Ralegh from the Tower.[30] Spenser, who dedicated works to Mary Sidney and encouraged Daniel, was on intimate terms with Ralegh. In 1590, he addressed his 'Letter of the author' to Ralegh which acts as a preface to *The Faerie Queene*, and in 1595 he dedicated *Colin Clouts Come Home Againe* to Ralegh. It is in this poem that Spenser also famously praised Daniel.[31]

We know that Ralegh thought highly of Daniel's work. While in the Tower, Ralegh wrote his *History of the World* (1614) and in the section on Alexander, Ralegh directly quoted the first fourteen lines of the Act III Chorus of Daniel's *Philotas* (1605). The lines speak of court intrigue and jealous Princes:

> See how these great men cloathe their private hate,
> In these faire colours of the publike good,
> And to effect their ends, pretend the State,
> As if the State by their affection stood,
> And arm'd with power and Princes jealousies,
> Will put the least conceit of discontent
> Into the greatest ranke of treacheries,
> That no one action shall seeme innocent;
> Yea valour, honour, bountie, shall be made
> As accessaries unto ends unjust:
> And even the service of the State must lade
> The needfull'st undertaking with distrust,
> So that base vilensse; idle Luxurie,
> Seeme safer farre, than to doe worthily.[32]

It is easy to see how these words, from a play that had become so specifically associated with the fall of his rival Essex, also spoke to Ralegh in his downfall. This had similarly been instigated by 'great men' who cloaked their hatred in terms of the 'publike good', so ensuring 'That no one action shall seeme innocent'. In fact, Daniel is the only contemporary English writer from whom Ralegh quotes, stating that 'Heereof a Poet of our owne hath given a note as much better, as it is more generall in his *Philotas*'.[33] That Ralegh chose to praise a play written and performed during his incarceration is, as Gazzard notes, both intriguing and strongly suggestive. It points to *Philotas* being deciphered not only by the Privy Council for its commentary on the Essex case, but also by readers such as Ralegh, who saw an 'application to his own position'.[34]

On his coronation, James I proclaimed himself 'Caesar Augustus' of Britain, wanting to base his *Pax Britannica* on Augustus's *Pax Romana*. Daniel used this association in his *Panegyrike Congratularie*, addressing James in April 1603 as 'one Imperiall Prince'.[35] With the identification of James as Augustus coming from the King himself, and his known fondness for Rome, Daniel's 'prowd tyrant Caesar' easily lent itself to use in topical political commentary.[36] Did the Raleghs appropriate lines from Daniel, a poet they knew, for the connection of Augustus with the King?

While this would be an interesting theory, the portrait's subject remains doubtful. Apart from the lack of similarity in looks between any of Lady Ralegh's known portraits and this picture, Lady Ralegh's age is also a factor; she would be too old to be the Cleopatra. Born in 1565, she was already forty-two in 1607, the earliest possible date for the painting. She would thus be markedly older than the young woman depicted in the portrait. Women were, of course, frequently idealized in portraits and presented as younger than they were, a notable recent example being Elizabeth I. Nevertheless, the fact remains that there are also no similarities between Lady Ralegh's authenticated likeness in other paintings and this portrait (see Figure 12). The miniature worn by the sitter in the painting, and described by Christie's as Sir Walter Ralegh, also does not provide any corroboration. Portraits of Ralegh show him with a more angular chin line and do not resemble the miniature (see Figures 13 and 14). Lady Ralegh therefore cannot plausibly be the Cleopatra of the portrait.

FIGURE 12 Portrait of Lady Raleigh (née Elizabeth Throckmorton 1565–1647), *artist unknown, 1603. Photo © National Gallery of Ireland, Dublin.*

Although the identification of Lady Ralegh as the portrait's sitter is undermined by the above discussion, the identification of the painting's inscription, as coming from Daniel's 1607 *Cleopatra*, adds to the portrait's significance. The portrait

FIGURE 13 Sir Walter Ralegh, *attributed to 'H' monogrammist, 1588.* © *National Portrait Gallery, London.*

presents us with an extraordinary image – a picture of an early seventeenth-century English aristocratic woman, costumed as Daniel's Cleopatra, holding the asp, in a moment of resistance to Caesar. The portrait might record a private performance of a closet drama, or it might represent a Jacobean lady imagining herself as Cleopatra, as an expression of female self-definition

FIGURE 14 *Detail of painting illustrated in Fig. 10 showing miniature worn by the sitter. Photograph © National Portrait Gallery, London.*

and agency. This is also a kind of performance, suggesting the Egyptian queen might have represented a model of elite female heroism for women in the period. Both these possibilities are explored in this chapter; in either case, this young aristocratic woman identified with Cleopatra and wanted to speak through Daniel's lines.

Lady Anne Clifford as Cleopatra?

If the sitter of the portrait is not Lady Ralegh, then who might she be? In trying to solve this puzzle, it is useful to take a different approach and look at the young women within Daniel's circle of aristocratic patrons who might have had some reason for playing Cleopatra, while employing lines that ask to be recognized as his.[37] More than anyone, Lady Anne Clifford, the Countess of Dorset (1590–1676), stands out for her close attachment to Daniel. He was Anne's tutor from around 1600 for about two years, and was an important influence in her formative years. Although she was a precocious child and known throughout her life for her stubborn willfulness, their relationship grew to become one of mutual esteem and affection. In 1603, Daniel wrote two of his finest verse epistles for Lady Anne and her mother, Margaret Clifford (née Russell), Countess of Cumberland. Daniel's affection for Anne Clifford is evident throughout the epistle, as he emphasizes the great privilege of being descended from two such noble families, the Cliffords and the Russells, and provides gentle advice on how to approach her status. Daniel's *Rosamond* (1592), which as discussed inaugurated the vogue for English female complaints, centred on Rosamond Clifford, and might have kindled Anne Clifford's early interest in family history.[38]

Daniel remained a trusted advisor and friend to Clifford throughout his life. In his biography of Anne Clifford, Richard T. Spence suggests that she held Daniel in such high regard not only because he was a diligent tutor, but also because she might have seen him as a surrogate father figure.[39] Her own parents were estranged and she saw little of her father, George Clifford, 3rd Earl of Cumberland. Daniel's importance to her might also lie in the fact that he had taught her how to read and write well – two skills that sustained her through the isolated and difficult periods of her life. Mary Ellen Lamb argues that Clifford's diaries and portraits reveal that her reading of male-authored works written for male readers helped her assert herself in a dominant patriarchal society and resist the immense pressures she faced.[40] Towards the end of 1608, Daniel also played a role in negotiations for her marriage to Edward Seymour, grandson of the Earl of Hertford, advising the Clifford ladies on behalf of the Earl to continue with the proposed match.[41] Lady Cumberland, however, decided against this, and on 25 February 1609 Anne Clifford was married to Richard Sackville, Lord Buckhurst, who two days later, on his father's death, became 3rd Earl of Dorset. Daniel's part in these delicate marriage negotiations, as Pitcher observes, shows an unusual intimacy with his aristocratic patrons for someone of his class. It points to the value placed in his good judgement and sensitivity and to the fact that his writing mattered to his dedicatees.[42]

Clifford's regard for Daniel is evident even decades after his death, not only in the Great Triptych, painted in 1646, in which she memorialized him as 'Samuel Daniel Tutour to this Young Lady a man of an Upright and excellent Spirit', but also in the monument she had erected to him in St George's Church in Beckington, Somerset. Apart from these larger public gestures, we also have glimpses of more private moments, reflecting Clifford's attachment to Daniel and the high esteem she held for poets. A copy of her 1605 edition of Sir Philip Sidney's *Arcadia* (now in the Bodleian Library), annotated in her own hand, illustrates this.[43] The edition, designed and commissioned by Mary Sidney, was a kind of *magnum opus* of her brother's work, bringing together Sidney's prose, poetic theory and poetry. It is interesting that in Clifford's copy the most frequent notes are in the *Defence of Poesie*, with the rest of the book more sparsely annotated. In the section discussing the high status of poets among the Romans, she has underlined the phrase 'a Poet was called *Vates*' (or prophet), and emphasizes in a note, 'Poets no lyers', by Sidney's words 'but truely, I thinke truely: that of all writers under the sun the poet is the least lyer'.[44] We also know she had manuscript copies of some of Daniel's unpublished poems and 'Part of the Civile Wars', now lost.[45] Her long-serving secretary, George Sedgewick, described an interview with

Clifford (*c*.1670) in which, concerned for his future well-being, she was 'often repeating to me a verse of Mr. Samuel Daniel, the famous poet and historiographer, who had been her instructor in her childhood and youth'. The lines are 'To have a silly home I do desire, / Loth still to warm me by another's fire', and indicate the couplet might have been part of a poem Daniel wrote for her when she was a young girl under his charge.[46]

Another clue to a more likely identification of the Cleopatra sitter's identity lies in a sonnet dedicated by Daniel to Clifford in the 1607 *Certaine Small Workes*, which does not fit as a dedicatory piece to any composition.[47] The sonnet seems to imply that Daniel is dedicating the entire edition to her, because he cannot leave her any of the major works, which are already dedicated to others. Daniel writes:

> I Cannot give unto your worthines
> Faire hopefull Lady these my legacies
> Bequeath'd to others, who must needs possesse
> The part belonging to their dignities.
>
> (sig. A7r)

However, Daniel then goes on to nominate her as guardian of all his works and his literary executor. It is a sign of his high regard for Clifford, who was only seventeen at this time, but, as discussed in Chapter 2, Daniel was also deeply shaken after *Philotas*. By 1607 he had become unwell and was already thinking in terms of his legacy:

> I here desire
> To make you supravisor of my will
> And do intreat your goodnesse to fulfill
> My last desires left unto you in trust
> I know you love the Muses, and you will
> Be a most faithfull Guardian and a just.
> And therefore I do so leave all to you
> That they may both have theirs & you your due.
>
> (sig. A7r)

In the 1607 prefatory poem 'To the Reader', Daniel said of his work, 'It is the building of my life the fee / Of Nature, all th'inheritance that / I Shal leave'.[48] In dedicating his entire edition to her, Daniel was leaving to her the most valuable inheritance he had to give – his work – 'the building of his life'. Clifford's life was dominated by an inheritance dispute since 1605 when her father died. The vast lands and castles of Westmorland and North Yorkshire that could have been passed to her, were left to her uncle Francis Clifford, instead, as the closest male heir.[49] In making her the heir to his works, Daniel gracefully alluded to her 'due'. This is the collection that also includes the version of *Cleopatra* quoted in the portrait's inscription, and thus provides us with a direct connection between the 1607 *Cleopatra* and Clifford. She might have seen the play as hers, having now moved from Mary Sidney's patronage to being under her aegis. Might the couple in the portrait be Lady Anne Clifford and her first husband, Richard Sackville, 3rd Earl of Dorset?

Clifford and the Cleopatra

There are plausible resemblances between Anne Clifford's younger portraits and the young woman in the Cleopatra portrait. They share the same round face, dark, long curly hair, a small mouth with a full lower lip and a dimpled chin. Although the idea of likeness across Renaissance portraits can be contentious in art history,[50] authenticated portraits of Clifford as a young woman all show these highly distinctive features. We can see these similarities in the often-reproduced left-hand panel of the Great Triptych, which states this represents her in 1605, aged fifteen. Karen Hearn has shown that a little-known head-and-shoulders portrait of a young girl (in a private collection), inscribed with the date 1605, could be the prototype for the panel.[51] Clifford's young features in the Great Triptych are also similar to a mid-to-late seventeenth-century engraving by Robert White, based on a 1603 image

(Figure 15). The resemblance between her features in this engraving and the sitter of the Cleopatra portrait can be said to be even more pronounced.

Clifford was born in 1590 and so would be the right age to be the Cleopatra of the portrait and, although she developed a severe look in later years, she retained this rather full-cheeked, baby-faced aspect into her thirties. The William Larkin portrait of Clifford, painted *c.*1618–19, when she was about twenty-eight years old, also supports this and shows similarities to the Cleopatra portrait.[52]

The miniature worn by the sitter of the Cleopatra portrait does not in this case serve to exclude the identification. There is a certain likeness between the portrait by Larkin of Richard Sackville and the miniature, which would suggest that he may represent the same man (see Figure 16). The portrait's miniature echoes the contemporary elite fashion for miniatures done in this antique style. An Isaac Oliver miniature, *c.*1610–11, depicts Prince Henry similarly attired in antique Roman manner.[53] Renaissance classicism was popular at the court of Prince Henry, and a feature of many of Inigo Jones's masque designs.[54] Philip Herbert, a favourite of James's and later Clifford's second husband (m. 1630), along with his brother William, who was attached to the court of Anna of Denmark, are also depicted in the antique style by Gheeraerts, *c.*1610.[55] This brings the fashion for this style of miniature to the very heart of the Dorsets' social circle. The Pembrokes were friends and Kent neighbours at Penshurst. Sackville was famously fashionable, had taken part in a number of court masques, including *Prince Henry's Barriers* (1610), and was certainly young enough to be the sitter in the miniature.

Clifford was encouraged to take part in fashionable entertainments and court masques. Her parents were patrons of drama and music, and her education included training in these, as befitting a young lady of her rank.[56] Aemilia Lanyer might have taught her music while she lived at the royal manor of Cookham with Lady Cumberland sometime around 1603 to

FIGURE 15 Anne, Countess of Pembroke. *Engraving by Robert White, mid-to-late seventeenth century.* © National Portrait Gallery, London.

FIGURE 16 Richard Sackville, 3rd Earl of Dorset, *by William Larkin (c.1613). Kenwood House, London, UK/© Historic England/ Bridgeman Images.*

1605.[57] Clifford is known to have performed in Ben Jonson's *Masque of Beauty* (1608) and *Masque of Queens* (1609), and Daniel's *Tethys' Festival* (1610), in which Daniel cast her as the nymph of Aire, the river that flows past Skipton Castle. Masque participation for aristocrats was in non-speaking roles, while actors spoke the lines.

Intriguingly, in *The Masque of Queens*, performed at Shrovetide, 2 February 1609, Clifford was given the role of Berenice – like Cleopatra a queen of Egypt. There are similarities between the Cleopatra portrait and the masque costume designed by Inigo Jones for Clifford as Berenice (see Figure 17).[58] The costume reflects the Italian influences on Jones's designs and bears striking similarity to the late seventeenth-century Cleopatra cameo discussed in the Introduction (see Figure 3). Clifford was chosen for the beauty and richness of her hair to play Berenice, who sacrificed her hair as a votive offering. She tells us that when she was young her hair 'was Browne and verie thicke and so long as that it reached the Calfe of my Legges when I stood upright'.[59] There is a remarkable likeness between the headdress designed to cover the 'mutilated' hair, depicted in Jones's sketch for the costume, and the mitre-like headdress worn by the Cleopatra in the portrait. Strong similarities can also be seen in the drapery of the robes, the necklaces and the translucent covering of the breasts. However, in the masque design there is also a baldric across the chest and no ermine.

What we see in the portrait might be an adaptation of the Berenice costume for playing Cleopatra, although of course the costume could also have changed somewhat between its design and manufacture. In examining the costume in the Cleopatra portrait, Jenny Tiramani finds that 'the artist has definitely depicted the wearer in a realistic clothing', and that 'there is nothing impossible or improbable here' to exclude performance.[60] The Isaac Oliver miniature of Clifford, from the same period and also showing her in masque dress, provides some additional corroboration.[61] Resemblances can be found in the miniature's face and in the dark, loose hair adorned by a coronet, which is not unlike the coronet worn with Cleopatra's headdress.

FIGURE 17 *Masque design,* Lady Anne Clifford as Berenice, Queen of Egypt, *by Inigo Jones, 1609. © Devonshire Collection, Chatsworth. Reproduced by permission of Chatsworth Settlement Trustees.*

Reassigning the portrait sitter's identity to Lady Anne Clifford then leads us to a different understanding of the significance of the painting. Clifford might have found elements in Cleopatra worthy of emulation and inspiration in her own identity projection (as discussed below). With the intimacy of her association with Daniel, this personal investment offers a different lesson from what we would learn if the sitter was Lady Ralegh.

A performance of *Cleopatra*?

If the sitter in the portrait is Clifford, possibly in the Berenice masque costume (or an adaptation of it), then this would add to the occasion of an already remarkable visual image and its possible interpretations. Clifford might have used the costume of one Egyptian queen to dress as another. Might she have actually played Cleopatra in Daniel's closet drama? These neo-Senecan plays were thought in older literary criticism to have been written only to be read aloud in a coterie circle, and not intended for performance. However, recent scholarship has shown that our knowledge and understanding of closet drama may not be complete and that these plays might have been fully performed in elite private settings. Marta Straznicky points out that closet plays were 'not in general opposed to theatricality' as they were part of the same elite, private culture as academic drama, which was 'not only read but performed at the universities'.[62] Research projects, such as productions of Elizabeth Cary's *The Tragedy of Mariam* (1994) by Stephanie Hodgson-Wright, Margaret Cavendish's *The Convent of Pleasure* (1995) by Gweno Williams, Mary Sidney's *Tragedie of Antonie* (1999) by Marion Wynne-Davies and Alison Findlay, the Rose Theatre Company's performances of Jane Lumley's *Iphigenia at Aulis* (2013) and Elizabeth Schafer's stagings of *Mariam* (2013), have established that such dramas were performable and might well have been written with the intention of performance.[63] In her biography of Mary Wroth, Margaret Hannay examined the possible conditions for a private performance of *Love's Victory*, which Findlay tested in a staged reading at Penshurst in 2014.[64]

Closet drama is increasingly being recognized as an important and innovative sub-genre of early modern English drama. Written for a private elite audience, it allowed for the use of more daring topical political commentary, within the safety of a like-minded circle and distance from the censure of the Revels Office and Privy Council. Women were not only writing and commissioning these plays as devisers, they might also have performed in them in the great country houses, using them to explore models of female heroism.[65] In her study of Elizabethan country-house entertainment, Elizabeth Zeman Kolkovich shows that these events enabled elite female participation in performance and authorship. Both the 1592 performances offered for Elizabeth I's visits to Bisham Abbey and Sudeley Castle included female speaking roles. Lady Elizabeth Russell (Anne Clifford's aunt by marriage) oversaw the entertainment at Bisham, in which her daughters performed the roles of political advisors. Writing about Mary Sidney, Kolkovich argues that the Countess used country-house entertainments to strengthen her authorial identity and promote 'a more radical Protestant foreign policy'.[66]

In looking at Mary Sidney's *Antonie*, Findlay states that although 'how the play was realised in a private or communal reading or in a household performance is unknown', there is strong 'evidence of a tradition of reading and performance in the Pembroke household'. She believes a staging of *Antonie* in a setting such as Penshurst, Wilton or Ramsbury was possible, by imagining 'a small coterie production drawing on clothes and objects from the household itself'.[67] As a result of recent scholarship, Hannay changed her opinion that 'a stageable *Antonie* would have taxed the resources of the Wilton Household' and thought that both Mary Sidney's *Antonie* and Daniel's *Cleopatra* could have been staged in private settings.[68]

The Cleopatra portrait may make a new contribution to this debate, providing a possible record of a private staging. The painting shows what a coterie performance of Daniel's *Cleopatra* might have looked like, showing that in such private stagings masque costumes were used. Although household accounts require further investigation, some evidence suggests that masquers paid for their own expensive costumes, and retained them afterwards. Clifford's husband, the Earl of Dorset, for instance, is recorded as having yellow silk masquing stockings in his possession in a 1617 Knole inventory.[69] It would seem logical that aristocrats would try to use these expensive and glamorous masque costumes again, whether in portraits or in privately held performances.

The early Jacobean era was a time of cultural experimentation and a perceived loosening of rules – even perhaps of pleasure in sophisticated transgression. That there was a European queen consort, Anna of Denmark, for whom women's performance was culturally acceptable, led to innovative court masques in which the Queen herself chose to perform. Daniel was in fact commissioned to write the first masque for Anna, *The Vision of the Twelve Goddesses*, in which the Queen and her ladies performed at Hampton Court in January 1604. Sophie Tomlinson points out that the female theatrical culture of the early Stuart Court was in its elite sphere 'profoundly inspiring to literary and theatrically minded women'.[70] Daniel, an important influence on Clifford, was thus at the forefront of this cultural shift.[71]

These masques were extravagant fashionable affairs, and afforded a new licence with revealing costumes. Although the dress in the Cleopatra portrait may strike us as startlingly revealing today, there are fairly numerous instances of contemporary, early seventeenth-century masque designs, demonstrating that even queens of England could appear with bare or visible breasts in performance.[72] That Clifford had appeared in the Berenice costume (and perhaps even in an adaptation of it after 1609) is strongly suggested by the case of Anthony Stafford's *Niobe* (1611). The first part of this was dedicated to Robert Cecil and appeared without any problem. The second part, *Staffords Niobe Dissolv'd into a Nilus: Or, His Age drown'd in her owne teares*, was dedicated to Clifford and seems to have caused great displeasure to the Dorsets. In all except three copies the dedication has been removed. Stafford discourses on suicide and also complains bitterly about immodest women, whose

> bodies they pinch in, as if they were angrie with nature for casting them in so gross a mould: but as for their looser parts, them they let loose to prey upon whatsoever their lust-darting eyes shal seize-upon. Their brests they laye to the open viewe, like two faire apples: of which whosoever tasteth shall be sure of the knowledge of evill.[73]

We do not know why the dedication was hurriedly cancelled. However, if Clifford had recently appeared dressed as Cleopatra in the Berenice costume, then the explanation for the offence could lie there.

Shifting perspectives

Would Anne Clifford have been comfortable going from silent masque roles to playing Cleopatra, and speaking lines about suicide and lust? The late sixteenth and early seventeenth centuries were a time of shifting perspectives when humanism and the revival of classical philosophy modified views on death and self-slaughter. As discussed in the Introduction, a different reading of Antony's and Cleopatra's suicides was made possible with the translation of Montaigne, who felt that suicide could be a glorious act in cognitive, metaphysical terms, even though it was condemned under Christian law. In his essay 'On Judging Someone Else's Death', Montaigne cited a Stoic as saying, 'It is no great thing to be alive ... the great thing is to die honourably, wisely and with constancy'.[74] Clifford records in her *Diary* having Montaigne's *Essays* read to her in November 1616: 'Upon the 9th I sat at my work and heard Rivers and Marsh read Montaigne's Essays, which Book they have read almost this fortnight.'[75] That the 1603 translation by Florio also included a dedicatory poem by Daniel must have further recommended the work to her. The work is prominently displayed among the books in the left-hand panel in the Great Triptych – the books that formed an influential part of her reading in her youth and were important to her – along with Daniel's *Works* and *Chronicles of England*.[76]

In 1616 John Donne was granted the benefice of St Nicholas's Church, located at the edge of the Dorsets' estate Knole Park, in Sevenoaks, at the behest of Sackville. Donne had completed his treatise on suicide, *Biathanatos* (written 1607-8, published after his death in 1631), well before taking up the position.[77] He had, however, deliberately kept the circulation of this self-consciously provocative work, viewing suicide as not always a sin, limited. Although it seems unlikely that he would have shared such a work with a formidable social superior like Clifford, on whom he was dependent for patronage, we know that he regularly visited Knole in his capacity as Rector of the local church. Clifford records in her *Diary* not only hearing his sermons, but also Donne's visiting and staying for dinner.[78] We also know that Donne conversed with her on intellectual subjects, because in her funeral sermon he was reported to have said, 'That she knew well how to discourse of all things, from predestination, to Slea-silk. Meaning, that although she was skilful in housewifery, and in such things in which women are conversant, yet her penetrating wit soared up to pry into the highest mysteries: looking at the highest example of female wisdom.'[79] It is possible that the 'the highest mysteries' alluded to might have included topics such as death and suicide.

Just as views towards death and suicide were becoming more complicated in the early modern era, so was the handling of the Antony and Cleopatra story. With her translation of Garnier, Mary Sidney introduced to the English dramatic canon a Cleopatra who had moved away from the scheming seductress of the Augustan narrative, providing a model of tragic female heroism. Daniel's play, the first original English drama on the subject of Cleopatra, evoked the vulnerability, grace and suffering of a great queen in defeat, as she delays her suicide to try and desperately save her children. Daniel's commission to explore the tragedy of Cleopatra in greater depth from the female perspective, as I have argued, placed the Egyptian queen into direct contact with the genre of female complaint, giving her a powerful voice.

The sensibility associated with tragedy and the rewritten Cleopatra of early modern drama – as a figure suitable for tragedy – might have been more appealing to aristocratic women's subjectivities than previously thought. Findlay observes that the Garnier-Sidney representation of a constant Cleopatra 'legitimised the passion of the individual woman, in contrast to the public role of a monarch, as a fit subject for the self-fashioned female speaking part'.[80] Mary Ellen Lamb points out that Cleopatra's resolution to die exemplifies the same 'heroics of constancy as these concerned women' in the period.[81] Cleopatra's final line in *Antonius*, 'fourth my soule may flowe', constitutes a powerfully perverse form of independence, since her self-slaughter is in fact the bold affirmation of an autonomous self.[82] This stoic idea, of death as a liberation of the soul, is taken up in Daniel both in the line reproduced in the portrait's inscription, 'witness my soule parts free to Anthony', and in Cleopatra's words, 'I must my selfe force open wide a dore / To let out life, and to unhouse my spirit.'[83] Shakespeare leads us to associate the Egyptian queen primarily with sensuality, but Mary Sidney's and Daniel's play remind us of the alternative early modern view of her as a neo-stoic heroine.

The portrait underscores the dramatic power of Daniel's play, demonstrating that his Cleopatra, in particular, had emerged as a figure that elite women could look to for agency. It shows that early modern aristocratic women identified with Cleopatra, seeing her as a figure of powerful female sovereignty and resistance. The women of Clifford's circle were rich and powerful and active in patronage and cultural production, and in some cases also engaged in irregular sexual relationships. Lady Wroth, Clifford's friend, had an adulterous affair with her cousin William Herbert, 3rd Earl of Pembroke. Lady Penelope Rich, as mentioned previously, the thinly veiled Stella of Sidney's sonnets, had a relationship with Daniel's patron Charles Blount, Lord Mountjoy. They had five children, while she openly maintained households both with her husband and Mountjoy (from 1590 to 1605). Frances Howard (a cousin of Sackville's) and Robert Carr, the Earl of Somerset (a former suitor of Clifford's), were involved in a notorious divorce and marriage, and implicated in the murder of Sir Thomas Overbury who opposed the marriage (1613–16).[84] The Cleopatra of neo-Senecan tragedy, even with her adulterous liaisons and suicide, would not have seemed so shocking to early women's sensibilities.

Daniel and the portrait

In answering whether Clifford might have played Daniel's Cleopatra, and with the Berenice costume helping to date the portrait to 1609 or after (if we accept that this is the dress worn in the portrait), then Daniel's own circumstances around this time, including the trouble over *Philotas*, have to be taken into consideration. As previously discussed, *Philotas* was performed at the Blackfriars Theatre in 1604–5 by the Children of the Queen's Revels, and its apparently sympathetic allusions to the Earl of Essex led to Daniel's being summoned before the Privy Council. In the *Apology* that Daniel felt compelled to attach to the play on its publication, he states that his intention was to have the play performed privately at Bath by children, but that he was driven by necessity to let the commercial stage 'bee the mouth of my lines'. He wrote two letters: one to Robert Cecil, the prime mover against him, the other to his patron the Earl of Devonshire, reiterating that he was forced by necessity to stage the play and 'doo a thing unworthy of mee, and much against my harte'.[85]

Although we know that in 1608 Daniel was involved in Clifford's marriage negotiations on behalf of the Earl of Hertford and visited Lady Cumberland at her London home,[86] he was staying in his publisher Simon Waterson's house in town and was generally unwilling to go far from it.[87] Expressing the reason for this reluctance, he wrote in a letter to James Kirton, Hertford's man, that 'to be often seene in ye Cittie, at this tyme, of some I would not see, might much prejudice mee'.[88] By 1611, Daniel's health had deteriorated and, believing he was dying, he lost interest in publishing poetry. Instead, he produced only work that he had to, such as *Tethys' Festival* (in 1610) and *Hymen's Triumph* (in 1614) for the Queen, and instead concentrated on the *Histories*. While it seems unlikely that Daniel would be personally involved in the portrait, it still seems plausible that even without his involvement or presence, a group of his aristocratic patrons might have mounted a private staging of *Cleopatra*, either at Knole or at Penshurst. Since Daniel's *Cleopatra* was written at Mary Sidney's behest, and was now under Anne Clifford's aegis, they might have felt they had authority to use the play for their own purposes.

The portrait raises several important questions regarding a performance of *Cleopatra* about which we can only speculate: if the portrait is a record of a performance, then does the excerpted inscription suggest that an abridged version of the closet play was staged? Or was Cleopatra's long final speech simply excerpted to allow the lines to fit in the inscription? If the inscription is seen as a thumbed and worn copy of a player's lines, then might Clifford have actually spoken these words? Or would she have struck the pose of Cleopatra during the performance while, as in masques, professional players or perhaps the sons of gentlemen (as Daniel claimed his original intention was with *Philotas*) spoke the lines? In his study of tragedy and the children's theatre, R. A. Foakes has shown that it was the children's companies, such as at Blackfriars, rather than the adult companies, who were boldly experimenting with tragedy. This included the performance of classical and serious tragedy during the first decade of the 1600s.[89] They might thus be important if we think of the portrait in terms of a performance. It is also, of course, possible that rather than a full realization of the play a presentation was made of some select scenes.

We can only speculate about whether the portrait records a performance and, if so, what kind this might have been. The painting, based on a scene from Daniel's play, is crucially performative and adds new insight into what a coterie production at this date might have looked like. If the portrait is a record of a performance of *Cleopatra*, then, as René Weis comments, 'what we may have here is a Rolls Royce version of the *Titus Andronicus* Peacham drawing (assuming it does indeed echo a scene in *Titus*), in that here it is a particular person who might be shown in full costume' with actual lines from the play.[90]

Imagining Cleopatra

If Anne Clifford is the sitter of the portrait and she is not in role for a coterie performance, then it seems she is *playing* Cleopatra, imagining being the Egyptian queen for a personal reason, using lines from Daniel that she considered hers. As mentioned earlier, Clifford's life was dominated by a notorious dispute over her inheritance caused by her father, who left all his estates and titles to his brother, bequeathing her a jointure of £15,000 instead.[91] Probably believing that her mother's death in May 1616 was caused by the stress this protracted dispute for her daughter's inheritance placed on her health, Clifford vowed never to give up her lands. She withstood all kinds of pressure and condemnation from the Archbishop of Canterbury and from James and his courtiers, among others. The King personally involved himself in deciding the case to preserve the patriarchal status quo. Her marriage, initially a happy one, suffered as her husband wanted her to agree to a settlement that would provide him with funds to maintain his own estate and extravagant habits. Clifford writes in her *Diary* of an audience with the King, in which she boldly withstood his pressure to force her to consent to an agreement, saying: 'Sometimes he used fair means & persuasion, & sometimes foul means, but I was resolved before so as nothing would move me.'[92]

Inheritance and motherhood are prominent themes in Daniel's *Cleopatra* and it seems plausible that this portrait might have something to do with the King's decision, which in 1617 went against Clifford, with Sackville accepting £17,000 in compensation. Clifford regarded James's Award as 'being as ill for me as possible'.[93] She might have found in Caesar's treatment of Cleopatra – 'But Caesar it is more than thou canst doe / Promise, flatter, threaten extreamities' (sig. H3r) – and her struggle to negotiate some form of grace for her children, affinities with James's tyranny over her own inheritance struggle. If so, she could have seen in Cleopatra's words, 'And now prowd tyrant Cæsar doe thy worst', a defiance that matched her own. If the Cleopatra portrait is from this period, then the Larkin portrait of Clifford, *c.*1618–19, shows that she could still have plausibly been the sitter into her late twenties. The Cleopatra portrait could also date from the early years of Clifford's widowhood following Sackville's death in 1624 when she was more independent.

Although Daniel had dedicated his *Letter from Octavia to Marcus Antonius* (1599) to Clifford's mother, Lady Cumberland, in which he touched on her husband's well-known philandering, he also saw a splendour and complexity in the Egyptian queen. Daniel's sensitivity towards the situation of elite women and his ability to give voices to women, especially women in crisis, is evident here both in his dealings with his aristocratic female patrons and in his female characterizations. *Cleopatra*, as previously discussed, was the subject of Daniel's sustained authorial interest over thirteen years. Its importance to Daniel, would suggest it would be important to Clifford too, especially as the work was now under her guardianship. Having not been averse to playing one Egyptian queen, Berenice, Clifford might have found affinities with Cleopatra as a woman and a mother in crisis, seeing in her a heroic resistance figure to James's self-identification with Augustus.

As pressure for her to agree to a settlement intensified from May 1616, Clifford documented her sense of isolation, and of betrayal by her husband, in her *Diary*. She writes of 'being condemned by most folks because I would not consent to the Agreement, so I may truly say, I am like an Owl in the Desert'.[94] In one of the severest actions against her, Sackville had their two-year-old daughter, Margaret, taken away from her. Clifford describes how distraught she was on that 'grievous and sorrowful day'.[95] She might have found echoes of her own painful parting from her daughter in Cleopatra's wrenching parting from her son: 'That blood within thy vaines came out of mine, / Parting from thee, I part from part of me' (sig. G6v). Within a few weeks of this punishment, she also lost her beloved mother who was her support. Her well-known comment that 'the marble pillars of Knole and Wilton were to mee oftentimes, but the gay Arbours of Anguish', written during her second marriage, might well have also been looking back to this particularly traumatic time.[96]

In many ways, the description of Cleopatra's resistance to Caesar would have resonated with Clifford's own situation:

Onely this Queene, that hath lost all this all,
To whom is nothing left, except a mind,
Cannot into a thought of yielding fall,
To be dispos'd as chance hath her assign'd ...
Will yet this womans stubborne heart be woone?

(sig. H5v–H6r)

The lines might echo her resolution not to yield to the King's pressure and to the wide condemnation she faced for her stubbornness. It was her mind and her reading that had given her the strength to be assertive in a patriarchal society, and during this difficult time it must have seemed that this was all she had left to sustain her.[97] With the Queen advising calm and patience, including offering messages of advice through Daniel, Clifford (if she is the sitter) might have had this portrait painted just for her husband in order to send a personal message. She might have used the painting to say privately what she could not say publicly about the King's award and her husband's self-interest. Daniel's portrayal of Cleopatra was a model of tragic heroism Clifford could perhaps aspire to.

The painting reveals something about the kinds of self-representation aristocratic English women might attempt in this period. As Keir Elam notes, it 'opens up new ways of understanding the intimate three-way dialogue between portraiture, performance, and politics' in early Jacobean England.[98] Interestingly, in looking at the idea of women's cultural production, Davidson and Stevenson, whose concept of devisership is explored in Chapter 2, find that:

> the person above all whose life and work becomes more comprehensible if she is identified as a deviser is Lady Anne Clifford ... Her personal agenda is eloquently declared by a whole set of artefacts, none of which is from her own hand: the 'Great Picture' that she commissioned; the buildings she created or repaired; and, not least, the highly elaborate tombs of herself and her mother, and the very markedly plainer tomb of the father who had been estranged from her mother and who had tried to divert her inheritance to male relatives.[99]

Clifford acted as a deviser throughout her life, preserving key moments from her biography. It was also typical of her to put a panel of writing on a picture, as in the Great Triptych. If she is the sitter in the portrait it would not be out of character for her even at this young age to have commissioned such a work. The portrait, with its appropriation of Daniel's lines, is carefully conceived, including the sceptre in the sitter's left hand, which reflects Cleopatra's refusal to let 'Rome behold my sceptre-bearing hand / behind me bound, and glory in my teares' (sig. H3v). The mystery and coded messages embedded in the portrait in many ways follows the Tacitean tradition of *obscura verba* found in closet plays, a deliberately obscure manner of speaking and of style.[100] This suggests its deviser must have been well-versed in closet drama.

This carefully staged painting displays a poignant eloquence. Miniatures were the most private and personal of art forms and were usually worn closed. The wearing of an openly displayed jewelled miniature suggests a mourning conceit.[101] Cleopatra is wearing a miniature of Antony who is already dead as a symbol of mourning. However, if the portrait is plausibly of Clifford and was painted for a personal reason, then the miniature adds to its message of Clifford mourning not only the loss of her inheritance, but also perhaps her relationship with her husband as she knew it. The portrait might then express her sense of isolation within the limits of her agency. Alternatively, if we see the portrait as a record of a performance of *Cleopatra*, then might Sackville have been her Antony and the portrait part of a diptych?

The painting appears to be a rare example of a full-scale portrait from this period showing clearly visible breasts, under a sheer fabric. This was usually the sign of an unmarried young woman, and exposed breasts are found depicted in miniatures, then considered to be the most private and elite of art forms. Clare McManus points out that 'the frank representation of the female body was confined to an art form commissioned and owned by the aristocracy, and to the elite theatricals of the masque'.[102] This suggests that the portrait might have been meant as a private record and not for display in more public spaces. An early seventeenth-century painting of Frances Howard, Duchess of Lennox (*c*.1615) by Gheeraerts is useful for purposes of comparison. It shows Howard in a similar type of coronet with loose-flowing hair and a low neckline, with almost exposed breasts.[103]

Although the identification of the woman in the portrait can only be speculative thus far, the occasion of its execution will probably always remain so, at least until new evidence is discovered. Reassigning the sitter's identity to Clifford reveals different lessons about the significance of the painting. It is curious that it became associated with Lady Ralegh, since there are known connections between Anne Clifford and Elizabeth Throckmorton, which are documented by Clifford herself. She writes in her *Diary* of visiting Lady Ralegh in the Tower in January 1616, during Sir Walter's incarceration, and then of visiting Lady Ralegh again in April 1619 after her husband's execution.[104] In his study of a previously misidentified portrait of Mary Rogers – Lady Harington – John Stephen Edwards discusses how the destruction and re-purposing of English stately homes in the twentieth century led also to the breakup of historic local collections of portraits. As a result, many of these portraits, particularly those of women, lost their identity, and were often arbitrarily relabeled to suit the demands of a new context.[105] It seems something similar may have happened in the case of the Cleopatra portrait. The Dixwell-Oxenden's Kent connection, however, does perhaps support a connection to Knole and Clifford. Finding the painting may help answer some of these questions. Was there something written on the back of the portrait that led to it being labelled as Lady Ralegh?

A British literary portrait of some significance, the painting furnishes possible evidence of a performance of *Cleopatra*, and even stronger evidence of a Jacobean lady wanting to role-play as Daniel's Cleopatra. The painting supports the idea that Cleopatra and her story were somehow taken up by a circle of elite cognoscenti. The fact that Mary Sidney chose to translate Garnier and that a poet of Daniel's stature was writing about Cleopatra suggests her story must have been of interest in informed aristocratic circles. Although the portrait's current whereabouts are still to be discovered, the record of this painting adds to our knowledge of the elite female response to Cleopatra in the period and plausibly to our knowledge of Lady Anne Clifford, an indomitable early modern woman. The painting demonstrates that Cleopatra represented a model of powerful sovereignty and heroism that aristocratic women could aspire to. We now have strong evidence to suggest that elite women, particularly those in distress, found sympathy and affinities with Cleopatra, underlining how divergent, complex and multivalent the response was to the Egyptian queen in the period.

This chapter explored the occasion and significance of this fascinating painting and its possible interpretations. In the following chapter, we will look at the UCL staging of *Cleopatra* undertaken in 2013 to test the feasibility of an elite private performance of Daniel's closet drama, as possibly recorded in the portrait.

4

'Then thus we have beheld': Staging Daniel's *Cleopatra*

> The conquering cause hath right, wherein thou art,
> The overthrowne must be the worser part.
> Which part is mine, because I lost my part,
> No lesser than the portion of a crowne.
> (Cleopatra to Caesar, sig. I3r)[1]

The portrait of a Jacobean lady, plausibly Lady Anne Clifford, in role as Daniel's Cleopatra provides us with one of the most remarkable, and unique, survivals from the English Renaissance of elite representations of the Egyptian queen. The painting alters our outlook about the reception of Cleopatra in the period and furnishes possible evidence of an elite private performance of a closet drama. It provides even stronger evidence of an aristocratic lady imagining herself as Cleopatra, as an expression of female self-definition and agency. This is also a kind of performance, suggesting that the Egyptian queen might have offered a model of female heroism for early modern women. If the painting is a record of a staging of Daniel's play, then it is important to bring its true significance fully into the light. The portrait may be the evidence scholars have been seeking in calling into question the traditional assumption that closet drama was never intended for performance. It has been widely held as a truism that neo-Senecan closet drama with its high rhetoric does not have the emotional range and drama necessary for performance. Daniel's tragedy, however, may help in challenging this presupposition.[2]

To test these hypotheses, I led a project to stage Daniel's closet drama to see if it was performable. In March 2013, as producer, I mounted a performance of *The Tragedie of Cleopatra*, with Emma Whipday as director and Helen Hackett as executive producer.[3] As far as we know, this was the first such staging of Daniel's play in around four hundred years, and certainly the first in modern times.[4] The performance was presented by the UCL Centre for Early Modern Exchanges and held at the Great Hall of Goodenough College, in Bloomsbury, London, with a cast and crew made up mainly of current and former UCL students of varied experience and disciplines. Auditions yielded a predominantly female cast. Two alumni, now professional actors, played the lead roles: Charlotte Gallagher as Cleopatra (see Figure 18) and Beth Eyre as Caesar. The project aimed to test the performability of Daniel's closet drama; to draw attention to an early modern representation of Cleopatra that is fascinatingly different from Shakespeare's Cleopatra in her nobility and stoicism, while also showing that Shakespeare was in dialogue with earlier iterations; and, since the play centres on a non-European queen, to explore early modern conceptions of race and gender.[5]

We also wanted to draw attention to the fact that there was female participation in drama in this period. Women not only wrote and devised closet drama, but they might have also performed in these plays in the great country houses. Such plays were regarded as designed only for reading aloud in a coterie circle and consequently thought of as less worthy of attention than plays written for the commercial playhouses.[6] Scholars, however, have increasingly recognized that closet plays were probably privately staged, and were an innovative current in English drama, allowing for female participation, dramatic experiment and the use of topical commentary within

FIGURE 18 *Charlotte Gallagher as Daniel's Cleopatra, recreating the pose in the Cleopatra portrait.* © *Yi Ling Huang.*

a close, elite circle. As discussed in Chapter 3, much valuable work has been done on the performability of early modern women's closet drama in the ongoing effort to recover texts by women writers. Closet drama by men, however, remains mostly overlooked.[7] This project aimed to bring attention to Daniel's *Cleopatra*, which is significant as the first original drama about the Egyptian queen in English, and important for its influence on Shakespeare's *Antony and Cleopatra*. It is also distinct for its connection to two women writers, Mary Sidney and Anne Clifford, and their role of 'devisership' in relation to the play.[8] Daniel's play, along with Mary Sidney's translation of Garnier, gave Cleopatra's story dramatic currency in England and helped establish her tragedy as a subject for discerning elite readers. Although largely unknown outside the academy today, many scholars working on the genre regard it as the best play to have been written in the neo-Senecan tradition in the period.[9]

As much as possible, we wanted to replicate the probable conditions of an elite Jacobean-style country-house performance. Our venue, the Great Hall of Goodenough College, was specifically chosen to evoke the feeling of mingled intimacy and grandeur of a great hall in a country house where elite drama might have been staged.[10] The performance text was the 1607 edition of *Cleopatra*, since this is the source of the portrait's inscription.[11] The edition, as previously discussed, is Daniel's final and most major revision of his tragedy and, as argued below, also the most performable. While there have been other stagings of rarely performed early modern plays, most of these were staged readings with script in hand. We wanted to move beyond this by having our actors learn the lines, to demonstrate the performability and dramatic power of Daniel's play.

This chapter explores the many insights gained about Daniel's *Cleopatra* from this project. It examines what was learnt during the script preparation and rehearsal process, and how certain themes and ideas, discussed in previous chapters, became prominent in performance. Apart from the full performance at Goodenough, we also held performances of selected scenes at the Shakespeare Institute, in Stratford-upon-Avon, and at Knole House, in Kent, where Anne Clifford might have played Daniel's Cleopatra.[12] These are discussed later in the chapter. Since this chapter presents the decisions we made in staging Daniel's tragedy and in imagining his Cleopatra, it adopts a more personal voice than other chapters.

Early views on performability: *Cleopatra, Philotas* and performance experience

That Daniel's 1607 *Cleopatra* readily lends itself to performance became apparent in early read-throughs. The perception that closet drama is static, with lengthy soliloquies rendering it inaccessible to staging, did not seem applicable in this case. Daniel's revised and restructured *Cleopatra* is significantly different from his earlier versions. The impetus for this major reworking, I would argue, came both from Daniel's natural growth and development as a poet and dramatist, and from the disaster over *Philotas*. As previously discussed, this resulted in nostalgia for Elizabeth, and a further softening in Daniel's characterization of Cleopatra.

My intention in this section is not to argue that Daniel was preparing his tragedy for performance – this seems unlikely within a couple of years of the humiliation suffered over *Philotas* – but rather to demonstrate that his closet drama reflects traces of performance experience (as discussed below) and is performable. As such, my intention is not to show evidence of performance but evidence of performability. For this project, it was important to define 'performability' and to see what might constitute evidence of this. To this end, we looked at the practical feasibility of staging the play, such as evidence within the text of embedded directorial cues, references to props and other material traces of possible performance. It should, of course, be acknowledged that trained actors and talented student performers will do the work of rendering any text performable. Our production, therefore, does not stand as proof that Daniel's play was written for full performance. I wanted to discover what might be revealed about the play through performance and, potentially, to challenge assumptions that it would not be compelling or engaging as a performance piece.

Hidden performance cues in the text allow for movement and action. The vacillation and hesitancy apparent in Cleopatra's words on the page – the sense of her 'majestie confus'd, and miserie' (sig. H6r) – translates easily into dramatic action. This was evident from the first scene, newly added in this revised edition. In previous versions, the play begins with Cleopatra's eight-page soliloquy, which forms the entire first act, but the very opening lines of Daniel's 1607 version, 'Come *Rodon*, here' (sig. G5r), command movement, and signify gesture. This is powerfully demonstrated in Cleopatra's desperation to save Caesario and her struggle to part with him:

O my divided soul what shall I doe
Whereon shall now my resolution rest? ...
When both are bad, how shall I knowe the best?
Stay; I may hap to worke with *Cæsar* now,
That he may yield him to restore thy right.
Goe, *Cæsar* never will consent that thou
So neere in blood shall be so great in might
Then take him *Rodon*, goe my sonne, farewell
But staye: there's something I would gladly say.
Yet nothing now. But O God speed you well,
Lest saying more, that more might make the[e] staye.

(sig. G6v)

Cleopatra's words allow an opportunity for movement and action, reflecting the inner turmoil of her 'divided soule' in the commands: 'Stay', 'Goe' and 'take him'. In the plaintive 'But staye' that follows, a further moment of vacillation, there is also the presence of a colon, highlighting and lifting the words.[13]

In the lines that follow, we have the most deeply personal and anguished part of Cleopatra's speech:

> Yet let me speake, perhaps it is the last
> That ever I shall speake to thee, my sonne,
> Doe mothers use to part in such post haste?
> What must I end when I have scarce begun?
> Ah no (deare heart) tis no such slender twine
> Wherewith the knot is tyde twist me and thee:
> That blood within thy vaines came out of mine,
> Parting from thee, I part from part of me.
>
> (sig. G6v)

Implicit performance cues in the text tell us that in this moment Cleopatra is emotionally and physically close to Caesario. She addresses him as 'sonne' and speaks of 'mothers', with a reference to 'twine' and 'knot' that is almost umbilical, as she speaks of the blood they share. The presence of brackets around 'deare heart' also serve to highlight the words to an actor's eye, inviting the possibility for Cleopatra to enfold her son in her arms,[14] before she sends him far away, knowing she may never see him again. Amid this despair, there are also flashes of hope, as Cleopatra lets herself momentarily think that Caesario may perhaps survive and 'give limits to the boundlesse pride / Of fierce *Octavius*, and abate his might' (sig. G5r). After Caesario's departure, and his effort to be strong and comfort his mother, the stage direction tells us that Cleopatra is '*sola*', alone. We witness her grief at their catastrophic situation, 'To thinke, that by our meanes they are undone, / On whom we sought our glory to convay' (sig. G7r).

From its first act, *Cleopatra* afforded an opportunity for a range of dramatic action and emotions as the Egyptian queen's suffering, as a mother and a queen, are foregrounded.[15] The emotional range that enhances the performability of the play also works as a powerful tool for challenging and re-writing earlier stereotypes of the *meretrix regina* (whore-queen) image,[16] showing, instead, a very complex and different side of Cleopatra. In his restructuring of the play's opening, Daniel repositioned II.i in previous editions to I.ii of the 1607 edition. Its shift to the Roman camp establishes the tense dichotomy between Egypt and Rome, with Proculeius's account to Caesar of Antony's death. With this, Daniel deftly positions Cleopatra away from harsher classical representations. We learn in this report from a Roman officer of Cleopatra's tenderness for the dying Antony, as she 'Calles him her Lord, her Spouse, her Emperor, / Forgets her owne distresse, to comfort his / And interpoints each comfort with a kisse' (sig. H1r). She sees herself as Antony's wife, and the reader's and audience's attention is drawn away from previous condemnatory views of her to see, instead, the suffering of a great queen in defeat and a model of female heroism. Cleopatra's confusion and suffering in the preceding scene are vividly contrasted with Caesar's cold and calculating, almost clinical, instructions to Proculeius to 'Supple her heart with hopes of kinde relief / Give words of oyle, unto her wounds of griefe' (sig. H1v), as he plans all the while to lead her as a trophy in his triumph.

In his final reworking of *Cleopatra* (discussed in Chapter 2), Daniel moved away from narration to more dramatic action, by adding characters such as Caesario, Charmion, Eras and Diomedes to the list of speaking parts, and eliminating the neo-classical Nuntius (or Messenger). The importance of these changes to the performability of *Cleopatra* became evident during our rehearsal process. Some of the most memorable lines and moments in performance were contributed by the addition of these characters (see below). Caesario's character allowed for the new opening scene and the later moving execution speech. The addition of Cleopatra's hand-maidens, Charmion and Eras, mentioned previously only in the Nuntius's report of Cleopatra's death, helped create a sense of a domestic female space and an aura of vulnerability around Cleopatra. This could be powerfully contrasted with the uniform masculinity of the Roman military presence around Caesar and his rapacious might.

The move towards action and performability in Daniel might have been the result of his experience as Licenser of plays at the Blackfriars Theatre for the Children of the Queen's Revels from 1604–5. It is around this period that he can be seen developing from a poet into a dramatist. Daniel's *Philotas* is significant for its apparent allusions to the Earl of Essex and unique in its distinction of being the only closet drama known to have been performed publicly in the Jacobean period. The Children of the Queen's Revels, as Lucy Munro observes, appropriated 'the elite mode of a closet drama, adapting it to the requirements of commercial drama'.[17] As previously discussed, in the *Apology* that Daniel felt compelled to attach to *Philotas* on its publication, he stated that his original intention was to have the play presented in Bath by children, 'as a private recreation'.[18]

Although Daniel was uncomfortable with a public performance, his words show that *Philotas*, a closet drama, was intended for a private performance (though here by gentlemen's sons). It was therefore not designed merely to be read aloud in a coterie circle. Daniel stated that he had written the first three acts of the play in 1600, and then set it aside, completing it in 1604. The move from poet to dramatist becomes visible in *Philotas* from around Acts III–IV with his inclusion of various dramatic devices, such as the use of fewer soliloquy; increased dramatic action; shifts to different locations within the Macedonian camp; and the metatheatrical use of the Chorus discussed further below. Daniel's revised *Cleopatra*, published two years after *Philotas*, shows certain similar traces of his performance experience with *Philotas* and may owe something to the experience of Blackfriars as well.

Daniel was not opposed to private performances, and in his contributions to the genre can be seen as an innovator in English Renaissance drama. *The Vision of the Twelve Goddesses* (1604) was the first masque written for Anna of Denmark, and the first masque staged at the Jacobean court in which the Queen and her ladies performed.[19] Although it was performed at Hampton Court on 8 January 1604, John Pitcher has discovered PRO manuscripts and payment receipts which show that Daniel was present at the Palace from the third week of November, perhaps to oversee the musicians and rehearsals.[20] Daniel's *The Queenes Arcadia*, the first Italian style pastoral tragi-comedy written in English, was performed in August 1605 before the Queen and Prince Henry, during the royal family's visit to Christ Church, Oxford. The university performance implies that Daniel regained the favour of his royal patron fairly quickly after the crisis over *Philotas*.[21] He wrote two other court masques for the Queen: *Tethys' Festival* (1610) and *Hymen's Triumph* (1614).

In masque performances women had silent roles, while professional actors spoke the lines. Daniel's Cleopatra has many lines, and we do not know if Anne Clifford – if she is the lady in the Cleopatra portrait – actually spoke the lines or simply held a pose as in a masque while players spoke the lines. It was not unusual for aristocrats to dress up and present performances and entertainments. We can only speculate about how the closet drama might have been staged and acted in Daniel's time, or even if it was staged. The portrait, as previously discussed, is intriguing as it provides us with a visual image of what a coterie performance of *Cleopatra* might have looked like. My purpose was to test the performability of Daniel's closet drama and to see whether an intimate circle of young aristocrats with personal connections to the text, such as Clifford, could have staged it in some way.[22]

Editing for performance, adapting for performance

In staging Daniel's *Cleopatra*, an essential first task was to prepare a script. As there are no modern printed editions of Daniel's 1607 edition, this was compiled from the 1607 copy in the British Library and the 1611 edition printed in

Bang's Materialien, a series known for its textual accuracy.[23] We decided to abridge the play script to reduce the play's running time from about two-and-a-quarter hours to under two hours, thus making it more accessible to a modern audience. Lukas Erne has demonstrated that the printed editions of plays written for the commercial playhouse were often longer and more literary than the actual play script performed.[24] This might apply to elite private country-house performances as well, and with this reasoning, a stanza was cut from each Chorus, and some additional lines from a few long speeches.

The Chorus cuts presented no problem since these stanzas were cut in specific places where the lines are a recapitulation of what is already dramatically apparent. It is interesting to note, however, that it was exactly in the places where we carefully cut the incidental lines that our Cleopatra and Rodon (actors Charlotte Gallagher and Elspeth North) would stumble in rehearsal and their concentration was disrupted. They both wondered why Daniel's logical thought sequence was not present in those moments to help them remember the lines. The play from its 1594 edition is largely written in quatrains with an unusual *abab* rhyme scheme. We discovered that this worked as an important device in helping our actors learn their lines. In certain instances, the actors' difficulties were at points where a cut left the text with half of a bifurcated quatrain. It appeared we were overly enterprising as editors, and most of these lines were restored.[25]

Certain minor roles were also cut and amalgamated, and others doubled, thus reducing the cast list from the nineteen suggested by Daniel's text to our more manageable company of fifteen. It seems plausible that for a Jacobean country-house performance aristocratic players might also have similarly cut, amalgamated and doubled roles, depending on the number of people available in the household.[26] We doubled four of the Egyptian roles to form the Chorus: Charmion and Eras (Cleopatra's handmaids), Seleucus (Cleopatra's treasurer) and Rodon (Caesario's tutor). This seemed appropriate since the

Chorus in Daniel is 'all Egyptian'. As members of the Chorus these characters now also became the *vox populi*, the voice of the Egyptian people, directly addressing the audience and speaking of the disaster of monarchical confusion and foreign occupation.

In bringing Daniel's play to life, we realized in our first read-throughs that there are three flashback scenes embedded in, and implied by, the text. In these moments, the poignancy and grace of Cleopatra's condition, words and gestures are described by another character; they are, however, not imagined as reported speech, but rather as performed by the sorrowful Egyptian queen herself. We found that an effective way of staging these moments was as flashback scenes accompanied by lute music. Although in neo-Senecan drama characters narrate the offstage action of others, and the idea of 'flashbacks' is a modern cinematic invention, our decision to incorporate this device is akin to dramaturgical adjustments made to stage all plays. The first of these flashback scenes, Proculeius's report of Antony's death, an impressive and lengthy piece of storytelling, could be broken up by lute music and performed without the necessity for an actor to play Antony, who is not included in the list of characters. In our staged version, we had the continual spectre of Antony's body (a cloth dummy covered by a sheet) in the background. The other two scenes were moving accounts of Cleopatra by Roman officers to other Romans (Proculeius to Caesar and Titius to Dolabella), and these worked more effectively with Cleopatra's presence on stage, speaking her own imagined lines.

Although we found that the play-text needed a little adaptation for performance, this is always the case for any play-text and need not imply unperformability. Thus, in early read-throughs, we cut the script to under two hours, amalgamated and eliminated certain roles, doubled some of the Egyptian characters as the Chorus, and identified possibilities for performing some scenes as flashbacks. We then proceeded to think about the staging itself.

A Jacobean-style production: Music, costumes, props

We initially aspired to a form of 'original practices' production, recognizing that even those conceived as such for the newly reconstructed Shakespeare's Globe, on Bankside in London, 'cherry-picked particular elements' of this concept, 'while rejecting others'.[27] The term 'original practices' was coined in 2002 to describe the pioneering work of Mark Rylance, Jenny Tiramani and Clare van Kampen in exploring stage conventions of the late sixteenth and early seventeenth centuries, at the Globe. Tiramani's focus was specifically on costume, based on the large body of evidence which 'suggests that much of the playing apparel of the late-sixteenth-century actor was contemporary dress'. The early modern mode, in fact, was to add little to change the look of the stage for a particular play, with the story-telling choices focused more on the performers' dress.[28] Farah Karim-Cooper describes 'original practices' as including carefully researched details of movement, music and socially correct deportment, while taking into account material culture and objects, such as props, textiles and make-up.[29]

In line with the idea of an 'original practices' production, I organized two workshops for our cast. The first, on moving in Jacobean costume, was run by Evienna Goodman, an expert on historical dress who has done work for the Globe and the Victoria and Albert Museum.[30] The second, on Jacobean acting, was held by Philip Bird, a Globe actor-director, whose teaching centres on early modern practices.[31] He was able to show the cast how to look within the lines for clues the writer is giving, directing them what to do. These workshops exposed our cast to lessons on deportment and socially appropriate codes of conduct, rhetoric and performance style that young aristocrats, especially those taking part in elite stagings, might have received. Anne Clifford is known to have performed in three court masques, and her husband, Richard Sackville, the Earl of Dorset, appeared in at least five masques and masquing cognates.[32] Masquers were well prepared for court performances, and it seems received rehearsal practice from the playwrights themselves and from tutors. It is probable that Daniel was at Hampton Court, overseeing the rehearsals of *The Vision* (see above). We also know from a letter written by Sir Thomas Edmond to Gilbert Talbot, Earl of Shrewsbury, that Hugh Sanford, the former tutor of William Herbert, Earl of Pembroke, was brought in especially for the masque to 'direct the order and course of the Laydies'.[33] In later court masques, of course, the aristocratic participants also had the benefit of Inigo Jones's vision and involvement. Although we do not know what Jacobean acting style might have been, these workshops provided some introduction to the type of training received by young aristocrats involved in elite entertainments.

Music would have formed an intrinsic part of an elite staging, and we sought to incorporate lute music into the performance, which would be historically accurate and representative of such an occasion. The lute was considered one of the most prestigious of instruments and was 'at its most fashionable during the Elizabethan and Jacobean period'.[34] Our lutenist, Sam Brown, of the Royal College of Music, was seated onstage throughout, as lutenists traditionally were in court masques and elite performances. He was occasionally integrated into the fictional world of the play when Cleopatra gestured to him to start or stop playing, but mainly he remained outside the action, playing during the flashbacks scenes and as a lead-in to each of the Choruses. Simon Smith, our musical director, who has researched music for the Globe, and Brown selected appropriate musical accompaniments, including by John Danyel, Samuel Daniel's brother.[35]

The Cleopatra portrait provided a unique visual image of what a coterie performance of Daniel's play might have looked like. In preparing to mount the production, we very much wanted to reproduce the costume in the portrait, but original practices costumiers provided an estimate which was prohibitive for an academic production. We were also cognizant of the fact that adapting the play to engage a modern audience was inevitably an obstacle to any kind of original practices performance. So rather than an 'original practices staging', our production evolved into a 'Jacobean-style production', where we selected what we could of the concept, striving to be as authentic as possible to probable Jacobean country-house playing conditions.

For costuming decisions, we drew inspiration from the portrait and the fact that the sitter appeared to be in rich contemporary masque dress, with the sitter in the painting's miniature depicted in the antique style. We particularly drew on the painting in making costuming choices for Cleopatra and turned to a costumier who rented authentic-looking Elizabethan and Jacobean dress. We also rented a richly embroidered silk gown worn by the actress Helen Mirren as Elizabeth I in the eponymous Channel 4 TV drama.[36] Although worn by a modern-day Elizabeth I, this seemed a fitting choice both as a gown reused from a past glamorous court performance (as perhaps with the Berenice costume), and as a nod to the fact that Elizabeth's clothes were recycled as costumes in Anna's masque (albeit here from a TV series). While the use of the not-long-deceased Elizabeth's gowns is well known, what is not so widely known is that this was undertaken for Daniel's *Vision of the Twelve Goddesses*. Arbella Stuart, who was present at Hampton Court in December 1603, reported that 'The Queene intendeth to make a mask this Christmas to which end my Lady of Suffolk and my Lady of Walsingham have warrants to take of the late Queenes best apparel out of the Tower at theyr discretion.'[37] The Countess of Suffolk was Katherine Howard, and Lady Walsingham was Audrey Walsingham, the Guardian and Keeper of the Robes.

Apart from the portrait, we were also guided by Henry Peacham's well-known 1590s sketch of *Titus Andronicus* and by Philip Henslowe's inventories in making costuming decisions for the rest of the cast.[38] These indicate that theatrical costumes in the period were basically Elizabethan or Jacobean with small details and exotic touches and drapery added, alluding to the necessary historical and locational association. Since we had a number of long-haired female actors playing male roles, including Caesar, we dealt with this by sweeping their loose hair over one shoulder, as in the somewhat androgynous portraits of Henry Wriothesley, 3rd Earl of Southampton.[39] In line with Findlay's view that it is possible to imagine a country-house performance as 'a small coterie production drawing on clothes and objects from the household itself',[40] the cast was attired in Jacobean aristocratic dress, with the Roman officers, apart from Caesar, costumed all in black. Small touches of armour that would be available in a great country house were added to augment the idea that they were part of the Roman war machine, portraying the *all'antica* Renaissance version of classical Roman dress.[41]

A props list was easily compiled while preparing the script. Among other items, this included: a basket of figs; two asps; letters from Dolabella to Cleopatra and from Cleopatra to Caesar; and, perhaps a little more unexpectedly, purple flowers. Some cues for props in Daniel are more implicit than others. While the text calls, for example, for 'two Aspicks' (sig. I7r), other prop cues are more embedded. In IV.ii, Cleopatra, offering last rites and final goodbyes to the dead Antony, says 'My heart blood should the purple flowers have been / Which here upon thy tombe to thee are offred' (sig. K1r). Cleopatra scattering flowers on Antony's tomb provides a powerfully poignant visual image, adding action and movement to the scene, and this implicit prop cue was incorporated into our list. To apply Findlay's idea of a coterie performance drawing on 'objects from the household itself', the props which were not purchased were supplied from our own households.[42] Although a purist kind of historical authenticity was impossible, nevertheless in mounting our production within practical limitations and by drawing on domestic resources, we were able to feel that we were doing something analogous to (even if not identical to) what might have happened in an elite household performance.

Our stage setting, following the early modern practice of not altering the permanent look of the stage, was a wooden table, with a white sheet covering a body (a cloth dummy) to represent Antony's tomb and Cleopatra's monument. This was flanked by a silver urn, and two chairs; a silver bowl with purple petals was placed on a nearby pedestal, and next to this, as a symbol of Egypt, rested a large brass shield decorated with two intertwined snakes. With all this in place, we were ready for the performance to begin and to see what insights were gained in the process.

Cleopatra in rehearsal and performance: What was learned

Producing Daniel's *Cleopatra* provided a remarkable opportunity to test the performability of the play and to see whether the portrait could possibly be a record of an elite staging. It also afforded an exceptional opportunity to study the closet drama in performance. Since there were no past precedents to compare or draw from, both the rehearsal process and performance were an exciting and illuminating experience. Certain ideas and themes in the play became reinforced or newly prominent during staging. These are discussed below.

Cleopatra as complaint

The idea of *Cleopatra* as complaint, which I explored in Chapter 2, became more compelling during the rehearsal process and performance. Daniel's changes and the dramatic devices introduced in 1607 suggest his strengthening of the characteristics of complaint in his closet drama. Cleopatra's long soliloquy in II.i can be seen as a lament for her own loss of self, for Antony's downfall, for her children's fate and for the Egyptian state. She realizes that all that now remains is 'This monument, two maides, and wretched I' (sig. H3r). In previous editions, this was the opening soliloquy, but Daniel's reworking allowed him to put the dramatic action first, foregrounding the Egyptian queen's calamitous situation. By the end of the first act, we have thus seen Caesario sent far away, heard the report of Antony's suicide and know that Caesar is within the walls of Alexandria desiring Cleopatra as his triumph's 'onely ornament' (sig. H1v). The First Chorus, which follows the end of the act, has also condemned their queen's 'disordred lust' for having 'her state, her selfe, and us undonne' (sig. H2r). Daniel heightens the pathos and grace of Cleopatra's suffering by showing us the catastrophic events she has been through before we actually hear her lament her condition. The sense of female complaint is established more firmly in II.ii, with Cleopatra placing herself in this tradition. Referring to Caesar, she says 'Tell him my frailtie, and the gods have given / Sufficient glory, could he be content' and 'leave me here in horror to lament' (sig. H6v). Her sense of loss of both self and state is emphasized in the lines 'Now he hath taken all away from me, / What must he take me from my selfe by force?' (sig. H6v). As Gallagher's voice rose, tautening with emotion and flashing with anger, the above lines stood out in performance. This was one of the scenes we staged as a flashback, and the decision to accompany this with lute music highlighted its effect, mirroring the words while emphasizing moments of despair and hope.

The music chosen for the flashback scenes was John Danyel's pavan *Rosa* and this worked somewhat fortuitously to reinforce the idea of *Cleopatra* as complaint.[43] A pavan is a slow, stately, elegant dance, often with a solemn mood and a repetitive theme that does not steal the limelight from the words. It seemed hard not to wonder if Danyel's *Rosa* relates in some way to his brother's *Complaint of Rosamond*. The brothers were known to be close, and they collaborated on several occasions – such as when they provided an entertainment for the new King and Queen in 1603 for their visit to the Hertfords at Tottenham Lodge, in Wiltshire[44] – but their work together has rarely been explored. It seemed to be more than a coincidence that both brothers would have an interest in the same subject, and unlikely that this would not be a collaborative effort of some kind.[45] Interestingly, *Rosa*, like Daniel's *Delia and Rosamond* (1592), was also dedicated to Mary Sidney. According to lutenist Brown, *Rosa* 'has a very specific theme and rhythm scheme, almost exactly like stanzas'. He reiterates that the music certainly fits the poem; plaintive, despairing, with rays of hope on a melancholy background. No wonder it also fitted *Cleopatra* so well.[46] *Rosamond* and *Cleopatra* are spatially next to each other in all the editions from 1594 on, bringing the play into direct contact with the genre of complaint (this proximity is discussed in Chapter 2 above).

The Chorus

In mounting a production of Daniel's *Cleopatra*, the Chorus, a requisite feature of the neo-Senecan mode, seemed at first the hardest aspect of the closet drama to stage. In performance, however, the Chorus was particularly compelling, manifesting remarkable energy. The cast members were initially unsure of how to work on this classical element since, as a feature not present in Shakespeare, it is not as familiar to non-classicists. They were directed in rehearsals to let the Chorus be free-flowing, stepping in to say the lines wherever they felt comfortable. The four actors eventually began to make different lines their own, and what developed from this initial improvisation was an almost ritualistic intertwining of speeches, as they began moving around each other in dance-like movements. As Philip Bird observed, the 'surprising and aurally delightful rhyming schemes' of the Choruses became far more prominent in rehearsals and performance than in a reading. The Choruses use twelve- or fourteen-line stanzas, sometimes based on sonnet form, and always with intricate interlocking rhyme-patterns. The opportunity for contact with the audience was essential for these passages to work.[47] While the metatheatrical use of the Chorus in *Philotas* has been recognized by scholars (in the Chorus placing themselves in the same position as the audience by expressing views on the action, and by referring to themselves as 'Spectators'),[48] our production made apparent that the Chorus in *Cleopatra* also provides a metatheatrical framework. The Chorus engages the audience throughout, adds variation to the longer speeches within the scenes and provides transitions between the acts.

Writing about *Cleopatra*, Joan Rees notes that although the Chorus 'combine commentary on the moral implications of the drama with statements appropriate to the individuals composing' it, the 'result is only intermittently successful'. While acknowledging the careful crafting of each Chorus in form and diction as making a particular contribution to the play, she finds 'they try to do too much'.[49] Rees's comments, in an otherwise sympathetic reading of the play, underscore the importance of the illumination provided by staging. Each Chorus worked well in performance and was highly effective.

The question, raised in Chapter 2 above, of whether we should see the Chorus in Daniel as impartial observers of history, or as those who jump to a quick moralizing condemnation of Cleopatra, was not a factor in the production. The directorial decision to double four of the Egyptian roles also to form the Chorus, with two members loyal to Cleopatra (Charmion and Eras), and two who betray her (Rodon and Seleucus), introduced a new element in the performance. By providing a voice for the Egyptian characters who were both players in, and victims of, this unfolding tragedy, the Chorus reflected the chaos and confusion that would have ensued with Octavius's victory and Antony's suicide in the Ptolemaic dynasty's final days. With Egypt's fall, many previously loyal citizens must have been deciding how best to survive by ingratiating themselves with the new regime. Seleucus admits as much in the exchange of betrayals with Rodon, regretful now that 'in this late shifting of our state' he was not loyal to his generous queen, following instead 'the fortune of the present time' (sig. I6v). With our performance choice, each individual Chorus member was already a biased participant (honourable or otherwise) in the drama.

The final Chorus's opening lines, delivered here by Rodon and Seleucus, reflect the sense of loss just experienced by the audience:

> Then thus we have beheld
> Th'accomplishment of woes
> The full of ruine and
> The worst of worst of ills.

(sig. K6v–K7r)

By this point in the performance, we have seen young Caesario led to his death and witnessed Cleopatra's suicide, followed by that of her handmaidens. We sympathize with the Egyptians, who have 'seene all hope expeld' (sig. K7r) from their land and feel the impending harshness of Octavius's new regime.

Power in performance

Certain lines and scenes had an unexpected power in performance. Among these were speeches by Caesario and Charmion, two characters newly added in 1607, demonstrating Daniel's move towards performability as he turned away from reported speech. As written on the page, Caesario's execution speech comes across as an exercise in rhetoric about the cyclical rise and fall of kingdoms. In rehearsals and in performance, the speech became one of the most moving and memorable moments of the play, identifying a new emotional core in the play. As Emily Stiff, our Caesario, looked up to the heavens and knelt down to touch 'Nylus earth' (sig. K2r), she was able to find implicit performance cues, infusing her words with emotion and movement. The speech no longer seemed about symbolic ideas, but about the human suffering that follows the fall of a dynasty. Caesario's lines 'Kings will alone, competitors must downe, / Neere death he stands, who stands too neere a crown' (sig. K2v) reverberated in performance.

Charmion's final lines, after Cleopatra's and Eras's suicides, were also surprisingly affecting in performance. The presence of an audience added a new dimension to Charmion's speech. Although the audience foresees Cleopatra's suicide, their collective stunned silence added an impact not previously recognized in a reading of this speech. A sense of 'Desolation' (sig. K7r) permeated the Great Hall at Goodenough, as Charmion (Lucy Jennings) tenderly straightened Cleopatra's crown, defiantly stating that her queen's grace and beauty in death show that 'shee skorns both death & Cesar' (sig. K6v).

Daniel's play centres on tensions between Egypt and Rome, leading to the end of a dynasty and foreign rule. In 1607, this thematic concern would have spoken to English fears and anxieties. With the union of the two crowns, as previously discussed, there was now a foreign king on the English throne, and many looked back nostalgically to the Tudor dynasty.[50] Lines about race rang out in performance, with Cleopatra's plea for Caesar's grace for her son, 'A mixed issue yet of Romane race' (sig. H7r). The lines must have held a particular resonance in the period as England dealt with its own issues of national identity. Although the play focuses on a non-European heroine and the consequences of monarchical confusion, Daniel's ambivalence towards the European Romans is clear, as he portrays them in a less than complimentary light. Caesario speaks of 'greedie Rome' (sig. G6r), and asks, 'What Kings? What States? hath not the Romane pride / Ransackt, confounded, or els servile bought' (sig. G6r). The identification of the Romans with the Scots was made easy by James's own identification with Augustus. The comments about Roman greed would have resonated with the English, who had become increasingly appalled by Scottish favouritism at the Jacobean court. In a polemic work of the period, *Traditional Memoyres on the Raigne of King James I* (published 1658), Francis Osborne describes the Scots as hanging on to James like 'horseleeches' – symbols of greed – as 'They beg our lands, our lives. / They switch our nobles, and lye with their wives.'[51]

Among the couplets that reverberated in performance were also ones emphasizing Cleopatra's tragic heroism as she determines to die. Cleopatra's lines, 'But I will find where ever thou doest lie / For who can stay a mind resolv'd to die' (sig. K1r), rang out in the Great Hall at Goodenough. Just before this resistance to Caesar, we see a vulnerable Cleopatra at Antony's tomb offering her final rites, sensing Antony's ghost is with her. Opportunities for performability were present throughout the text, as in this moment in the change in focus in performance indicated by the change in pronoun in the lines:

> Then why doe I complaine me to the aire?
> But tis not so, my *Antony* doth heare.
> His ever living Ghost attends my praier
> And I do know his hovering spirit is neere
> And I will speake and pray, and mourn to thee,
> O pure imortall soule, that deign'st to heare.
>
> (sig. I8v)

In these lines, Cleopatra goes from saying 'His Ghost' to 'thee'. The couplet 'His ever living Ghost attends my prayer / And I do know his hovering spirit is neere' (sig. I8v) provides an opportunity for two direct lines of address to the audience.[52] For Gallagher, these lines were particularly moving to perform, as she looked out at the audience. The idea of Cleopatra as a tragic heroine, explored in previous chapters, becomes reinforced in performance.

One of the most dynamic scenes in performance was III.ii, the scene where Caesar and Cleopatra meet for the first time, and Seleucus betrays his queen. What emerged in rehearsals and performance was a power play between Caesar (Eyre) and Cleopatra (Gallagher) replete with political and sexual tension and utter disgust, as Cleopatra, at least outwardly, concedes to Caesar 'Thanks thrice renowned *Cesar*, / Poore *Cleopatra* rests thine owne for ever' (sig. I4r). Performance cues tell us that Cleopatra is prostrated in front of Caesar, as she ironically states 'now here at thy conquering feet I lie' (sig. I2v). Caesar's repeated, irritable insistence that she 'Rise madame, rise' (sig. I2v) shows that even in the moment that should have been completely his – entry as victor into her inner sanctum – she is still able to play a political chess game, placing him at a disadvantage. The scenic echoes in Shakespeare of this meeting are discussed in Chapter 5. We chose to stage this scene with Cleopatra lying down provocatively in front of Caesar, with Gallagher's intensely sardonic and exaggerated performance heightening the sense of power play. A number of performance choices were available for this scene. We experimented with these, both in rehearsals, as well as at a workshop held at the UCL Academy with Year 12 students, and at the Shakespeare Institute's 'Reanimating Playbooks' symposium, which included academics and members of the Royal Shakespeare Company and the Globe Education team.[53]

Among the ideas that became even more prominent in performing this scene was the power of Cleopatra's metatheatrical glance forward to later representation of her as a feeble ruler. Shakespeare, of course, also has Cleopatra glance forward to later representations of her, but with the public stage in mind it is to the boy actor who will play her 'I'th' posture of a whore' (5.2.219), rather than to history's judgement of her rule. In the *Civil Wars*, Daniel expressed his particular brand of historiography and warned of the dangers of distorting the past to find quick and easy scapegoats, rather than giving due attention to all causal factors:

> So much unhappie do the Mightie stand ...
> That if by weakenesse, folly, negligence,
> They do not coming miserie withstand,
> They shall be deemed th'authors of th'offence,
> And to call in, that which they kept not out;
> And curst, as they who brought those plagues about.
> (*Civil Wars*, V.66)

Daniel's Cleopatra is well aware that this will be her fate:

> How easie *Cesar* is it to accuse,
> Whom fortune hath made faultie by their fall,

> They who are vanquished may not refuse
> The titles of reproch th'are charg'd withall.
>   The conquering cause hath right, wherein thou art,
>   The overthrowne must be the worser part.
> Which part is mine, because I lost my part,
> No lesser than the portion of a crowne ...
> But weaker powers may here see what it is,
> To neighbour great competitors so neere,
> If we take either part we perish thus.
> If newtrall stand, both parties we must feare.
>
> (sigs. I3r–I3v)

The Egyptian queen realizes that she will be seen as the sole author of her country's subjugation, regardless of the fact that the Roman war machine ploughing through 'Europe, Afrique, Asia' (sig. G6r) allowed little hope of survival for 'weaker powers' (sig. I3v). As printed on the page, the couplet 'The conquering cause hath right, wherein thou art, / The overthrowne must be the worser part' (sig. I3r) seems to be deliberately and functionally indented to draw significance to the lines as an epigrammatic *sententia*.[54] In a scene otherwise full of high drama and political one-upmanship, these lines include a self-revelatory moment as Cleopatra recognizes the role of infamy that history will assign her: 'Which part is mine, because I lost my part, / No lesser than the portion of a crowne' (sig. I3r). Knowing that history is written by the victors, she is cognizant that she will be blamed for the end of her dynasty, regardless of the impossibility of her situation: 'If we take either part we perish thus, / If newtrall stand, both parties we must feare' (sig. I3v).

Cleopatra thus afforded many moving moments and fresh insights in performance. Daniel's closet drama has been regarded as dense and difficult on the page. In performance, lines that seemed repetitive worked to enhance the power and emotional intensity of a play previously thought unperformable. The sense of confusion and hesitancy apparent in Cleopatra's words became intensified in dramatic action. The neo-Senecan

Chorus also worked to emphasize the performability of the play. We were able to show the audience at Goodenough a different Cleopatra from the one they have become so familiar with from Shakespeare. Instead, they saw a queen and a mother struggling to save her son as she prepares for a noble death.

Staging *Cleopatra* at the Shakespeare Institute and at Knole House

We were invited by the Shakespeare Institute in Stratford-upon-Avon in November 2013, and by the National Trust at Knole House in Sevenoaks in Kent in June 2014, to give a presentation about the production and stage selected scenes from the play. These events afforded an opportunity to test the performability of *Cleopatra* at two additional spaces, allowing us to take Daniel's closet drama to the centre of Shakespeare study, and to Anne Clifford's home. Due to budgetary constraints, our cast performed at both these events mainly in modern black dress, with a few small embellishments. We were thus able to test the performability of the play, based purely on its dramatic effectiveness, without the added magnificence and splendour of costumes.

The Shakespeare Institute is based at Mason Croft in Stratford, a large townhouse with Tudor roots that was greatly expanded in the eighteenth century. The event was held in the large oak-panelled hall, the Music Room, now used for lectures and performances. Among the scenes selected were: I.i (Cleopatra's emotional parting with Caesario, as he is sent away with Rodon); II.ii (Proculeius's account of Cleopatra and his taking the dagger from her hand staged as a stylized flashback scene); III.ii (Cleopatra and Caesar's meeting and Seleucus's betrayal); IV.iii (Caesario's speech as he is led to his death); and V.ii (Cleopatra's death scene). The scenes had the same dramatic intensity in performance in the Stratford setting as they did at Goodenough. In discussions after the event, many audience members commented on how moving Daniel's Cleopatra was, on the poignancy of Caesario's speech and on the emotive power of the lute music.

The presentation at Knole provided an exciting opportunity to perform scenes from *Cleopatra* at one of the great houses where the play might have been originally staged. Anne Clifford came to Knole as the young wife of Richard Sackville, 3rd Earl of Dorset, in 1609, and was mistress of the house until 1624, when, with her husband's death, the estate and title passed to his younger brother, Edward Sackville. If the portrait depicts Clifford in role as Daniel's Cleopatra, dressed in the Berenice masque dress, then this helps date the painting and the possible performance to 1609 or after.[55] Knole would thus have been a likely location for a country-house staging.

Our event was in the Great Hall at Knole, an impressive space with its tall stained-glass windows emblazoned with the arms of Elizabeth I, elaborately carved screen and portraits of Sackvilles hanging on the walls above the wood-panelling.[56] Since the event took place some fifteen months after our original performance at Goodenough, both our lead actors were unavailable due to professional commitments. The roles of Cleopatra and Caesar were taken up by cast members Elspeth North and James Phillips, who previously had supporting roles at Goodenough. The audience saw a more vulnerable Cleopatra and an intensely brooding Caesar as these actors brought their own interpretation to the roles, drawing on performance aspects available in Daniel. In doing so, they demonstrated that the lead roles have a depth and complexity that provides materials for different interpretations and could be performed well by cast members of varied experience. The event at Knole thus presented an occasion also to assert the performability of the play in a new and unexpected way, using different lead actors.

At Goodenough, many audience members commented on the fact that our Cleopatra performed in front of a large portrait of Elizabeth II, each representing very different concepts of female sovereignty.[57] At Knole, it was hard not to think of Anne Clifford, with the portrait of Thomas Sackville prominently centered on the wood-panelling directly behind us, and that of Edward Sackville, 4th Earl, hanging above the door to the upstairs rooms.[58] Both men played pivotal roles in Clifford's life; the 1st Earl, Richard's grandfather, negotiated her marriage, while her brother-in-law Edward's 'malicious hatred' caused much misery, as her marriage fell apart under the strain of her inheritance dispute.[59] As III.ii, one of the selected scenes, unfolded before us, it was difficult not to feel – surrounded as we were by symbols of patriarchal dynastic power – the resonance Clifford, and other aristocratic women, might have found in Cleopatra's lines: 'What, *Cesar*, should a woman doe, / Opprest with greatnesse?' (sig. I3r). The same sparks flew between North and Phillips in this dynamic scene as had been present between Gallagher and Eyre. The intense political and sexual tension apparent in the staging of this scene seems a deliberate feature of Daniel's verse, becoming greatly emphasized in performance.

Each of the three venues offered opportunities and challenges in testing the performability of Daniel's tragedy. By also staging the performances at the Shakespeare Institute and at Knole, we were able to experiment with the performability of the play in different spaces, with and without the aid of costumes, and with different actors playing the leads. We thus demonstrated that while the locations and cast may vary, Daniel's *Cleopatra* remained highly performable and captivating for audiences.

Conclusion and actors' response

I began the project of staging Daniel's *Cleopatra* to see if his closet drama was performable, to determine whether the portrait might possibly be a record of an elite private staging. Although we can only speculate if the play was ever performed in its time or if this was its premiere, the full performance at Goodenough and the selected scenes at the Shakespeare Institute and at

Knole show that it is performable. The play has a heightened emotional impact in performance that is not evident by reading alone. Its emotional range, along with implicit directional cues and references to an easily manageable number of props, make it a drama that readily lends itself to performance.

Daniel's neo-Senecan tragedy is an important play to stage, not only as the first original drama about Cleopatra in English, but because it imagines a Cleopatra who in her emotional range and interiority is different from Shakespeare's Cleopatra. In her review of this production, Mary Ellen Lamb found *Cleopatra* to be a 'drama of a character's interior states', and sees more of Daniel's Cleopatra in Shakespeare's Hamlet than in his Cleopatra. She wonders if this aspect of the closet drama might, in fact, have been an influence on *Hamlet*.[60] The portrait is significant as it shows an early modern aristocratic woman imagining herself as Cleopatra, so changing our outlook about the reception of the Egyptian queen in the period. If the lady in the portrait is Anne Clifford, then it is intriguing to think that she might have played Daniel's Cleopatra, a resistance figure to Caesar, as she stood up to James (who identified with Caesar) and the patriarchal system. The painting takes the anti-Cleopatra and anti-female theatricality admonitions typical of early modern conduct books, to 'be all you Octavias' and to 'make your Chamber your private theatre, wherein you may act some devout scene to God's honour', and subverts them.[61] Inspired by the portrait, our production demonstrates the potent and innovatory force women brought to early modern drama.

Staging *Cleopatra* was an exciting and enlightening journey for all involved. It also afforded a unique opportunity to collate the actors' responses regarding the performability of the closet drama. On various dates after the production, I interviewed some of our cast members – Charlotte Gallagher (Cleopatra), Beth Eyre (Caesar), Emily Stiff (Caesario), Mike Waters (Proculeius) and Elspeth North (Rodon at Goodenough, and Cleopatra at Knole) – about their thoughts on performing in *Cleopatra*. Without exception, all found the experience to be challenging and rewarding and the play performable. Gallagher, who loved playing Cleopatra, stated that although the number of her lines was initially overwhelming, she could see 'a professional director staging this, as a fresh new play'. For her, the best parts of the play are those that are divergent to the Egyptian queen's myth, where Cleopatra is vulnerable and doubtful, when the sense of self is lost. She discovered that 'Daniel's logical thought progression helps you remember the lines'. Eyre also noted being initially struck by how long the speeches were, before then observing in rehearsals how performable they actually were. She was surprised at how 'dynamic the scenes are between Cleopatra and Caesar, and how clear and natural the dialogue felt', finding Daniel 'even quite concise'. Although closet drama has been thought inaccessible for actors, Stiff and Waters both commented on the quality of Daniel's verse, with their speeches now ingrained in their minds. They felt Daniel's use of rhyme was contributory to this. After playing Cleopatra at Knole, North reflected that 'there is more room for sympathy in Daniel's Cleopatra because the audience gains an insight into her genuine feelings'. In Shakespeare 'you don't see Cleopatra on her own', whereas in Daniel 'you witness her private moments where she is not performing for anyone but trying to work out what her performance will be'.[62]

There are of course inevitable limitations to the project as a speculative exercise. We simply do not know if and how the closet play would have been staged in the period, and if it was mounted as an elite private entertainment whether it was fully realized or some extract presented. The performance raises several questions about which we can only conjecture: we do not know much about early modern country-house rehearsal practices – would aristocrats have put in the time and effort to learn the lines? Would professional actors have been brought in to speak the lines as for court masque performances? And would any alterations have been made to the closet drama to adapt it for staging? Although what we learned from the performance remains speculative, mounting the production was an important experiment. The illumination provided by staging shed new light on the Chorus and underscored or made newly apparent emotional cores and themes in the play. As the first staging of Daniel's *Cleopatra* in at least four hundred years, the production makes a significant contribution to the history of early modern performance.

In *Motives of Woe* John Kerrigan, looking at complaint in Renaissance tragedy, questioned the stage-worthiness of grief.[63] Daniel's *Cleopatra*, examining the Egyptian queen's different emotional states in her final hours, is about profound grief and loss. Our production goes some way in establishing the stage-worthiness of *Cleopatra* and showing how moving this fascinating play is in performance. The production underscored the deep complexity and subtlety of Daniel's Cleopatra. With the end of this chapter, we move from looking at Cleopatra in elite cultures to Shakespeare's representation in *Antony and Cleopatra*.

5

'She did make defect perfection': The paradox and variety of Shakespeare's Cleopatra

> I saw her once
> Hop forty paces through the public street
> And, having lost her breath, she spoke, and panted,
> That she did make defect perfection,
> And, breathless, pour breath forth.
> (*Antony and Cleopatra*, 2.2.239–42)[1]

Shakespeare's *Antony and Cleopatra* was entered in the Stationers' Register on 20 May 1608, and although we do not have an exact date for the composition of the play, most scholars agree that it was probably written in late 1606 or early 1607, after *King Lear* and *Macbeth*.[2] Epic in its scale and in the portrayal of its legendary protagonists, it was richly poetic and fluid in its language. It was also the first dramatization of the Antony and Cleopatra story in non-elite circles in English. Shakespeare's play, closely following North's Plutarch and centring on Cleopatra, begins with the news of Fulvia's death. It covers Antony's marriage to Octavia and ends after Actium with the double catastrophe of the lovers' suicides in the last two acts. Shakespeare took the potential for a duality of perspectives built into Cleopatra's tragedy by Mary Sidney and Daniel, and melded this with other aspects of the Egyptian queen's historical and literary myth. The shifting locations between Alexandria and Rome (twenty-three in the first three acts alone) underscore the opposition and tumult of constantly varying perspectives of Cleopatra and of the Egyptian and Roman worlds provided throughout the play. Cleopatra is both the 'Rare Egyptian' (2.2.228) and the 'foul Egyptian' (4.12.10); a 'whore' (3.6.68), a 'boggler' (3.13.115) and 'a most triumphant lady' (2.2.194). Thus, although judgement is uncertain in other Shakespearian tragedies such as *Othello* and *Lear*, it is particularly complex and occluded in *Antony and Cleopatra*.[3]

Shakespeare's Cleopatra is not the ennobled figure of high tragedy until after Antony's death and the long final act. Instead, she is depicted as a seductive siren, with a glamour, theatricality and paradox in her that makes 'the holy priests / Bless her when she is riggish' (2.2.249–50). Cleopatra is unlike any other woman in Shakespeare. Always performing to her audience within the world of the play, and with few glimpses of interiority, she is at once so elusive and complex that she works particularly well as a dramatic persona. She is, as Eggert observes, both 'the Cleopatran enigma' and 'the Cleopatran spectacle'.[4] She is, therefore, widely perceived to be among Shakespeare's most powerful characterizations, and ranked with Hamlet and Falstaff as 'inexhaustible'.[5] Her sighs and tears are 'greater storms and tempests than almanacs can report' (1.2.156), she has 'a celerity in dying' (1.2.151), even staging her own faked death in Act 4, and she hops 'forty paces' through the street (2.2.239), yet she is regal and heroic in her end. She is, in fact, at her most theatrical in her final moments when she instructs her ladies-in-waiting to 'Show me, my women, like a queen' (5.2.226).[6] The carefully conceived elegance of her self-presentation in death is designed to emphasize her queenliness, ensuring that her suicide is 'well done, and fitting for a princess / Descended of so many royal Kings' (5.2.325–6). In so doing, she upstages Caesar even in defeat.

It is Shakespeare's Cleopatra who has come to dominate our impression of the Egyptian queen today. His play has so successfully captured our consciousness that even classical historians have relied on his narrative and descriptions when writing about the real historical events and characters.[7] In this chapter, I explore how Shakespeare's Cleopatra was influenced by Mary Sidney's and Daniel's Cleopatras, and how he departed from them. I also look at how Shakespeare drew on the infinite variety of Cleopatras that were available to him for his characterization. Although clearly different in many ways, I suggest that Shakespeare's play is also more like the closet dramas that preceded it than has been previously considered. By resituating Shakespeare's Cleopatra and his play in its Jacobean context, the chapter underscores the historical-political contextualization of his tragedy. The chapter begins by examining the publication history of *Antony and Cleopatra* and investigates its significance in its own time.

Publication history: Delay and forgetting

Despite its current recognition, in its own time, *Antony and Cleopatra* remained unpublished for fifteen years after its registration until 1623 and the printing of the First Folio. The play had been registered in May 1608, when 'A booke Called. Anthony. *and* Cleopatra' was entered in the Stationers' Register by Edward Blount, with 'The *booke* of Pericles *prynce of Tyre*'. Scholars agree that these are the plays we know. While *Pericles* was published in 1609 (although by another publisher), Blount seems to have forgotten his ownership of *Antony and Cleopatra*.[8] It was this same Blount who with Isaac Jaggard received the licence as principal publishers of the Folio in November 1623, some seven years after Shakespeare's death. In his study of the First Folio, Blayney points out that as far as Blount and Jaggard knew there were sixteen unregistered plays, including *Antony and Cleopatra*. However, when they had the titles copied into the Stationers' Register they carefully restricted their claim to 'soe manie of the said Copies as are not formerly entred to other men', paying an extra fee for a search of any other recorded rights.[9] The search would have shown that, in fact, there were only fourteen previously unregistered plays: *As You Like It* had been provisionally registered by James Roberts. On his retirement, Roberts' titles had been passed to William Jaggard, and only recently inherited by William's son Isaac. The other play was, of course, *Antony and Cleopatra*, and as Blayney comments: 'it is striking testimony to the nature of Blount's interest in Shakespeare that although he had himself registered the play in 1608, by 1623 he had apparently forgotten that he owned it'.[10] The delay in publication may also tell us something about the reception of *Antony and Cleopatra* in the period.

We can establish whether this delay in the play was unusual, by examining W. W. Greg's *Bibliography* of printed drama, looking at plays from 1592 to 1623 (the year of *Antonius*'s publication to the printing of First Folio, using Greg's numerical system of plays, Nos. 105–406).[11] For the analysis, I looked at the first registration date of plays and their publication date. Of the 301 plays listed in the period, I included 296. Among the exclusions were: *Antony and Cleopatra* as the test play, along with *As You Like It* as the second work found previously entered in the Stationers' Register (SR). The other plays excluded were those with no entry dates. As many lost plays also had no entry dates, these were omitted from the analysis.[12] The results showed that 82 per cent of the plays (244 of 296 plays) were published in twelve months or less of their registration and that almost 99 per cent of the plays were published within sixty months or less. Only 1.4 per cent of plays (4 out of 296 plays) took longer to publish. The results are summarized in Table 1 (below):

Table 1. Time between registration and publication of English printed drama (1592–1623)

Number of Months	Number of Plays	Percentage of Plays
12 months or less	244	82.4%
13 to 24 months	42	14.2%
25 to 60 months	6	2.0%
More than 60 months	4	1.4%
Total	296	100%

The four plays (1.4 per cent) that took sixty months or longer in this period are:

- 205. *Dr Faustus*, SR 18 December 1592; published 1604 (taking 132 months).
- 213. *King Leir*, SR 14 May 1594, re-entered 8 May 1605; published 1605 (128 months).
- 279. *Troilus and Cressida*, SR 7 February 1603; published 1609 (83 months).
- 336. *English Men for My Money*, SR 3 August 1601; published in 1616 (184 months).

Antony and Cleopatra, in comparison with these plays, took 186 months between its date of entry and publication, making it an outlier as well.

The only other play that took longer was *As You Like It*, which formed part of the famous staying entry of 4 August 1600. It had been entered in the Stationers' Register with *2 Henry IV, Much Ado About Nothing* and *Every Man in His Humour*, according to which the printing of the plays was 'to be staied'. This staying entry has traditionally thought to be when the Chamberlain's Men used a friendly publisher to block piratical printing of their plays, leaving them unpublished as valuable performance properties. Blayney, however, finds the theory that acting companies viewed print publication as going against their interests as an unfounded myth.[13] Drawing on Blayney, Erne convincingly argues that the fact that the three other plays entered with *As You Like It* were formally registered within twenty days and printed within a year suggests that the company's policy was not to prevent publication. Rather, *As You Like It* remained unpublished since three other romantic comedies of Shakespeare's appeared in 1600, supplying the demand for subsequent years. The staying entry was thus in place as the plays had lacked 'authorization', a regulatory compliance necessary from the state or church before permission for publication was granted.[14] While providing a plausible explanation for *As You Like It*, Erne did not explore the possible reasons for the delay in *Antony and Cleopatra*. The theory that it might also have been a staying or blocking entry on behalf of the King's Men is somewhat problematic.[15] There is no evidence of a significant prior relationship between Blount and the company – his only previous King's Men play was *Sejanus* (1604), which he most probably got from Jonson. That *Antony and Cleopatra* was licensed by Sir George Buc, Master of the Revels, rather than a deputy also points to a more serious intention than just going through the motions of a blocking entry.[16] The fact that the delay in *Antony and Cleopatra*'s publication was unusual, and that Blount registered the play, suggests that there might be a story behind it.

Blount was a leading literary publisher of the period. Apprenticed to William Ponsonby, he became a junior partner with Simon Waterson, Daniel's publisher and friend. His dramatic publications, like Ponsonby's and Waterson's, were for an elite readership. They included neo-Senecan drama and university plays, Florio's translation of Montaigne's *Essays* (1603), a number of Daniel's works, such as *A panegyrike congratulatory to the Kings Majestie* (1603) and *Philotas* (1605), and Marlowe's *Hero and Leander* (1617).[17] He liked to publish plays based on classical history. Although we can only speculate about why Blount forgot about *Antony and Cleopatra* to such an extent that he spent a shilling to discover that he already owned the play,[18] it is interesting to explore the gradations of possibilities as to why he initially delayed its publication. Marvin Spevack observes that the fact that Blount moved his shop within St Paul's Churchyard in 1608 due to the plague only accounts for a slight delay since by 1609 Blount was back to printing his usual four to five titles per year.[19]

Blount's delay in publishing the play raises three intriguing questions. First, could Blount have seen Shakespeare's play as an investment to hold on to until it increased in value, but then forgot that he owned it? Shakespeare was a success in the theatre and print: *Henry IV, Part I* (1598) went through seven editions in a twenty-five-year period and *Richard III* (1597) through five.[20] Unlike Ponsonby and Waterson, who only registered books they printed, Blount also bought titles to sell on for a higher return. Secondly, did he suppress *Antony and Cleopatra* because he considered the Egyptian queen as belonging to the elite circle he worked for? Ponsonby, the Sidneys' publisher of choice, had published *Antonius*, and the story of Cleopatra was very much associated with Daniel and Waterson at the time. As discussed in Chapter 2, Daniel's *Cleopatra* went through seven editions between 1594 and 1607 and was a best-seller in its time. These editions were all published by Waterson, with the 1605 *Certaine Small Poems* (which included *Philotas* and *Cleopatra*) co-published with Blount. In 1607 Blount also brought out a separate edition of *Philotas* with additions from *Certaine Small Poems*.[21] He was thus closely connected to Waterson, to Daniel and to *Cleopatra*, and might not have wanted to step on his senior partner's turf.

Thirdly, might he have held back Shakespeare's play as it was still seen as politically too dangerous? We know that Greville burnt his own tragedy of Antony and Cleopatra, fearing it could be perceived as commentary on Elizabeth and Essex. As Greville says, this stirred second thoughts in him 'to bee careful (in his owne case) of leaving faire weather behind'.[22] He saw danger in the lovers' story and its association with Essex. Scholars, such as Geoffrey Bullough and James Shapiro, view Shakespeare's delay in writing a possible Elizabethan sequel to *Julius Caesar* (1599), following on with the story of the triumvirate, as directly linked to the dangers of being seen to comment on Essex.[23] While this might explain Shakespeare's delay in not writing the play soon after *Julius Caesar*, it might also account for the delay in its publication when he did. Although Greville did not write his 'Dedication to Sidney' until around 1610–12, in which he discussed the fate of his tragedy, it seems highly probable that Blount would have become aware of its destruction through Waterson because of Daniel's ties with Greville. In 1605 Daniel had been summoned in front of the Privy Council for apparent sympathetic allusions to Essex in *Philotas* (co-published by Blount), and it is likely that Greville burnt his tragedy sometime after the trouble over this. Where Daniel's *Cleopatra* was afforded cover as it focused on events after Antony's death, Shakespeare's tragedy in 1608 might have been seen as too risky to publish as it depicted the lovers privileging private passion over public duty and showed the fall of a great general.

While we can only speculate about the reasons for its delay, the fact that Blount forgot about his ownership of *Antony and Cleopatra* suggests that it was also perhaps rarely performed. Although the plague closed the theatres for intermittent periods between 1603 and 1613, we do know that many of Shakespeare's plays were revived in the first decades of the seventeenth century.[24] John Russell Brown notes that *Richard III* and *Hamlet* were theatrical favourites in the period, as were a dozen other of Shakespeare's works.[25] There is no record, however, of a performance of *Antony and Cleopatra* in the commercial playhouse or at court in Shakespeare's lifetime,[26] and no records survive about a performance before the theatres were closed in 1642. A note in the Lord Chamberlain's records of 1669 states that 'it had been formerly performed in the Blackfriars', the small indoor playhouse.[27] Shakespeare's plays were usually staged at court and the Globe in the early seventeenth century, until the acquisition of the Blackfriars by the King's Men in 1608. *Antony and Cleopatra* is also significantly the only Shakespearian tragedy not to be staged for over 150 years, between 1660 and 1759, when it was briefly revived by David Garrick for six performances.[28] By then John Dryden's *All for Love, or the World Well Lost* (1678) had taken over as the Cleopatra play of choice. This preference could have been due to the possibility that Shakespeare's play was seen as overly long and experimental, and it defied the classical unities.[29]

Erne writes about how Shakespeare was not only a playwright writing for the stage but also a literary dramatist who cared about producing a reading text for the page. He suggests that Shakespeare wrote his longer plays as literary texts with a future readership in mind and the expectation that an abridged version would be prepared for the stage.[30] Frank Kermode points out that the fact that Shakespeare 'was a poet has somehow dropped out of consideration'.[31] By 1606 Shakespeare was prosperous, a shareholder in his company and a publishing success. This prosperity allowed him the freedom to write not only to meet the demands of the King's Men's schedule, but also to push boundaries and innovate. Was *Antony and Cleopatra* a play that Shakespeare had written to explore what could be done in a textual, literary way? Was this perhaps the *feliciter audax*, or 'happy valiancy' that Coleridge famously recognized in its language and style?[32]

Shakespeare experimented with structure and language and the breaking of generic rules. That he might have written *Antony and Cleopatra* more as a literary play and less for the stage could perhaps help account for some of its famous staging problems. It is certainly among Shakespeare's longer plays at 3,636 lines and usually requires some cutting in the theatre.[33] Its rapid scene changes (forty-two in all), numerous shifts to multiple geographical locations, the challenge in handling the change in tone between the more comedic first and tragic latter half of the play, the large number of speaking parts (65–8) and the need to find larger-than-life actors to fill the title roles – especially when we think in terms of the boy actor needed to carry off the role of Cleopatra – make it a difficult play to stage.[34]

In an interview for *The Guardian* to mark the 400th anniversary of Shakespeare's death, Harriet Walter emphasizes the theatrical challenges presented by the play, even as she found the role of Cleopatra energizing. She describes the play as a 'hard one to do' and speaks of the need to perform the many scenes and locational shifts very fast, or 'it starts to fall apart'. Walter states that 'the language is always powerful in Shakespeare, but with Antony and Cleopatra the speeches are so big and muscular and rich' that they are 'exhausting to speak'.[35] In his Introduction to the play, René Weis looks back at the play in performance from the 1880s to the 1980s and discusses how no modern production has been fully satisfactory even though it does have magnificent parts. For Weis one of the play's most important features 'is a rhetorical inventiveness, which turns excess into sheer aesthetic pleasure', so making the play consistently 'more successful in the study than on the stage'.[36]

Richard Dutton recently contributed a different angle to this debate, suggesting that Shakespeare wrote his longer, more rhetorically complex plays for court performances rather than the playhouse. Emphasizing the importance of the court in shaping Shakespeare's texts, and his tendency to imagine performances within his own plays in elite settings, Dutton hypothesizes that Shakespeare primarily thought of himself as writing for the court and elite patrons. He argues, therefore, that we should see Shakespeare as a court dramatist rather than the literary dramatist Erne posits.[37] We will never really know if *Antony and Cleopatra* was written as a literary or court play, since there is no record of either a court or stage performance in Shakespeare's lifetime. Although there are other plays for which there are no performance records (and records are incomplete), the fact that Blount forgot about his ownership of the play supports the idea that it must not have been performed that frequently.

Drama, as Erne comments, has always 'existed on the intersection of theatricality and literariness'.[38] Although *Antony and Cleopatra* is now widely recognized as being among Shakespeare's greatest imaginative achievements, its unusual publication history provides us with some possible insight as to how the play and his rendering of the Egyptian queen might have been received in its time. Shakespeare played with the instability of genre throughout his career. He might also have experimented with seeing what could be done in a literary way while creating in his Cleopatra a figure who is always performing and aware of her own self-display. In a period of continuous innovation, writers might have seen boundaries between and within different forms of drama as fluid and less defined than we see them today. As such, a play assumed to be for the commercial playhouse might, in fact, have been composed without much of an eye to the public stage.

Creating Cleopatra: Influences and departures

The primary source for Shakespeare's play was the 'Life of Marcus Antonius' in *Plutarch's Lives of the Noble Grecians and Romans*, as translated by Sir Thomas North from the French of Jacques Amyot. Where Mary Sidney's neo-Senecan *Antonius* concentrated on the last day of Antony's life, and Daniel's *Cleopatra* on the final hours of the Egyptian queen's life, Shakespeare's *Antony and Cleopatra* covered a ten-year span of the lovers' story. His play begins, not long after the protagonists had met at Tarsus, with Antony already captivated by Cleopatra and living in Alexandria. It spans the years 40 BC to 30 BC: the year of Fulvia's death to that of Antony's and Cleopatra's suicides.[39] Unrestrained by the classical unities, the wide arc of Shakespeare's epic allowed him to imagine his protagonists as lovers and rulers, and to portray them in despair and defeat. His play, while epic, is thus also strangely intimate. This section looks at Shakespeare's use of Plutarch, and of the two dramas that preceded his.

As discussed in the Introduction above, Plutarch's method of comparing the virtues and vices of his subjects – with his ability to wonder at the lovers, even as his rational tone condemned them – provided complexity and paradox to the Cleopatra story. The final pages of the 'Life' give a moving account of Cleopatra's death after Antony and the fate of her dynasty. This inherent duality in her story had been built upon in the Garnier-Sidney interpretation and seized upon in Daniel. The scope of Shakespeare's play allowed him to draw on a larger swath of Plutarch's account in creating his Egyptian queen, adding to the variety of her personality. It is from hints and details in Plutarch that Shakespeare created the Cleopatra who would be with Antony day and night, playing dice and sports with him, feasting with him, taunting him, using her womanly wiles and going with him into the streets at night in disguise.[40] It is also from Plutarch that we learn of Antony's noble mind, his propensity for extravagance and flattery and his essential generosity to his men. Shakespeare shows Antony's magnanimity even in defeat with his sending Enobarbus's treasure and spoils of war after him, even though Enobarbus (developed from a minor character in the 'Life' as a Choric figure) has deserted him. The dispassionate and sceptical Enobarbus dies from a broken heart at his betrayal of Antony.[41] Plutarch mentions playful and spontaneous moments, showing a more human side of the lovers, which Shakespeare captures and enhances in his tragedy. Examples of these include the fishing incident when Cleopatra jokingly has a salt fish put on Antony's hook, or when he is left alone at Cydnus in the marketplace as the people rush to see the queen. In Shakespeare's hands, Antony whistles to hide his embarrassment.[42]

To manipulate the canvas in Plutarch for dramatic purposes, Shakespeare omits some details and condenses others. He was already practised at doing this, both with Plutarch (*Julius Caesar*) and with English chronicle history sources (primarily Holinshed). In *Antony and Cleopatra*, he omitted the account of the disastrous Parthian campaigns under Antony's command;

compressed details of the wars Fulvia and his brother Lucius were waging against Octavius, and of Fulvia's death; and suppressed Antony's part in Pompey's assassination. To focus attention on Antony and Cleopatra, he also reduced the role of Octavia. In Plutarch, there are eight years of separations and attempted reconciliations between the two, until Octavia is expelled from Antony's house. By excising such details, Shakespeare effectively avoids any mention of her pregnancies and their children, with Antony saying 'Have I my pillow left unpressed in Rome, / Forborne the getting of a lawful race' (3.13.111–12). These manipulations keep the play fast-paced, while also diminishing some of the most negative aspects of Antony and his relationship with Cleopatra. Apart from his passion for Cleopatra, Shakespeare provides two added motivations for Antony's leaving Octavia, both of which made his life with her untenable: her 'holy, cold / and still conversation' (2.6.124–5) – a virtue from the Roman perspective – and, as R. H. Case notes, the 'subjection of his genius to Caesar's'.[43] That this subjection was already on Shakespeare's mind as he was writing *Macbeth* is suggested by the somewhat unexpected comparison Macbeth makes between his own situation with Banquo, and Antony's with Caesar:

> There is none but he,
> Whose being I do fear; and under him
> My genius is rebuked, as it is said,
> Mark Antony's was by Caesar.

(3.1.53–6)

Plutarch does not describe Octavius in any detail in his 'Life', he is, however, as Wilders observes, revealed through his actions. Octavius's cold efficiency and calculated politicking contrast with Antony's nobleness and magnanimity, and this is reflected in Shakespeare's portrayal.[44]

More than in any other play, Shakespeare closely follows his principal source's descriptions and language.[45] There are numerous examples throughout the play of lines that

Shakespeare uses without much alteration. He seems to have worked with North's Plutarch open in front of him, as in the scene when the dying Charmian is confronted by the Roman soldier: 'Is that well done Charmion? Verie well sayd she againe, and meete for a Princes discended from the race of so many noble kings.'[46] In Shakespeare, this becomes: 'What work is here, Charmian? Is this well done?', with Charmian replying 'It is well done, and fitting for a princess / Descended of so many royal Kings' (5.2.324–6). This is also very close to Daniel, and it is possible that Shakespeare may here be drawing on Plutarch as filtered through Daniel (1599 *Cleopatra*, sig. K3r).

Plutarch, importantly, described the manner in which Antony fell in love with Cleopatra when they met at Tarsus – this poetic description was invaluable for Shakespeare as the centrepiece of his play:

> She disdained to set forward otherwise, but to take her barge in the river of Cydnus, the poope whereof was of gold, the sailes of purple, and the owers of silver, which kept stroke in rowing after the sounde of the musicke of flutes, howboyes, citherns, violls, and such other instruments as they played upon in the barge. And now for the person of her self: she was layed under a pavilion of cloth of gold of tissue, apparalled and attired like the goddesse Venus, commonly drawen in picture: and hard by her, on either hand of her, pretie faire boyes apparalled as painters doe set forth god Cupide, with little fannes in their hands, with the which they fanned winds upon her.[47]

In Enobarbus's celebrated evocation of Cleopatra this becomes:

> The barge she sat in, like a burnished throne,
> Burned on the water; the poop was beaten gold;
> Purple the sails, and so perfumed that
> The winds were love-sick with them; the oars were silver,
> Which to the tune of flutes kept stroke, and made
> The water which they beat to follow faster,
> As amorous of their strokes. For her own person,

> It beggared all description: she did lie
> In her pavilion, cloth-of-gold of tissue,
> O'erpicturing that Venus where we see
> The fancy outwork nature. On each side her
> Stood pretty dimpled boys, like smiling cupids,
> With divers-coloured fans, whose wind did seem
> To glow the delicate cheeks which they did cool,
> And what they undid did.
>
> (2.2.201–15)

While the verbal parallels with Plutarch are remarkable, Shakespeare transforms his description of Cleopatra's arrival on the Cydnus into pure seduction, overwhelming even the elements. Music fills the air, and the sails 'are so perfumed that / The winds were lovesick with them' (2.2.203–4), and even the water becomes 'amorous' of the barge's oar strokes (2.2.207). Cleopatra is portrayed as more beautiful than a work of art. Yet, paradoxically, Enobarbus can only explain her beauty in terms of art; she 'o'erpictures' even the perfection of the Venus of the great artists' imaginations, such as Apelles, Titian and Botticelli.[48] She is more beautiful and erotic than the goddess of beauty and desire herself.

To create his Cleopatra, however, Shakespeare at some point decided to depart from Plutarch. Case observes that his Egyptian queen of the first four acts is a much coarser, grubbier version than the one that features in the 'Life'.[49] Plutarch emphasizes Cleopatra's 'good grace' and 'her curteous nature that tempered her words and dedes', and writes of her finely taunting Antony for his soldierly humour and coarseness.[50] By contrast, in Shakespeare 'vilest things / Become themselves in her' (2.2.248–9). She is shown employing every manipulative technique to keep Antony from leaving for Rome:

> See where he is, who's with him, what he does.
> I did not send you. If you find him sad,
> Say I am dancing; if in mirth, report
> That I am sudden sick.
>
> (1.3.3–6)

She tells Charmian that the way to keep a man is through persistent frustration; she violently attacks the messenger bringing news of Antony's marriage (2.5); and flirts with Caesar's messenger Thidias (3.13). Shakespeare, similarly, forsakes Plutarch in the creation of his elevated and noble Cleopatra of the final act. Although Plutarch's biography had an ambiguity not found in other classical accounts of the story, he saw her as 'the last and extremest mischiefe of all other' for Antony, so that 'if any sparke of goodness or hope of rising were left him, Cleopatra quenched it straight, and made it worse then before'.[51] Plutarch viewed Antony's affair as a self-destructive infatuation rather than a transcendent love, with his wasting away time in the 'childish sports' and 'idle pastimes' of the Egyptian court.[52] Shakespeare gave voice to Plutarch's condemnation in the play as the distinctly Roman perspective, as in Demetrius's and Philo's comments at the beginning of the play. However, he found the vision of tragic greatness and an ennobling love in Mary Sidney's and Daniel's works. They had seen the pathos and duality in Cleopatra's story, and the potential for a heroic queen. As discussed below, previous scholars have been uncertain about Mary Sidney's and Daniel's influence on Shakespeare. Although this is more accepted today, there is still a continuing debate, with Martin Wiggins recently listing their plays only as possible sources.[53] I would argue that a much stronger case can be made for their influence.

The influence of Mary Sidney on Shakespeare

That Shakespeare read Mary Sidney's translation of Garnier during the research or composition of his play is suggested by the many verbal and conceptual parallels between the two works. While early critics, such as Willard Farnham, concluded that if Shakespeare 'read *Antonius*, the reading produced no telltale effects upon *Antony and Cleopatra*', Bullough prints it as an analogue and Spevack includes it among the major sources and influences.[54] Ernest Schanzer has shown that echoes of Mary Sidney's *Antonius* – from almost the opening lines of her Argument to the final lines of her translation – run through Shakespeare's play. These include: the bond of 'amity' that Antony's marriage to Octavia is supposed to 'knit' with Caesar; Cleopatra's explanation to Antony that she 'dare not' open the monument door lest she is taken in Caesar's triumph (a fear emphasized in Daniel, but not in Plutarch); and Antony's lament at being defeated by the cowardly novice Caesar.[55] They are also echoes in Antony's fear that Cleopatra has 'packed cards with Caesar'; and Cleopatra's grief-stricken comparison of Antony's eyes to the sun and the moon.[56] These comparisons are compelling and do not occur in other sources or analogues available to Shakespeare. Mary Sidney's selection of the word 'slime' to describe the Nile's fertile flooding is also seen as unusual and an influence on Shakespeare (*Antonius*, 2.763–8; *AC*, 2.20–2). However, Spenser uses the word seven times in the *Faerie Queene*, usually to describe fertile raw matter, so the choice of word could also have come through him.[57] Most striking is the echo of Cleopatra's final lines of the play, 'A thousand kisses, thousand thousand more / Let you my mouth for honors farewell give' (5.2019–20). In Shakespeare, these words resonate in Antony's dying words as he says farewell to Cleopatra: 'Of many thousand kisses the poor last / I lay upon your lips' (4.15.21–2).

While the verbal echoes are essential in establishing that Shakespeare read *Antonius*, of even greater interest are, perhaps, the conceptual and thematic parallels. It is in Mary Sidney rather than in Plutarch that Shakespeare would have found a portrayal of Antony's and Cleopatra's despair after the naval catastrophe at Actium. As discussed in Chapter 1, Garnier captured something new in representations of the Cleopatra story, showing Antony's anguish, remorse and suspicions in defeat. Shakespeare's Antony shares the same sense of loss of self, and believes, similarly, that he has been betrayed by the woman he sacrificed everything for, with Fortune abandoning him. In *Antonius*, set after Actium, Antony recognizes that with 'All thoughts of honor trodden under foote / So I me lost' (3.1168–9). His loss of honour and of self anticipates that in Shakespeare: 'If I lose my honour, / I lose myself' (3.4.22–3).

In both plays, Antony feels the need to 'break' away from the enchantress, and after Actium, his emotions tumultuously swing between rage at Cleopatra, a desire for vengeance upon her, and love for her.[58] The sense of self-loathing running through the plays, of being trapped by one's own consent in a destructive love, echoes that of the persona of Shakespeare's dark lady sonnets, and this might have spoken to what Shakespeare already had in mind with his Antony. Shakespeare also follows Mary Sidney in associating Antony's connection to Hercules with the story of the mythic hero unmanned by his infatuation for Omphale, and of his dressing in 'Maides attire' (*Antonius*, 3.1234; *AC*, 2.5.22). While Plutarch mentions Antony's reputed descent from Hercules, the idea of cross-dressing is not present in his account nor in Garnier. Mary Sidney might have added this, not just because it was a familiar aspect of the myth, but because Philip Sidney had specifically referred to Hercules dressing in 'women's attire' while under the infatuation of Omphale.[59] For Shakespeare there might also have been some influence of the *Faerie Queene* here, from Artegall's enthralment by Radegund and the cross-dressing in Book V. This could not have been an influence on Mary Sidney as it appears for the first time in the 1596 *Faerie Queene*, but it might perhaps have reinforced Shakespeare's sense that the comparison with the cross-dressing Hercules was appropriate.[60]

Antonius is noteworthy for its sympathetic portrayal of Cleopatra and its boldly eroticized final scene. Although Shakespeare does not follow the Garnier-Sidney representation in creating a Cleopatra who reveals any sense of interiority (unusual in a Shakespearean tragic protagonist) or self-blame for Antony's downfall, he employs many of the same strategies to soften his characterization. Shakespeare follows Mary Sidney in providing Cleopatra with fear as a motive for her disastrous decision to flee at Actium (a motive not found in

Plutarch). He also follows the order of events in *Antonius*, rather than in Plutarch, by moving Antony's resolution to die before, rather than after, the false report of Cleopatra's death.[61] Shakespeare's Cleopatra, like the Sidney-Garnier Cleopatra, almost dies at the news of Antony's attempted suicide, and is revived by her maids. In both plays, it is in her arms that Antony lies bleeding as he dies, heightening their tragic love.[62] Shakespeare might have got the idea for the erotic language and power of Cleopatra's death scene from *Antonius*. The Garnier-Sidney Cleopatra sees herself as Antony's wife, speaking of 'our holy marriage' and of the 'knot of our amitie' (5.1969–70) that truly binds them. Shakespeare provides the same sanctity and truth to their love, elevating it in his Cleopatra's 'Husband, I come!' as she prepares to join Antony in death (5.2.286).

It is interesting to see how Shakespeare plays with two elements that are central to the Garnier-Sidney interpretation – the impact of Cleopatra's absence on Antony and the idea of her constancy. In *Antonius*, Mary Sidney enhanced the persistence of Cleopatra's 'Image' for Antony and how she 'haunts' him when he is away from her.[63] Antony describes this longing as an all-consuming desire: 'Her absence thee besottes: each hower, each hower' (1.114). Shakespeare's Cleopatra is very well aware of this effect and knows how to use it. Like the dark lady of Shakespeare's sonnets, she knows how 'to make the taker mad. / Mad in pursuit and in possession so'.[64] The general exploration in the sonnets of passion and its effects on subjectivity has much in common with *Antony and Cleopatra*. Bridget Escolme observes that 'The production of desire by absence is central to Cleopatra's theatricality': in 1.2 she leaves as soon as she hears Antony approaching even though she was seeking him before; she frequently feigns illness and fainting (as in 1.3.6, and 72); and is fatally absent in Act 4, causing Antony to kill himself for loss of her.[65]

Shakespeare unsettles the idea of constancy and inconstancy in his tragedy. Where the Garnier-Sidney Cleopatra is positioned as a figure of constancy from her very first lines, Shakespeare's Antony and Cleopatra of the first four acts are both inconstant or are perceived as such. Escolme notes that inconstancy, or less pejoratively changeability, are a crucial part of the play's plot and structure.[66] Although Antony makes immense claims for his love – 'Let Rome in Tiber melt, and the wide arch / of the ranged empire fall! Here is my space!' (1.1.34–5) – these are dispensed with when political expediency in Rome demands he marry Octavia. He accuses Cleopatra of inconstancy, but she is actually more constant than him; she defends herself to Proculeius – 'Rather a ditch in Egypt / Be gentle grave unto me!' (5.2.56–7) – in very similar terms to the Garnier-Sidney Cleopatra's defence of her constancy: 'Rather may I to deepest mischief fall: / Rather the opened earth devower me' (2.401–2). Her inconstancy in Shakespeare can be equated with her changeability rather than disloyalty, and, paradoxically, is a positive force for the play. Her tempest-like shifts in mood and her innate theatricality add to the infinite variety of her personality. She is Antony's 'wrangling queen',

> Whom everything becomes – to chide, to laugh,
> To weep; whose every passion fully strives
> To make itself, in thee, fair and admired!
>
> (1.1.50–2)

This changeability, for Escolme, 'is central to the pleasure Cleopatra produces for Antony – and to the theatrical pleasure produced by this play'.[67]

The influence of Daniel on Shakespeare

While Cleopatra's changeability is an essential part of what mesmerizes us, her tragic greatness and heroism lie in her grief and devastation for Antony, and in the strength of her intention to commit suicide. It is in Daniel that Shakespeare found a sense of Cleopatra's suffering and nobility as a great queen in defeat. Writing the *Complaint of Rosamond* and exploring the elite lady's lot prepared Daniel for writing about Cleopatra. Shakespeare would have been interested in Daniel's sensibility, and how he handled a great passion. Daniel's *Letter from Octavia* (1599) would also have been of interest, especially with Shakespeare's own experimentation with female modes of complaint such as in 'A Lover's Complaint' (1609). Shakespeare had already turned to *Rosamond* (first published in 1592, and revised in 1594) as an inspiration for the *Rape of Lucrece* (1594) and for some of his early plays of the mid- to late 1590s, such as *Romeo and Juliet, Love's Labour's Lost* and *2 Henry IV*.[68] It seems likely that with his interest in *Rosamond* he would also know Daniel's *Cleopatra* when it first appeared in *Delia and Rosamond augmented* (1594).

Although scholars generally regard *Cleopatra* as more of an influence on Shakespeare than *Antonius*, the level of this influence is still debated. In his recent book on the year 1606 which also looked at *Antony and Cleopatra*, Shapiro states that although Shakespeare certainly read Daniel, he did not draw much from it. Bullough, however, prints *Cleopatra* as a probable source, and Spevack prints it as a major source.[69] It can be argued that Shakespeare created his version of Cleopatra with Daniel's early *Cleopatra* in mind. It is Daniel's Cleopatra, uniquely in her 'beauties waine' with 'wrinkles of decling' (sig. C2r), who helps fashion Shakespeare's middle-aged Egyptian queen, 'Wrinkled deep in time' (I.5.30). Plutarch, as discussed in Chapter 2, describes Cleopatra as meeting Antony 'when a womans beautie is at the prime' – when she was twenty-four years old.[70] It is also in Daniel that we first have the idea of the return to Cydnus, and of Cleopatra approaching death as though she were preparing to meet her lover (*Cleopatra*, sig. I3v; *AC*, 5.2.227–8). Daniel's treatment of Cleopatra as a subject suitable for tragedy might have inspired Shakespeare's conception of his Cleopatra and led to his devoting the long final act to her personal tragedy.[71]

Echoes of Daniel's words and poetic thought infuse Shakespeare's play: the resolve of Shakespeare's Cleopatra to die and the association of this with her hands, 'My resolution and my hands I'll trust', echo the words of Daniel's Cleopatra,

'I have both hands, and will, and I can die'; the opposition of Rome's strict austerity and Egypt's luxury and 'lascivious court'; and Cleopatra's idealization of Antony as the 'demi-Atlas of this earth'.[72] Reverberations are also found in the shared horror of the Roman triumph, underscored for both Cleopatras by the humiliating fear of being led in front of Octavia (5.2.53–4; sig. B4v); in Dolabella's falling in love with Cleopatra (5.2.198; sig. G4r); and in her acknowledgement, that 'I shall remain your debtor' (5.2.203) for warning her of Caesar's intent. This sense of indebtedness is remarkably close to Daniel's Cleopatra: I will 'die his debtor' (sig. G4r), and unlike anything in Plutarch, who describes Dolabella only as bearing Cleopatra no ill will.[73] Most striking is the idea of Cleopatra's grace in death: in Daniel, Charmion speaks of 'a grace that graceth death' (sig. K2v), and in Shakespeare Caesar describes her 'strong toil of grace' (5.2.347).[74]

There are also scenic echoes between the two plays. Is Shakespeare perhaps 'visualizing' the implicit scenography built into Daniel's play? This is particularly so in the scenic echoes in 5.2 in Proculeius's interaction with Cleopatra and in Caesar's meeting with her (as also highlighted by the staging of Daniel's play). The Egyptian queen's kneeling and apparent submission to Caesar in a tense power play reflect his somewhat irritated command, 'rise. Rise, Egypt' (5.2.114) and closely echo Daniel (sig. E3r). Cleopatra's protest to Caesar in Shakespeare at her treasurer's betrayal 'That I some lady trifles have reserved, / Immoment toys' (5.2.164–5), seems to paraphrase Daniel's 'resrv'd some certain woman's toies ... / In trifling ornaments' (sig. E4v) that she might 'mediate' her case with Livia and Octavia.[75] There are many other examples of conceptual parallels and echoes between the two works, suggesting that Daniel did leave his mark on Shakespeare.

The most significant departure from Daniel in *Antony and Cleopatra* is in the idea of the Egyptian queen's motherhood. Shakespeare mentions Cleopatra's children only in passing, whereas Daniel's tragedy centres on her motherhood. They do not appear on the stage or in the list of roles (in *Antonius* 'The children' are included in the list of actors, and Caesario has a speaking part in the 1607 *Cleopatra*). Shakespeare's Cleopatra, unlike Daniel's and Mary Sidney's Cleopatras, shows no emotion towards her children; indeed, she wishes Caesarion dead to prove her love to Antony (3.13.167). The hesitation and vulnerability of Daniel's Cleopatra – her 'devided soule' (sig. G1r) – arise because she is a mother as well as a queen. She is only living while there is any hope that she might be able to save Caesario and her dynasty. She has no doubt otherwise about her resolve. Shakespeare hints at this when Cleopatra tells Proculeius:

> If your master
> Would have a queen his beggar, you must tell him
> That majesty, to keep decorum, must
> No less beg than a kingdom. If he please
> To give me conquered Egypt for my son,
> He gives me so much of mine own as I
> Will kneel to him with thanks.
>
> (5.2.15–21)

However, when the children are mentioned in Shakespeare's play it is usually as political bargaining chips as above, and when Caesar threatens them should Cleopatra harm herself. Shakespeare's focus is more on eroticizing the Egyptian queen than depicting her as a mother. She is very much a lover and a queen in Shakespeare's play, and in her end a wife. One of the most poignant images in the play is of Cleopatra holding the asp to her breast, as she likens it to the baby 'That sucks the nurse asleep' (5.2.309). Even here, though, her thoughts turn to death 'as a lover's pinch' (5.2.294) and to the husband she is about to join.

Shakespeare's Cleopatra not only surpasses the goddess of beauty and desire in her eroticism, but she also wants everyone to desire her, including the messenger. She is envious of the horse who bears Antony's weight – as she has – and longingly remembers Antony's murmurings calling her his 'serpent of Old Nile' (1.5.26).[76] Plutarch describes Cleopatra as beautiful and graceful, but not eroticized: 'her beawtie (as it is reported) was not so passing, as unmatchable of other women, nor yet suche, as upon present viewe did enamor men with her: but so sweete was her companie and conversacion, that a man could not possiblie but be taken'.[77] In Mary Sidney, and especially in Daniel, Cleopatra is weary of her beauty. No consolation comes to her at all in the fact that even in her extreme distress the soldier Dolabella, who is supposed to be helping her, finds her desirable.

Daniel's *Letter from Octavia* (1599), which preceded *Cleopatra* in *The Poeticall Essayes* (1599), is also regarded as a possible source for Shakespeare.[78] That he read the work is suggested by various echoes, including the reference in the Argument to 'Antonie having yet upon him the fetters of Aeygpt' (sig. B1r), from which Shakespeare's Antony knows he must break free (1.2.122). It is also seen as the source for the first scene in the play. In the second stanza of Daniel's *Letter*, Octavia writes to Antony to make him realize the suffering he is causing her, but she then suddenly imagines Antony blushing to receive a letter from his wife while he is with Cleopatra. In Shakespeare, Cleopatra taunts Antony about the messenger from Rome:

> You must not stay here longer; your dismission
> Is come from Caesar; therefore hear it, Antony.
> Where's Fulvia's process? – Caesar's, I would say. Both?
> Call in the messengers! As I am Egypt's Queen,
> Thou blushest, Antony, and that blood of thine
> Is Caesar's homager; else so thy cheek pays shame
> When shrill-tongued Fulvia scolds.
>
> (1.1.27–33)

There is no suggestion of such a scene in Plutarch, as Holger Norgaard points out. Shakespeare might have found staging the reception of a letter from home in this manner an effective device.[79]

Most intriguingly, perhaps, Daniel's Octavia might also lie in some way behind Shakespeare's picture of Octavia. In his Cleopatra, Daniel created a sophisticated intellect 'To whom', as Caesar says, 'is nothing left but a minde' (sig. C4v).[80] When Daniel's Cleopatra speaks, it is in the most elaborate language, since all she has left are her words. Daniel's Octavia, although she speaks movingly of her circumstances in the *Letter*, speaks in a moral Roman tone. Shakespeare's comment about Octavia's 'holy, cold / and still conversation' (2.6.124–5) might have been inspired by the contrast between the two characterizations in Daniel.[81]

Examining these sources shows something of how Shakespeare worked in creating his own Cleopatra. While Plutarch, as Shakespeare's primary source, is often discussed, the neo-Senecan dramas by Mary Sidney and Daniel remain largely neglected. A recent sourcebook on Cleopatra and the reception of her image and literary afterlife does not even include them, with Mary Sidney's voice strikingly absent from a chapter devoted to 'Women's Voices' on the Egyptian queen.[82] As demonstrated in this section, these tragedies resonate in the text of Shakespeare's play. In explorations of the relationship of *Antony and Cleopatra* with *Antonius* and *Cleopatra*, what emerges is that Shakespeare's play, while different in many ways, is also much closer to these neo-Senecan dramas than has been previously considered.

Infinite variety and race

Apart from the above sources, Shakespeare also had an infinite variety of Cleopatras and many extremities of opinion about the Egyptian queen available to him in the works produced in the period. As shown in the Introduction, Cleopatra appears not only in catalogues of women from myth and history who were morally dubious, such as Helen of Troy and Delilah, but also with women who have immortal praise, such as Penelope and Lucrece. She is the representation of decadence and intemperance and is a whore and a harlot. Antony's obsession with her is seen as the worst kind of bondage. She is an example of love and loyalty and stands with noble wives, such as Portia and Artemesia, who killed themselves after their husbands died.[83] She is also an example of women's evil inclination and their ability to feign crying.[84] She is the embodiment of grace and beauty with golden hair; yet she is also a 'nutbrowne lady' whose 'country breeds none bright', and a 'Black Egyptian'.[85]

Shakespeare's play evokes these widely varying versions of Cleopatra in different sixteenth-century sources, and this might have helped shape his idea of her particularly occluded moral status. Echoes of the Augustan narrative in these sources – of Cleopatra as 'the verie miraculous monster of all her sexe' – reverberate in the Roman perspective in the play.[86] This Augustan view manifests itself in Antony's enraged declaration that she is 'of all thy sexe; most monster-like' (4.12.36). Shakespeare's play is not only about the legendary love story, and Rome's victory over Egypt, but it is also about the struggle with the Augustan view of Cleopatra.[87] Shakespeare interrogates this narrative by looking at Cleopatra from different perspectives.

The idea of Cleopatra's changeability and elusiveness might also have been reinforced by Shakespeare's reading of Plutarch's essay 'Isis and Osiris' in his *Moralia*. Shakespeare must have known of Philemon Holland's 1603 translation. It is likely that it is from here that he drew a sense of the mysteries of Egypt and of how chameleon and feminine the Egyptian world was as opposed to the male world of Rome.[88] The idea of an encoded culture was associated with Egypt in the Renaissance and we see this both in the *Faerie Queene* in Spenser's mention of 'Ægyptian Wisards old' (V.8) and in Ben Jonson's *The Alchemist* (1610) where he associates the use of allegory and coded meaning with the Egyptian 'mystic symbols', or hieroglyphics.[89]

Just as Shakespeare drew on the varieties of Cleopatra for his characterization of the Egyptian queen, so too he drew on the varying views of her race. Although modern post-colonial and Afro-centric feminist critics have taken up Shakespeare's Cleopatra as being black, this reading is not fully supported by the text.[90] She is alternatively described as having a 'tawny front' and as a 'gipsy' (1.1.6, 10), and describes herself as 'with Phoebus's amorous pinches black' (1.5.29); yet her whiteness is also emphasized by Antony in his anger that Thidias dare kiss her ladylike 'white hand' (3.13.143). Cleopatra's being a gypsy also does not particularly support the idea of the darkness of her skin. Although gypsies were often thought to be Egyptians, views on this matter are also conflicted in the period. For example, Thomas Dekker's *Lanthorne and candle-light* (1609) specifically challenges the idea of gypsies as Egyptians:

> If they be Egiptians, sure I am they never descended from the tribes of any of Those people that came out of the land of *Egypt*: Ptolomey (king of the Egiptians) I warrant never called them his subjects: no nor Pharao before him.
>
> (sig. H1v)

The judgement about Cleopatra's race as with everything else about her in Shakespeare is also occluded. Shakespeare employs all the varying views of her race and disrupts them. His Cleopatra is deliberately racially ambiguous. She is neither black nor white, whereas Mary Sidney's and Daniel's Cleopatras are definitely white. As discussed below, she moves through the course of the play from being dark and exotic to white English, and she is seen to blush.

In drawing from the variety of Cleopatras available to him, Shakespeare created a complex, mesmerizing and glamorous queen: 'Age cannot wither her, nor custom stale / Her infinite variety' (2.2.245–6).

Antony and Cleopatra and the 1607 *Cleopatra*

Over the years, scholars have unquestioningly accepted the view that Shakespeare's play influenced the alterations in Daniel's 1607 version. The two plays are seen as being in dialogue with each other, with Shakespeare borrowing from Daniel's 1594/9 edition, and Daniel borrowing back from Shakespeare in 1607. In looking at Daniel's changes, Case was the first to cautiously suggest that 'although the evidence is by no means overwhelming' it is consistent with a 'hypothesis that Daniel re-wrote his play because he had just seen another treatment of it'.[91] This hypothesis was subsequently taken up by E. K. Chambers and J. Dover Wilson and became expressed, as Schanzer notes, as 'a certainty'.[92] It has since become the favoured view of critics, as they began using Daniel's 1607 *Cleopatra* to help establish the date of Shakespeare's *Antony and Cleopatra*. Although Leavenworth argued against Shakespeare's influence on Daniel's revisions, he saw the revised *Cleopatra* and its poetic thought as influencing Shakespeare's play.[93] I want to offer an alternative view to these readings. I would suggest that there is no sign of *Antony and Cleopatra* in the 1607 *Cleopatra*, and none of the 1607 *Cleopatra* in *Antony and Cleopatra*.

Recent scholarship shows that in 1605 to 1606, when *Antony and Cleopatra* was in gestation or being composed, Shakespeare was reading Daniel's *Philotas* (1605) and being influenced by *The Queenes Arcadia* (performed 1605; printed 1606). Kevin Curran has found verbal echoes in *Antony and Cleopatra* 2.5 from *Philotas*, specifically in the reactions to bad news in both plays.[94] Warren Boutcher has shown that Shakespeare's use of a passage from Florio's translation of Montaigne's 'Of the Caniballes' (1603) in 2.1 of *The Tempest* (*c*.1611–12), should be viewed as a theatrical response to Daniel's use of the same passage in 3.1 of *The Queenes Arcadia*, describing an Arcadia for Anna that is compared to a golden age.⁹⁵ His work reveals that Shakespeare borrows from Montaigne in precisely the same pattern that Daniel does. Shakespeare might have read the play or seen it when it was performed at Oxford at Christ Church in 1605. Daniel had become the Queen's writer, and his writing mattered publicly. Although Daniel had faced trouble over *Philotas*, his standing remained unaffected, as evidenced by his being invited to write the *Queenes Arcadia* and by its being mounted for the royal visit. As Boutcher states, 'the prominence of Samuel Daniel in literary, dramatic, and intellectual culture ... in the period *c.*1603–6, has not been given due recognition'.⁹⁶ What Boutcher's work indicates is that during this period the borrowing between Daniel and Shakespeare was going one way.

Daniel's changes centre on his movement away from soliloquy and narration to dialogue, his inclusion of extra characters and speaking parts – especially that of Caesario – and the restructuring of his play to include a new opening scene. As I discussed in Chapter 2, his emphasis is on foregrounding Cleopatra's motherhood and her suffering from the beginning of the play. The impetus of these changes can be seen as coming from his development as a dramatic writer. In the 1603 *Defence of Ryme*, Daniel is thinking about what a tragedy might be. He concedes that it 'would best comport with a blank Verse', with the Chorus in rhymed verse.⁹⁷ *Cleopatra* is in verse, but Daniel had moved to seeing that tragedy is best worked in speech that is more comparable with everyday language. In his 1611 dedication to Mary Sidney, Daniel explained that he was trying to reimagine Cleopatra's tragedy when she 'spake distresse' rather than have it narrated by another character.⁹⁸

Shakespeare was an influence on Daniel, but this came later and can be seen in Daniel's *Histories* (1612). Most critics think Shakespeare influenced Daniel since they see Shakespeare as the greater, more dominant author. This insistence, however, might have distorted their readings. Shakespeare's gargantuan reputation is, as Michael Dobson has shown, very much a product of the late seventeenth and eighteenth centuries.⁹⁹

'A lass unparalleled': Nostalgia, politics, and national identity

Towards the end of her farewell speech, Shakespeare's Cleopatra holding the asp in the dramatic moment of her suicide wishes, 'O, couldst thou speak, / That I might hear thee call great Caesar ass / Unpolicied!' (5.2.305–6). This is a remarkable statement at a time when James I associated his own image so closely with Caesar Augustus. The *OED* defines 'unpolicied' as 'not politically organised'. Caesar, Bevington notes in his commentary, has been 'outmanoeuvred' in the contest of 'policy' or craft, including statecraft, for Cleopatra has foiled his ambitions'.[100] This last scene – unlike anything else in Shakespeare both for the complex and spectacular nature of Cleopatra's death, and for her sense of victory in defeat – opens with her saying:

> My desolation does begin to make
> A better life. 'Tis paltry to be Caesar.
> Not being Fortune, he's but Fortune's knave,
> A minister of her will. And it is great
> To do that thing that ends all other deeds,
> Which shackles accidents and bolts up change,
> Which sleeps and never palates more the dung,
> The beggar's nurse and Caesar's.
>
> (5.2.1–8)

When Cleopatra declares ''Tis paltry to be Caesar' (5.2.2), she is not just dismissing Octavius; she is, as Hopkins observes, 'rejecting earthly power', and the very symbol of supreme authority appropriated by James.[101]

The King's cultivation of his Augustan image readily lent itself to topical commentary (as explored in Chapters 2 and 3), and could hardly be missed by a dramatist in 1606 or early 1607, when Shakespeare wrote *Antony and Cleopatra*.[102] In the play, Caesar declares that 'the time of universal peace is near' when 'the three-nooked world / Shall bear the olive freely' (4.6.5–7). James's coronation medal depicted him wearing a laurel wreath and proclaimed him 'Caesar Augustus of Britain, Caesar the heir of Caesar', with his wanting to base his *Pax Britannica* on Augustus's *Pax Romana*. Daniel, as previously discussed, used this association in his *Panegyrike Congratulatorie*. Other poets, such as Henry Petowe, highlighted the connection, with titles such as *Englands Caesar: His Majesties Most Royall Coronation* (1603). James's entry into London, delayed until March 1604 because of the plague, was celebrated with a distinctly 'Augustan' theme. At Temple Bar, he passed under a triumphal arch representing a temple with the main figure of Peace, and hailed as *Augustus Novus*, the new Augustus. At the Strand, two magnificent seventy-foot-high pyramids, evocative of Egypt, were erected to represent the unification of England and Scotland, with lines provided by Ben Jonson, comparing '*Brittaines King*' to Augustus.[103]

Written some two years after James's coronation, Shakespeare's *Antony and Cleopatra* needs to be read in the light of the emerging disillusionment with James and nostalgia for Elizabeth I, as reflected both in Daniel's contemporaneous 1607 *Cleopatra* and in the wider literary culture. Although this might seem impolitic for a member of the King's Men, who were dependent on James for patronage, Shakespeare's use of shifting perspectives provided a cover of ambiguity. As I pointed out in Chapter 2, disenchantment with the King and his peace policy set in early. The long-desired ideal of masculine rule after fifty years of female sovereignty (Elizabeth and her sister Mary before her) was quickly compromised and deflated by experience. James's court, with his Scottish entourage, his penchant for heavy drinking and favourites, his extravagance and his periods of inertia, was seen as debauched, scandalous and lazy. English anxieties and fears quickly grew about issues of national identity and sovereignty, with a foreign king seated on the English throne, and with his hated peace-making policy towards Catholic Spain.[104] As early as July 1604, James was also aware of the attitude against him when he bitterly complained to Parliament:

> In my government bypast in Scotland (where I ruled upon men not of the best temper) I was heard not only as a king but as a counsellor. Contrary here nothing but curiosity from morning to evening to find fault with my propositions.[105]

In a letter dated June 1606, Sir Henry Neville wrote 'that the kingdom generally wishes this peace be broken, but *Jacobus Pacificus* I believe will scarce incline to that state'.[106] English Protestants urgently felt that James should revoke the peace with Spain, negotiated in 1604, and adopt a more militant posture towards an untrustworthy enemy.

Growing nostalgia and praise for Elizabeth was often a cover for criticism of James. Michael Dobson and Nicola J. Watson stress that the public stage 'became one of the most important sites of Elizabeth's posthumous rehabilitation'.[107] They note that the Elizabeth who is first heralded on the stage is the figure portrayed in John Foxe's *Actes and Monuments of the English Martyrs*, an exemplary and pure Protestant – more often a helpless victim, rather than a symbol of absolute power.[108] After the Gunpowder Plot of 1605, however, she is portrayed as a militant queen, with the failed Catholic plot paralleled to the failed invasion of the Spanish Armada.[109] Of the five plays produced about Elizabeth during the first decade of James's reign, the first four were written between 1604 and 1607 and were immediately contemporaneous to *Antony and Cleopatra*. These include: Simon Rowley's *When You See Me, You Know Me* (first performed 1604, printed 1605), which gave voice to Elizabeth's Protestantism through a letter to her brother Edward; Thomas Heywood's *If You Know Not Me, You Know Nobody: or, The Troubles of Queen Elizabeth* (first performed 1604, published 1605), which examined Elizabeth's suffering during Mary's reign, and ended with her being crowned onstage; Heywood's *If You Know Not Me, You Know Nobody* part II (first performed 1605, published 1606), which portrayed a militaristic queen at Tilbury and the victory over the Spanish Armada; and Thomas Dekker's allegory of a corrupt Catholic Rome, *The Whore of Babylon* (first performed 1606, published 1607), which praised Elizabeth's Protestant stance and personates her in the figure of the fairy queen, Titania.[110]

The English queen had emerged as a symbol of anti-Stuart and anti-Rome resistance.[111] Sympathy for embattled and under-siege queens was also drawn on in this period. In *England's Sorrow, or, A Farewell to Essex* (1606), William Herbert compares Elizabeth to Bonduca, or Boudica, the legendary Briton warrior queen, who resisted Roman expansionism. According to Tacitus, she chose to commit suicide like Cleopatra, rather than to live a slave.[112] In elite circles, Mary Sidney's *Antonius* and Daniel's *Cleopatra* had already evoked affinities not only between Cleopatra and Elizabeth, but also between Egypt and England and the avaricious imperial designs of Rome and Spain.

Read in the context of this nostalgia, Shakespeare's Cleopatra also reflects certain aspects of Elizabeth. Helen Morris points to two scenes that are not in Plutarch and could have parallels to topical events. The first is the famous example of Elizabeth's anxious queries of the emissary of Mary Queen of Scots about her rival's appearance, just as Cleopatra enquires about Octavia's age, hair colour and height when she learns that Antony is married. The second cites Elizabeth's speech at Tilbury in 1588, 'I know I have the bodie of a weak and feeble woman, but I have the heart and stomach of a King, ... I myself will be your general', to show echoes in Cleopatra as a militaristic queen.[113] It is difficult, however, to say if Elizabeth's exchange with the emissary was widely known and how topical this was since it took place some fifty years earlier. Elizabeth's speech at Tilbury was also not printed in this form until 1654. In his commentary on the speech, Steven W. May notes that there are debates as to its accuracy.[114]

That Shakespeare had the English queen on his mind as he conceived his Egyptian queen is suggested by his following Daniel in ageing her, and by Enobarbus's description of Cleopatra as 'this great fairy' (4.8.12), evoking Spenser's *Faerie*

Queene and its many Elizabeth-figures. It is also supported by Cleopatra's comparison of herself in her grief over Antony's death to being no more than 'the maid that milks' (4.15.78). Elizabeth had wished in a speech to Parliament in 1576 that she could exchange places with a milkmaid and be afforded a more private life. This speech, as May notes, was circulated widely in the late sixteenth and early seventeenth centuries. She used this comparison again in her speech to Parliament in 1586, wishing she and Mary Queen of Scots could have resolved matters as 'two milkmaids with pails upon our arms'.[115] The direct association of Elizabeth as a milkmaid had also recently been made in Heywood's *If You Know Not Me* Part I, where the young Elizabeth in captivity dreams of life as a milkmaid.[116]

As with the shifting perspectives that underpin *Antony and Cleopatra*, there are shifting topical allusions that enhance the ambiguity of the play. We can add Shakespeare's portrayal of the drunken revelry of the triumvirs on Pompey's ship to the list of invented scenes reflecting possible topical events. It might have suggested the drunken entertainments held during the state visit of James's brother-in-law Christian IV of Denmark to England in the summer of 1606, including those on the King's own ships. As a King's Man, Shakespeare had a more formal role at court, including attendance at court events, and it is likely he would have witnessed these occasions and other similar ones at first hand.[117]

Lisa S. Starks argues that Shakespeare's Cleopatra becomes 'more white English and less black Egyptian through the course of the play'. She moves from embodying aspects of the dark lady of Shakespeare's sonnets to reflecting those of Elizabeth. Cleopatra is seen as the 'exotic Other' by the Romans; however, her changeability, violent temper and the sumptuousness of her royal barge recall the English queen and the spectacle and theatricality of her female rule.[118] Like Daniel's Cleopatra, Shakespeare's Cleopatra blushes (5.2.148), implying light-coloured skin, and is seen to do so by Caesar when he comes to take account of her treasure. Blushing, as we have seen, was viewed as an automatic biological reaction, and considered a sign of a person's honest response and lack of duplicity. By contrast, Cleopatra knows that Caesar is lying to her about her fate so that she 'should not / Be noble to myself' (5.2.190–1). Shakespeare's play reflects the preoccupation with martial virtue in the period.[119] Just as Cleopatra becomes more noble, Caesar's Roman virtue becomes diminished. In the nobility of her death, she becomes 'A lass unparalleled' (5.2.315), much as Elizabeth was remembered in a poem:

Glorious in Life,
    Deplored in her death
Such was unparallel'd
    ELIZABETH.[120]

A sense of nostalgia and loss of past greatness permeates the play. Antony feels his loss of self so profoundly that he senses his own disintegration, saying 'Here I am Antony, / Yet cannot hold this visible shape' (4.14.13–14). Cleopatra remembers Antony as a 'demi-Atlas' whose 'legs bestrid the ocean; his reared arm / Crested the world' (5.2.81–2) and recalls when 'Eternity was in our lips and eyes, / Bliss in our brows' bent' (1.3.36–7). However, as Eggert comments, when Caesar's power engulfs Egypt, memory becomes all Cleopatra has left,[121] much as her mind is all that Daniel's Cleopatra has left. The Egyptian queen's death becomes an exercise in 'performative thought' as she takes the time to plan and stage the grandeur of her death, so that she, rather than Caesar, authors her self-presentation in death.[122]

Shakespeare's play ends with Caesar's speech, in which the hitherto coldly political Caesar declares his intention to hold a funeral for Cleopatra:

                Take up her bed,
And bear her women from the monument.
She shall be buried by her Antony.
No grave upon the earth shall clip in it
A pair so famous. High events as these

Strike those that make them, and their story is
No less in pity than his glory which
Brought them to be lamented. Our army shall
In solemn show attend this funeral,
And then to Rome.

(5.2.355–64)

This unexpected magnanimity for the Egyptian queen (whom Caesar has referred to as a whore) is noteworthy, especially since there is no mention of this in Plutarch, nor of Cleopatra's body being moved from the monument. Julia M. Walker views Caesar's order to move Cleopatra as referring to James's 1606 architectural revisions of Elizabeth's tomb. As such, she concludes that 'a number of James Stuart's concerns and goals [were] foregrounded by the Roman conquest of Cleopatra', and that 'in both the play and in politics' the concept of 'male-defined dynastic continuity ... is built upon the space created by the marginalization of a dead woman icon'.[123] Yuichi Tsukada convincingly argues that by not taking into account the emerging nostalgia for Elizabeth, Walker misinterprets the play's support for James, and simplifies Shakespeare's dramatization of Cleopatra's death and its significance.[124] As I suggested in Chapter 2, nostalgia for Elizabeth and accompanying disdain for James arose quite early in the new regime; it can be seen in Daniel's revised 1607 *Cleopatra*, and is shared by Shakespeare's play.

Although at first glance a topical reading of *Antony and Cleopatra* seems remote, this becomes more evident when Shakespeare's tragedy is situated in its Jacobean context and against the historical-political backdrop of the 1590s Cleopatra plays. The play, and particularly its complex final scene, holds a mirror to James and his policies.[125] With Cleopatra's death, we are left with both a sense of loss and a sense of exhilaration at her defiance and outmanoeuvring of Caesar. Just as Cleopatra becomes a figure of resistance, so Shakespeare shows that the memory of a great queen cannot be contained by new imperial powers.

Epilogue and conclusion: Cleopatra after Shakespeare

> We princes are set ... upon stages in the sight
> and view of the world.
>
> (Elizabeth I)[1]

If we accept that Cleopatra as queen could be used as a vehicle for comments on aspects of Elizabeth I, as argued in this book, and demonstrated by Greville's destruction of his play, then this analogy carries immediate ramifications that turn her into a politically charged icon. Two examples of this in English drama are the neo-Senecan plays of Mary Sidney and Daniel. In the early Jacobean period – in Daniel's 1607 *Cleopatra*, in the portrait of the Jacobean lady depicted as Cleopatra and plausibly identified as Anne Clifford, and in Shakespeare's *Antony and Cleopatra* – we see that the Egyptian queen is used to reflect on contemporary politics and on James I's policies.

The political utility in Cleopatra's story meant that she could be used for topical commentary across both the late Elizabethan and the early Jacobean periods. The duality and splendour in her tragedy, the possibility for sympathy and condemnation, the conflict between the public and private selves of a monarch, the end of a great dynasty and the rise of imperial Rome made Cleopatra such a flexible figure that her story could be made to serve different functions. Writers could thus invoke her to highlight succession fears and perceived monarchical neglect; yet they could also find a deeper sympathy in her after Elizabeth's death to express nostalgia for female sovereignty and disenchantment with James's Scottish court and his pacifist policies.

The Egyptian queen continued to fascinate poets and dramatists writing after Shakespeare in the seventeenth century. She appeared in a number of published works, which were each influenced in some way by Mary Sidney's, Daniel's or Shakespeare's characterizations, and which reflected the shifting, conflicted, and widely varied views of her that were prevalent in the sources in the period surveyed. As the seventeenth century progressed she was used for arguing both Royalist and anti-Royalist positions. This epilogue briefly surveys these works before summing up the conclusions of this book.

Early in the seventeenth century, Cleopatra appeared in the work of two women writers, in Aemilia Lanyer's long poem *Salve Deus Rex Judæorum* (1611), and in Elizabeth Cary's neo-Senecan drama *The Tragedie of Mariam* (1613). Lanyer, who might have taught Anne Clifford music, probably knew Daniel when he was tutor to Clifford.[2] Her work indicates that she was familiar with his *Rosamond*, *Letter from Octavia*, and *Cleopatra*. Lanyer also had possible connections to Shakespeare through her relationship with Lord Hunsdon, the Lord Chamberlain, and is, according to A. L. Rowse and more recently René Weis, a possible candidate for the 'dark lady' of Shakespeare's sonnets.[3] In *Salve Deus*, Lanyer meditates on the categorization of women and the difficulties of interpretation in the debates over their worthiness. The idea of the burden of beauty in Mary Sidney (one of her dedicatees), and in Daniel, discussed in Chapters 1 and 2 above, is echoed in Lanyer's poem. Cleopatra is the main focus of the section on women who have been entrapped by male desire. She is catalogued with Helen of Troy and Lucrece, and immediately followed by Rosamond and Matilda.[4] Lanyer refers to the Egyptian queen as 'Great Cleopatra' (ll. 215), and 'Poore blinded Queene' (ll. 219) finding pathos in her situation. Although she views Cleopatra's suicide as 'That glorious part of Death, which last shee plai'd' (ll. 1417), a reference perhaps to either Daniel's or Shakespeare's play, her assessment is in the end deeply conflicted. She sees Octavia as more virtuous, concluding that in her actions, Cleopatra 'a blacke Egyptian do'st appeare' (ll. 1431).

In contrast to Lanyer's preoccupation with Cleopatra, Elizabeth Cary deals only tangentially with the Egyptian queen in *Mariam*. Cary's play was the first original tragedy written in English by a woman. It reflects the influence of *Antonius* and the Sidney circle's neo-Senecan dramas and their emphasis on Stoic values of self-reliance and self-determination.[5] Her play contributes to the differing views of Cleopatra's race in the period. Mariam's mother states that if only Antony had been sent her daughter's portrait, he would have left 'the browne *Egyptian*' (I.ii.196) and Mariam would have been in a '*Roman's* Chariot set / In place of *Cleopatra*' (I.ii.200–1).

Cleopatra was also the subject of drama written for the commercial playhouse which focused on her tragedy and continued to produce extremely divergent views of her.[6] Among these, the cunning and evil Cleopatra of the Augustan sources reappeared in Thomas May's *The Tragedie of Cleopatra Queen of Ægypt* (performed 1626, published 1639). May drew on Shakespeare by setting his play before Actium, but he excluded the shifting perspectives on Cleopatra that contribute so much in Shakespeare to her complexity. He was known in the period for his translation of Lucan's *Pharsalia* (1627), which as discussed in the Introduction included one of the most critical accounts of Cleopatra. His Egyptian queen is depicted grasping for a Roman monarchy, robbing 'Temples of God' and cold-bloodedly testing poisons on prisoners.[7] May was a republican, and Norbrook views his play as a proto-republican work, with Pettegree seeing it as 'making visible an alternative form of national politics to Charles I's personal rule'.[8] May's association with the republican cause further supports the argument in this book that the story of Cleopatra was used in drama for contemporary political commentary. Here, aspects of her myth as a decadent and monstrous queen were deployed to comment on monarchical corruption.

Sir Charles Sedley's *Antony and Cleopatra* (performed and published 1676) followed in the Restoration with the re-emergence of a more sympathetic and refined Egyptian queen. Sedley's protagonists are represented as heroic and faithful lovers.[9] While positioning his play as an adaptation of Shakespeare's work by using the same title and setting his play after Actium, Sedley returned to a neo-classical model. Bevington notes that the neo-classical mode seems to have been the preference for Restoration acting companies and audiences.[10] Sedley's play was successful in performance and is regarded as an inspiration for Dryden's decision to follow with his own version.

Of the Cleopatra plays written after Shakespeare, the most important adaptation is John Dryden's heroic tragedy *All for Love, or the World Well Lost* (performed and published 1678). Dryden's tragedy, which also returned to observing the neo-classical unities, was so successful that, as discussed in Chapter 5, it became the Cleopatra play of choice for performance in the period. Although Dryden acknowledges his debt to Shakespeare, both in the title as 'an imitation of Shakespeare's stile' and in the preface stating that 'the death of Antony and Cleopatra, is a Subject which has been treated by the greatest Wits of our Nation after Shakespeare', he does not acknowledge the dramatists who preceded Shakespeare.[11] While drawing on the Shakespearean legacy, his work, I would argue, is also striking for its similarities to Daniel's *Cleopatra*. Among these are Cleopatra's opening line in Dryden's Act II, 'What shall I do, or wither shall I turn?', which echoes the vacillation of Daniel's Cleopatra, 'what shall I do? / Whereon shall now my resolution rest?'; Cleopatra's line 'Tis sweet to die, when they wou'd force life on me' which paraphrases the resolve of Daniel's Cleopatra 'Tis sweete to die when we are forc'd to live'; and the final words of Dryden's Cleopatra '*Caesar*, thy worst; / Now part us, if thou canst' match the defiance of the final words of Daniel's Cleopatra, 'Cæsar doe thy worst'.[12] These lines do not occur in Shakespeare, suggesting that Daniel was a direct source for Dryden and that the words of his neo-Senecan drama echoed on the Restoration stage. Dryden also contributes to the varied views of Cleopatra's race, with Antony's reference in the opening line of Act III that he thought longingly of her and 'how those white arms would fold me in'.

There were also examples of continuities of interest in Cleopatra within Bess of Hardwick's family. During the English Civil War, Lady Jane Cavendish and Lady Elizabeth Brackley, the two eldest daughters of William Cavendish, Duke of Newcastle, composed a play in manuscript entitled *The Concealed Fancies* (*c*.1645).[13] Like their great-grandmother, Bess of Hardwick, whose Hardwick Hall tapestries included Cleopatra (see Introduction above), the Cavendish sisters also draw attention in their work to the idea of the Egyptian queen as a type of virtuous resistance. They had been left to manage the family estates at Bolsover and Welbeck while their father and two brothers were away fighting for the Royalist cause. In July 1644, the Cavendish men were exiled, and in August of that year Welbeck fell to the parliamentary forces (being only briefly regained). Scholars believe that the play was written during the sisters' captivity at Welbeck Abbey since it provides a backdrop to the play.[14] *The Concealed Fancies* is written as a female complaint and is, as Lisa Hopkins and Barbara MacMahon note, comparable to the narratives of female suffering written during the Civil War.[15] Most interestingly, it draws on the figure of Cleopatra as a woman in crisis. Within the play the sisters discuss performing the Egyptian queen:

> I practised Cleopatra when she was in her captivity, and could they have thought me worthy to have adorned their

triumphs, I would have performed his gallant tragedy, and so made myself glorious for time to come.

(III.iv.14–18)

Like Cleopatra, who was held under siege in her monument by the Roman forces, the Cavendish sisters were under threat in a domestic feminine space by an occupying (if native) force. S. P. Cerasano and Marion Wynne-Davies believe the reference in the lines above to 'his gallant tragedy' is to Shakespeare, since the authors make other references to his plays.[16] Bess of Hardwick's wall hanging of Cleopatra had depicted her flanked by two figures of the virtues Fortitude and Justice. While four of the five tapestries of the noble women series survive, the one of Cleopatra is no longer extant. Hopkins and MacMahon question whether the sisters might have taken the wall hanging to Bolsover or Welbeck, which were both later plundered by the Parliamentarian forces.[17] Although we can only speculate, this might perhaps help explain why the Cleopatra hanging no longer survives. In negotiating the Civil War and the ensuing siege at Welbeck, the Cavendish sisters would have found affinities with Cleopatra as a figure of female heroism, and in the virtues of Fortitude and Justice. Produced some seventy-two years after Bess's tapestry, their play underlines the continuing resonance elite women found in the Egyptian queen. The adaptability within her story also meant that just as Cleopatra could be depicted in May's proto-republican play as a symbol of decadence, she re-emerged here in a Royalist play as a figure of resistance.

Conclusions

This study began by suggesting that modern perceptions of Cleopatra are dominated by a reductive version of Shakespeare's depiction of the Egyptian queen as the sultry, exotic other. I have argued that Shakespeare's Cleopatra is far more complex than this simplified image, and that his complexity derives from sources and precedents – including Mary Sidney and Daniel – which already offered sophisticated and subtle versions of Cleopatra. Then behind them stand numerous references to Cleopatra in sixteenth-century sources that create widely divergent and even contradictory images of her, deriving from different traditions and deploying her for different rhetorical and political purposes. That the story of Cleopatra was of some interest to the Sidney and Essex circles and those closely associated to them is emphasized by her tragedy being taken up by Mary Sidney, Daniel and Greville. Mary Sidney's translation of Garnier, along with Daniel's play, gave dramatic currency to Cleopatra's story in England and helped establish her tragedy as a subject for discerning elite readers. Although their neo-Senecan plays have been thought of as somehow lesser works since they were not intended for the commercial stage, this book has demonstrated how innovative and important a current they were in English drama.

There was also more sympathy for Cleopatra in the Renaissance than previously realized. This recuperation is reflected in the response to the *Cleopatra* statue and the art and literary works it inspired, revealing the pathos and sorrow in her tragedy. It is also reflected in the striking response by women to the Egyptian queen. The evidence in my book shows that while she was condemned as an example of women's evil inclination in some early modern works, Cleopatra and her story actually spoke to elite and educated women, who found affinities with her. This is demonstrated by Bess of Hardwick's wall hanging of a noble Cleopatra; Françoise Hubert's poem prefixed to Garnier's *Marc Antoine*, in which she is crucially a woman speaking to another woman, finding empathy in Cleopatra's condition; and in Mary Sidney's portrayal of the Egyptian queen in *Antonius*. We also saw how the sitter of the Cleopatra portrait, plausibly Anne Clifford, encodes the Egyptian queen as a symbol of defiance. In the later *Concealed Fancies*, the Cavendish sisters identified with Cleopatra as another woman in captivity. While scholars recognize

Cleopatra as a figure of female heroism, the above examples, and the portrait in particular, strongly suggest that she was seen as such by women, especially those in distress.

The evidence presented in this book shows that Renaissance Cleopatras in drama were mainly white, as in the works of Garnier, Mary Sidney and Daniel, but existed as white, black, and brown in other sixteenth-century sources. In Shakespeare, who drew on the possibilities of this varied colouring, Cleopatra is alternatively described as having a 'tawny front' and as a 'gipsy' (1.1.6, 9), and describes herself as 'with Phoebus's amorous pinches black' (1.5.30), yet her whiteness is also emphasized by Antony in his description of her ladylike 'white hand' (3.13.42). In this, my findings are consistent with Aebischer, and question modern post-colonial and Afro-centric critics who, as I discussed in Chapter 5, preoccupied with later important histories of colonialism and intolerance, have taken up Cleopatra as a symbol of the other and a black queen.[18] While their readings apply to colonial and post-colonial periods, I would suggest that they do not seem as applicable to the social and political contexts in which the Cleopatra plays of the late sixteenth and early seventeenth century were produced. Although still portrayed as an exotic queen in these works, Cleopatra was deliberately rendered more English and white in Mary Sidney's and in Daniel's works to foreground similarities with Elizabeth and enhance ideas of her nobility and beauty (according to conventional sixteenth-century standards). The evidence in this book shows that Cleopatra and her story spoke to elite European women who found empathy with her and saw her sympathetic qualities.

The most rewarding aspect of this research has been those findings that are contrary to Cleopatra's Augustan reception. It was surprising to find that the Egyptian queen was a figure of emulation for women, and that Cleopatra's motherhood and her sense of vacillation and confusion are given such prominence in Daniel's play, which, as discussed in Chapter 2 above, was a bestseller in its time.[19] The association of Cleopatra – a woman held so culpable in history for the perceived failings of women – with complaint is also striking. The idea of *Cleopatra* as complaint became more evident and compelling during the project to stage Daniel's closet play. In the rehearsal process and performance, we saw Daniel take us through the various stages of grief and complaint – bereavement, the loss of state, the idea of living beyond the moment when life has ended, anger, self-blame and regret, betrayal, and a sense of isolation. In staging Daniel's *Cleopatra*, we discovered new emotional cores in the play, including the power and importance of Caesario's execution speech. Although Daniel's play has been seen by some feminist critics as a regressive departure from Mary Sidney's portrayal of the Egyptian queen, this book shows that Daniel's portrayal is deeper and subtler in its sympathy than previously recognized.

In looking at Cleopatra in classical history, it is noteworthy how overreaching and established the Augustan narrative continued to be, and remarkable to see the ways in which Shakespeare's version of her has been followed by later historians. For example, *A Commentary on Horace: Odes Book I* (1975) ends its note on Ode 37 with the astonishing statement: 'Cleopatra was 39 when she died, and an ugly and vindictive woman.'[20] While the 1930 *Cambridge Ancient History* famously used quotations from Shakespeare in its section on Antony and Cleopatra, they were removed from later editions. However, in the 1996 edition, Christopher Pelling in discussing their suicides, still found that 'Plutarch and after him Shakespeare tell the story magnificently'.[21] Although Anna Jameson, the Victorian literary critic, had 'no doubt that Shakespeare's Cleopatra is the historical Cleopatra', it is surprising to see this reliance on Shakespeare in the work of twentieth-century classical historians.[22] The conflation of the historical Cleopatra with Shakespeare's Cleopatra continues but is now also deployed in the opposite direction. It was deliberately undertaken by Janet Suzman, Escolme observes, as a feminist re-appropriation of the Egyptian queen in her production of *Antony and Cleopatra* (2012). Suzman cited her use of recent biographies of Cleopatra in her programme note, which self-consciously distanced themselves from Shakespeare's narrative, so that the queen could be seen undertaking the duties of state, 'with a country to consider'.[23]

In *Antonius*, Mary Sidney added the idea of the persistence of Cleopatra's image haunting Antony. In many ways, Cleopatra's image haunts us still today many centuries later, since it is so firmly fixed in the public consciousness. A study undertaken in 1995, and updated in 2010, estimates that until then over 200 plays and novels, 45 operas, 5 ballets and 43 films have been inspired by her. This number would now, of course, be larger. The study also records the production of no fewer than 230 paintings and statues of Cleopatra in the seventeenth and eighteenth centuries alone.[24] Among the plays written about the Egyptian queen after the seventeenth century, the ones of most interest are perhaps Bernard Shaw's *Caesar and Cleopatra* (1899) and the Egyptian poet Ahmed Shawqi's *Maṣra' Kiliyūpātrā*, or *The Death of Cleopatra* (1920).[25] These plays reflect the contradictory and divergent views of the queen as continuing and even more pronounced across different nations. While Shaw portrayed Cleopatra as a sex kitten, Shawqi depicts her assiduously working on matters of state. His play opens in the palace library in Alexandria with Cleopatra attending to her duties, much as Suzman recently showed her. Shawqi's work, a rare Egyptian representation, was written as topical commentary on British colonial forces and his Cleopatra is a figure of resistance to the occupying army. Inspired by Jodelle's and Garnier's dramatizations, it offers a response to Shakespeare's *Antony and Cleopatra*, positioning Cleopatra as a serious and committed ruler.[26] Shawqi's play, which remains largely unexplored in the English-speaking world, and which exists only in a translation that is now largely unavailable, presents new and unexplored areas for research.

Three major biographies of Cleopatra have been published since I began this study. Adrian Goldsworthy's account is written from the perspective of a military historian; Duane W. Roller's biography uses only ancient sources; and Stacy Schiff's book is aimed at a non-academic readership.[27] Each author is keenly aware of the need to present something of the historical Cleopatra and not rely on Shakespeare like past classical historians. There have also been major exhibitions devoted to Cleopatra and Egypt held in important world cities every year of this study, emphasizing that interest in the myth of Cleopatra and in the new archaeological discoveries from her world continue unabated.[28]

This book considered why Cleopatra VII, Queen of Egypt, captured the literary imagination in late sixteenth- and early seventeenth-century England. It asked: what were the implications of writing about the Egyptian queen when there was an English queen on the throne, and when the country was experiencing its own complicated response to queenship? We have seen that Cleopatra's story spoke to the conflict between public duties and the private selves of a monarch. It lent itself to the Sidney and Essex circles' use of Roman history for topical commentary, to support the Protestant cause at home and abroad, to the use of Taciteanism, and to address succession anxieties at a time when with the death of a queen power passed from one dynasty to another. The inherently performed nature of Cleopatra's roles and identities and the self-consciousness that underpins these roles is evidenced not only in the dramatization of her story in the period, but also in the portrait of the Jacobean lady and the Cavendish sisters' later play. It supports the idea that Cleopatra and her story was somehow taken up by a circle of elite cognoscenti and that she held an appeal for women. This study has shown that we need to look back beyond Shakespeare's Cleopatra to understand the sources and cultural contexts that produced her. While it is the case that Cleopatra was portrayed as an example of unbridled female sexuality, ambition and luxury, she was also seen as a mother, a heroic role model and a positive emblematic figure in the period.

Appendix: The *Cleopatra* statue and the poems at the Vatican

This appendix looks in more detail at the Vatican *Cleopatra* (now known as Ariadne) discussed in the Introduction and elsewhere in this book, and at the poems it inspired in Italy during the sixteenth and seventeenth centuries.

The statue of the sorrowful *Cleopatra*, a second-century BC Roman version of a Hellenistic work, was acquired by Pope Julius II on 2 February 1512, following months of negotiations after its discovery. The Pope paid such a substantial acquisition fee that the payments continued into the papacy of Paul III (1534–49). Already regarded as a masterpiece by collectors and artists, the *Cleopatra* was believed to be the actual replica of the Egyptian queen carried in Augustus's triumph. For Julius II, who identified himself as the second Julius Caesar, both the statue and his newly built Belvedere sculpture court represented a 'triumphal monument', glorifying and fulfilling the Papacy's and Rome's destiny. The statue was installed the following year in the sculpture court, part of the Belvedere Papal villa complex. Set on an antique sarcophagus and mounted as a fountain, it was placed in a niche in the Belvedere with other prominent ancient statues, such as the *Laocoon*, *Apollo*, *Venus*

Felix and *Commodus as Hercules*. By the 1530s the statue's niche was decorated to look like a grotto.[1]

The Belvedere sculpture courtyard became a highlight for visitors to the Vatican and was mentioned in influential books. William Thomas describes the *Cleopatra* and its setting in *The Historie of Italie* (1549):

> The garden walled rounde about, is full of faire oringe trees, and hath in the middest a goodlie fountaine with perfeite plottes in molde of the river of *Nile in Ægypt*, and of *Tyber*, that renneth through Rome. Besides the images of fine marble of *Romulus* and *Remus* plaiyng with a wovlfes teates, of *Apollo* with his bowe and arowes, of *Laocoonte*, with his. ii. children wrapped about with serpentes, of *Venus* beholdyng little *Cupido*, of the sorowfull *Cleopatra*, liyng by the river side, and of divers other to long to reherse. (40–1)

In 1540, casts were taken of the important Belvedere statues, by Francesco Primaticcio for the King of France's gardens at Fontainebleau. Primaticcio's mould exaggerated the *Cleopatra*'s reclining pose and became the model for many other replicas well into the nineteenth century. The statue defined the image of the Egyptian queen in the Renaissance. In the 1550s, at Giorgio Vasari's advice, Paul III had the *Cleopatra* moved to a specially built and elaborately decorated room, which became known as the 'Stanza della Cleopatra'. Francis Haskell and Nicholas Penny note that this was 'an early (perhaps earliest) example of a sculpture giving its name to a room'.[2]

The statue inspired many poems in the sixteenth and seventeenth centuries, including ones by Baldassare Castiglione (1478–1539), Bernadino Baldi (1553–1617) and Agonisto Favoriti (1642–82), which were inscribed on pilasters framing it. These poems express the sympathy and interest that was being felt for Cleopatra, with the discovery of the statue. The installation of the poems at the Vatican signals their influence and the statue's further consecration.[3]

In its presentation, the statue looked almost like a secular shrine, with Cleopatra as a secular Renaissance saint and martyr, even as she was still a triumphal monument (see Figure 1). Castiglione's poem gives Cleopatra's statue a voice and speaks of her sorrow and fear of the Roman triumph. The poem printed and widely circulated in Italy from the 1530s on inspired Baldi's and Favoriti's works.[4] The duality of perspectives in Cleopatra's story continued even in the presentation of the Vatican *Cleopatra*.

The poems by Castiglione and Favoriti are in Latin and the sonnet by Baldi in Italian. While Alexander Pope translated Castiglione's poem into English (*c.*1710, published 1717), the other two works remain untranslated and relatively unknown in Anglophone culture. Pope's translation compresses several moments and reworks the poem's meaning slightly at times. This Appendix presents new translations of all three poems, undertaken specifically for the purposes of this study. The poems of Castiglione and Favoriti are translated by Jaime Goodrich, and the Baldi sonnet is co-translated by Jason Lawrence and Selene Scarsi.

Notes on the text

The three poems are transcribed in Taja D'Agostino, *Descrizione Del Palazzo Apostilico Vaticano* (Rome, 1750): Baldassare Castiglione, 'Cleopatra', 388–92; Bernadino Baldi, 'On the statue of Cleopatra in the Vatican', 392; and Augustini Favoriti, 'Cleopatra in the Vatican Gardens', 393–8. The translations follow the text in D'Agostino. The notes are my own. I have added line numbers as per modern editing conventions for ease of reference.

Baldassare Castiglione
CLEOPATRA

Marmore quisquis in hoc saevis admorsa colubris
Brachia, & aeterna torpentia lumina nocte
Aspicis, invitam ne crede occumbere letho.
Victores vetuere diu me abrumpere vitam,
Regina ut veherer celebri captiva triumpho,
Scilicet & nuribus parerem serva Latinis.
Illa ego progenies tot ducta ab origine Regum,
Quam Pharii coluit gens fortunata Canopi,
Delitiis fovitque suis Ægyptia tellus
Atque Oriens omnis Divum dignatus honore est
Sedulitas, pulchraeque necis generosa cupido
Vicit vitae ignominiam, insidiasque Tyranni.
Libertas nam parta nec est, nec vincula sensi
Umbraque Tartareas descendi libera ad undas.
Quod licuisse mihi indignatus perfidus hostis
Saevitiae insanis stimulis exarsit, & ira,
Namque triumphali invectus Capitolia curru
Insignes inter titulos, gentesque subactas
Extinctae infelix simulacrum duxit, & amens
Spectaclo explevit crudelia lumina inani.

APPENDIX

You whoever see in this marble statue arms bitten at
By savage snakes, and eyes sluggish with eternal night,
Do not believe that she met death against her will.
For a long time the victors forbade me to cut life short,
So that as a captive queen I would be carried in a well-attended triumph,   5
And, naturally, as a slave I would wait on Roman brides.
I am that offspring drawn from the lineage of so many Kings,
Whom the prosperous race of Egyptian Canopus cherished
And the Egyptian land nurtured with its delights
And the whole Orient thought worthy of the honour of Gods.   10
Assiduity and the noble-minded desire of a beautiful death
Conquered the dishonour of life and the plots of a Tyrant.
For liberty is not acquired, and I did not feel chains,
And, a free shade, I sank into the Tartarean waves.
Angry at what was permitted to me, the treacherous enemy   15
Blazed with wrath and the outrageous stings of rage,
For carried to the Capitol on a triumphal chariot
Among the distinguished titles and conquered races,
Unhappy he led the image of the dead one, and, foolish,
Filled [his] cruel eyes with empty spectacle.   20

1–2   *arms bitten ... eternal night* Propertius, *Elegies*, 3.11.52–6,
     describes Cleopatra's statue in the triumph in similar terms.
3   *She* Cleopatra.
4   Plutarch mentions Octavius's threat to her children should she
     harm herself after Antony.
5   *well-attended triumph* It was a three-day triumph, with the Egyptian
     Day the most celebrated, well-attended and richest.
6–7   Alexander Pope compresses and reworks this moment.
7   *so many Kings* echoes Charmian's line to the soldier in Plutarch.
8   *Canopus* Ancient town in the Nile Delta.
12   *Tyrant* Octavius became Augustus after his triumphal return.
14   *free shade ... Tartarean* Death brings her freedom as a spectre.
     Tartarean, pertaining to purgatory or infernal.
19   *image ... one* refers to the effigy of Cleopatra carried after her death
     in the triumph. Mentioned in Plutarch, Propertius and Dio.
20   *ancient ... deed* The speaker is perhaps referring here to the
     Augustan writers, who in spite of the rhetoric of the victor could not
     diminish the fame of her suicide.

Neu longaeva vetustas facti famam aboleret,
Aut seris mea sors ignota Nepotibus esset!
Effigiem excudi spiranti e marmore jussit
Testari, & casus fatum miserabile nostri.
Quam deinde ingenium artificis miratus Julus
Egregium celebri visendam sede locavit:
Signa inter veterum Heroum, saxoque perennes
Supposuit lacrimas aegrae solatia mentis,
Optatae non ut deflerem gaudia mortis;
Nam mihi nec lacrimas lethali vipera morsu
Excussit, nec mors ullum intulit ipsa timorem,
Sed charo ut cineri, & dilecti conjugis umbrae
Aeternas lacrimas, aeterni pignus amoris
Maesta darem, inferiasque inopes, & tristia dona.
Has etiam tamen insensi rapuere Quirites.
At tu, magne Leo, Divum genus, aurea sub quo
Saecula, & antiquae redierunt laudis honores,
Si te praesidium miseris mortalibus ipse
Omnipotens Pater aethereo demisit Olympo,
Et tua si immensae virtuti est aequa potestas,
Munificaque manu dispensas dona Deorum,
Annue supplicibus votis, nec vana precari
Me sine, parva peto, lacrimas. Pater optime redde,
Redde, oro, fletum: fletus mihi muneris instar;
Improba quando aliud nil jam Fortuna reliquit.
At Niobe ausa Deos scelerata incessere lingua,

APPENDIX

And ancient antiquity would not destroy the fame of the deed,
Or would my fate be unknown to later Descendants!
He ordered a likeness to be hammered out from living marble
And to bear witness to the wretched fate of our downfall.
Which Julus – having wondered at the artist's surpassing genius – then   25
Placed in a well-frequented seat so that it must be seen:
Among the figures of the old Heroes, and in the rock
He buried perennial tears, the comforts of a troubled mind –
Not that I would lament the joys of a wished-for death,
For the viper with its fatal bite did not stir my tears   30
Nor did death itself introduce any fear –
But that to the dear ashes and shade of a beloved spouse,
Eternal tears, a pledge of eternal love,
I (sorrowful) would give, both meagre funeral rites and sad obsequies.
Yet I perceived that the Romans stole even those.   35
But you, great Leo, descendant of the Gods, under whom the golden
Ages and honours of ancient praise have returned,
If as a defence for miserable mortals
The omnipotent Father himself sent you down from divine Olympus,
And if your power is equal to [your] boundless virtue   40
And you dispense the gifts of the Gods with a liberal hand,
Grant humble prayers, and to pray for vain things
Do not allow me; I seek small things, tears. Best father, restore,
Restore, I beg, tears: tears [are] as good as a gift to me
Since cruel Fortune has left nothing else now.   45
But Niobe, who dared to assault the Gods in wicked speech,

23 *Julus* Pope Julius II (1443–1513) first acquired the statue for the Vatican.
24 *Placed ... seat* The statue was placed in a corner niche in the Belvedere. The statue court became a huge attraction for visitors to the Vatican.
25 *old Heroes* It was placed with Hercules and the Laocoon etc.
30 *beloved spouse* Antony.
33–35 She wishes for tears so she can properly honour and lament Antony.
36 *great Leo* Pope Leo X (1475–1521) succeeded Julius II in 1513.
46 *Niobe* The Queen of Thebes was a tragic figure of Greek mythology. She turned into a rock after all fourteen of her children were killed, due to her mocking the goddess Leto, who only had the twins Apollo and Artemis. The rock was known as the weeping rock. See Ovid's *Metamorphoses*, Book IV.

Induerit licet in durum praecordia marmor,
Flet tamen, assiduusque liquor de marmore manat.
Vita mihi dispar, vixi sine crimine, si non
Crimen amare vocas: fletus solamen amantum est:
Adde quod afflictis nostrae jucunda voluptas
Sunt lacrimae, dulcesque invitant murmure somnos;
Et quum exusta siti Icarius Canis arva perurit
Huc potum veniunt volucres, circumque, supraque
Frondibus insultant: tenero tum gramine laeta
Terra viret, rutilantque suis poma aurea ramis.
Hic ubi odoratum surgens densa nemus umbra
Hesperidum dites truncos non invidet hortis.

May have covered her heart in hard marble,
Yet she weeps, and continual fluid trickles from the marble.
My life [was] different, I lived without crime, if
You do not call it a crime to love: tears [are] the solace of lovers: 50
Moreover, to the downhearted our tears are a delightful pleasure,
And they invite sweet sleep with a murmur;
And when the Icarian Dog Star scorches the fields dry with thirst,
The birds come here to drink; both around and above
They gambol in the leafy boughs: then happy with tender grass   55
The earth is green, and the golden apples redden on their branches.
Here where the fragrant grove, rising with thick shade,
Does not begrudge the gardens of the Hesperides their splendid trunks.

49   *without crime* asserts she is blameless. Her only crime is loving too much.
53   *Icarian Dog Star* Canicula, the dog of Icarus was translated to the heavens as a star for his faithfulness. Ovid *Elegia* XVI.
54–55   Describes the setting of her statue in a shady court, cooled by many fountains.
57   *fragrant grove* The court was lined with symmetrical rows of orange trees, whose scent filled the air. Described also in
58   William Thomas *Historie of Italie*.
        Hesperides The nymphs of the night or sunset in Greek mythology, who tend a blissful garden.

Bernadino Baldi
On the statue of Cleopatra in the Vatican
SONNET

Io, cui giá tanta lieta il Nilo accolsse
  Quant' or mesta, e dolente el Tebro mira,
  Del Latin vincitore il fasto e l'ira
  Fuggendo el mio fin corse, e non men doles.

Il mio collo real soffrir non volse
  Catena indegne, onde il velen, he spira
  L'angue che al nudo mio freddo s'aggira
  Ringrazio, e lei, ch'indi il mio stame sciolse.

Non può tuto chi vince. Il suo superbo
  Trionfo non ornai, bench'egli bianco
  Marmaro intagliasse, ch'il mi overo admosbra.

Libera fui Regina, e'l fato acerba
  Libertà non mi tolse, onde scesi anco
  Sciolto spirto all'Inferno, e'libre ombra.

APPENDIX

I, as happy when welcomed by the Nile
Am now as sad and sorrowful, watched by the Tiber,
Fleeing the pomp and anger of the Roman victor,
I ran to my end, and it grieved me no less.

My royal neck did not wish to suffer 5
An unworthy chain, so the poison, which the snake
That wraps itself around my cold flesh breathes,
I thank, and her, who then released my soul.

He who wins cannot achieve everything. His proud
Triumph I did not embellish, even though 10
He engraved the white marble, which conceals the truth of me

Free was I as a Queen, and cruel fate
Could not deprive me of freedom, so I descended,
A released spirit, to Hell, a free shadow.

1–2   Nile and Tiber may refer not just to Egypt and Rome, but also to the huge statues of the rivers installed near her.
3   *Fleeing ... Roman victor* As in Castiglione, the statue gives the triumph as a reason for Cleopatra's suicide. This motive is not in Plutarch.
5   The snake is wrapped around the statue's upper left arm like an armlet.
8   *Her* The figure of Death, who releases her soul.
9   *He* Octavius.
11   *white ... me* A sympathetic and provocative statement. It asserts that the truth about her has been hidden in this statue, as it has in the Augustan nationalistic rhetoric controlling her image.
14   *free shadow* echoes Castiglione l.14, free shade.

Augustini Favoriti
Cleopatra in the Vatican Gardens
To Christina, Queen of the Swedes, Goths, and Vandals

> Si te spectaclum infelix, si tristia tangunt
> Fata meae duro bene sculptae in marmore sortis,
> O nostros dignata lares invisere mundi
> Cardine ab extremo patria, Regnoque relictis,
> Regina, heroum nulli virtute secunda,
> Aurea quos olim tulit aetas maxima Olympi,
> Numina quum humanos non dedignantia coetus
> Tecta frequentabant mortalia, castaque gentis
> Pectora, non falsae complebant laudis amore.
> Huc ades; illa ego sum Latiis celeberrima Fastis
> Femina, nosti angues, animumque in morte ferocem.
> Quo properas? saltem alloquio solare dolentem
> Reginam Regina; nec est indigna videri
> Forma loci, & sacris regio gratissima Musis,
> Quae nemus hoc, fontes*que* colunt, jugaq*ue* lata viretis

Favoriti's poem follows Castiglione in giving the *Cleopatra* statue a voice, representing its subject. The poem is addressed to Queen Christina of Sweden, and presents a great queen addressing another great queen. Only the poem's opening and end directly focus on the Egyptian queen's sorrow. In the rest of the work, Cleopatra's statue highlights the location and splendour of the Vatican sculpture collection. Although the date of the poem is unknown it was probably written in 1654 when Christina was first welcomed to Rome. She was known for her support of the arts, and Favoriti might have been soliciting her patronage.

If an unhappy sight, if the sad fates of my destiny,
Well sculpted in hard marble, touch you,
O, one who thought it worthy to visit our household gods
From the outermost pole of the world, with fatherland and
    Kingdom left behind,
Queen second in virtue to none of the heroes   5
Whom the greatest golden age of Olympus once bore,
When deities, not disdaining human company,
Frequented mortal roofs, and the pure hearts
Of people were not full with love of false praise.
Be present here; I am that woman most celebrated in Roman Annals,   10
You have known the snakes, and the fierce courage in death.
Where do you hasten? At least with speech console,
Queen, a Queen grieving; and it is not unworthy to be seen –
The place's beauty, and a region most pleasing to the sacred Muses
Who haunt this grove, and springs, and the broad hills,   15

4   *fatherland... behind* Queen Christina (1626–89) succeeded
        to the throne at age six, becoming queen regnant at the age of
        eighteen. Insisting on staying single, she abdicated her throne in
        1654 in favour of her cousin and converted to Catholicism, moving
        to Rome.
10–11   If Cleopatra is the most celebrated woman in Roman history, then
        her statue can assume that Christina knows of her story and the
        snakes used in her heroic death.
13   *Queen ... grieving* The statue of the Egyptian queen seeks
        consolation from another queen, Christina.
15   *broad hills* The Belvedere was built on high grounds behind the
        Vatican complex.

Cyrrhae posthabitis, & verticibus Parnassi.
Hic ubi Grajorum artificum miranda videbis
Signa antiqua, tuae Gentis, quibus ira pepercit,
Abstinuitque manus artem mirata vetustam,
Ut de me sileam, viden hos, qui robore multo
Luctantem, ingratosque Deos, arasque vocantem
Arrecti miserum spiris ingentibus hydri
Laocoonta ligant: ut anhelat, ut ore supremum
Ingemit, ut socios implorant opemque propinqui
Herculis. Ipse quidem casum dolet, & cupit angues
Elisisse manu, ac primos iterare labores,
Phidiacus labor, Alcides, sed enim aspera Juno
Heroa immeritum dum grandine pulsat, & imbri,
Non tantum orbavit clava exuviisque leonis,
Verum & poplitibus nervos humerisque torosa
Brachia divellit, fecitque ex Hercule monstrum
Informe, ignaraeque nefas ludibria turbae.
Ast illum informem licet, & sine nomine truncum
Miratum huc Ararim veniunt, Rhenumque bibentes,
Et vivos illinc discunt effingere vultus.

Having neglected the verdant peaks of Cyrrha and Parnassus.
Here where you will see things of Greek craftsmen to be wondered at:
Ancient statues, which the wrath of your People spared,
And, having admired the ancient art, withheld its hands.
So that I say nothing about myself, look at these snakes   20
Arisen with huge coils who bind wretched Laocoon,
Struggling with much strength and calling on thankless Gods and altars,
How he gasps, how he groans his last from the mouth,
How they beg allies and the help of neighbour
Hercules. Indeed Alcides himself, that Phidian   25
Labour, grieves the mishap, and desires to crush
The snakes with his hand, and to repeat first labours,
But since harsh Juno batters the hero
Undeservedly with hail and rain,
Not only has she stripped away the cudgel and lion's skin,
But also the sinews from the knee and the muscular   30
Arms from the shoulders she has plucked, and she has made
Of Hercules a shapeless monster, and – a crime – play things for
    an ignorant crowd.
But surely for that trunk – shapeless, without name, and
Admired – they come here, drinking the Saône and Rhine,
And thence they learn to shape living faces.   35

16   *Cyrrha and Parnassus* Associated with Apollo, Cyrrha is the peak of Mount Parnassus.
17   *Here ... see* The statue begins introducing the Vatican collection.
25   *Alcides, Phidian* Another name for Hercules. Phidias was an ancient Greek sculptor and artist.
26–30   The *Cleopatra* is describing the statue of *Commodus as Hercules* in the Belvedere statue court.
35   *Saône* is a tributary of the Rhone, running through Eastern France.

Cetera quid memorem Nilum, Tibrimque parentem
Spirantes docto in silice, Eridanumque, Tagumque,
Nativo fulgentem auro, Gangemque superbum
Eois opibus, quos omnes Daedala & ipsi
Æmula naturae finxit manus. hic habitant Dii,
Aurato hic Phoebus percurrit pectine chordas,
Hic gelidam fundit proles Semeleia lympham,
Pocula deliciasque tuas, hic otia degunt,
Mercuriusque minaxque rubenti casside Mavors
Et magni Æneae genitrix, & candida Phebe,
Omnes aut Divi, aut Divum genus, unaque deerat,
Quam studiis vultuque refers, factisque, Minerva.
Huc & Alexander Fabium tunc nomine dici
Audieram, indocti fugeret quum murmura vulgi,
Nobiliumque manus juvenum comitata solebant
Ferre pedem, hic tristes animo deponere curas,
Dulcia securae ducentes gaudia mentis.
Vidi ego, & in cubitum surrexi oblita doloris,
Incessumque viri observans, & lumina dixi:
Aut Babylon ignara futuri, aut hic erit hic vir
Olim qui Latiam regnando restituat rem,
Qui veteres artes, & secula prisca reducat,
Iratasque pio componat foedere gentes,
Quamquam animi flecti indociles, & vulnera tactu
Crudescant, medicamque manum impacata
recusant
Quo properas? ne Diva oculis te subtrahe nostris,

Why should I mention the rest: Nilus and father Tiber
Breathing in learned flint, and Po, and Tagus
Gleaming with native gold, and Ganges haughty
With Eastern wealth, all of whom a Daedalean hand, 40
Striving after nature itself, has shaped. Gods live here,
Here Phoebus runs through chords with a golden plectrum,
Here Semele's child pours cold water,
Drinking cups and your delights, here they spend free time,
Both Mercury and threatening Mars with red metal helmet, 45
And the mother of great Aeneas, and shining Phoebe,
All either Gods, or the race of Gods, and one was absent,
Whom you call to mind in face, and by studies and by deeds – Minerva.
And here then I had heard Alexander to be called
Fabius by name, when he would flee the murmurs of the
    unlearned crowd, 50
And an accompanying band of noble youths was accustomed
To set foot, here to put aside sad cares from the mind,
Leading the sweet joys of the carefree mind.
I have seen, and forgetful of grief I have risen in bed,
And watching the walk and eyes of the man, I have said: 55
'Either Babylon was ignorant of the future, or this, this will be the man
Who could someday restore the Roman state by reigning,
Who could bring back the old arts, and earlier ages,
Who could reconcile angry peoples with pious treaty,
Although their minds cannot be taught to bend, and wounds
Grow worse with touch, and unquiet things refuse a healing hand. 60
Where do you hasten? Goddess, do not withdraw yourself from our eyes,

---

40   *Daedalean hand* An artistic, craftsman-like hand. Daedalus was the father of Icarus.
43   *Semele's child* A reference to Dionysus (Bacchus), whom Semele became pregnant with as a result of an affair with Zeus.
46   *mother ... Aeneas* Reference to the statue of Venus in the Belvedere.
48   *Minerva* Christina was known for her learning and support of the arts and compared to Minerva or Pallas Athena.
49   *Alexander* This links Cleopatra's Macedonian heritage with Christina's known admiration for Alexander.

Namque ego te rerum seriem, eventusque
  docebo,
Qui super Heroum sedes, super aethera
  tollent
Nomen Alexandri: sub mortem plurima quando,
Et longe faciem venientis cerminus aevi.
An te proxima silva trahit, studiumque ferarum?
Non ibi torvus aper, non duris unguibus ursi,
Quos jaculo cecidisse tuo saepe horruit Arctos
Utraque, sed cervi imbelles, capraeque fugaces
Pictarumque cohors non invadenda volucrum.
Quin etiam casus, & mors ingloria ab altis
Imminet arboribus, nam quae nux pinea curvo
Strata jacet campo, Satyros quam ludere circum
Metirique vides thyrso, sua ab arbore nuper
Decidit, & magno tellurem perculit ictu.
Adde, quod inclusus Boreas, Eurusque, Notusque,
Et quotquot saevis agitant plangoribus aequor,
Illa turre fremunt eversuri omnia late,
Quamvis sub tanto cohiberi Principe venti
Non indignentur, veniantqe ad jussa volantes;
Iamque parent iterum Scythicas illidere puppes
Leucatae, ab diram Leucatam, & conscia luctus
Saxa mei, heu dolor! heu cladis monumenta nefandae.

Palazzetto privato d' Innocenzio VIII. in Belvedere

For I will teach you the order, and outcome of things,
Who will lift the name of Alexander above the seats of Heroes,
Above the heavens: when subject to death, we see very many things
And the face of the coming age from afar.   65
Or do the adjoining forests, and an enthusiasm for wild animals
    draw you?
Not there the grim boar, not the bears with hard claws
Whom the Great and Little Bear often trembled to see felled by your spear,
[Not] either of them, but peaceful stags, and timid goats   70
And a crowd of colourful birds that are not to be seized.
In fact, also mishap, and an inglorious death
Threaten from tall trees, for the pine-nut which lies
Strewn on the curved meadow, which you see the Satyrs
Play around and measure with a thyrsus, lately from its
    tree   75
Has fallen, and struck the earth with a great blow.
Add that the enclosed North, East, and South winds,
And the sea toss with whatever savage beatings,
They roar at that tower, about to overturn all things widely,
Although they do not disdain to be confined under   80
Such a Prince of winds, and they come willingly on command;
And already they prepare again to crush the Scythian ships
Of Leucata, from dreadful Leucata, and the rocks [are] aware
Of my sorrow, alas grief! Alas the monuments of an unspeakable disaster.

Private Palazzo of Innocent VIII at the Belvedere

62	*Where ... hasten?* Echoed from l. 11.
64	*Alexander* is repeated again from l.62. Alexandra was also the last name taken by Christina on her baptism after her abdication, honouring both the reigning Pope Alexander VII, and her lifelong hero.
66–70	The Vatican's menagerie had greatly expanded, and included many colourful parrots.
75	*thyrsus* A staff of giant fennel wound with ivy leaves, topped with a cone.
82	*Scythian* An ancient people from Iran.
83	*Leucata* lay slightly north of Actium in the Mediterranean. In the *Aeneid* (3.274–5, 8.677), Virgil identifies mons Leucata with Actium as the place of Antony and Cleopatra's defeat.
84	**unspeakable disaster** The naval catastrophe at Actium.

Castiglione's poem, foregrounding Cleopatra's grief, represents a shift in the conception and treatment of the Egyptian queen from the earlier Italian works of Dante and Boccaccio.[5] In Castiglione's and Baldi's poems, Cleopatra fears the dishonour of the Roman triumph, and in the former the further humiliation of serving Roman ladies. Both poems speak of the queen's spirit as free (l. 14 in each). Favoriti's later poem highlights Cleopatra's 'fierce courage in death' (l. 11). These ideas are also shared by the Garnier-Sidney interpretation and in Daniel, and in Shakespeare. Cleopatra wishes to avoid the humiliation of the triumph and sees death by her own hand as a form of freedom and resistance to tyranny. If Daniel knew the Cleopatra poems through Florio and his Italian connections, then Shakespeare, in turn, might have also been influenced by these poems though Daniel.[6]

The *Cleopatra* statue also appears to have a connection to the Sidney-Herbert family. In the early 1630s, Mary Sidney's second son Philip Herbert commissioned a major restoration of Wilton House and its gardens. This project was undertaken by Inigo Jones, with Isaac de Caus working mainly on the garden. Caus records four fountain statues purchased for Wilton as: replicas of Venus, Diana with Cupid, Susanna, and Cleopatra (no longer believed extant). In writing about the Wilton garden, Dianne Duggan observes that Cleopatra was 'unexpected' in this group as she 'was an unusual character to have in the gardens at this time in England'.[7] She suggests Herbert might have been 'honouring the rich literary heritage and patronage of the family'. It is intriguing to note that he married Anne Clifford in 1630, and with her interest in architecture she became deeply involved in the restoration programme at Wilton in the early happy years of her second marriage.[8] The 'unexpected inclusion' of Cleopatra might also have something to do with Clifford's influence – both because of Mary Sidney's and her own connection to the Egyptian queen.

References in notes

Bostock, Stephen St C., *Zoos and Animal Rights* (2004; rpt., London: Routledge, 2014), 20–1.

Buckley, Veronica, *Christina Queen of Sweden: The Restless Life of a European Eccentric* (London: Fourth Estate, 2004), 53, 92–104, 183.

Ziolkowski, Jan M., and Michael Putnam, *The Virgilian Tradition: The First Fifteen Hundred Years* (New Haven: Yale University Press, 2008), 281.

NOTES

Introduction

1 Marilyn L. Williamson, *Infinite Variety: Antony and Cleopatra in Renaissance Drama and Earlier Tradition* (Mystic, CT: Lawrence Verry, 1974), 1.

2 See Maria Wyke, *Projecting the Past: Ancient Rome, Cinema and History* (1997; rpt., London: Routledge, 2013), 75; Coppélia Kahn, *Roman Shakespeare: Warriors, Wounds, Women* (London: Routledge, 1997), 112; Lucy Hughes-Hallett, *Cleopatra: Histories, Dreams and Distortions* (London: Bloomsbury, 1990), 21–143; and Mary Hamer, *Signs of Cleopatra: History, Politics, Representation* (London: Routledge, 1993), xiv–xv, 1–23.

3 'Soda-pop celebrity', *The Economist*, 14 September 1991, 89.

4 See http://www.tatler.com/news/articles/june-2016/a-history-of-ball-breaking-women. The original article featuring Clinton and her image as Cleopatra has been changed and republished 6 February 2018. *Washington Post* cartoonist Ann Telaneas' work was displayed at the RSC's exhibition of political cartoons, Draw New Mischief. Barbican, London, 3 November 2017–21 January 2018. https://officiallondontheatre.com/news/rscs-rome-season-transfers-to-the-barbican-111405709/amp/. Information about the cartoon kindly supplied by Rathika Muthukumaran.

5 Plutarch, 317.

6 Duane W. Roller, *Cleopatra: A Biography* (New York: OUP, 2010), 2. An interview with Roller forms an appendix in my thesis.

7 Wyke, *Projecting the Past*, 75.

8 Roller, *Cleopatra*, 130–1; Maria Wyke, *The Roman Mistress* (Oxford: OUP, 2002), 202.

9. Ibid., 195–6.
10. Horace, see Epode 9 written soon after Actium, and Ode I.37 celebrating Cleopatra's death.
11. Roller, *Cleopatra*, 2; Wyke, *Roman Mistress*, 195, 205.
12. Mary Beard, *Women and Power: A Manifesto* (London: Profile, 2017), esp. 58–9.
13. Roller, *Cleopatra*, 7–8.
14. Plutarch, 273.
15. Roller, *Cleopatra*, 146, 170; Wyke, *Roman Mistress*, 204.
16. Al-Masudi quoted in Hughes-Hallett, *Histories, Dreams and Distortions*, 70. See also Okasha El Daly, *Egyptology: The Missing Millennium: Ancient Egypt in Medieval Arab Writings* (London: UCL Press, 2005), 131–5.
17. Roller, *Cleopatra*, 177.
18. Dante Alighieri, *Inferno: A New Verse Translation*, trans. Michael Palma (New York: Norton, 2002), v.63. Hughes-Hallett, *Histories, Dreams and Distortions*, 70.
19. Giovanni Boccaccio, *On Famous Women*, trans. Guido A. Guarino (London: Italica, 1964), 192.
20. Bullough, 220.
21. Geoffrey Chaucer, *The Legend of Good Women, The Riverside Chaucer*, foreword Christopher Cannon, 3rd rev. edn (Oxford: OUP, 2008), 604–5.
22. Ibid., 588–603.
23. Williamson, *Infinite Variety*, 2.
24. See Mary Morrison, 'Some Aspects of the Treatment of the Theme of Antony and Cleopatra in Tragedies of the Sixteenth Century', *Journal of European Studies* 4, no. 2 (1974): 114. Paul Taylor, Warburg Institute, helped with the Vatican *Cleopatra* image, 11 November 2011.
25. Mary Beard, *The Roman Triumph* (Cambridge, MA: Harvard University Press, 2007), 143–5.
26. Plutarch, 316.
27. See Brian A. Curran, 'Love, Triumph, Tragedy: Cleopatra in High Renaissance Rome', in *Cleopatra: A Sphinx Revisited*, ed.

Margaret M. Miles (Berkeley: University of California Press, 2011), 116, n. 93, for paintings inspired by the statue. See also Mary Hamer, 'The Myth of Cleopatra since the Renaissance', in *Cleopatra of Egypt: From History to Myth*, ed. Susan Walker and Peter Hughes (London: British Museum Press, 2001), 304.

28 See the Appendix for these poems.

29 Francis Haskell and Nicholas Penny, *Taste and the Antique: The Lure of Classical Sculpture 1500–1900* (1981; rpt., New Haven: Yale University Press, 1998), 10, 184–6.

30 Curran, 'Love, Triumph', 117.

31 Morrison, 'Some Aspects', 114.

32 Ibid.

33 For details of these works, see ibid., 114–25; Bullough, 222–8.

34 Samuel Daniel, *The Poeticall Essayes of Sam. Danyel* (London, 1599), sig. A1r.

35 Greville, xxiv–xxx, 166–7.

36 Bullough, 225.

37 Morrison, 'Some Aspects', 118.

38 Bullough, 228.

39 Seneca is quoted in Escolme, 100.

40 Ibid., Escolme is referring here to Shakespeare's Cleopatra, but this assessment also applies to the historical Cleopatra.

41 This was exactly the context for Shakespeare's 'Rape of Lucrece' (1594).

42 See Michel de Montaigne, 'The tale of Spurina' and 'On judging someone else's death', in *The Complete Essays*, trans. and ed. M. A. Screech (1987; rpt., London: Penguin, 2003), 830, 684–91.

43 See Michel de Montaigne, 'On Vanity', in *The Complete Essays*, trans. and ed. M. A. Screech (1987; rpt., Penguin: London, 2003), 1113.

44 Negative accounts of Augustus are available in Tacitus's *Annals*, bk 1. 9–10, in *Histories: Books 4–5. Annals: Books 1–3*, trans. Clifford H. Moore and John Jackson (Cambridge, MA: Loeb Classical Library, Harvard University Press, 1931).

45 René Weis, xxxv–vi.

NOTES

46 From the British Museum's description of the cameo.

47 See Gianmaria Mosca (after), *Antony and Cleopatra*, sixteenth-century marble, Italy. https://www.ngv.vic.gov.au/explore/collection/work/3291/. H. R. Woudhuysen kindly brought this piece to my attention.

48 Information kindly supplied by Crosby Stevens, art historian at Bolsover Castle. Private correspondence, 22 November 2014.

49 Santina M. Levey, *Elizabethan Treasures: The Hardwick Hall Tapestries* (London: National Trust, 1998), 69. These strong female figures, excluding Cleopatra, feature in Christine de Pizan's *City of Ladies*.

50 Susan Frye, *Pens and Needles: Women's Textualities in Early Modern England* (Philadelphia: University of Pennsylvania Press, 2010), 60–1, 68.

51 Ibid., 61.

52 See for example, George Turberville, *Epitaphes, epigrams, songs and sonets* (London, 1567); Pierre Boaistuau, *Certaine secrete wonders of nature prophane* (London, 1569); and Girolamo Cardano, *Cardanus comforte translated into Englishe* (London, 1573).

53 Baldassare Castiglione, *The Courtier*, trans. Sir Thomas Hoby (London, 1561).

54 See Bernard Gilpin, *A godly sermon preached in the court at Greenwich* (London, 1581); and William Fulbecke, *A booke of christian ethicks or moral philosophie* (London, 1587).

55 See William Bullein, *Bulleins bulwarke of defence* (London, 1579). See Magnus Albertus, St, *The boke of secretes of Albertus* (S. l, 1560).

56 For examples in the order given, see Robert Wedderburn, *The Complaynt of Scotland* (Paris: s. n., *c*.1550); John Lydgate, *The serpent of division* (London, 1559); and Castiglione, *The Courtier*. See W. Averell, *A dyall for dainty darlings, rockt in the cradle of securitie* (London, 1584); and Thomas Lodge, *An alarum against usurers* (London, 1584). See Lodowick Lloyd, *The pilgrimage of princes* (London, *c*.1573); Robert Greene, *The Spanish masquerado* (London, 1589); and William Rankins, *The English Ape* (London, 1588).

57 For Cleopatra as whore and loyal lover, see Stephen Batman, *The golden booke of the leaden goddes* (London, 1577); Giovanni Boccaccio, *Thirtene most plesant and delectable questions* (London, 1571); and Anthony Munday, *A courtly controversie, betweene loove and learning* (London, 1581). For Cleopatra's colour, see Walter Darell, *A short discourse of the life of servingmen* (London, 1578); Robert Greene, *Ciceronis amor· Tullies love* (London, 1589); George Gascoigne, *A hundreth sundrie flowres* (London, 1573); and Richard Robinson, *A golden mirrour conteining certaine pithie and figuratiue visions* (London, 1589).

58 Rankins, *English Ape*, sig. B1v.

59 Thomas Elyot, *Bibliotheca Eliotæ Eliotis librarie* (London, 1542).

60 Thomas Cooper, *Thesaurus lingua Romanae et Britannicae* (1565; rpt., London, 1578).

61 Thomas Nashe, *The anatomie of absurditie* (London, 1589), sig. A4v.

62 Holger Norgaard, response to John D. Reeves, 'A Supposed Indebtedness of Shakespeare To Peele', *N&Q* 197, no. 21 (1952): 442. G. Watson, 'The Death of Cleopatra', *N&Q* 223 (1978): 412, for the literary history of Cleopatra's suicide.

63 Marcia Pointon, *Brilliant Effects: A Cultural History of Gem Stones and Jewellery* (New Haven: Yale University Press, 2009) 117–18.

64 Ibid.

65 Ad Putter, 'Pearl', in *The Literary Encyclopedia*, vol. 1.2.1.02: *Medieval and Early Modern England, 1066–1485*, ed. Kate Ash-Irisarri, David Fuller, Hugh Magennis et al., online edn, 30 March 2001, http://www.litencyc.com/php/sworks.php?rec=true&UID=13215.

66 See Matthew 13.45–6, in the *Geneva Bible* (London, 1599), 'Again, the kingdom of heaven is like to a merchant man that seeketh good pearls, who having found a pearl of great price, went and sold all that he had and bought it.' https://www.biblegateway.com/passage/?search=Matthew+13:45&version=GNV. See Pointon, *Brilliant Effects*, 365, 114. Elizabeth is represented in many portraits bedecked in pearls.

67 Thomas Stapleton, *A counterblast to M. Hornes vayne blaste against M. Fekeham* (London, 1567), 524.

68 Sebastian Münster, *A briefe collection and compendious extract* (London, 1572).

69 *The Phoenix Portrait*: http://www.npg.org.uk/research/ programmes/making-art-in-tudor-britain/the-phoenix-and-the-pelican-two-portraits-of-elizabeth-i-c.1575.php.

70 See Theodora A. Jankowski, *Women in Power in the Early Modern Drama* (Chicago: University of Chicago Press, 1992), Chapter 5 on Dido. Samantha Frénée-Hutchins, *Boudica's Odyssey in Early Modern England* (Farnham: Ashgate, 2014); Sharon L. Jansen, *Debating Women, Politics, and Power, in Early Modern Europe* (Basingstoke: Palgrave, 2008).

71 Greville, 93.

72 Janet Adelman, *The Common Liar: An Essay on Antony and Cleopatra* (New Haven: Yale University Press, 1973). The *AC* editions and handbook are in the List of Abbreviations, cited by the editor's name.

73 See Hughes-Hallett, *Histories, Dreams and Distortions*; Hammer, *Signs of Cleopatra*; Williamson, *Infinite Variety*.

74 For New Historicist readings of Shakespeare, see for example, Louis Montrose, '"Shaping Fantasies": Figurations of Gender and Power in Elizabethan Culture', *Representations* 2 (1983): 61–94. For other topical readings, see Alexandra Gajda, *The Earl of Essex and Late Elizabethan Political Culture* (Oxford: OUP, 2012), Chapter 6, for representations of Essex on the stage.

75 Katherine Eggert, *Showing Like a Queen: Female Authority and Literary Experiment in Spenser, Shakespeare, and Milton* (Philadelphia: University of Pennsylvania Press, 2000), 1–3.

76 Marta Straznicky, *Privacy, Playreading and Women's Closet Drama 1550–1700* (Cambridge: Cambridge University Press, 2004), 14–15.

77 Hannay, 120–9.

78 See Danielle Clarke, *The Politics of Early Modern Women's Writing* (Harlow: Pearson, 2001), 88–95; Wendy Piatt, 'Politics and Religion in Renaissance Closet Drama' (unpublished D.Phil. thesis, Bodleian Library, MS. D.Phil. c.15286. University of

Oxford, 1998), 85–90; Paulina Kewes, '"A Fit Memorial For The Times To Come ...": Admonition and Topical Application in Mary Sidney's *Antonius* and Samuel Daniel's *Cleopatra*', *RES* 63, no. 259 (2012); and Pettegree.

79 Julie Crawford, *Mediatrix: Women, Politics, & Literary Production in Early Modern England* (Oxford: OUP, 2014).

80 Malcolm Smuts, 'Court-Centred Politics and the Uses of Roman Historians, c.1590–1630', in *Culture and Politics in Early Stuart England*, ed. Kevin Sharpe and Peter Lake (Basingstoke: Macmillan, 1994), 36.

81 From the Tacitean aphorisms attributed to Henry Savile, in BL Harley MS 1327, to the letters and poetry of Essex and his circle, we see the same type of phrases used to describe their concern and anxieties, including with flattery and greatness, 'evil counsellors' and 'factions'.

82 Pietro Martire d' Anghiera, *The decades of the new worlde or west India* (London, 1555), 95.

83 See Norbrook. See Annabel Patterson, *Censorship and Interpretation: The Conditions of Reading and Writing in Early Modern England* (Madison: University of Wisconsin Press, 1984). See Worden.

84 Wynne-Davies and Findlay staged *Tragedie of Antonie* in 1999. S. P. Cerasano and Marion Wynne-Davies, eds, *The Tragedy of Antonie*, in *Renaissance Drama by Women: Texts and Documents* (London: Routledge, 1996); Alison Findlay, *Playing Spaces in Early Women's Drama* (Cambridge: CUP, 2006); Straznicky, *Privacy, Playreading*, 16.

85 Hackett, esp. Chapter 6.

86 Chris Laoutaris, *Shakespearian Maternities: Crises of Conception in Early Modern England* (Edinburgh: Edinburgh University Press, 2008), 19.

87 A catalogue of these sources forms an appendix in my thesis.

88 See Chapter 4 for a link to view the production of Daniel's *Cleopatra*.

89 Hamer, *Signs of Cleopatra*, xv.

90 Ania Loomba, *Shakespeare, Race, and Colonialism* (Oxford: OUP, 2002), 28, 31–6, 41; Wyke, *Projecting the Past*, 75.

91 Margaret M. Miles, ed., *Cleopatra: A Sphinx Revisited* (Berkeley: University of California Press, 2011), 5.

Chapter 1

1 This quotation and the title quotation (I.112) are taken from Antony speaking of the impact and persistence of Cleopatra's 'image' and how it haunts him. See *Antonius* in *Works*, 154–209.

2 *Works*, 147. Robert Garnier (1545–90) died two months earlier on 20 September 1590. Mary Sidney had started her translation before Garnier's death.

3 Philippe de Mornay (1549–1623), see *A Discourse* in *Works*, 209, 229–54.

4 Mary Sidney's work went through two editions in her lifetime. It was reprinted singly in 1595 as *The Tragedie of Antonie*. The possible reason for this de-classicizing of Antony's name is discussed in Chapter 2. The play is referred to as either *Antonie* or *Antonius* in the literature, depending on which edition scholars prefer to use. I use *Antonius* as the edition on which the Countess asked Daniel to base his companion piece.

5 Marie-Alice Belle and Line Cottegnies, eds, *Robert Garnier in Elizabethan England: Mary Sidney's Hebert's Antonius and Thomas Kyd's Cornelia* (Cambridge: MHRA, 2017), 17; Jondorf, 9–10; Cerasano and Wynne-Davies, *Antonie*, 15. For the use of Stoicism, see also Daniel Cadman's important study *Sovereigns and Subjects in Early Modern Neo-Senecan Drama* (Farnham: Ashgate, 2015).

6 Garnier, 9.

7 See *Les Tragedies de Robert Garnier* (Paris, 1585), BL 1073.d.6. Translations in this paragraph are my own.

8 Garnier, 1; Jondorf, 4–5.

9 For uses of history in the period, see Smuts, 'Court-Centred Politics'.

10 Hannay, 127. *Works*, 43, lists the neo-Senecan plays that followed in the period.

11 Samuel Brandon's *Octavia* is considered to be a lesser play and imitated both Mary Sidney's and Daniel's Cleopatras. The influence of *Antonius* on Shakespeare and varying scholarly views are explored in Chapter 5.

12 Greville, 93; Norbrook, 151.

13 John Guy, *Elizabeth: The Forgotten Years* (Viking: London, 2016), focuses on succession anxieties and fears of a Catholic threat during this period. See also Penry Williams, *The Later Tudors: England, 1547–1603* (Oxford: Clarendon, 1995), 305–87; Kewes, 'Admonition', 259.

14 Worden, xxii; Clarke, *Politics*, 13.

15 H. R. Woudhuysen, 'Sidney, Sir Philip (1554–1586), Author and Courtier', in *Oxford Dictionary of National Biography*. Oxford University Press, 2004; online edn, 2011, paras 25, 34, http://www.oxforddnb.com/view/article25522.

16 Victor Skretkowicz, 'Mary Sidney Herbert's *Antonius*, English Philhellenism and the Protestant Cause', *Women's Writing* 6, no. 1 (1999): 7–25 (8).

17 For Mary Sidney's education, see Hannay, 27–8. She was taught Latin, French, Italian and probably Greek. For the Cleopatra tragedies written in the period, see the Introduction above.

18 *Works*, 140.

19 Morrison, 'Some Aspects', 120.

20 Ibid., 120.

21 Bullough, 222–8.

22 Mary Sidney's father died on 5 May, mother on 9 August, and brother on 17 October 1586.

23 Gabriel Harvey quoted in Worden, 244.

24 For a contemporary view of Sidney's death and its cultural impact, see Woudhuysen, 'Sidney', para. 47; Katherine Duncan-Jones, *Sir Philip Sidney: Courtier and Poet* (London: Hamish Hamilton, 1991). For Mary Sidney, see Hannay, 55–60.

25 Hannay, 59, from *CSP, Spanish* 4:488.

26 Michael G. Brennan, *The Sidneys of Penshurst and the Monarchy, 1500–1700* (Aldershot: Ashgate, 2006), 101, 105. Their younger brother Thomas Sidney was underage at this time.

27 Hannay, 60.

28 Mary Ellen Lamb, 'The Countess of Pembroke's Patronage', *ELR* 12, no. 2 (1982): 162–77 (177); Hannay, 112–14; Findlay, *Playing Spaces*, 24; Laoutaris, *Shakespearian Maternities*, 242.

29 Sir Philip Sidney, *An Apology for Poetry (or The Defence of Poesy)*, ed. Geoffrey Shepherd, rev. and exp. 3rd edn by R. W. Maslen (Manchester: Manchester University Press, 1989), 110. 32–3. All references are to this edition. Hannay, 121. Joan Rees, *Samuel Daniel: A Critical Biography* (Liverpool: Liverpool University Press, 1964), 45, discusses the fears of civil war in Eubulus' final speech in *Gorboduc*.

30 Gavin Alexander, *Writing After Sidney: The Literary Response to Sir Philip Sidney, 1586–1640* (Oxford: OUP, 2006).

31 Woudhuysen, 'Sidney', para. 46. Sir Francis Walsingham, Sidney's father-in-law, was bankrupted covering Sidney's funeral costs and debts. See William H. Bond, 'The Epitaph for Sir Philip Sidney', *Modern Language Notes* 58, no. 4 (1943): 253–7. H. R. Woudhuysen kindly brought this article to my attention.

32 Laoutaris, *Shakespearian Maternities*, 242.

33 Peter Burke, 'Cultures of Translations in Early Modern Europe', in *Cultural Translation in Early Modern Europe*, ed. Peter Burke and R. Po-chia Hsia (Cambridge: CUP, 2007), 12.

34 See, for example, Chris Laoutaris, 'Translation/Historical Writing', in *The History of British Women's Writing, 1500–1610*, vol. 2, ed. Caroline Bicks and Jennifer Summit (Basingstoke: Palgrave Macmillan, 2010), 296. Jaime Goodrich, *Faithful Translators: Authorship, Gender, and Religion in Early Modern England* (Evanston, IL: Northwestern University Press, 2014), 5–9.

35 For Lumley, see Marion Wynne-Davies, 'The Theatre', in *The History of British Women's Writing, 1500–1610*, vol. 2, ed. Caroline Bicks and Jennifer Summit (Basingstoke: Palgrave Macmillan, 2010), 180–4. For Elizabeth I and Parr, see Micheline White, 'Pray for the Monarch: The Surprising Contributions of Katherine Parr and Queen Elizabeth I to the Book of Common Prayer', *TLS* 5844 (3 April 2015): 14–15.

36 Burke, *Cultures of Translation*, 34; Warren Boutcher, 'The Renaissance', in *The Oxford Guide to Literature in English Translation*, ed. Peter France (Oxford: OUP, 2000), 46.

37 Brenda M. Hosington, 'Translation as a Currency of Cultural Exchange in Early Modern England', in *Early Modern Exchanges: Dialogues between Nations and Cultures (1550–1750)*, ed. Helen Hackett (London: Routledge 2015), 27–8.

38 Goodrich, *Faithful Translators*, 114, 116–17.

39 *Works*, 210; Norbrook, 96.

40 See Patterson, *Censorship and Interpretation*, 18–19, 50–2. See J. R. Tanner, *Tudor Constitutional Documents, A.D. 1485–1603* (1930; rpt., Cambridge: CUP, 2013), 413–21.

41 Hannay, 126. See also Stubbs, *The Discovery of a Gaping Gulf* (London, 1579).

42 Hannay, 127.

43 Jonathan Bate, *Soul of the Age: The Life, Mind and World of William Shakespeare* (London: Viking, 2008), 114. Bate is referring here to plays written for the public stage, but similar concerns applied to closet drama.

44 Cerasano and Wynne-Davies, *Antonie*, 15.

45 Tina Krontiris, *Oppositional Voices: Women as Writers and Translators of Literature in the English Renaissance* (London: Routledge, 1992), 69; Eve Rachelle Sanders, *Gender and Literacy on Stage in Early Modern England* (Cambridge: CUP, 1998), 92–4.

46 Margaret P. Hannay, '"Princes you as men must dy": Genevan Advice to Monarchs in the Psalmes of Mary Sidney', *ELR* 19, no. 1 (1989): 22–41. Skretkowicz, 'English Philhellenism', 8.

47 For recent critics who do not see a political significance in *Antonius*, see Alexander, *Writing After Sidney*, 97–106; Richard Hillman, 'De-Centring the Countess's Circle: Mary Sidney Herbert and Cleopatra', *Renaissance and Reformation* 28, no. 1 (2004): 61–79.

48 Hannay, 120–9; *Works*, 38–42; Skretkowicz, 'English Philhellenism', 25; Clarke, *Politics*, 95; Kewes, 'Admonition', 243–64; Crawford, *Mediatrix*, 74, 49.

49 Elizabeth Pentland, 'Philippe Mornay, Mary Sidney, and the Politics of Translation', *Early Modern Studies Journal* 6 (2014): 66–99, recently adopted a similar approach, focusing on Mornay.

50 Hannay, 69.

51 Antony Grafton and Lisa Jardine, '"Studied for Action": How Gabriel Harvey Read his Livy', *Past and Present*, 129 no. 1 (1990): 55.

52 Worden, 395.

53 *Works*, 141; Rees, *Samuel Daniel*, 46.

54 For Hubert's prefatory poem to *Marc Antoine*, see Garnier, 106. I am grateful to Jaime Goodrich for her generous help in translating the poem. Sanders, *Gender and Literacy*, 97, also cites the quatrain, interpreting it as Garnier's recognition 'that a female reader could be not only a lover, mother and wife, but also a subject: queen or a poet'.

55 See Elizabeth D. Harvey, *Ventriloquized Voices: Feminist Theory and English Renaissance Texts* (London: Routledge, 1995), 1–17. Hannay, 138. Chris Laoutaris generously discussed the idea of memorial voices with me.

56 For differing views of Mary Sidney's translation, see Alexander M. Witherspoon, *The Influence of Robert Garnier on Elizabethan Drama* (1926; rpt., New York: Phaeton, 1968), 98; Alexander, *Writing After Sidney*, 96–9; and *Works*, 150.

57 *Works*, 146. Coburn Freer, *The Poetics of Jacobean Drama* (Baltimore, MD: Johns Hopkins University Press, 1981), 206–7.

58 This paragraph is based on changes to the Argument outlined in *Works*, 147–9, and Sanders, *Gender and Literacy*, 108–9.

59 *Works*, 149. Amyot's translation of Plutarch was the immediate source for both Garnier and Sir Thomas North.

60 Sanders, *Gender and Literacy*, 115.

61 Findlay, *Playing Spaces*, 30. Belle and Cottegnies, *Robert Garnier in Elizabethan England*, 34, discuss 'vomissant'. They present an alternative viewpoint of Cleopatra's death.

62 See, for example, *CSP, relating to Ireland*, vol. 4: August 1588–September 1592. February 1589. 'Declaration of Richard Fitz Symons, of Drogheda,...., of a new Spanish Armada under

preparation with 100 gallies, with intentions of landing this in Ireland'. See *CSP*, vol. CCXXXI, 94, April 1590.

'Intelligence given by an Italian in the service of Mr. Richard. Drake, of the Spanish and the Duke of Parma attempting to liaise with Scotland and Ireland in launching a new attack'. In SPO.

63 Williams, *Later Tudors*, 321, gives details of the Armada fleet and possible Spanish invasion plans.

64 Pettegree, 31.

65 Quoted in Williams, *Later Tudors*, 313.

66 Ibid., 312–13.

67 Skretkowicz, 'English Philhellenism', 19.

68 See Catherine Bates, *The Rhetoric of Courtship in Elizabethan England* (1992; rpt., Cambridge: CUP, 2006).

69 Edmund Spenser, *The Faerie Queene*, ed. Thomas P. Roche, Jr. and C. Patrick O'Donnell, Jr. (1978; rpt., London: Penguin, 1987), 238–40, II.3.22–30.

70 Lisa Hopkins, *The Female Hero in English Renaissance Tragedy* (Basingstoke: Palgrave Macmillan, 2002), 151.

71 Pascale Aebischer, 'The Properties of Whiteness: Renaissance Cleopatras From Jodelle to Shakespeare', *Shakespeare Survey* 65 (2011): 221–38 (231).

72 Ibid., 232. Farah Karim-Cooper, *Cosmetics in Shakespearean and Renaissance Drama* (Edinburgh: Edinburgh University Press, 2006), 18.

73 Joyce Green MacDonald, *Women and Race in Early Modern Texts* (Cambridge: CUP, 2002), 37.

74 Alexander, *Writing After Sidney*, 82 n. 19; Skretkowicz, 'English Philhellenism', 16–17.

75 John Florio, *Worlde of Wordes* (London, 1598), sig. b1v.

76 Caroline Ruutz-Rees, 'Some Notes of Gabriel Harvey's in his Copy of Hoby's Translation of Castiglione's Courtier (1561)', *PMLA* 25, no. 4 (1910): 617. The Newberry Library kindly allowed me sight of Harvey's copy, Y 712.C27495, fol. Zz iiij ro. Ruutz-Rees made a slight error in transcription of a comma instead of a bold full stop between 'Cleopatra' and 'The Queen'. This suggests that Harvey was thinking of the two distinct queens in his comparison.

77 See Weis, xxxv–vi.

78 *Works*, 333, l. 1530, Agrippa states, 'No guard so sure, no forte so strong doth prove, / No such defence, as is the people's love' (IV.1529–30). See also Crawford, *Mediatrix*, 74.

79 Sanders, *Gender and Literacy*, 110.

80 Kewes, 'Admonition', 252–3.

81 Woudhuysen, 'Sidney', para. 1.

82 Marie Tanner, *The Last Descendant of Aeneas: The Hapsburgs and the Mythic Image of the Emperor* (New Haven, CT: Yale University Press, 1993). Alexander Samson kindly brought this work to my attention. For the Pompeii Leoni statue see https://s-media-cache-ak0.pinimg.com/236x/a9/26/2c/a9262c101ea0b3cf40aa1a9903f5ad1d.jpg.

83 Greville, 106, 109.

84 The quotation from the *OED* is in Walter R. Davis's entry on 'Allegory', in *The Spenser Encyclopedia*, ed. A. C. Hamilton, Donald Cheney, W. F. Blisset et al. (Toronto: University of Toronto Press, 1997), 16.

85 Edmund Spenser, *The Shepheardes Calender*, in *The Shorter Poems*, ed. Richard A. McCabe (London: Penguin, 1996), 23–156.

86 Pettegree, 38.

87 Worden, 192, 246.

88 Mary Sidney also used repetition to enhance the play's fire motif. Doubling 'enflamde' and 'burne' in Garnier's comparison of Hercules's passion for Omphale to Antony's for Cleopatra. Skretkowicz, 'English Philhellenism', 20.

89 See, for example, Margreta de Grazia, *'Hamlet' without Hamlet* (Cambridge: CUP, 2007), and Katharine Eisaman Maus, *Being and Having in Shakespeare* (Oxford: OUP, 2013).

90 Sanders, *Gender and Literacy*, 115.

91 See the Introduction above, and the appendix for these poems.

92 Garnier, 1; Jondorf, 35; Pettegree, *Foreign and Native*, 27.

93 Paul E. J. Hammer, *The Polarisation of Elizabethan Politics: The Political Career of Robert Devereux, 2nd Earl of Essex, 1585–1597* (Cambridge: CUP, 1999), 92.

94 *Works*, 212–13, 253.

95 Pentland, 'Phillipe Mornay', 67, 72.

96 Mack P. Holt, *The French Wars of Religion 1562–1629* (Cambridge: CUP, 2005), 81–9; Duncan-Jones, *Philip Sidney*, 60–2; Charlotte Arbaleste de Mornay, *A Huguenot Family in XVI Century France: The Memoirs of Philippe du Mornay, Souer du Plessis Marly*, trans. Lucy Crump (London: Routledge, n.d.), 104–10, 124–30.

97 Duncan-Jones, *Philip Sidney*, 80–2; Worden, 52–4.

98 *Works*, 210. See *Excellent discours de la vie et la mort* (Geneva, 1576), sig. A2, for the dedication to Mademoiselle Du Plessis. Mornay adopted the traditional language of co-sanguinity in his dedication to his then fiancée Charlotte Arbaleste. See Pentland, 'Phillipe Mornay', 72, 87; Arbaleste de Mornay, *Huguenot Family*, 145, vii, 288.

99 *Works*, 212, 217–18; *Discourse*, 239; Kewes, 'Admonition', 262.

100 Arbaleste de Mornay, *Huguenot Family*, 145.

101 Williams, *Later Tudors*, 339–40. Pettegree, 33.

102 Arbaleste de Mornay, *Huguenot Family*, 271–2.

103 Skretkowicz, 'English Philhellenism', 26.

104 Cicero is quoted in Worden, 140.

105 Robert Sidney's signed copy of *C. Cornelii Taciti Opera Quae Extant* (Antwerp, 1585) is dated 20 Jan. 1588. BL C.142.e.13. For the section on 'vertu', see 4.

106 Worden, 140, 260–1; Norbrook, 153.

107 John Lydgate, *The serpent of division* (London, 1559), sig. D1r.

108 Hannay, 127.

109 Paulina Kewes, 'Henry Savile's Tacitus and the Politics of Roman History in Late Elizabethan England', *HLQ* 74, no. 4 (2011): 515–16.

110 Worden, 260.

111 Daniel, *The Civil Wars* (London, 1609), sig A2v.

112 Daniel, *The Complaint of Rosamond* in *Delia. Containing certaine Sonnets: with the Complaynt of Rosamond* (London, 1592), sig. A1v. All references to *Rosamond* are to this edition, unless otherwise stated.

Chapter 2

1 Proculeius describing Cleopatra's condition to Caesar, in Daniel's *The Tragedie of Cleopatra*, in *Poeticall Essayes* (1599). All further references in this chapter to *Cleopatra* are to this edition, unless otherwise stated. The choice of the 1599 edition is explained later in the chapter.

2 John Pitcher, 'Daniel, Samuel (1562/3–1619)', *ODNB*, Oxford University Press, 2004; online edn, 2011, para. 5, http://www.oxforddnb.com/view/article/7120.

3 Peter Davidson and Jane Stevenson, 'Elizabeth I's Reception at Bisham (1592): Elite Women as Writers and Devisers', in *The Progresses, Pageants, and Entertainments of Queen Elizabeth I*, ed. Jayne Elisabeth Archer, Elizabeth Goldring and Sarah Knight (Oxford: OUP, 2007), 223–4.

4 In *Mediatrix*, Crawford also considers the idea of co-authorship between poet and female patrons, and discusses Mary Sidney and Daniel, 4.

5 Dedication to Mary Sidney, sig. H4r, in *Delia and Rosamond augmented. Cleopatra* (London, 1594).

6 *Works*, 41.

7 Edmund Spenser, 'Colin Clouts Come Home Againe', in *Shorter Poems*, ed. Richard A. McCabe (London: Penguin, 1996), 345–71 (ll. 416–17, 424–7).

8 1594 Dedication to Mary Sidney, sig. H4r.

9 *OED*, see State 1.b, 21.b.

10 Worden, 254.

11 I am grateful to René Weis for the discussion of this point.

12 See Russell E. Leavenworth, *Daniel's Cleopatra: A Critical Study* (Salzburg: Institut für Englische Sprache und Literatur, Universität Salzburg, 1974), 19–21. For example, lines 1–2, in 1594 read: 'Yet do I live, and yet doth breath possess / This hateful prison of a loathsome soule.' In 1599, the thought is subtler: 'Yet do I live, and doth breath extend / My life beyond my life?' elaborating on the idea of 'whether the body persists in life when the soul is dead'.

13 Ibid., 16–22. See John Pitcher, 'Samuel Daniel's Occasional and Dedicatory Verse: A Critical Edition', 2 vols (unpublished D.Phil. thesis, Bodleian Library, MS. D.Phil. d. 6440, University of Oxford, 1978), 190–5. Daniel's bibliography is hugely complicated with scholars using different methods to count his editions, which has led to some confusion.

14 Kewes, 'Admonition', 255.

15 Aebischer, 'Properties of Whiteness', 235.

16 Peter W. M. Blayney, 'The Publication of Playbooks', in *A New History of Early English Drama*, ed. John D. Cox and David Scott Kastan (New York: Columbia University Press, 1996), 388. With Daniel's *Philotas* already on the list of bestsellers, Blayney notes that the professional stage only produced one play capable of outselling Daniel's verse, *Mucedorus* (1598).

17 Daniel, *Cleopatra* in *Certaine Small Workes* (London, 1607), BL C.34.a.46. All further references to this edition are referred to as the 1607 *Cleopatra*.

18 *Cleopatra* (1599) in Bullough, 406–49.

19 Philip Sidney, *Astrophil and Stella*, Sonnet 45, in *The Major Works*, ed. Katherine Duncan-Jones (1989; rpt., Oxford: OUP, 2008), 170.

20 Eric Langley, *Narcissism and Suicide: in Shakespeare and his Contemporaries* (Oxford: OUP, 2009), discusses self-referential terms and their isolating and self-destructive nature.

21 Laoutaris, *Shakespearian Maternities*, 255.

22 Marie Axton, *The Queen's Two Bodies: Drama and the Elizabethan Succession* (London: Royal Historical Society, 1977). See also Louis Montrose, *The Subject of Elizabeth: Authority, Gender, and Representation* (Chicago: Chicago University Press, 2006), 149, 219.

23 See for example, Elizabeth's speeches of 5 November 1566, 15 March 1576 and 12 November 1586 in Leah S. Marcus, Janel Mueller and Mary Beth Rose, eds, *Elizabeth I: Collected Works* (Chicago: Chicago University Press, 2000), 97, 170, 186. In the latter two, Elizabeth wishes for the simpler life of a milkmaid as discussed in Chapter 5 below.

24 Ibid., 30, n. 1–2. Steven May, ed., *Queen Elizabeth I: Selected Works* (New York: Washington Square Press, 2004), 13, states that all five extant manuscripts of the poem attribute it to the Queen. It is therefore possible that this very personal poem was written by Elizabeth and discovered only after her death.

25 Langley, *Narcissism and Suicide*, 17–24, discusses the use of 'myself myself'. Here, I would argue that with the trope of the queen's two bodies, this becomes: 'from myself, my other self'.

26 Pitcher, 'Occasional and Dedicatory Verse', 3–4.

27 Hugh Gazzard finds a similar dualism in *Philotas* in '"Those Graue Presentiments of Antique": Samuel Daniel's *Philotas* and the Earl of Essex', *RES* 51 (2000): 423–50 (445).

28 Helen Hackett, 'The Rhetoric of (In)fertility: Shifting Responses to Elizabeth I's Childlessness', in *Rhetoric, Women and Politics in Early Modern England*, ed. Jennifer Richards and Alison Thorne (London: Routledge, 2007), 168–9.

29 Peter Wentworth, *A Pithie Exhortation to her Majestie for establishing her successor to the crowne* (Edinburgh, 1598), sig. B4v.

30 André Hurault Sieur de Maisse, *A Journal of All That was Accomplished by Monsieur De Maisse Ambassador in England from King Henri IV to Queen Elizabeth Anno Domini 1597*, trans. and ed. G. B. Harrison and R. A. Jones (London: Nonesuch, 1931), 115.

31 Quoted in Linda Levy Peck, 'Peers, Patronage and the Politics of History', in *The Reign of Elizabeth: Court and Culture in the Last Decade*, ed. John Guy (Cambridge: CUP, 1995), 87.

32 I am grateful to Chris Stamatakis for bringing these lines, which also form the epigraph, to my attention.

33 John Guy, *Queen of Scots: The True Life of Mary Stuart* (New York: Houghton Mifflin, 2004), 182–3. Mary's words are quoted from Randolph's letter in SP 52/9, no. 18.

34 William Fulke, *Praelictions vpon the sacred and holy Reuelations of St. Iohn* (London, 1573), 21. For specific applications to Mary Stuart, see James Emerson Phillips, *Images of a Queen: Mary Stuart in Sixteenth-Century Literature* (Berkeley: University of California Press, 1964). See Hackett, 139–41, for allusions to Mary Stuart as the whore of Babylon in Spenser.

35 Pettegree, 28, 33.

36 See Norbrook, 101–15; Hackett, 142–4, 163–6; and Thomas M. Cain's entry on 'Elizabeth, Images of' in *The Spenser Encyclopedia*, ed. A. C. Hamilton (London: Routledge, 1991), 621–5.

37 Montaigne, *Essays*, see 'On the uncertainty of our judgement', 314–20.

38 See, for example, Joan Rees, 'Samuel Daniel's *Cleopatra* and Two French Plays', *MLR* 47, no. 1 (1952): 1–10.

39 See the Appendix.

40 William Thomas, *Historie of Italie* (1549; rpt., London, 1561), sig. L1r. Grafton and Jardine, 'Studied for Action', 49–50, note that Thomas's *Historie* was one of the important works on Gabriel Harvey's book wheel.

41 June Schlueter, 'Samuel Daniel in Italy: New Documentary Evidence', *HLQ* 75, no. 2 (2012): 283–90; Mark Eccles, 'Samuel Daniel in France and Italy', *Studies in Philology*, 34, no. 2 (1937): 148–67. Daniel was one of the few people with access to Italian sources in England at this time. He studied Italian at Oxford with Florio, and his sister married Florio.

42 Rees, *Samuel Daniel*, 55–6.

43 Pitcher, 'Daniel, Samuel', para. 14.

44 1611 Dedication to Mary Sidney, sig. E3v, in *Certaine Small Workes* (London, 1611), BL C.34.a.1.

45 I am grateful to John Pitcher for his insight on Cleopatra's language. Private conversation, 12 October 2015.

46 Following Daniel, these female complaints were printed between 1592 and 1594 in England: Thomas Churchyard's *The Tragedy of Shore's Wife* (1593); Anthony Chute's *Beautie Dishonoured* (1593); Thomas Lodge's *The Complaint of Elstred* (1593); Richard Barnfield's *The Complaint of Chastite* (1594); William Drayton's *Matilda* (1594); and Shakespeare's *Lucrece* (1594). List kindly supplied by Chris Stamatakis. For the tradition of female complaint, see John Kerrigan, ed., *Motives of Woe: Shakespeare and 'Female Complaint'. A Critical Anthology* (Oxford: Clarendon, 1991).

47 See the Appendix for these poems.

48 Kewes, 'Admonition', 255.

49 Spenser, 'Colin Clouts', ll. 426–7.

50 See Kerrigan, *Motives of Woe*, 23, 52–63. See Chapter 4 for discussion of Danyel's music used in the *Cleopatra* production and how this worked in the complaint tradition.

51 Lucy Munro, *Children of the Queen's Revels: A Jacobean Theatre Repertory* (Cambridge: CUP, 2005), 139, also notes Daniel's interest in 'generic experimentation' in his tragicomedies and *Philotas*.

52 See Kerrigan, *Motives of Woe*, 1–65, for some general characteristics of complaint.

53 Harvey, *Ventriloquized Voices*, 140. Daniel's affinity can be contrasted to some poets, such as Breton's ventriloquizing of Mary Sidney, as discussed in Chapter 1.

54 Leavenworth, *Daniel's Cleopatra*, 21.

55 Rees, *Samuel Daniel*, 81.

56 These date boundaries are from when *The Letter* was first published to the last collected edition printed in Daniel's lifetime. I examined the 1599, 1602, 1603, 1605, 1607 and 1611 editions.

57 Mimi Still Dixon, 'Not Know Me Yet?' in *The Female Tragic Hero in English Renaissance Drama*, ed. Naomi Conn Liebler (New York: Palgrave, 2002), 81, 84; Sanders, *Gender and Literacy*, 121.

58 Catherine Belsey's influential study, *The Subject of Tragedy: Identity & Difference in Renaissance Drama* (London: Methuen, 1985) explores 'the construction of subjectivity' in drama of the period. It does not look at Daniel's *Cleopatra* or Mary Sidney's representation, but covers Shakespeare's.

59 Plutarch, 273.

60 Norbrook, 135–9; Hackett, 182–6, 191–7.

61 Roy Strong, *The Cult of Elizabeth: Elizabethan Portraiture and Pageantry* (London: Pimlico, 1999), 146–51. See Hurault, *A Journal*, 25, for his description of an aged Elizabeth.

62 Kewes, 'Admonition', 254.

63 See, for example, Anton Raphael Mengs, *Octavian and Cleopatra* (*c.*1759), http://www.nationaltrustcollections.org.uk/object/732099.

64 John Pitcher, 'Benefiting from the Book: The Oxford Edition of Samuel Daniel', *Yearbook of English Studies* 29 (1999): 74. Daniel stopped revising Delia after 1601.

65 H. R. Woudhuysen, *Sir Philip Sidney and the Circulation of Manuscripts 1558–1640* (Oxford: Clarendon, 1996).

66 Clarke, *Politics*, 137.

67 Woudhuysen, *Circulation of Manuscripts*, 15. See Alexander, *Writing After Sidney*, for the interest in Sidneian incompletion (*aposiopesis*), and the way Sidney's works were tweaked, revised and supplemented after his death.

68 See Arthur M. Z Norman, 'Daniel's *The Tragedie of Cleopatra* and *Antony and Cleopatra*', *Shakespeare Quarterly*, 9 no. 1 (1958): 11–18; Kevin Curran, 'Shakespeare and Daniel Revisited: *Antony and Cleopatra* II. v. 50–4 and *The Tragedy of Philotas* V. ii. 2013–15', *N&Q* 54, no. 2 (2007): 318–20.

69 Cecil C. Seronsy, *Samuel Daniel* (New York: Twayne Publishers, 1967), 50. See Chapter 4 below for the impact of Caesario's speech in performance.

70 Samuel Daniel, *The Tragedy of Philotas*, ed. Michel Laurence (1949; rpt., New Haven: Yale University Press, 1970), 27, 41–2.

71 Dedication to Prince Henry, sig. A4v, in *Certaine Small Poems* (1605). All further references are to this edition.

72 Michel, *Philotas*, 50–1, convincingly argues that Daniel had access to actual trial proceedings, probably through Camden. See also John Pitcher, 'Samuel Daniel and the Authorities', *MaRDiE*, 10 (1998): 113–48 (117–18); Gazzard, 'Those Grave Presentiments', 443–5; Daniel Cadman, '"Th'accesion of these mighty States": Daniel's *Philotas* and the Union of Crowns', *Renaissance Studies* 26, no. 3 (2012): 365–84.

73 Spenser, *Prothalamion*, 491–8 (ll.160), in *Shorter Poems*; Pitcher, 'Daniel, Samuel', para. 6.

74 See John Guy, ed., *The Reign of Elizabeth: Court and Culture in the Last Decade* (Cambridge: Cambridge University Press, 1995), 1–19; Hackett, 167–93.

75 Norbrook, 173–5, cites Cyril Tourneur's satire *The Transformed Metamorphosis* (1600) as prophesying such a transformation.

76 Hackett, Chapters 6 and 7, details this sense of delay.

77 Worden, 355–6; John Watkins, *Representing Elizabeth in Stuart England: Literature, History, Sovereignty* (Cambridge: Cambridge University Press, 2002), 56–86; Michael Dobson and Nicola J. Watson, *England's Elizabeth: An Afterlife in Fame and Fantasy* (Oxford: Oxford University Press, 2002), 46–61.

78 Worden, 356.

79 Watkins, *Representing Elizabeth*, 84.

80 Jenny Wormald, 'James VI and I: Two Kings or One?', *History* 68, no. 223 (1983): 189–90.

81 Anne Clifford, *The Memoir of 1603 and The Diary of 1616–1619*, ed. Katherine O. Acheson (Ontario: Broadview, 2007), 45.

82 Pauline Croft, *King James* (Basingstoke: Palgrave, 2003), 55. See 'Sir John Harington, on the Entertainment at Theobalds 1606', in *The Progresses, Processions and Magnificent Festivities of King James the First*, ed. John Nichols (London, 1828), 73.

83 Worden, 355–9. See Watkins, *Representing Elizabeth*, 76–86, for Greville's complicated response to Elizabeth.

84 John Gouws, 'Greville, Fulke, First Baron Brooke of Beauchamps Court (1554–1628)', *ODNB*, Oxford University Press, 2004; online edn, 2011, para.10, http://www.oxforddnb.com/view/article/11516.

85 1605 Dedication to Prince Henry, sig. A5v.

86 Gazzard, 'Those Grave Presentiments', 428.

87 Pitcher, 'Daniel and the Authorities', 118.

88 Christopher Maginn, 'Blount, Charles, Eighth Baron Mountjoy and Earl of Devonshire (1563–1606)', *ODNB*, Oxford University Press, 2004; online edn, 2011, para. 11, http://www.oxforddnb.com/view/article/2683.

89 See Chapters 3 and 5 for more on James's association with Augustus.

90 1599 *Cleopatra* (sig. E1v); 1607 *Cleopatra* (sig. I1v).

91 Smuts, 'Court-Centred Politics', 37.

92 John Pitcher, *Samuel Daniel: The Brotherton Manuscript: A Study in Authorship* (Leeds: University of Leeds Press, 1981), 136, 36.

93 *Taciti Opera*, 4, 19.

94 Quentin Skinner, *Machiavelli: A Very Short Introduction* (Oxford: OUP, 2001), 86.

95 See Katherine A. Craik, *Reading Sensations in Early Modern England* (Basingstoke: Palgrave, 2007), and Katherine A. Craik and Tanya Pollard, eds, *Shakespearean Sensations: Experiencing Literature in Early Modern England* (Cambridge: CUP, 2013). See Alan Stewart, *Shakespeare's Letters* (Oxford: OUP, 2008), 193–230. I am grateful to Chris Laoutaris for his guidance on this paragraph.

96 University of London Library, MS 187, f. 13v. See also Paul E. J. Hammer, 'Essex and Europe: Evidence from Confidential Instructions by the Earl of Essex, 1595–1596', *English Historical Review* 3, no. 431(1996): 357–81.

97 Paul E. J. Hammer, *The Polarisation of Elizabethan Politics: The Political Career of Robert Devereux, 2nd Earl of Essex* (Cambridge: CUP, 1999), 107; Alexandra Gajda, *The Earl of Essex and Late Elizabethan Political Culture* (Oxford: OUP, 2012), 237; Cecil C. Seronsy, 'The Doctrine of Cyclical Recurrence and Some Related Ideas in the Works of Samuel Daniel', *Studies in Philology* 54, no. 3 (1957): 387–407.

98 Greville, 93.

99 Ibid.

Chapter 3

1 The quotation used in the chapter title is of Caesar speaking about Cleopatra in Daniel's 1607 *Cleopatra*, sig. H5v. All references to *Cleopatra* in this chapter are to this edition.

2 See Figure 1, the Vatican *Cleopatra*. The statue defined the image of Cleopatra in the period.

3 See Introduction.

4 This was confirmed by H. R. Woudhuysen (UCL/Lincoln College, Oxford), who examined the inscription in detail, and under whose generous guidance much of the auction-related work in this chapter and early drafts of Yasmin Arshad, 'The Enigma of a

Portrait: Lady Anne Clifford and Daniel's *Cleopatra*', *The British Art Journal* 11, no. 3 (2011): 30–6, were undertaken.

5 The painting was kindly examined by Sandra Romito (Christie's), Catherine Daunt and Catherine MacLeod (NPG), Karen Hearn (Tate Britain/UCL) and Diana Dethloff (UCL).

6 Nashe, *anatomie of absurditie*, sig. A4v.

7 For example, see *Kitty Fisher as Cleopatra Dissolving the Pearl*, by Sir Joshua Reynolds (*c*.1759), English Heritage, Kenwood.

8 Catherine MacLeod and Julia Marciari Alexander, eds, *Painted Ladies: Women at the Court of Charles II* (London: National Portrait Gallery, 2001), 78.

9 Kim F. Hall, *Things of Darkness: Economies of Race and Gender in Early Modern England* (Ithaca: Cornell University Press, 1995), 179–87; Anna Beer, *My Just Desire: The Life of Bess Ralegh, Wife of Sir Walter* (New York: Ballantine, 2003), 129–30; Pamela Allen Brown, 'New Fable of the Belly: Vulgar Curiosity and the Persian Lady's Loose Bodies', in *The Impact of Feminism in English Renaissance Studies*, ed. Dympna Callaghan (Basingstoke: Palgrave, 2007), 171–92.

10 Beer, *Bess*, 130.

11 Christie's, *Catalogue of Early English Portraits: The Property of Lady Capel Cure; Also Old Pictures & Drawings from Various Sources Nov. 20, 1931* (London: Christie, Manson & Woods, 1931), lot 4. In private correspondence (15 November 2009), Hugo Capel Cure confirmed that the Lady Capel Cure in question was Muriel Oxenden, who had married Sir Edward Capel Cure. The painting has no connection with the Cheney collection housed at Blake Hall, Essex.

12 *Debrett's Peerage, Baronetage, Knightage and Companionage* (London: Dean & Son, 1901), 453. For Greville's heir, see Gouws, 'Greville, Fulke', para. 18.

13 Christie's, *Catalogue of Old Pictures: The Properties of The Rt. Hon. The Earl of Southesk, Admiral Robert Hathorn Johnson Stewart ... and Others, 23 July 1948* (London: Christie, Manson & Woods, 1948), lot 77.

14 Confirmed by Catherine Daunt (NPG), email correspondence 24 September 2009. The NPG also confirmed that the damage

on the print is on the painting itself and not the negative; email correspondence 1 October 2009.

15 Information kindly supplied by Stephen Conrad to Robin Simon, September 2011.

16 The Cleopatra painting was not listed in Leonard Dent's will, examined 11 October 2009. Gerard Dent was located through the kind assistance of the churchwarden at St Mary's Burghfield. Private correspondence, 1 January 2010.

17 Leonard Dent, *Hillfields: Notes on the Contents* (London: The Author, 1972), 1, 28.

18 Email correspondence with Jean Bray, archivist at Sudeley Castle, 13 February 2010. The Bridgeman Art Library, Philip Mould & Company, the Wallace Collection and the Weiss Gallery were also not familiar with the portrait or its whereabouts.

19 Hall, *Things of Darkness*, 183.

20 Ibid., 187.

21 1607 *Cleopatra*, sigs K6v–K7r.

22 Email correspondence with John Pitcher, 13 October 2009.

23 This dating would not change much even if the sitter or the painter had access to a manuscript copy of the play, since Daniel would have worked on this major revision after his last edition of 1605.

24 Hall, *Things of Darkness*, 185–7.

25 Mark Nicholls and Penry Williams, *Sir Walter Raleigh: In Life and Legend* (London: Continuum, 2011), 196, 230–2.

26 Ibid., 230.

27 Brown, 'New Fable', 184.

28 Beer, *Bess*, 129.

29 Ibid., 130.

30 Hannay, 123.

31 See Andrew Hadfield, *Edmund Spenser: A Life* (Oxford: OUP, 2012), 240–2, 313–15. See Spenser's 'Letter of the author expounding his whole intention … ', in *The Faerie Queene*, 15–16; also Spenser, *Colin Clouts*, Dedication, in *Shorter Poems*, 344, 345–71 (ll. 416–17). See also Chapter 2 above.

32 Walter Ralegh, *Historie of the World* (London, 1614), 199. Lines from *Philotas* as quoted.

33 Ibid.

34 Gazzard, 'Those Graue Presentiments', 449.

35 Daniel, *A panegyrike congratulatorie to the Kings Majestie. Also certaine epistles* (London, 1603), sig. A1r.

36 See Edward Chaney, 'Roma Britannica and the Cultural Memory of Egypt: Lord Arundel and the Obelisk of Domitian', in *Roma Britannica: Art Patronage and Cultural Exchange in Eighteenth-Century Rome*, ed. David Marshall, Susan Russell and Karin Wolfe (Rome: British School, 2011), 147–70, for James's programme to Romanize London.

37 I am grateful to John Pitcher for pointing me in this direction. Email correspondence, 5 November 2009.

38 Spence, 12–17.

39 Ibid., 13.

40 Mary Ellen Lamb, 'The Agency of the Split Subject: Lady Anne Clifford and the Uses of Reading', *ELR* 223 (1992): 347–68 (349).

41 John Pitcher, 'Negotiating a Marriage for Lady Anne Clifford: Samuel Daniel's Advice', *RES* 64, no. 267 (2013): 770–94.

42 Ibid., 791. See Jessica Stoll, 'Petrarch's *De Vita Solitaria*: Samuel Daniel's Translation *c.* 1610', *MLR* 109, no. 2 (2014): 313–32, for a discussion of Daniel's *The Prayse of Private Life* which he presented to Lady Cumberland. Daniel added Senecan *sententiae* to present solitude as a moral way of life, permitting life to be endured. This manuscript appears to be the one Clifford read in 1619 at a time of great difficulty in her life.

43 Sir Philip Sidney, *The Countess of Pembrokes Arcadia* (London, 1605), Bodleian Library, Oxford, Juel-Jensen Sidney 13.

44 Ibid., 493, 508. See also Paul Salzman, 'Anne Clifford's Annotated Copy of Sidney's *Arcadia*', *N&Q* 56, no. 4 (2009): 554–5.

45 Pitcher, *Brotherton*, 15.

46 Ibid., 16, quoted from George C. Williamson, *Lady Anne Clifford* (Kendall: Titus, Wilson and Son, 1922), 206.

47 This sonnet was generously brought to my attention by John Pitcher.

48 *Certaine Small Workes* (1607), sig. C3v.

49 Spence, 40–54.

50 See, for example, Harry Berger, 'Fictions of the Pose: Facing the Gaze of Early Modern Portraiture', *Representations* 46 (1994): 87–120.

51 See https://www.artfund.org/supporting-museums/art-weve-helped-buy/artwork/2506/the-lady-anne-clifford-collection-of-portraits-including-the-great-picture. Karen Hearn, 'Lady Anne Clifford's Great Triptych', in *Lady Anne Clifford: Culture, Patronage and Gender in 17th-Century Britain*, ed. Karen Hearn and Lynn Hulse (Leeds: Yorkshire Archaeological Society Occasional Paper No. 7, 2009), 12.

52 See https://www.artfund.org/supporting-museums/art-weve-helped-buy/artwork/12470/portrait-of-lady-anne-clifford.

53 See http://www.fitzwilliamprints.com/image/803819/oliver-isaac-i-henry-frederick-prince-of-wales-by-isaac-oliver.

54 Karen Hearn, *Marcus Gheeraerts II: Elizabethan Artist in Focus* (London: Tate Publishing, 2002), 26–7.

55 Ibid.

56 Spence, 15.

57 See *The Poems of Aemilia Lanyer: Salve Deus Rex Judæorum*, ed. Susanne Woods (Oxford: OUP, 1993), 29, 31.

58 This was pointed out to me by Helen Hackett.

59 Spence, 20.

60 I am grateful to Jenny Tiramani for her comments. Email correspondence 3 March 2016.

61 Spence, 22.

62 Straznicky, *Privacy, Playreading*, 16.

63 Alison Findlay, Stephanie Hodgson-Wright and Gweno Williams, *Women and Dramatic Production 1550–1700* (Harlow: Pearson, 2000). Findlay is part of the Rose Theatre Company and *Iphigenia at Aulis* was directed by Emma Rustcastle. See Romana Wray, 'Performing *The Tragedy of Mariam* and Constructing Stage History', *Early Theatre* 18, no. 2 (2015): 149–66, for Schafer's stagings of *Mariam*. A staged

reading of Margaret Cavendish's *Convent of Pleasure* was performed in March 2014 in New York, dir. Elysee Singer.

64 Margaret P. Hannay, *Mary Sidney, Lady Wroth* (Farnham: Ashgate, 2010); Findlay, *Playing Spaces*, 83–94. The staged reading of *Love's Victory* was held at the 'Dramatising Penshurst: Site, Script, Sidneys' Conference, 8–9 June 2014, Penshurst, Kent.

65 See Chapter 2 above, for Mary Sidney as a deviser in relation to Daniel's *Cleopatra*.

66 Elizabeth Zeman Kolkovich, *The Elizabethan Country House Entertainment: Print, Performance and Gender* (Cambridge: CUP, 2016), 51–2, 209.

67 Findlay, *Playing Spaces,* 23.

68 Private correspondence with Margaret Hannay, 13 November 2009.

69 Martin Wiggins and Catherine Richardson, *British Drama: Vol. 11* (forthcoming, OUP), Appendix 2, Works Excluded from the Catalogue, Section B, Duplications, describes the stockings from the 2 June 1617 inventory. I am grateful to Martin Wiggins for giving me sight of this. Email correspondence, 22 August 2018. For examples of aristocrats in portraits in masque dress, see Captain Thomas Lee (*c.*1594), by Marcus Gheeraerts, Tate Gallery; Lucy Harington, Countess of Bedford, attributed to John de Critz, *c.*1606, Woburn Abbey; and Lady Thyme, by William Larkin, Longleat.

70 Sophie Tomlinson, *Women on Stage in Stuart Drama* (Cambridge: CUP, 2005), 8, 19. Although the Jacobean court masques involved the participation of the Queen and her ladies, W. R. Streitberger in *The Master of the Revels and Elizabeth I's Court Theatre* (Oxford: OUP, 2016), 75, shows that there is evidence of earlier amateur female participation in the form of theatrical performance in the Elizabethan court and in 'masques for women'.

71 Chapter 4 below discusses Daniel's involvement in staging *The Vision*.

72 This was notably a feature of Inigo Jones's designs. See, for example, the design for Tethys or a nymph (the part played by Anna of Denmark), 1610; Henrietta Maria as Chloris; and the Isaac Oliver miniature of a lady dressed as Flora, early seventeenth century. See Stephen Orgel and Roy Strong, *Inigo*

Jones: *The Theatre of the Stuart Court*, 2 vols (London: Sotheby Parke Bernet, 1973).

73 Dedication to Stafford's *Niobe: or His Age drown'd in her owne teares* (London, 1611). Robert Harding at Maggs Brothers generously gave me sight of these lines and the information on which this paragraph is based. Private correspondence 17 July 2011. Of the three surviving dedications, we know about two: the only intact one is in a private collection, and the other is a partly mutilated copy at the Bodleian Library, Oxford, BOD 8°S14(2) Art.

74 *Essays*, 'On Judging Someone Else's Death', 690.

75 See *The Diaries of Lady Anne Clifford*, ed. D. J. H. Clifford (Stroud: Sutton, 2003), 43.

76 Spence, 190–1, lists the books in the Triptych.

77 John Donne, *Biathanatos*, ed. Ernest W. Sullivan II (London: University of Delaware Press, 1984).

78 Clifford, *The Memoir*, 141, entries of 26 and 27 July 1617.

79 Ibid., 259, for Edward Rainbow, Bishop Carlisle's funeral sermon.

80 Findlay, Hodgson-Wright and Williams, *Women and Dramatic Production*, 7.

81 Mary Ellen Lamb, *Gender and Authorship in the Sidney Circle* (Madison: University of Wisconsin Press, 1990), 119.

82 Findlay, *Playing Spaces*, 30; *Antonius* (V.2022).

83 *Cleopatra* (1607), sigs H5v, K1r.

84 Clifford, *The Memoir*, 'Introduction', ed. Acheson, 28–9.

85 Daniel, *Philotas*, 36–9.

86 Pitcher, 'Negotiating', 770.

87 Woudhuysen, *Circulation of Manuscripts*, 240.

88 Rees, *Samuel Daniel*, 123.

89 R. A. Foakes, 'Tragedy at the Children's Theatres after 1600: A Challenge to the Adult Stage', in *The Elizabethan Theatre II*, ed. David Galloway (Toronto: Macmillan, 1970), 39. John Pitcher kindly brought this to my attention.

90 I am grateful to René Weis for his comments on my work. See Henry Peacham, 'Enter Tamora pleadinges for her sonnes going to execution', Longleat House, Wiltshire, PO/ Vol. I: 1516–1612, item 54.

91 Spence, 40–58.

92 Clifford, *Diaries*, 37, 47.

93 Ibid., 62.

94 Ibid., 35, 60–4.

95 Ibid., 34.

96 Ibid., 99.

97 Clifford, *The Memoir*, 14; Lamb, 'Agency', 349.

98 See Keir Elam's important study, *Shakespeare's Pictures: Visual Objects in the Drama* (London: Bloomsbury Arden Shakespeare, 2017), 29.

99 Davidson and Stevenson, 'Elizabeth I's Reception', 224–5.

100 See Chapter 2 above for the Tacitean idea of obscurity. If everything in the portrait is carefully staged, then a ring visible on the fourth finger of the sitter's raised right arm would also be included for some deliberate reason. We know that the wearing of rings held a special symbolism in portraiture of the period. We can only speculate, but if the sitter is Clifford then it may be one of the rings she refers to in her *Diary*, see, for example, 35.

101 For use of miniatures in portraits, see Graham Reynolds, 'The Painter Plays the Spider', *Apollo*, April 1964, 279–84.

102 Clare McManus, *Women on the Renaissance Stage* (Manchester: Manchester University Press, 2002), 130.

103 See Philip Mould Gallery, Historical Image Library, for the painting of Frances Howard. http://www.historicalportraits.com/Gallery.asp?Page=Item&ItemID=968&Desc=Duchess-of-Lennox-|-Marcus-Gheeraerts-the-Younger,-Circle-of.

104 Clifford, *Diaries*, 28, 77.

105 John Stephan Edwards, 'A New Portrait of Mary Rogers, Lady Harington', *British Art Journal* 12, no. 2 (2011): 54–7.

Chapter 4

1 The quotation used in the title is from Daniel's 1607 *Cleopatra*, sig. K7v. All references to *Cleopatra* in this chapter are to this edition unless otherwise stated.

To watch the performance of Daniel's *Tragedie of Cleopatra*, visit: https://vimeo.com/bloomsburymethuendrama/review/302836585/f61cac9e5d.

The performance was generously supported by the UCL Centre for Early Modern Exchanges and sponsored by the UCL Grand Challenge of Intercultural Interaction; The Malone Society; Oxford Journals: *Music and Letters*; Goodenough College; UCL European Institute; UCL Faculty of Arts and Humanities, including FIGS (the Faculty Institute of Graduate Studies); UCL English Department and the UCLU Drama Society. It was preceded by a UCL Early Modern Exchanges seminar 'Women and Drama' in February 2013, chaired by Helen Hackett, with speakers Alison Findlay, Marion Wynne-Davies, Yasmin Arshad and Emma Whipday. See Yasmin Arshad, Helen Hackett and Emma Whipday, 'Daniel's Cleopatra and Lady Anne Clifford: From a Jacobean Portrait to Modern Performance', *Early Theatre* 18, no. 2 (2015): 167–86. See the *Staging Cleopatra* project blog, Arshad and Whipday, http://thetragedieofcleopatra.wordpress.com.

2 See Chapter 3 on the changing scholarly view about the performability of closet drama.

3 The performance has received the following reviews: Mary Ellen Lamb, 'Play and DVD Reviews: *The Tragedie of Cleopatra*', *Early Modern Women* 9, no. 2 (Spring 2015): 148–52; Marion Wynne-Davies, 'Review of Samuel Daniel's *Tragedie of Cleopatra*' (directed by Emma Whipday for the UCL Centre for Early Modern Exchanges) at the Great Hall, Goodenough College, London, 3 March 2013, *Shakespeare* 12, no. 4 (2016): 443–7, doi: 10.1080/17450918.2013.833982; Derek Dunne, 'Play Review: *The Tragedie of Cleopatra*', *Cahiers Élisabéthains* 83 (Spring 2013): 43–4.

4 Confirmed in email correspondence with Alison Findlay and Margaret Hannay, 13 December 2010 and 4 June 2011 respectively.

5 See Yasmin Arshad, 'Bursary Funded Research: Staging Daniel's *Cleopatra*', 9 October 2013, malonesociety.com/2013/10/09/bursary-funded-research-staging-daniels-cleopatra/; and, '*Tragedie of Cleopatra* – The Premiere?', 26 February 2013, http://bloggingshakespeare.com/tragedie-of-cleopatra-the-premiere.

6 For example, Peter W. M. Blayney, *A New History of Early English Drama*, ed. John D. Cox and David Scott Kastan (New York: Columbia University Press, 1996), does not include *Antonius* or *Cleopatra*.

7 See Chapter 3 for the various performances and the scholars involved. The special issue of *Early Modern Theatre* 18, no. 2 (2015) looked at performances of plays written, translated and commissioned by women. Regarding men's closet drama, Shakespeare's Globe staged a reading of *Philotas* in 2003 and of selected scenes presented by the Edward's Boys company in September 2018. However, as discussed below, *Philotas* is the only closet drama known to have been publicly performed in its time.

8 See Chapter 5 for Daniel's influence on Shakespeare, and Chapters 2 and 3 for Mary Sidney and Anne Clifford.

9 See for example, Williamson, *Infinite Variety*, 134; Witherspoon, *Influence of Robert Garnier*, 99; and Seronsy, *Samuel Daniel*, 45.

10 The Great Hall at Goodenough College, a postgraduate residence, was built the 1930s in the Jacobethan style. It is where royalty and foreign ambassadors are entertained when visiting Goodenough. http://events.goodenough.ac.uk/function-rooms/the-great-hall.

11 See Chapter 3.

12 A presentation was also made at the UCL Festival of the Arts in April 2013.

13 The discussion of hidden performance cues in this and the following paragraph is closely based on actor-director Philip Bird's generous email exchange with me on 11 February 2013 and 26 August 2018. Bird's workshop for our actors is discussed later in the chapter.

14 Ibid., Bird, email correspondence, 26 August 2018.

15 Seronsy, *Samuel Daniel*, 46, notes that *Cleopatra* 'possesses a surprising amount of variety and stage action for a play of its kind'.

16 Propertius, *Elegies*, 3.11. 39.

17 Munro, *Children of the Queen's Revels*, 138.

18 See the *Apology* in *Philotas*, 156. See Chapters 2 and 3 above.

19 See Chapter 3.

20 John Pitcher, 'Samuel Daniel's Masque *The Vision of the Twelve Goddesses*: Texts and Payments', *MaRDiE* 26 (2013): 17–42 (32).

21 Pitcher, *Daniel, Samuel*, para. 15.

22 See Chapter 3 above.

23 *Cleopatra* in *Certaine Small Workes* (London, 1607), STC (2nd ed.) 6240, BL C.34.a.46, was used as our copy-text. I also used *The Tragedie of Cleopatra: nach dem Drucke von 1611*, ed. M. Lederer, *Materialien zur Kunde des älteren Englischen Dramas von W. Bang; Bd.31* (1911; rpt., Louvain: Uystpruyst, 1969), since the portrait's inscription comes from the 1607 edition or the reprint based on this.

24 Lukas Erne, *Shakespeare as Literary Dramatist* (2003; rpt., Cambridge: CUP, 2013), 196, 216–18. Looking at variant texts of *Romeo and Juliet, Henry V* and *Hamlet*, Erne contends that Shakespeare produced longer, more literary texts for readers, which were abridged for theatrical performance.

25 At my discussion of this point at the Shakespeare Institute's 'Reanimating Playbooks' symposium, in May 2013, Martin Wiggins interestingly observed that the play is written in a kind of 'complex double helix of sense and rhyme scheme', and that 'the two don't always coincide; the rhyme beats away beneath the surface without necessarily imposing itself on the conscious mind' since what one is listening to is the sense. This double helix made it difficult to cut without disrupting either. Email correspondence, 23 May 2013.

26 We know that commercial playhouses and touring companies at the time followed this practice. See Peter H. Greenfield, 'Touring', in *A New History of Early English Drama*, ed. John D. Cox and David Scott Kastan (New York: Columbia UP, 1996), 260.

27 Jenny Tiramani, 'Exploring Early Modern Stage and Costume Design', in *Shakespeare's Globe: A Theatrical Experiment*, ed. Christie Carson and Farah Karim-Cooper (Cambridge: CUP, 2008), 58. For a view of the contested definitions and debate surrounding 'original practices', see Alan C. Dessen, '"Original Practices" at the Globe: A Theatre Historian's View', in *Shakespeare's Globe: A Theatrical Experiment*, ed. Christie Carson and Farah Karim-Cooper (Cambridge: CUP, 2008), 45–51.

28 Tiramani, 'Costume Design', 58, 60.

29 Farah Karim-Cooper, 'Props', in *Shakespeare and the Making of Theatre*, ed. Stuart Hampton-Reeves and Bridget Escolme (Basingstoke: Palgrave, 2012), 91.

30 The idea for this workshop came from my attendance at the Globe's 'Gesture Lab' on 5–7 November 2010, exploring gesture and movement on the early modern stage. The workshop with Goodman was held on 27 January 2013. Eleanor Lowe kindly introduced me to Goodman.

31 The workshop with Bird was held on 10 February 2013. Farah Karim-Cooper kindly facilitated this.

32 See Chapter 3 above for Clifford's masque performances. Sackville's known masquing and cognate appearances are: *Prince Henry's Barriers* and a tilt for the Prince's creation in 1610; *The Caversham Entertainment* and *The Masque of Squires* in 1613; he was also a participant in the tilt for the Somersets' wedding in 1614; and in the Accession Day Tilt in 1620. Information kindly supplied by Martin Wiggins, email correspondence, 17 March 2013.

33 Quoted in Pitcher, '*The Vision*', 35. The letter, dated 23 December 1603, was written from Hampton Court two weeks before the masque performance.

34 Christopher Marsh, *Music and Society in Early Modern England* (Cambridge: CUP, 2010), 14, 16.

35 Samuel Daniel signed his name as 'Daniel' whereas John used 'Danyel'. I use 'Danyel' as the preferred spelling for John's last name, since he is known by this tag in the music world.

36 *Elizabeth I*, dir. Tom Hooper, written by Nigel Williams (Channel 4 TV, 2005). Permission kindly granted by Angels the Costumiers.

37 In a letter addressed 'To the right honorable my very good uncle the Earle of Shrewsbury' dated 18 December 1603, in *The Letters of Arbella Stuart*, ed. Sara Jayne Steen (New York: OUP, 1994), 197. Pitcher, '*The Vision*', 32.

38 Peacham, 'Enter Tamora'; Philip Henslowe, Diary and Account Book, 1592–1609, *Henslowe-Alleyn Digitisation Project* MSS7, http://www.henslowe-alleyn.org.uk/catalogue/MSS-7.html.

39 See, for example, *Henry Wriothesley, 3rd Earl of Southampton*, c.1600, http://www.npg.org.uk/collections/search/portrait/

mw05918/Henry-Wriothesley-3rd-Earl-of-Southampton?LinkID=mp04202&role=sit&rNo=0.

40 Findlay, *Playing Spaces*, 90.

41 The 2014 production of *Antony and Cleopatra* at the Globe, starring Clive Wood and Eve Best, made similar costuming choices, with Roman officers in black Jacobean dress.

42 Findlay, *Playing Spaces*, 90.

43 *Rosa* was selected by Sam Brown, without his having any familiarity with the story of Rosamond Clifford or Daniel's poem. Email correspondence, 2 July 2014.

44 See Pitcher, *Negotiating*, 780.

45 The idea of exploring the collaboration between the Daniel brothers, which came out of the *Cleopatra* production, led to my co-producing 'Samuel Daniel and John Danyel: An Evening of Music and Poetry' at the Britten Theatre on 10 September 2015, and co-organizing the 'Samuel Daniel, Poet and Historian' Conference held at the Royal College of Music, London, 10–11 September 2015, both with John Pitcher.

46 The discussion of the music in this paragraph is closely based on conversations with Sam Brown and email correspondence, 6 November 2013.

47 Email correspondence with Philip Bird, 3 March 2013.

48 See, for example, Cadman, 'Daniel's *Philotas*', 374–5. See Munro, *Children of the Queen's Revels*, 140.

49 Rees, *Samuel Daniel*, 61.

50 Wormald, 'James VI and I', 189.

51 Ibid., 190, quoted from Osborne, 217. The idea of the horse leech as an emblem of greed comes from the Bible, Proverb 30.15: 'The horseleach hath two daughters, *crying*, Give, give.'

52 Email correspondence with Philip Bird, 11 February 2013.

53 The UCL Academy workshop was held in February 2013. See n. 25 above for 'Reanimating Playbooks' symposium.

54 That this indentation is deliberate is supported by the fact that this does not occur often in the play-text.

55 See Chapter 3.

56 For detail of how the space worked in performance, see Arshad, Hackett, Whipday, 'From a Jacobean Portrait to Modern Performance', 179–80. For the Great Hall, see Robert Sackville-West, *Knole: Kent* (1998; rpt., Swindon: National Trust, 2011).

57 Portrait of Elizabeth II, by Henry Mee. Purchased by Goodenough College in 1987.

58 Portrait of Thomas Sackville, 1st Earl of Dorset (1536–1608), attributed to John De Critz. Edward, 4th Earl of Dorset (1589–1652), attributed to the Studio of Sir Anthony van Dyck.

59 See, for example, Clifford, *Diaries*, 92.

60 Lamb, 'Review: *Cleopatra*', 148–52.

61 Richard Brathwaite, The *English Gentlewoman* (London, 1631), 44, 48.

62 North, Stiff and Waters were interviewed on 14 March 2013; Gallagher on 6 June 2013; and Eyre on 22 May 2014. The Interview with North post-Knole was conducted on 8 July 2014.

63 Kerrigan, *Motives of Woe*, 55.

Chapter 5

1 The quotation used in the chapter title is from Enobarbus's description of Cleopatra, in *Antony and Cleopatra*, ed. John Wilders (1995; rpt., London: Arden, 2006). All further references are to this edition, unless otherwise stated.

2 See Wilders, 1; Bevington, 1; Martin Wiggins and Catherine Richardson, *British Drama: 1533–1642: A Catalogue: Volume V, 1603–1608* (Oxford: OUP, 2015), 325. See James Shapiro, *William Shakespeare and the Year of Lear* (London: Faber and Faber, 2015).

3 Adelman, *Common Liar*, 29, 45.

4 Eggert, *Showing Like a Queen*, 140.

5 A. C. Bradley, *Oxford Lectures on Poetry* (London: Macmillan, 1920), 299.

6 Eggert, *Showing Like a Queen*, 7; Kahn, *Roman Shakespeare*, 138.

7 See, for example, Christopher Pelling, 'The Triumviral Period', in *The Cambridge Ancient History*, 2nd edn, ed. Alan K. Bowman, Edward Champlin and Andrew Linnot (Cambridge: CUP, 1996), 1–69. I discuss the extraordinary tendency of classical historians to cite Shakespeare in the Epilogue.

8 Bevington, 1. Spevack, 379–80, notes that *Pericles* went into a second edition in the same year and, since no prosecution charges were brought, this indicates that it was published with Blount's permission.

9 Peter W. M. Blayney, *The First Folio of Shakespeare* (Washington, DC: Folger Shakespeare Library, 1991), 19–20.

10 Ibid., 21.

11 W. W. Greg, *A Bibliography of the English Printed Drama to the Restoration. Vol. 1, Stationers' Records, Plays to 1616: Nos. 1–349* (London: Bibliographical Society, 1939). I am grateful to Martin Wiggins and H. R. Woudhuysen for their guidance on the delay in publication. Email correspondence 29 September 2015 and 30 September 2015, respectively.

12 The lost plays that had an entry date were printed within the year, not altering the overall result.

13 Blayney, 'Playbooks', 383–4.

14 Erne, *Literary Dramatist*, 7, 127. The three other plays Erne refers to as appearing in print in 1600 are: *Much Ado About Nothing*; *A Midsummer Night's Dream* and *The Merchant of Venice*. See Blayney, 'Playbooks', 396–7 for the concept of 'authority'.

15 W. W. Greg, *Some Aspects and Problems of London Publishing Between 1550 and 1650* (Oxford: Clarendon, 1956), 121–2, forwards the theory originally suggested by A. C. Pollard in *Shakespeare's Folios and Quartos: A Study in the Bibliography of Shakespeare's Plays 1594–1685* (London: Methuen, 1909).

16 Wiggins, email correspondence, 29 September 2015.

17 Marta Straznicky, ed., *Shakespeare's Stationers: Studies in Cultural Bibliography* (Philadelphia: University of Pennsylvania Press, 2013), Appendix B, 235; Emma Smith, *The Making of*

Shakespeare's First Folio (Oxford: Bodleian, 2015), 115. I am grateful to John Pitcher for his generous discussion of Blount. Private conversation, 12 October 2015.

18 Blayney, *First Folio*, 21.

19 Spevack, 397.

20 Blayney, 'Playbooks', 388.

21 Daniel, *Certaine Small Poems Lately Printed* (London, 1605); *The Tragedie of Philotas* (London, 1607).

22 Greville, 93.

23 Bullough, 214–17, Shapiro, *1606*, 263–5.

24 Leeds Barroll, *Politics, Plague and Shakespearian Theatre: The Stuart Years* (Ithaca, NY: Cornell UP, 1995), 173, shows that the theatres were fully open for 20 months and partially open for 11 months out of the 94-month period.

25 John Russell Brown, *Shakespeare: Antony and Cleopatra: A Casebook* (London: Macmillan, 1968), 12–13.

26 There is some circumstantial evidence suggesting that *AC* was possibly performed in late 1606 or early 1607. The play appears to have influenced Barnabe Barnes's *The Devil's Charter*, staged at court by the King's Men in February 1607 and printed later that year. Barnes references the 'aspicks' brought to kill the two sleeping princes as '*Cleopatræs* birds' (ll. 2547–8), and echoes Shakespeare's repeated use of 'Nilus's slime'. This, combined with the fact that the asps are applied to the breast as in Shakespeare, and not to the arm as in Plutarch, suggests that Barnes might have seen the play or had access to it. As mentioned in the Introduction, this alternative tradition about Cleopatra's death was prominent in art, although it had not featured in the English Cleopatra plays.

27 Spevack, 758; Neill, 24.

28 Sara Munson Deats, 'Shakespeare's Anamorphic Drama: A Survey of *Antony and Cleopatra* in Criticism, on Stage, and on Screen', in *New Critical Essays*, 35.

29 Weis, lxix. I discuss Dryden briefly in the Epilogue.

30 Erne, *Literary Dramatist*, 45.

31 Frank Kermode, *Shakespeare's Language* (New York: Farrar, Straus and Giroux, 2000), vii, 3–8.

32 Samuel Taylor Coleridge, *Shakespeare Criticism*, ed. T. M. Raysor, 2 vols (1930; rpt., New York: Dutton, 1960), 76–9.

33 Wiggins and Richardson, *British Drama*, 329.

34 For staging difficulties, see Wilders, 4; Neill, 24; Deats, 'Anamorphic Drama', 34. For the list of speaking parts, see Wiggins and Richardson, *British Drama*, 327. See also Andrew Gurr, *The Shakespearean Stage 1574–1642* (Cambridge: CUP, 2009), 113–14, who believes that probably the same boy played Lady Macbeth and Cleopatra. Boy actors were taken on by the adult companies at 11–12 years of age to play female roles until their voice broke.

35 Andrew Dickson, 'Harriet Walter on *Antony and Cleopatra*: You Have to Play it Fast, or it Falls Apart', *The Guardian*, 4 January 2016, http://www.theguardian.com/stage/2016/jan/04/harriet-walter-on-antony-and-cleopatra-shakespeare-400-anniversary-interview.

36 Weis, lix, lxx–lxxxiii.

37 Richard Dutton, *Shakespeare Court Dramatist* (Oxford: OUP, 2016), 2–3, 81, 189–94. See also, Helen Hackett, 'Longer shall you gaze on't', review of W. R. Streitberger, *The Masters of the Revels and Elizabeth I's Court Theatre*, and Richard Dutton, *Shakespeare, Court Dramatist. Times Literary Supplement*, 28 October 2016, 7–8.

38 Erne, *Literary Dramatist*, 244.

39 Bullough, 239.

40 See Plutarch, 276, and compare to *AC*, 1.1.54–5, and 289 to *AC*, 1.3. Plutarch describes the fondness for going out at night in disguise as more Antony's interest.

41 See Plutarch, 272, and *AC*, 4.6.21–35. Adelman, *Common Liar*, 24.

42 See Plutarch, 277, and *AC*, 2.5.15–20; see 274, and *AC*, 2.2.224–5.

43 See Case, xxxi. See Bevington, 3–5; Wilders, 57–8.

44 Wilders, 61.

45 Shapiro, *1606*, 271.

46 Plutarch, 316.

47 Ibid., 274.

48 See Weis, xli. See Marguerite A. Tassi, 'O'erpicturing Apelles: Shakespeare's *Paragone* with Painting in *Antony and Cleopatra*', in *New Critical Essays*, 296. Apelles' Venus was mentioned in Pliny's *Natural History* translated by Philemon Holland in 1601, and it inspired Botticelli's and Titian's representations of Venus.

49 Case, xxxi.

50 Plutarch, 275.

51 Ibid., 273.

52 Ibid., 275; Neill, 13; Bevington, 4.

53 Wiggins and Richardson, *British Drama*, 329.

54 Willard Farnham, *Shakespeare's Tragic Frontier: The World of His Final Tragedies* (Berkeley: University of California Press, 1950), 155; Bullough, 229–31, 358–406; Spevack, 475–524.

55 Ernest Schanzer, '*Antony and Cleopatra* and the Countess of Pembroke's *Antonius*', *N&Q* 3, no. 4 (1956): 152–4. In order of the examples given, see the Argument to *Antonius*, ll. 3–4 and *AC*, 2.2.132–5; ll. 31–4 and 4.15.23–6; and *Antonius*, 3.1109–12 and *AC*, 3.11.35–40.

56 See *Antonius* 3.891, *AC* 4.14.19; *Antonius* 5.1963, *AC* 5.2.79. See Michael Steppat, 'Shakespeare's Response to Dramatic Tradition in *Antony and Cleopatra*', in *Shakespeare: Text, Language, Criticism: Essays in Honour of Marvin Spevack*, ed. Bernard Fabian and Kurt Tetzeli von Rosador (Hildesham and New York: Olms-Weidman, 1987), 255–79.

57 Mitsuharu Matsuoka, 'A Hyper-Concordance to the Works of Edmund Spenser', *The Victorian Literary Studies Archive*, 28 December 2003, http://victorian-studies.net/concordance/spenser/.

58 See *Antonius*, 1. 81, *AC* 1.2.125. See *Antonius* 3.890–5, 910, 920–32, compare to *AC*, 3.11, 4.12.16, and 3.13. See Steppat, 'Dramatic Tradition', 259.

59 *The Defence*, 112. 37–9.

60 Spenser, *The Faerie Queene*, V.5.20–6, 778–9.

61 Steppat, 'Dramatic Tradition', 262. Compare 1.8, 3.875, 1249 to *AC*, 4.14.27–33.

62 Spevack, 478.

63 See Chapter 1.

64 Sonnet 129, ll. 8–9, *Shakespeare's Sonnets*, ed. Katherine Duncan-Jones (1997; rpt., London: Arden, 2001), 260.

65 Bridget Escolme, *Emotional Excess on the Shakespearian Stage: Passion's Slaves* (London: Bloomsbury Arden Shakespeare, 2014), 155.

66 Ibid., 154–5.

67 Ibid., 155.

68 Norman, 'Daniel's *The Tragedie of Cleopatra* and *Antony and Cleopatra*', 11–18.

69 Shapiro, *1606*, 268; Bullough, 406–49; Spevack, 524–79. Bullough prints the 1599 *Cleopatra*, Spevack the 1594 edition. As in Chapter 2, the 'early *Cleopatra*' refers to the pre-1607 version, and all references here are to the 1599 edition.

70 Plutarch, 273.

71 Norman, 'Daniel's *The Tragedie of Cleopatra* and *Antony and Cleopatra*', 18.

72 In order of examples given see *AC*, 4.15.51, and Cleopatra, sig. B4r; see *Cleopatra* sig. C2r; and *AC*, 1.5.23 and sig. B3r.

73 Plutarch, 314.

74 Bullough, 235–7; Norman, 'Daniel's *The Tragedie of Cleopatra* and *Antony and Cleopatra*', 11–18.

75 Plutarch, 313–14, is a shared source for both writers, but there is no sense of the power play or use of the word 'rise', or 'toys'. Plutarch emphasizes Cleopatra's pitiful state.

76 Stanley Wells, *Shakespeare, Sex, & Love* (Oxford: OUP, 2010), 213.

77 Plutarch, 275.

78 Bullough, 237–8; Spevack, 530–1.

79 Holger Norgaard, 'Shakespeare, and Daniel's "Letter from Octavia"', *N&Q* 200 (1955): 56–7; Steppat, 'Dramatic Tradition', 531.

80 See Chapter 2.

81 This was suggested to me by John Pitcher. Private conversation, 12 October 2015.

82 Prudence J. Jones, *Cleopatra A Sourcebook* (Norman: University of Oklahoma Press, 2006).

83 See Introduction nn. 54–7 above.

84 Nashe, *The anatomie of absurditie*, sig. A4v.

85 William Painter, *The Palace of Pleasure* (London, 1566); Robinson, *A golden mirrour*; and Darell, *A Short Discourse*; Greene, *Ciceronis amor*; Gascoigne, *A hundreth sundrie flowres*.

86 Rankins, *The English Ape*, sig. B1v.

87 Kahn, *Roman Shakespeare*, 112.

88 Philemon Holland, *Plutarch's The Morals* (London, 1603), 1286–1319. See also *AC*, 3.6.18, where Caesar criticizes Cleopatra for appearing 'In th'habiliments of the goddess Isis'. I am grateful to Edward Chaney for pointing this line out.

89 Ben Jonson, *The Alchemist*, ed. Elizabeth Cook (London: Bloomsbury, 2010), 2.3.203.

90 See, for example, Loomba, *Shakespeare, Race, and Colonialism*. For Afro-centric readings, see MacDonald, *Women and Race in Early Modern Texts*; Hall, *Things of Darkness*; Francesca T. Royster, *Becoming Cleopatra: The Shifting Image of an Icon* (Basingstoke: Palgrave, 2003); and Carol Chillington Rutter, *Enter the Body: Women and Representation on Shakespeare's Stage* (London: Routledge, 2001). For an alternative view of Cleopatra's race, see Aebischer, 'Properties of Whiteness', 236–8.

91 Case, xxvii.

92 Ernest Schanzer, 'Daniel's Revision of His *Cleopatra*', *RES* 8, no. 37 (1957): 375–81 (375).

93 Leavenworth, *Daniel's Cleopatra*, 101–2, 108–9.

94 Curran, 'Shakespeare and Daniel Revisited', 318–20.

95 Warren Boutcher, *The School of Montaigne in Early Modern Europe: Volume Two: The Reader-Writer* (Oxford: OUP, 2017), 258–72.

96 Warren Boutcher, 'Shakespeare's Montaigne or Daniel's Montaigne? The King's Commonwealth and the *Queen's Arcadia*', Abstract, Samuel Daniel Poet and Historian Conference, London, 10–11 September 2015.

97 Daniel, *A Defence of Ryme*, in *A Panegerikye Congratulatorie* (London, 1603), sig. H6v.

98 1611 Dedication to Mary Sidney, sig. E3v.

99 Michael Dobson, *The Making of the National Poet: Shakespeare, Adaptation, and Authorship, 1660–1769* (Oxford: Clarendon, 1992).

100 Bevington, 266.

101 Lisa Hopkins, *The Cultural Uses of the Caesars on the English Renaissance Stage* (Ashgate: Farnham, 2008), 2.

102 H. Neville Davies, 'Jacobean *Antony and Cleopatra*', in *New Casebooks: Antony and Cleopatra*, ed. John Drakakis (Basingstoke: Macmillan, 1994), 128.

103 Ibid. See Ben Jonson, 'The Speech', in *His part of King James his royall and magnificent entertainement through his honorable cittie of London* (1604), sig. E1v.

104 Wormald, 'James VI and I', 189–90.

105 Ibid., 111, n. 75, *PRO. SP* 14/8/93.

106 Quoted in Davies, 'Jacobean *Antony and Cleopatra*', 130.

107 Dobson and Watson, *England's Elizabeth*, 46.

108 Ibid., 50.

109 Yuichi Tsukada, 'Shakespeare and the Politics of Nostalgia: Negotiating the memory of Elizabeth I on the Jacobean Stage' (unpublished PhD thesis, King's College London 2015), 103. I am grateful to Tsukada for letting me have sight of his chapter '*Antony and Cleopatra*: The Competition for Representing the Queen'.

110 A discussion of these plays is provided in Dobson and Watson, *England's Elizabeth*, 50–60; and Tsukada, 'Politics of Nostalgia', 102–7.

111 Watkins, *Representing Elizabeth*, 36.

112 Tacitus, *The Annals of Imperial Rome*, XIV, 29–39, in Frénée-Hutchins, *Boudica's Odyssey*, 21.

113 Helen Morris, 'Queen Elizabeth I "Shadowed" in Cleopatra', *HLQ* 32, no. 3 (1969): 271–8.

114 May, *Elizabeth I: Selected Works*, 78–83.

115 Ibid., 55, 59, 62.

116 Dobson and Watson, *England's Elizabeth*, 54.

117 Davies, 'Jacobean *Antony and Cleopatra*', 137, 145; Shapiro, *1606*, 295–9.

118 Lisa S. Starks, '"Immortal Longings": The Erotics of Death in *Antony and Cleopatra*', in *New Critical Essays*, 251. See also Morris, 'Elizabeth I "Shadowed"', 276–7.

119 Gajda, *Earl of Essex*, 268.

120 The above poem, inscribed at All Hallowes Church in London, is quoted in Julia M. Walker, 'Bones of Contention: Posthumous Images of Elizabeth and Stuart Politics', in *Dissing Elizabeth: Negative Representations of Gloriana*, ed. Julia M. Walker (Durham, NC: Duke University Press, 1998), 260. The inscription's date is unknown. It was recorded in John Stow's *Survey of London* (1633), originally published in 1598 (reprinted 1603), and expanded in the 1618 edition (SR 2 November 1613) to record inscriptions on tombs.

121 Eggert, *Showing Like a Queen*, 151.

122 Ibid.

123 Julia M. Walker, *The Elizabeth Icon: 1603–2003* (Basingstoke: Palgrave, 2004), 31–2.

124 Tsukada, 'Politics of Nostalgia', 96.

125 Pettegree, 50–1.

Epilogue

1 This well-known quotation of Elizabeth's is from her 12 November 1586 speech to Parliament, *Selected Works*, 65. Although she was referring to the critical eyes that were always on her, and to the performative nature of monarchy, these words also apply to Cleopatra who is among the historical figures whose story has been most judged and most often set on the stage.

2 Susanne Woods, *Lanyer: A Renaissance Woman Poet* (Oxford: OUP, 1999), 33–6.

3 A. L. Rowse, *Shakespeare's Sonnets: The Problems Solved. A Modern Edition with Prose versions, Introduction and Notes*, 2nd edn (London: Macmillan, 1973), xxxv–viii; René Weis, *Shakespeare Revealed: A Biography* (London: John Murray, 2007), 148–9.

4 Lanyer, *Salve Deus*. All references are to this edition. The reference to Matilda, who was pursued by King John, might be to Drayton's *Matilda* (1594), one of the complaints that followed Daniel's *Rosamond*.

5 Elizabeth Cary, *The Tragedy of Mariam 1613* (London: Malone Society Reprints, 1914/92).

6 Cleopatra appeared in other plays in the period which are not discussed here as being beyond the scope of this book. These are: Philip Massinger and John Fletcher's *The False One* (*c*.1620), which focused on earlier aspects of the story and the betrayal of Pompey by his officer, and featured Julius Caesar and Cleopatra; Katherine Philips' *Pompey. A Tragedy* (1663), a translation of Corneille's *La Mort de Pompéé* (Paris, 1644); and William Davenant's farce, *The Play House to be Let* (*c*.1663), in which Cleopatra appears in Act 5.

7 Thomas May, *The Tragedie of Cleopatra Queen of Ægypt* (London, 1639), sigs B7v, C6v, Act IV.

8 David Norbrook, 'Lucan, Thomas May and the Creation of a Republican Literary Culture', in *Culture and Politics in Early Stuart England*, ed. Kevin Sharpe and Peter Lake (Basingstoke: Macmillan, 1994), 45–66; Pettegree, 68.

9 Charles Sedley, *Antony and Cleopatra* (London, 1676), Newberry Library, Chicago, Y135S4572. See also Case, xxxviii.

10 Bevington, 44.

11 John Dryden, *All for Love, or, The World Well Lost* (London, 1678). All references are to this edition, except for the preface, which is quoted from the 1696 edition.

12 All examples from Daniel are from the 1607 *Cleopatra*, but these also occur in earlier editions. In order of examples given: see *All for Love*, sig. C4r and *Cleopatra*, sig. G5v; *All for Love*, sig. L2v and *Cleopatra*, sig. H3v; and *All for Love*, sig. L3v and *Cleopatra*, sig. K6v.

13 Bodleian Library, Oxford University, Rawlinson MS Poet. 16.
14 Jane Cavendish and Elizabeth Brackley, *The Concealed Fancies* (c.1645), in *Renaissance Drama by Women: Texts and Documents*, ed. S. P. Cerasano and Marion Wynne-Davies (London: Routledge, 1996), 127–9. All references are to this text.
15 Lisa Hopkins and Barbara MacMahon, '"Come, what, a siege?": Metarepresentation in Lady Jane Cavendish and Lady Elizabeth Brackley's *The Concealed Fancies*', *Early Modern Literary Studies* 16, no. 3 (2013): 1–17 (4).
16 Cavendish and Brackley, *Concealed Fancies*, 211, n. 38.
17 Hopkins and MacMahon, 'Come, what, a siege?', 5.
18 See Aebischer, 'Properties of Whiteness', 222, 237.
19 Blayney, 'Playbooks', 387–8.
20 R. G. M. Nisbet and Margaret Hubbard, *A Commentary on Horace Odes Book I* (1970; rpt., Oxford: Clarendon, 1975), 411.
21 W. W. Tarn and M. P. Charlesworth, 'The Triumvirs'; 'The war of the East against the West'; 'The triumph of Octavian', in *The Cambridge Ancient History*, 1st edn, vol. 10, ed. S. A. Cook, F. E. Adcock and M. P. Charlesworth (1930; rpt., Cambridge: CUP, 1934), 111. See Pelling, 'The Triumviral Period', 63. See also Wyke, *Roman Mistress*, 197; and Joyce Tyldesley, *Cleopatra: Last Queen of Egypt* (Perseus: New York, 2008), 258.
22 See John Russell Brown for Anna Jameson, in *Antony and Cleopatra: A Casebook*, 35.
23 Escolme, *Emotional Excess*, 148–9, provides a detailed discussion of Suzman's production at the 2012 Chichester Festival Theatre.
24 This list is cited in and expanded by Giuseppe Pucci, 'Every Man's Cleopatra', in *Cleopatra: A Sphinx Revisited*, ed. Margaret M. Miles (Berkeley: University of California Press, 2013), 195.
25 Bernard Shaw, *Caesar and Cleopatra* (Penguin: London, 2006). Ahmad Shawqi, *The Death of Cleopatra: Maṣrā Kiliyūpātrā*, trans. Jeanette W. S. Attiya (Cairo: Anglo-Egyptian Bookshop, 2006).

26 Rafik Darragi, 'Ideological Appropriation and Sexual Politics: Shakespeare's *Antony and Cleopatra*, and Ahmed Shawky's *Masra' Cleopatra*', in *Shakespeare's World/World Shakespeare: The Selected Proceedings of the International Shakespeare Association World Congress, Brisbane, 2006*, ed. Richard Fartheringham, Christina Johnson and R. S. White (Newark: University of Delaware Press, 2006), 361.

27 Adrian Goldsworthy, *Antony and Cleopatra* (New Haven, CT: Yale UP, 2010); Roller, *Cleopatra* (2010); and Stacy Schiff, *Cleopatra: A Life* (New York: Little, Brown and Company, 2010).

28 The cities are Bonn, 2011, http://www.bundeskunsthalle.de/en/exhibitions/cleopatra.html; Los Angeles, 2012, http://www.discoverlosangeles.com/blog/cleopatra-exhibition; Rome, 2013–14, http://www.romahouse.com/event/cleopatra-roma-e-lincantesimo-dellegitto/; Tokyo, 2015, http://www.tnm.jp/modules/r_free_page/index.php?id=1714&lang=en; and Singapore, 2015, http://sagg.info/singapore-pinacotheque-de-paris-opens-may-2015/.

Appendix

1 Curran, 'Love, Triumph', 107, 114, 119; Haskell and Penny, *Taste for the Antique*, 184–7.

2 Haskell and Penny, *Taste for the Antique*, 13.

3 Ibid., 186.

4 Curran, 'Love, Triumph', 116.

5 Ibid.

6 See Chapter 2.

7 'Pembrokes Arcadia: "Delicious Wilton ... that Arbour of the Muses"', *British Art Journal* 14, no. 3 (2013/14): 9–20 (14).

8 Clifford, *The Diaries*, 95–6.

SELECT BIBLIOGRAPHY

Primary sources

Manuscripts

London, British Library, Henry Cuffe. *Aphorisms gathered out of the life and out of that most noble Robert Earle of Essex*, BL Harley MS 1327.

London, University of London Library. *Instructions to a Secret Agent in France, circa 1595*, MS 187.

Printed books

Albertus, Saint Magnus. *The boke of secretes of Albertus*. S.l., 1560.

Averell, W. *A dyall for dainty darlings, rockt in the cradle of securitie*. London, 1584.

Batman, Stephen. *The golden booke of the leaden goddes*. London, 1577.

Boaistuau, Pierre. *Certaine secrete wonders of nature prophane*. London, 1569.

Boccaccio, Giovanni. *On Famous Women*. Translated by Guido A. Guarino. London: Italica, 1964.

Brathwaite, Richard. *The English gentlewoman*. London, 1631.

Bullein, William. *Bulleins bulwarke of defence*. London, 1579.

Cain, Thomas M. 'Elizabeth, Images of'. In *The Spenser Encyclopedia*, edited by A. C. Hamilton, 621–5. London: Routledge, 1991.

Cardano, Girolamo. *Cardanus comforte translated into Englishe*. London, 1573.

Cary, Elizabeth. *The Tragedy of Mariam 1613*. London: Malone Society Reprints, 1914/1992.

Castiglione, Baldassare. *The Courtier*. Translated by Sir Thomas Hoby. London, 1561.

Cavendish, Jane, and Elizabeth Brackley. *The Concealed Fancies*. In *Renaissance Drama by Women: Texts and Documents*, edited by S. P. Cerasano and Marion Wynne-Davies. 1996; rpt., London: Routledge, 1997.

Chaucer, Geoffrey. *The Legend of Good Women*. In *The Riverside Chaucer*, foreword by Christopher Cannon, 587–630. 3rd revised edn. Oxford: OUP, 2008.

Christie's. *Catalogue of Early English Portraits: The Property of Lady Capel Cure; Also Old Pictures & Drawings from Various Sources Nov. 20, 1931*. London: Christie's, 1931.

Christie's. *Catalogue of Old Pictures: The Properties of The Rt. Hon. The Earl of Southesk, Admiral Robert Hathorn Johnson Stewart ... and Others, July 23, 1948*. London: Christie's, 1948.

Clifford, Anne. *The Diaries of Lady Anne Clifford*. Edited by D. J. H. Clifford. 2003; rpt., Stroud: Sutton, 2009.

Clifford, Anne. *The Memoir of 1603 and The Diary of 1616–1619*. Edited by Katherine O. Acheson. Ontario: Broadview, 2007.

Coleridge, Samuel Taylor. *Shakespeare Criticism*. Edited by T. M. Raysor. 2 vols. 1930; rpt., New York: Dutton, 1960.

Cooper, Thomas. *Thesaurus lingua Romanae et Britannicae*. 1565; rpt., London, 1578.

D'Agostino, Taja. *Descrizione Del Palazzo Apostilico Vaticano*. Rome, 1750.

D'Anghiera, Pietro Martire. *The decades of the new worlde or west India*. Translated by Richard Eden. London, 1555.

Daniel, Samuel. *Certaine Small Poems lately printed, with the tragedie of Philotas*. London, 1605.

Daniel, Samuel. *Certaine Small Workes*. London, 1607. BL C.34.a.46.

Daniel, Samuel. *Certaine Small Workes*. London, 1611. 6243, BL C.34.a.1.

Daniel, Samuel. *The Civil Wars*. London, 1609.

Daniel, Samuel. *The Complaint of Rosamond*, in *Delia. Containing certaine sonnets: with the complaynt of Rosamond*. London, 1592.

Daniel, Samuel. *Delia and Rosamond augmented. Cleopatra*. London, 1594. BL C. 58.aa.14.

Daniel, Samuel. *A panegyrike congratulatory to the Kings Maiestie. Also certaine epistles*. London, 1603. BL C.116.1.f.1 (1).

Daniel, Samuel. *The Poeticall Essayes of Sam. Danyel*. London, 1599.

Daniel, Samuel. *The Tragedie of Cleopatra*, 1599. In *Narrative and Dramatic Sources of Shakespeare: Vol. V*. Edited by Geoffrey Bullough. London: Routledge and Kegan Paul, 1964.

Daniel, Samuel. *The Tragedie of Cleopatra: nach dem Drucke von 1611*. Edited by M. Lederer. In *Materialien zur Kunde des älteren Englischen Dramas von W. Bang; Bd.31*. 1911; rpt., Louvain: Uystpruyst, 1969.

Daniel, Samuel. *The Tragedy of Philotas*. Edited by Laurence Michel. 1949; rpt., New Haven: Yale University Press, 1970.

Dante Alighieri. *Inferno: A New Verse Translation*. Translated by Michael Palma. New York: Norton, 2002.

Darell, Walter. *A short discourse of the life of servingmen*. London, 1578.

Dekker Thomas. *Lanthorne and candle-light*. London, 1609.

Dent, Leonard. *Hillfields: Notes on the Contents*. London: The Author, 1972.

Donne, John. *Biathanatos*. Edited by Ernest W. Sullivan II. London: University of Delaware Press, 1984.

Dryden, John. *All for Love, or, The World Well Lost*. London, 1678.

Elizabeth I. *Elizabeth I: Collected Works*. Edited by Leah S. Marcus, Janel Mueller and Mary Beth Rose. Chicago: University of Chicago Press, 2000.

Elizabeth I. *Queen Elizabeth I: Selected Works*. Edited by Steven W. May. New York: Washington Square Press, 2004.

Elyot, Thomas. *Bibliotheca Eliotæ Eliotis librarie*. London, 1542.

Florio, John. *Worlde of Wordes*. London, 1598.

Fraunce, Abraham. *The Countess of Pembroke's Ivy Church*. London, 1591.

Fulbecke, William. *A booke of christian ethicks or moral philosophie*. London, 1587.

Fulke, William. *Praelictions upon the sacred and holy Reuelations of St. John*. London, 1573.

Garnier, Robert. *Les Tragedies de Robert Garnier*. Paris, 1585. BL 1073.d.6.

Garnier, Robert. *Two Tragedies: Hippolyte and Marc Antoine*. Edited by Christine M. Hill and Mary G. Morrison. London: Athlone Press, 1975.

Gascoigne, George. *A hundreth sundrie flowres*. London, 1573.

Gilpin, Bernard. *A godly sermon preached in the court at Greenwich*. London, 1581.

Greene, Robert. *Ciceronis amor· Tullies love*. London, 1589.
Greville, Fulke. *The Prose Works of Sir Fulke Greville, Lord Brooke*. Edited by John Gouws. Oxford: Clarendon, 1986.
Hurault, André, Sieur de Maisse. *A Journal of All That was Accomplished by Monsieur De Maisse Ambassador in England from King Henri IV to Queen Elizabeth Anno Domini 1597*. Translated and edited by G. B. Harrison and R. A. Jones. London: Nonesuch, 1931.
Jonson, Ben. *The Alchemist*. Edited by Elizabeth Cook. London: Bloomsbury, 2010.
Lanyer, Aemelia. *The Poems of Aemelia Lanyer: Salve Deus Rex Judæorum*. Edited by Susanne Woods. Oxford: OUP, 1993.
Lloyd, Lodowick. *The pilgrimage of princes*. London, c.1573.
Lodge, Thoma. *An alarum against usurers*. London, 1584.
Lydgate, John. *The serpent of division*. London, 1559.
May, Thomas. *The Tragedie of Cleopatra Queen of Ægypt*. London, 1639.
Montaigne, Michel de. *The Complete Essays*. Translated and edited by M. A. Screech. 1987; rpt., London: Penguin, 2003.
Mornay, Charlotte Arbaleste de. *A Huguenot Family in XVI century France: the memoirs of Philippe du Mornay, Souer du Plessis Marly*. Translated by Lucy Crump. London: Routledge, n.d.
Munday, Anthony. *A courtly controversie, betweene loove and learning*. London, 1581.
Münster, Sebastian. *A briefe collection and compendious extract of the straunge and memorable things*. London, 1572.
Nashe, Thomas. *The anatomie of absurditie*. London, 1589.
Nichols, John, ed. *The Progresses, Processions and Magnificent Festivities of King James the First*. London, 1828.
Painter, William. *The palace of pleasure*. London, 1566.
Plutarch. *Lives of the Noble Grecians and Romanes*. Translated by Sir Thomas North. In *Narrative and Dramatic Sources of Shakespeare: Vol. V*. Edited by Geoffrey Bullough, 254–318. London: Routledge and Kegan Paul, 1964.
Plutarch. *The Morals*. Translated by Philemon Holland. London, 1603.
Ralegh, Sir Walter. *The Discoverie of the Large, Rich, and Bewtiful empire of Guiana*. London, 1596.
Raleigh, Sir Walter. *Historie of the World*. London, 1614.
Rankins, William. *The English Ape*. London, 1588.
Robinson, Richard. *A golden mirrour conteining certaine pithie and figuratiue visions*. London, 1589.

Sedley, Charles. *Antony and Cleopatra*. London, 1676. Newberry Library, Chicago, Y13584572.

Shakespeare, William. *Antony and Cleopatra*. Edited by David Bevington. 1990; rpt., Cambridge: CUP, 2007.

Shakespeare, William. *Antony and Cleopatra*. Edited by Emrys Jones. Introduction by René Weis. London: Penguin, 2005.

Shakespeare, William. *Antony and Cleopatra*. Edited by Michael Neill. 1994; rpt., Oxford: OUP, 2008.

Shakespeare, William. *Antony and Cleopatra*. Edited by M. R. Ridley. Based on the 1906 Arden Shakespeare edition of R. H. Case. Cambridge, MA: Harvard UP, 1954.

Shakespeare, William. *Antony and Cleopatra*. Edited by John Wilders. London: Arden Shakespeare, 2006.

Shakespeare, William. *Antony and Cleopatra, A New Variorum Edition*. Edited by Marvin Spevack. New York: MLA, 1990.

Shakespeare, William. *King Lear*. Edited by R. A. Foakes. 1997; rpt., London: Bloomsbury Arden Shakespeare, 2016.

Shakespeare, William. *Macbeth*. Edited by Sandra Clark and Pamela Mason. London: Bloomsbury Arden Shakespeare, 2015.

Shakespeare, William. *Shakespeare's Sonnets*. Edited by Katherine Duncan-Jones. 1997; rpt., London: Arden, 2001.

Shaw, Bernard. *Caesar and Cleopatra*. London: Penguin, 2006.

Shawqi, Ahmad. *The Death of Cleopatra: Maṣrā Kiliyūpātrā*. Translated by Jeanette W. S. Attiya. Cairo: Anglo-Egyptian Bookshop, 2006.

Sidney, Mary, Countess of Pembroke. *The Collected Works of Mary Sidney Herbert, Countess of Pembroke, Volumes I and II*. Edited by Margaret P. Hannay, Noel J. Kinnamon and Michael G. Brennan. Oxford: Clarendon, 1998.

Sidney, Sir Philip. *An Apology for Poetry (or The Defence of Poesy)*. Edited by Geoffrey Shepherd, revised and expanded 3rd edn by R. W. Maslen. Manchester: Manchester University Press, 1989.

Sidney, Sir Philip. *The Countess of Pembrokes Arcadia*. London, 1605. Bodleian Library, Oxford, Juel-Jensen Sidney 13 (Lady Anne Clifford's copy with annotations in her own hand).

Sidney, Sir Philip. *The Major Works*. Edited by Katherine-Duncan Jones. 1989; rpt., Oxford: OUP, 2008.

Spenser, Edmund. *The Faerie Queene*. Edited by Thomas P. Roche, Jr. with C. Patrick O' Donnell, Jr. 1978; rpt., London: Penguin, 1987.

Spenser, Edmund. *The Shorter Poems*. Edited by Richard A. McCabe. London: Penguin, 1996.
Stafford, Antony. *Niobe: or His Age drown'd in her owne teares*. London, 1611.
Stapleton, Thomas. *A counterblast to M. Hornes vayne blaste against M. Fekeham*. London, 1561.
Stuart, Arbella. *The Letters of Arbella Stuart*. Edited by Sara Jayne Steen. New York: OUP, 1994.
Stubbs, John. *The Discovery of a Gaping Gulf*. London, 1579.
Tacitus, Cornelius. *Histories: Books 4–5. Annals: Books 1–3*. Translated by Clifford H. Moore and John Jackson. Cambridge, MA: Loeb Classical Library, Harvard UP, 1931.
Tacitus, Cornelius. *C. Cornelli Taciti Opera Quae Exstant*. Edited by Justius Lipsius. Antwerp, 1585. BL C.142. e.13 (Robert Sidney's copy with annotations in his own hand).
Thomas, William. *The Historie of Italie*. 1549; rpt., London, 1561.
Turberville, George. *Epitaphes, epigrams, songs and sonets*. London, 1567.
Wedderburn, Robert. *The Complaynt of Scotland*. Paris: s.n, *c*.1550.
Wentworth, Peter. *A pithie exhortation to her Majestie for establishing her successor to the crowne*. Edinburgh, 1598.

Secondary sources

Adelman, Janet. *The Common Liar: An Essay on Antony and Cleopatra*. New Haven: Yale University Press, 1973.
Aebischer, Pascale. 'The Properties of Whiteness: Renaissance Cleopatras from Jodelle to Shakespeare'. *Shakespeare Survey* 65 (2011): 221–38.
Alexander, Gavin. *Writing After Sidney: The Literary Response to Sir Philip Sidney, 1586–1640*. Oxford: OUP, 2006.
Arshad, Yasmin. 'Bursary Funded Research: Staging Daniel's *Cleopatra*', 9 October 2013. malonesociety.com/2013/10/09/bursary-funded-research-staging-daniels-cleopatra.
Arshad, Yasmin. 'The Enigma of a Portrait: Lady Anne Clifford and Daniel's *Cleopatra*'. *The British Art Journal* 11, no. 3 (2011): 30–6.
Arshad, Yasmin. '*Tragedie of Cleopatra* – The Premiere?', 26 February 2013. http://bloggingshakespeare.com/tragedie-of-cleopatra-the-premiere.

Arshad, Yasmin, Helen Hackett and Emma Whipday. 'Daniel's Cleopatra and Lady Anne Clifford: From a Jacobean Portrait to Modern Performance'. *Early Theatre* 18, no. 2 (2015): 167–86.

Arshad, Yasmin, and Emma Whipday. 'Staging Daniel's *Tragedie of Cleopatra* blog', 2012, http://thetragedieofcleopatra.wordpress.com.

Axton, Marie. *The Queen's Two Bodies: Drama and the Elizabethan Succession*. London: Royal Historical Society, 1977.

Barroll, Leeds. *Politics, Plague and Shakespearian Theatre: The Stuart Years*. Ithaca, NY: Cornell University Press, 1995.

Bate, Jonathan. *Soul of the Age: The Life, Mind and World of William Shakespeare*. London: Viking, 2008.

Beard, Mary. *The Roman Triumph*. Cambridge, MA: Harvard University Press, 2007.

Beard, Mary. *Women and Power: A Manifesto*. London: Profile, 2017.

Beer, Anna. *My Just Desire: The Life of Bess Ralegh, Wife of Sir Walter*. New York: Ballantine, 2003.

Belle, Marie-Alice, and Line Cottegnies, eds. 'Introduction'. In *Robert Garnier in Elizabethan England: Mary Sidney's Antonius and Thomas Kyd's Cornelia*, 1–84. Cambridge: MHRA, 2017.

Belsey, Catherine. *The Subject of Tragedy: Identity & Difference in Renaissance Drama*. London: Methuen, 1985.

Berger, Harry. 'Fictions of the Pose: Facing the Gaze of Early Modern Portraiture'. *Representations* 46 (1994): 87–120.

Blayney, Peter W. M. *The First Folio of Shakespeare*. Washington: Folger Shakespeare Library, 1991.

Blayney, Peter W. M. 'The Publication of Playbooks'. In *A New History of Early English Drama*, edited by John D. Cox and David Scott Kastan, 383–422. New York: Columbia University Press, 1997.

Bradley, A. C. *Oxford Lectures on Poetry*. London: Macmillan, 1920.

Brennan, Michael G. *The Sidneys of Penshurst and the Monarchy, 1500–1700*. Aldershot: Ashgate, 2006.

Brown, John Russell. *Shakespeare: Antony and Cleopatra: A Casebook*. London: Macmillan, 1968.

Brown, Pamela Allen. 'New Fable of the Belly: Vulgar Curiosity and the Persian Lady's Loose Bodies'. In *The Impact of Feminism in English Renaissance Studies*, edited by Dympna Callaghan, 171–92. Basingstoke: Palgrave, 2007.

Bond, William H. 'The Epitaph for Sir Philip Sidney'. *Modern Language Notes* 58, no. 4 (1943): 253–7.

Boutcher, Warren. 'The Renaissance'. In *The Oxford Guide to Literature in English Translation*, edited by Peter France, 45–55. Oxford: OUP, 2000.

Boutcher, Warren. *The School of Montaigne in Early Modern Europe: Volume Two: The Reader-Writer*. Oxford: OUP, 2017.

Burke, Peter. 'Cultures of Translations in Early Modern Europe'. In *Cultural Translation in Early Modern Europe*, edited by Peter Burke and R. Po-chia Hsia, 7–39. Cambridge: CUP, 2007.

Cadman, Daniel. *Sovereigns and Subjects in Early Modern Neo-Senecan Drama*. Farnham: Ashgate, 2015.

Cadman, Daniel. '"Th'accesion of these mighty States": Daniel's *Philotas* and the Union of Crowns'. *Renaissance Studies* 26, no. 3 (2012): 365–84.

Cerasano, S. P., and Marion Wynne-Davies, eds. *Renaissance Drama by Women: Texts and Documents*. 1996; rpt., London: Routledge, 1997.

Chaney, Edward. 'Roma Britannica and the Cultural Memory of Egypt: Lord Arundel and the Obelisk of Domitian'. In *Roma Britannica: Art Patronage and Cultural Exchange in Eighteenth-Century Rome*, edited by David Marshall, Susan Russell and Karin Wolfe, 147–70. Rome: British School, 2011).

Clarke, Danielle. *The Politics of Early Modern Women's Writing*. Harlow: Pearson, 2001.

Craik, Katherine A. *Reading Sensations in Early Modern England*. Basingstoke: Palgrave, 2007.

Craik, Katherine A., and Tanya Pollard, eds. *Shakespearean Sensations: Experiencing Literature in Early Modern England*. Cambridge: CUP, 2013.

Crawford, Julie. *Mediatrix: Women, Politics, & Literary Production*. Oxford: OUP, 2014.

Croft, Pauline. *King James*. Basingstoke: Palgrave, 2003.

Curran, Brian A. 'Love, Triumph, Tragedy: Cleopatra in High Renaissance Rome'. In *Cleopatra: A Sphinx Revisited*, edited by Margaret M. Miles, 96–131. Berkeley: University of California Press, 2011.

Curran, Kevin. 'Shakespeare and Daniel Revisited: *Antony and Cleopatra* II.v.50–4 and *The Tragedy of Philotas* V.ii.2013–15'. *N&Q* 54, no. 2 (2007): 318–20.

Darragi, Rafik. 'Ideological Appropriation and Sexual Politics: Shakespeare's *Antony and Cleopatra* and Ahmed Shawky's *Masra' Cleopatra*'. In *Shakespeare's World / World Shakespeare: The Selected Proceedings of the International Shakespeare Association World Congress, Brisbane, 2006*, edited by Richard Fartheringham, Christina Johnson and R. S. White, 358–70. Newark: University of Delaware Press, 2006.

Davidson, Peter, and Jane Stevenson. 'Elizabeth I's Reception at Bisham'. In *The Progresses, Pageants, and Entertainments of Queen Elizabeth I*, edited by Jayne Elisabeth Archer, Elizabeth Goldring and Sarah Knight, 207–26. Oxford: OUP, 2007.

Davies, H. Neville. 'Jacobean *Antony and Cleopatra*'. In *New Casebooks: Antony and Cleopatra*, edited by John Drakakis, 127–65. Basingstoke: Macmillan, 1994.

Davis, Walter R. 'Allegory'. In *The Spenser Encyclopedia*, edited by A. C. Hamilton, Donald Cheney, W. F. Blisset, David. A. Richardson and William W. Barker, 16–24. Toronto: University of Toronto Press, 1997.

Deats, Sara Munson, ed., *Antony and Cleopatra: New Critical Essays*. New York: Routledge, 2005.

Dessen, Alan C. '"Original Practices" at the Globe: A Theatre Historian's View'. In *Shakespeare's Globe: A Theatrical Experiment*, edited by Christie Carson and Farah Karim-Cooper, 45–51. Cambridge: CUP, 2008.

Dixon, Mimi Still. '"Not Know Me Yet?": Looking at Cleopatra in Three Renaissance Tragedies'. In *The Female Tragic Hero in English Renaissance Drama*, edited by Naomi Conn Liebler, 71–91. New York: Palgrave, 2002.

Dobson, Michael. *The Making of the National Poet: Shakespeare, Adaptation, and Authorship, 1660–1769*. Oxford: Clarendon, 1992.

Dobson, Michael, and Nicola J. Watson. *England's Elizabeth: An Afterlife in Fame and Fantasy*. Oxford: OUP, 2002.

Duggan, Dianne. 'Pembrokes Arcadia: "Delicious Wilton ... that Arbour of the Muses"'. *British Art Journal* 14, no. 3 (2013/14): 9–20.

Duncan-Jones, Katherine. *Sir Philip Sidney: Courtier Poet*. London: Hamish Hamilton, 1991.

Dunne, Derek. 'Play Review: *The Tragedie of Cleopatra*'. *Cahiers Élisabéthains* 83 (2013): 43–4.

Dutton, Richard. *Shakespeare Court Dramatist*. Oxford: OUP, 2016.

Eccles, Mark. 'Samuel Daniel in France and Italy'. *Studies in Philology* 34, no. 2 (1937): 148–67.

Edwards, John Stephan. 'A New Portrait of Mary Rogers, Lady Harington'. *British Art Journal* 12, no. 2 (2011): 54–7.

Eggert, Katharine. *Showing Like A Queen: Female Authority and Literary Experiments in Spenser, Shakespeare, and Milton*. Philadelphia: University of Pennsylvania Press, 2000.

Eisaman Maus, Katherine. *Being and Having in Shakespeare*. Oxford: OUP, 2013.

El Daly, Okasha. *Egyptology: The Missing Millennium: Ancient Egypt in Medieval Arab Writings*. London: UCL Press, 2005.

Elam, Keir. *Shakespeare's Pictures: Visual Objects in the Drama*. London: Bloomsbury Arden Shakespeare, 2017.

Erne, Lukas. *Shakespeare as Literary Dramatist*. 2003; rpt., Cambridge: CUP, 2013.

Escolme, Bridget. *Antony and Cleopatra*. Shakespeare Handbooks. Basingstoke: Palgrave Macmillan, 2006.

Escolme, Bridget. *Emotional Excess on the Shakespearian Stage: Passion's Slaves*. London: Bloomsbury Arden Shakespeare, 2014.

Farnham, Willard. *Shakespeare's Tragic Frontier: The World of His Final Tragedies*. Berkeley: University of California Press, 1950.

Findlay, Alison. *Playing Spaces in Early Women's Drama*. Cambridge: CUP, 2006.

Findlay, Alison, Stephanie Hodgson-Wright and Gweno Williams. *Women and Dramatic Production, 1550–1700*. Harlow: Longman, 2000.

Foakes, R. A. 'Tragedy at the Children's Theatres after 1600: A Challenge to the Adult Stage'. In *The Elizabethan Theatre II*, edited by David Galloway, 37–59. Toronto: Macmillan, 1970.

Frénée-Hutchins, Samantha. *Boudica's Odyssey in Early Modern England*. Farnham: Ashgate, 2014.

Freer, Coburn. *The Poetics of Jacobean Drama*. Baltimore: Johns Hopkins University Press, 1981.

Frye, Susan. *Pens and Needles: Women's Textualities in Early Modern England*. Philadelphia: University of Pennsylvania Press, 2010.

Gajda, Alexandra. *The Earl of Essex and Late Elizabethan Political Culture*. Oxford: OUP, 2012.

Gazzard, Hugh. '"Those Grave Presentiments of Antiquitie": Samuel Daniel's *Philotas* and the Earl of Essex'. *Review of English Studies* 51, no. 203 (2000): 423–50.

Goldsworthy, Adrian. *Antony and Cleopatra*. New Haven: Yale University Press, 2010.

Goodrich, Jaime. *Faithful Translators: Authorship, Gender, and Religion in Early Modern England*. Evanston: Northwestern University Press, 2014.

Gouws, John. 'Greville, Fulke, First Baron Brooke of Beauchamps Court (1554–1628)'. *ODNB*, Oxford University Press, 2004; online edn, 2011. http://www.oxforddnb.com/view/article/11516.

Grafton, Antony, and Lisa Jardine. '"Studied for Action": How Gabriel Harvey Read his Livy'. *Past and Present* 129, no. 1 (1990): 30–78.

Grazia, Margreta de. '*Hamlet*' *without Hamlet*. Cambridge: CUP, 2007.

Greenfield, Peter H. 'Touring'. In *A New History of Early English Drama*, edited by John D. Cox and David Scott Kastan, 251–68. New York: Columbia UP, 1996.

Greg, W. W. *A Bibliography of the English Printed Drama to the Restoration. Vol. 1, Stationers' Records, Plays to 1616: Nos. 1–349*. London: Bibliographical Society, 1939.

Greg, W. W. *Some Aspects and Problems of London Publishing Between 1550 and 1650*. Oxford: Clarendon, 1956.

Gurr, Andrew. *The Shakespearean Stage 1574–1642*. Cambridge: CUP, 2009.

Guy, John. Elizabeth: *The Forgotten Years*. Viking: London, 2016.

Guy, John, ed. *The Reign of Elizabeth: Court and Culture in the Last Decade*. Cambridge: CUP, 1995.

Guy, John. *Queen of Scots: The True Life of Mary Stuart*. New York: Houghton Mifflin, 2004.

Hackett, Helen. 'Longer shall you gaze on't.' Review of W. R. Streitberger, *The Masters of the Revels and Elizabeth I's Court Theatre*, and Richard Dutton, *Shakespeare, Court Dramatist*. *Times Literary Supplement*, 28 October 2016, 7–8.

Hackett, Helen. 'The Rhetoric of (In)fertility: Shifting responses to Elizabeth I's Childlessness'. In *Rhetoric, Women and Politics in Early Modern England*, edited by Jennifer Richards and Alison Thorne, 149–71. London: Routledge, 2007.

Hackett, Helen. *Virgin Mother, Maiden Queen: Elizabeth I and the Cult of the Virgin Mary*. Basingstoke: Macmillan, 1996.

Hadfield, Andrew. *Edmund Spenser: A Life*. Oxford: OUP, 2012.

Hall, Kim F. *Things of Darkness: Economies of Race and Gender in Early Modern England*. Ithaca: Cornell University Press, 1995.

Hamer, Mary. *Signs of Cleopatra: History, Politics, Representation*. London: Routledge, 1993.

Hamer, Mary. 'The Myth of Cleopatra since the Renaissance'. In *Cleopatra of Egypt: From History to Myth*, edited by Susan Walker and Peter Hughes, 302–11. London: British Museum Press, 2001.

Hammer, Paul E. J. 'Essex and Europe: Evidence from Confidential Instructions by the Earl of Essex, 1595–1596'. *English Historical Review* 3, no. 431 (1996): 357–81.

Hammer, Paul E. J. *The Polarisation of Elizabethan Politics: The Political Career of Robert Devereux, 2nd Earl of Essex*. Cambridge: CUP, 1999.

Hannay, Margaret P. *Mary Sidney, Lady Wroth*. Farnham: Ashgate, 2010.

Hannay, Margaret P. *Philip's Phoenix: Mary Sidney, Countess of Pembroke*. Oxford: OUP, 1990.

Hannay, Margaret P. '"Princes you as men must dy": Genevan Advice to Monarchs in the Psalmes of Mary Sidney'. *ELR* 19, no. 1 (1989): 22–41.

Harvey, Elizabeth D. *Ventriloquized Voices: Feminist Theory and English Renaissance Texts*. London: Routledge, 1995.

Haskell, Francis, and Nicholas Penny. *Taste and the Antique: The Lure of Classical Sculpture 1500–1900*. 1981; rpt., New Haven: Yale University Press, 1998.

Hearn, Karen. 'Lady Anne Clifford's Great Triptych'. In *Lady Anne Clifford: Culture, Patronage and Gender in 17th-Century Britain*, edited by Karen Hearn and Lynn Hulse, 1–24. Leeds: Yorkshire Archaeological Society Occasional, Paper No. 7, 2009.

Hearn, Karen. *Marcus Gheeraerts II: Elizabethan Artist in Focus*. London: Tate Publishing, 2002.

Hillman, Richard. 'De-Centring the Countess's Circle: Mary Sidney Herbert and Cleopatra'. *Renaissance and Reformation* 28, no. 1 (2004): 61–79.

Holt, Mack P. *The French Wars of Religion 1562–1629*. Cambridge: CUP, 2005.

Hopkins, Lisa. *The Cultural Uses of the Caesars on the English Renaissance Stage*. Ashgate: Farnham, 2008.

Hopkins, Lisa. *The Female Hero in English Renaissance Tragedy*. Basingstoke: Palgrave Macmillan, 2002.

Hopkins, Lisa, and Barbara MacMahon. '"Come, what, a siege?": Metarepresentation in Lady Jane Cavendish and Lady Elizabeth Brackley's *The Concealed Fancies*'. *Early Modern Literary Studies* 16, no. 3 (2013): 1–17.

Hosington, Brenda M. 'Translation as a Currency of Cultural Exchange in Early Modern England'. In *Early Modern Exchanges: Dialogues between Nations and Cultures (1550–1750)*, edited by Helen Hackett, 27–54. London: Routledge 2015.

Hughes-Hallett, Lucy. *Cleopatra: Histories, Dreams, Distortions*. London: Bloomsbury, 1990.

Jankowski, Theodora A. *Women in Power in the Early Modern Drama*. Chicago: University of Chicago Press, 1992.

Jansen, Sharon L. *Debating Women, Politics, and Power, in Early Modern Europe*. Basingstoke: Palgrave, 2008.

Jondorf, Gillian. *Robert Garnier and the Themes of Political Tragedy in the Sixteenth Century*. Cambridge: CUP, 1969.

Jones, Prudence J. *Cleopatra A Sourcebook*. Norman: University of Oklahoma Press, 2006.

Kahn, Coppélia. *Roman Shakespeare: Warriors, Wounds, Women*. London: Routledge, 1997.

Karim-Cooper, Farah. *Cosmetics in Shakespearean and Renaissance Drama*. Edinburgh: Edinburgh University Press, 2006.

Karim-Cooper, Farah. 'Props'. In *Shakespeare and the Making of Theatre*, edited by Stuart Hampton-Reeves and Bridget Escolme, 88–101. Basingstoke: Palgrave, 2012.

Kermode, Frank. *Shakespeare's Language*. New York: Farrar, Straus and Giroux, 2000.

Kerrigan, John, ed. *Motives of Woe: Shakespeare and 'Female Complaint'. A Critical Anthology*. Oxford: Clarendon, 1991.

Kewes, Paulina. '"A Fit Memorial For The Times To Come …": Admonition and Topical Application in Mary Sidney's *Antonius* and Samuel Daniel's *Cleopatra*'. *RES* 63, no. 259 (2012): 243–64.

Kewes, Paulina. 'Henry Savile's Tacitus and the Politics of Roman History in Late Elizabethan England'. *HLQ* 74, no. 4 (2011): 515–51.

Kolkovich, Elizabeth Zeman. *The Elizabethan Country House Entertainment: Print, Performance and Gender*. Cambridge: CUP, 2016.

Krontiris, Tina. *Oppositional Voices: Women as Writers and Translators of Literature in the English Renaissance*. London: Routledge, 1992.

Lamb, Mary Ellen. 'The Agency of the Split Subject: Lady Anne Clifford and the Uses of Reading'. *ELR* 22, no. 3 (1992): 347–68.

Lamb, Mary Ellen. 'The Countess of Pembroke's Patronage'. *ELR* 12 (1982): 162–79.

Lamb, Mary Ellen. *Gender and Authorship in the Sidney Circle*. Madison: University of Wisconsin Press, 1990.

Lamb, Mary Ellen. 'Play and DVD Reviews: *The Tragedie of Cleopatra*'. *Early Modern Women* 9, no. 2 (2015): 148–52.

Langley, Eric. *Narcissism and Suicide: in Shakespeare and his Contemporaries*. Oxford: OUP, 2009.

Laoutaris, Chris. *Shakespearian Maternities: Crises of Conception in Early Modern England*. Edinburgh: Edinburgh University Press, 2008.

Laoutaris, Chris. 'Translation / Historical Writing'. In *The History of British Women's Writing, 1500–1610*. Vol. 2, edited by Caroline Bicks and Jennifer Summit, 296–327. Basingstoke: Palgrave Macmillan, 2010.

Leavenworth, Russell E. *Daniel's Cleopatra: A Critical Study*. Salzburg: Institut für Englische Sprache und Literatur, Universität Salzburg, 1974.

Levey, Santina M. *Elizabethan Treasures: The Hardwick Hall Tapestries*. London: National Trust, 1998.

Loomba, Ania. *Shakespeare, Race, and Colonialism*. Oxford: OUP, 2002.

MacDonald, Joyce Green. *Women and Race in Early Modern Texts*. Cambridge: CUP, 2002.

MacLeod, Catherine, and Julia Marciari Alexander, eds. *Painted Ladies: Women at the Court of Charles II*. London: National Portrait Gallery, 2001.

McManus, Clare. *Women on the Renaissance Stage*. Manchester: Manchester University Press, 2002.

Maginn, Christopher. 'Blount, Charles, Eighth Baron Mountjoy and Earl of Devonshire (1563–1606)'. *ODNB*, Oxford University

Press, 2004; online edn, 2011. http://www.oxforddnb.com/view/article/2683.

Marsh, Christopher. *Music and Society in Early Modern England*. Cambridge: CUP, 2010.

Matsuoka, Mitsuharu. 'A Hyper-Concordance to the Works of Edmund Spenser'. *The Victorian Literary Studies Archive*, 28 December 2003. http://victorian-studies.net/concordance/spenser/.

Miles, Margaret M., ed. *Cleopatra: A Sphinx Revisited*. Berkeley: University of California Press, 2011.

Montrose, Louis. '"Shaping Fantasies": Figurations of Gender and Power in Elizabethan Culture'. *Representations* 2 (1983): 61–94.

Montrose, Louis. *The Subject of Elizabeth: Authority, Gender, and Representation*. Chicago: Chicago University Press, 2006.

Morris, Helen. 'Queen Elizabeth I "Shadowed" in Cleopatra'. *HLQ* 32, no. 3 (1969): 271–8.

Morrison, Mary. 'Some Aspects of the Treatment of the Theme of Antony and Cleopatra in Tragedies of the Sixteenth Century'. *Journal of European Studies* 4, no. 2 (1974): 113–25.

Munro, Lucy. *Children of the Queen's Revels: A Jacobean Theatre Repertory*. Cambridge: CUP, 2005.

Nicholls, Mark, and Penry Williams. *Sir Walter Raleigh: In Life and Legend*. London: Continuum, 2011.

Nisbet, R. G. M., and Margaret Hubbard, *A Commentary on Horace Odes Book I*. 1970; rpt., Oxford: Clarendon, 1975.

Norbrook, David. 'Lucan, Thomas May and the Creation of a Republican Literary Culture'. In *Culture and Politics in Early Stuart England*, edited by Kevin Sharpe and Peter Lake, 45–66. Basingstoke: Macmillan, 1994.

Norbrook, David. *Poetry and Politics in the English Renaissance*. Rev. edn 2002. 1984; rpt., Oxford: OUP, 2009.

Norgaard, Holger. 'Response to John. D. Reeves, "A Supposed Indebtedness of Shakespeare To Peele"'. *N&Q* 197, no. 21 (1952): 442–3.

Norman, Arthur M. Z. 'Daniel's *The Tragedie of Cleopatra* and *Antony and Cleopatra*'. Shakespeare *Quarterly* 9, no. 1 (1958): 11–18.

Orgel, Stephen, and Roy Strong. *Inigo Jones: The Theatre of the Stuart Court*. 2 vols. London: Sotheby Parke Bernet, 1973.

Patterson, Annabel. *Censorship and Interpretation: The Conditions of Reading and Writing in Early Modern England*. Madison: University of Wisconsin Press, 1984.

Peck, Linda Levy. 'Peers, Patronage and the Politics of History'. In *The Reign of Elizabeth: Court and Culture in the Last Decade*, edited by John Guy, 87–108. Cambridge: CUP, 1995.

Pelling, Christopher. 'The Triumviral Period'. In *The Cambridge Ancient History*, 2nd edn, edited by Alan K. Bowman, Edward Champlin and Andrew Linnot, 1–69. Cambridge: CUP, 1996.

Pentland, Elizabeth. 'Philippe Mornay, Mary Sidney, and the Politics of Translation'. *Early Modern Studies Journal* 6 (2014): 66–99.

Pettegree, Jane. *Foreign and Native on the English Stage, 1588–1611: Metaphor and National Identity*. Basingstoke: Palgrave, 2011.

Phillips, James Emerson. *Images of a Queen: Mary Stuart in Sixteenth-Century Literature*. Berkeley: University of California Press, 1964.

Piatt, Wendy. 'Politics and Religion in Renaissance Closet Drama'. Unpublished D.Phil. thesis, Bodleian Library, MS. D.Phil. c.15286. University of Oxford, 1998.

Pitcher, John. 'Daniel, Samuel (1562/3–1619)'. *ODNB*, Oxford University Press, 2004; online edn, 2011. http://www.oxforddnb.com/view/article/7120.

Pitcher, John. 'Negotiating a Marriage for Lady Anne Clifford: Samuel Daniel's Advice'. *RES* 64, no. 267 (2013): 770–94.

Pitcher, John. 'Samuel Daniel and the Authorities'. *MaRDiE* 10 (1998): 113–48.

Pitcher, John. 'Samuel Daniel's Masque *The Vision of the Twelve Goddesses*: Texts and Payments'. *MaRDiE* 26 (2013): 17–42.

Pitcher, John. 'Samuel Daniel's Occasional and Dedicatory Verse: A Critical Edition'. 2 vols. Unpublished D.Phil. thesis, Bodleian Library, MS. D.Phil. d.6440. University of Oxford, 1978.

Pitcher, John. *Samuel Daniel: The Brotherton Manuscript: A Study in Authorship*. Leeds: University of Leeds Press, 1981.

Pointon, Marcia. *Brilliant Effects: A Cultural History of Gem Stones and Jewellery*. New Haven: Yale University Press, 2009.

Pollard, A. C. *Shakespeare's Folios and Quartos: A Study in the Bibliography of Shakespeare's Plays 1594–1685*. London: Methuen, 1909.

Pucci, Giuseppe. 'Every Man's Cleopatra'. In *Cleopatra: A Sphinx Revisited*, edited by Margaret M. Miles, 195–207. Berkeley: University of California Press, 2013.

Putter, Ad. 'Pearl'. In *The Literary Encyclopedia*. Vol. 1.2.1.02: *Medieval and Early Modern England, 1066–1485*. Edited by Kate Ash-Irisarri, David Fuller, Hugh Magennis, Jamie McKinstry and Sarah Peverley, online edn, 30 March 2011. http://www.litencyc.com/php/sworks.php?rec=true&UID=13215.

Rees, Joan. *Samuel Daniel: A Critical Biography*. Liverpool: Liverpool University Press, 1964.

Rees, Joan. 'Samuel Daniel's *Cleopatra* and Two French Plays'. *MLR* 47, no. 1 (1952): 1–10.

Reynolds, Graham. 'The Painter Plays the Spider'. *Apollo*, April 1964, 279–84.

Roller, Duane W. *Cleopatra: A Biography*. New York: OUP, 2010.

Rowse, A. L. *Shakespeare's Sonnets: The Problems Solved. A Modern Edition with Prose versions, Introduction and Notes*. 2nd edn. London: Macmillan, 1973.

Royster, Francesca T. *Becoming Cleopatra: The Shifting Image of an Icon*. Basingstoke: Palgrave, 2003.

Rutter, Carol Chillington. *Enter the Body: Women and Representation on Shakespeare's Stage*. London: Routledge, 2001.

Ruutz-Rees, Caroline. 'Some Notes of Gabriel Harvey's in Hoby's Translation of Castiglione's *Courtier* (1561)'. *PMLA* 25, no. 4 (1910): 608–39.

Sackville-West, Robert. *Knole: Kent*. 1998; rpt., Swindon: National Trust, 2011.

Salzman, Paul. 'Anne Clifford's Annotated Copy of Sidney's *Arcadia*'. *N&Q* 56, no. 4 (2009): 554–5.

Sanders, Eve Rachelle. *Gender and Literacy on Stage in Early Modern England*. Cambridge: CUP, 1998.

Schanzer, Ernest. '*Antony and Cleopatra* and the Countess of Pembroke's *Antonius*'. *N&Q* 3, no. 4 (1956): 152–4.

Schanzer, Ernest. 'Daniel's Revision of His *Cleopatra*'. *RES* 8, no. 37 (1957): 375–81.

Schiff, Stacy. *Cleopatra: A Life*. New York: Little, Brown and Company, 2010.

Schlueter, June. 'Samuel Daniel in Italy: New Documentary Evidence'. *HLQ* 75, no. 2 (2012): 283–90.

Seronsy, Cecil C. 'The Doctrine of Cyclical Recurrence and Some Related Ideas in the Works of Samuel Daniel'. *Studies in Philology* 54, no. 3 (1957): 387–407.

Seronsy, Cecil C. *Samuel Daniel*. New York: Twayne Publishers, 1967.
Shapiro, James. *William Shakespeare and the Year of Lear*. London: Faber and Faber, 2015.
Skinner, Quentin. *Machiavelli: A Very Short Introduction*. Oxford: OUP, 2001.
Skretkowicz, Victor. 'Mary Sidney Herbert's *Antonius*, English Philhellenism and the Protestant Cause'. *Women's Writing* 6, no. 1 (1999): 7–25.
Smith, Emma. *The Making of Shakespeare's First Folio*. Oxford: Bodleian, 2015.
Smuts, Malcolm. 'Court-Centred Politics and the Uses of Roman Historians, c.1590–1630'. In *Culture and Politics in Early Stuart England*, edited by Kevin Sharpe and Peter Lake, 21–44. Basingstoke: Macmillan, 1994.
Spence, Richard, T. *Lady Anne Clifford: Countess of Pembroke, Dorset and Montgomery (1590–1676)*. Stroud: Sutton, 1997.
Starks, Lisa S. '"Immortal Longings": The Erotics of Death in *Antony and Cleopatra*'. In *Antony and Cleopatra: New Critical Essays*, edited by Sara Munson Deats, 243–53. New York: Routledge, 2005.
Steppat, Michael. 'Shakespeare's Response to Dramatic Tradition in *Antony and Cleopatra*'. In *Shakespeare: Text, Language, Criticism: Essays in Honour of Marvin Spevack*, edited by Bernard Fabian and Kurt Tetzeli von Rosador, 255–79. Hildesham and New York: Olms-Weidman, 1987.
Stewart, Alan. *Shakespeare's Letters*. Oxford: OUP, 2008.
Streitberger, W. R. *The Master of the Revels and Elizabeth I's Court Theatre*. Oxford: OUP, 2016.
Stoll, Jessica. 'Petrarch's *De Vita Solitaria*: Samuel Daniel's Translation *c*. 1610'. *MLR* 109, no. 2 (2014): 313–32.
Straznicky, Marta. *Privacy, Playreading and Women's Closet Drama 1550–1700*. Cambridge: CUP, 2004.
Straznicky, Marta, ed. *Shakespeare's Stationers: Studies in Cultural Bibliography*. Philadelphia: University of Pennsylvania Press, 2013.
Strong, Roy. *The Cult of Elizabeth: Elizabethan Portraiture and Pageantry*. London: Pimlico, 1999.
Tanner, J. R., ed. *Tudor Constitutional Documents, A.D. 1485–1603*. 1930; rpt., Cambridge: CUP, 2013.

Tanner, Marie. *The Last Descendant of Aeneas: The Hapsburgs and the Mythic Image of the Emperor*. New Haven, CT: Yale University Press, 1993.

Tarn, W. W., and M. P. Charlesworth. 'The Triumvirs'; 'The war of the East against the West'; 'The triumph of Octavian'. In *The Cambridge Ancient History*, 1st edn, Vol. 10, edited by S. A. Cook, F. E. Adcock and M. P. Charlesworth, 31–111. 1930; rpt., Cambridge: CUP, 1934.

Tassi, Marguerite A. '"O'erpicturing Apelles": Shakespeare's *Paragone* with Painting in *Antony and Cleopatra*'. In *Antony and Cleopatra: New Critical Essays*, edited by Sara Munson Deats, 291–308. New York: Routledge, 2005.

Tiramani, Jenny. 'Exploring Early Modern Stage and Costume Design'. In *Shakespeare's Globe: A Theatrical Experiment*, edited by Christie Carson and Farah Karim-Cooper, 57–65. Cambridge: CUP, 2008.

Tomlinson, Sophie. *Women on Stage in Stuart Drama*. Cambridge: CUP, 2005.

Tsukada, Yuichi. 'Shakespeare and the Politics of Nostalgia: Negotiating the memory of Elizabeth I on the Jacobean Stage'. Unpublished PhD thesis, King's College London, 2015.

Tyldesley, Joyce. *Cleopatra: Last Queen of Egypt*. Perseus: New York, 2008.

Walker, Julia M. 'Bones of Contention: Posthumous Images of Elizabeth and Stuart Politics'. In *Dissing Elizabeth: Negative Representations of Gloriana*, edited by Julia M. Walker, 252–76. Durham and London: Duke University Press, 1998.

Walker, Julia M. *The Elizabeth Icon: 1603–2003*. Basingstoke: Palgrave, 2004.

Watkins, John. *Representing Elizabeth in Stuart England: Literature, History, Sovereignty*. Cambridge: CUP, 2002.

Watson, G. 'The Death of Cleopatra'. *N&Q* 223 (1978): 409–14.

Weis, René. *Shakespeare Revealed: A Biography*. London: John Murray, 2007.

Wells, Stanley. *Shakespeare, Sex, & Love*. Oxford: OUP, 2010.

White, Micheline. 'Pray for the Monarch: The Surprising Contributions of Katherine Parr and Queen Elizabeth I to the Book of Common Prayer'. *TLS* 5844 (3 April 2015): 14–15.

Wiggins, Martin, and Catherine Richardson. *British Drama: 1533–1642: A Catalogue: Volume V, 1603–1608*. Oxford: OUP, 2015.

Williams, Penry. *The Later Tudors: England, 1547–1603*. Oxford: Clarendon, 1995.
Williamson, George C. *Lady Anne Clifford* (Kendall: Titus, Wilson and Son, 1922), 206.
Williamson, Marilyn L. *Infinite Variety: Antony and Cleopatra in Renaissance Drama and Earlier Tradition*. Mystic, CT: Lawrence Verry, 1974.
Witherspoon, Alexander M. *The Influence of Robert Garnier on Elizabethan Drama*. 1924; rpt., New York: Phaeton, 1968.
Woods, Susanne. *Lanyer: A Renaissance Woman Poet*. Oxford: OUP, 1999.
Worden, Blair. *The Sound of Virtue: Philip Sidney's 'Arcadia' and Elizabethan Politics*. New Haven: Yale University Press, 1996.
Wormald, Jenny. 'James VI and I: Two Kings or One?'. *History* 68, no. 223 (1983): 187–209.
Woudhuysen, H. R. 'Sidney, Sir Philip (1554–1586), Author and Courtier'. In *Oxford Dictionary of National Biography*. Oxford University Press, 2004; online edn, 2011. http://www.oxforddnb.com/view/article/25522.
Woudhuysen, H. R. *Sir Philip Sidney and the Circulation of Manuscripts 1558–1640*. Oxford: Clarendon, 1996.
Wray, Romana. 'Performing *The Tragedy of Mariam* and Constructing Stage History'. *Early Theatre* 18, no. 2 (2015): 149–66.
Wyke, Maria. *Projecting the Past: Ancient Rome, Cinema and History*. 1997; rpt., London: Routledge, 2013.
Wyke, Maria. *The Roman Mistress*. Oxford: OUP, 2002.
Wynne-Davies, Marion. 'Review of Samuel Daniel's *Tragedie of Cleopatra*' (directed by Emma Whipday for the UCL Centre for Early Modern Exchanges) at the Great Hall, Goodenough College, London, 3 March 2013. *Shakespeare* 12, no. 4 (2016): 443–7, doi: 10.1080/17450918.2013.833982.
Wynne-Davies, Marion. 'The Theatre'. In *The History of British Women's Writing, 1500–1610*. Vol. 2, edited by Caroline Bicks and Jennifer Summit, 175–95. Basingstoke: Palgrave Macmillan, 2010.

INDEX

Actium 4, 7, 48, 50, 60, 64, 177
   Augustan poetry written after 5, 247 n.10
   early modern drama set in aftermath of 36, 65, 193–4
   and allusion to Spanish Armada 50–2
Adelman, Janet 25, 251 n.72
Aebischer, Pascale 54, 220, 258 n.71, 287 n.90, 291 n.18
Alexander, Gavin 255 n.30, 256 n.47, 257 n.56
Alexander, Julia Marciari 109, 269 n.8
Alexander the Great 6, 54, 63
   in 'Cleopatra in the Vatican Gardens' (Favoriti), 236, 241, 243
   in *Philotas* (Daniel) 94
   in Ralegh 115
Albertus Magnus 249 n.55
all'antica style 15, 107, 160
allegory
   in Elizabethan literature 26
   and use in Garnier of political allegory 29, 30, 40, 53, 203, 209
   and use in Mary Sidney 40, 53, 57, 61
   and use in Spenser 25, 54, 57, 259 n.84
Al-Masudi 6

Amyot, Jacques 8, 50, 187, 257 n.59
Anna of Denmark 124, 131, 153–4, 159, 204
Anjou, Francis, Duke of Alençon
   proposed marriage to Elizabeth 38, 44, 76
   and poem on 76
Antony, Mark 4–5
   in Augustan narrative 5, 6, 10
   in Plutarch 188, 189, 190–2, 194
   and suicide 13
Antony, representation in literature 22, 23, 33, 194
   in Daniel 152, 156
   in Garnier-Sidney 39, 50, 51, 57, 58–60, 65
   impact of Cleopatra's image 51, 57, 59–60, 222
   and absence and longing 51, 60, 195
   mental and emotional state 39, 49, 50, 70
   loss of self (in Garnier-Sidney) 59, 193–4, 211
   in Shakespeare 187–9, 192, 193–4, 195, 211
   suicide 13, 36, 164
Arbaleste, Charlotte (de Mornay) 62–4, 260 n.96, 260 n.98
Ariadne 8, 225

INDEX

Arius 99, 100
ars moriendi 12
Arshad, Yasmin 268 n.4, 276 n.5, 280 n.45, 281 n.56
Artegall (*Faerie Queene*) 194
Artemisia/Artemesia 16, 17, 18, 202
Augustan narrative 1, 5–6, 13, 33, 221
   departure from 10, 39, 56, 134
Augustus 8–9, 22, 63 *see also* Octavius
   and affinities with Philip II 46, 56–7
   ambivalence towards 27, 63, 166, 206–11
   and in Sidney Circle 56, 63, 284 n.44
   James I's self-identification with 31, 99, 116, 139, 166, 206–7 *see also* James I
   triumph 5, 8–9, 23, 50, 59, 89, 152, 162, 193, 198, 225, 227
Averell, W. 249 n.46
Axton, Marie 75, 262 n.22

Baldi, Bernadino 9, 32, 61, 84, 226, 227, 244
   'On the statue of Cleopatra in the Vatican' 234–5
Barnes, Barnabe 283 n.26
Barnfield, Richard 264 n.46
Barroll, Leeds 283 n.24
Bate, Jonathan 256 n.43
Bates, Catherine 258 n.68
Batman, Stephen 250 n.57
Baynard's Castle 38, 46
Beard, Mary 5

beauty 6, 18, 23, 32, 53–4, 57, 166, 191, 199, 220
   and disenchantment 60, 89–91, 200
Beer, Anna 109, 114, 269 n.9
Belle, Marie-Alice 253 n.5, 257 n.61
Belphoebe (*Faerie Queene*) 26, 54
Belsey, Catherine 265 n.58
Berenice 127, 129, 131, 132, 135, 139, 159, 171
Berger, Harry 272 n.50
Bess of Hardwick, Elizabeth, Countess of Shrewsbury 16–17, 32, 67, 217, 218, 219
Best, Eve 280 n.41
Bevington, David 26, 206, 216
Bird, Philip 157, 163, 277 n.13, 279 n.31, 280 n.47, 280 n.52
Bisham Abbey, Elizabeth I's visit and female performance 130
Blackfriars Theatre 93, 135, 136, 153, 184
Blayney, Peter 74, 180, 181, 182, 262 n.16, 277 n.6, 282 n.9, 282 n.14
Blount, Charles, Lord Mountjoy and Earl of Devonshire 93, 94, 97–8, 100, 135
Blount, Edward 179, 180, 182, 183, 184, 186
Boaistuau, Pierre 249 n.52
Boccaccio, Giovanni 6–7, 244, 250 n.57
Bolingbroke, Henry 95
Bolsover Castle 217, 218, 249 n.48
Bond, William H. 255 n.31

Book of Common Prayer 43, 255 n.35
Boudica 25, 209
Boutcher, Warren 204–5, 287 n.95 and 287 n.96
Brackley, Lady Elizabeth 217–18 *see also* Cavendish, Lady Jane
Bradley, A. C. 281 n.5
Brandon, Samuel, *The Tragicomoedi of the Vertuous Octavia* 11,25, 37, 254 n.11
Bray, Jean 270 n.18
Brennan, Michael G. 254 n.26
Breton, Nicholas, 'The Countess of Penbroke's Love' 48, 265 n.53
Brown, John Russell 184, 283 n.25, 291 n.22
Brown, Pamela Allen 109, 114, 269 n.9
Brown, Sam 158, 163, 280 n.43, 280 n.46
Buc, Sir George 182
Bullein, William 249 n.55
Bullough, Geoffrey 39, 74, 183, 197, 286 n.69
Burke, Peter 255 n.33, 256 n.36

Cadman, Daniel 253 n.5, 266 n.72
Caesario 75, 91–3, 199, 205
    and Cleopatra's struggle to part with 92–3, 150, 162, 165–6
    and execution speech 110, 170–1
    and power of role in performance 151, 165, 221; 266 n.69; *see also* Stiff, Emily
Cain, Thomas M. 264 n.36
Caesar *see* Augustus; Octavius
Caesar, Julius *see* Julius Caesar
Calderinus, Domitius 24
Capel Cure, Sir Edward 269 n.11
Capel Cure, Hugo 269 n.11
Capel Cure, Lady Muriel Dixwell-Oxenden *see* Dixwell-Oxenden, Muriel
Cardano, Girolamo 249 n.52
Carr, Robert, Earl of Somerset 96, 113, 135
Cary, Elizabeth, *The Tragedie of Mariam* 129, 214, 215, 290 n.5
Case, R. H. 189, 191, 204
Casimir, John, Count Palatine 52
Castiglione, Baldassare 9–10, 32, 55, 61, 83–4, 226–7, 244
    'Cleopatra' 228–33
    The Courtier 55, 249 n.53, 249 n.56, 258 n.76
Catholic League 52
Caus, Isaac de 244
Cavendish, Lady Jane 217–18
    and Lady Elizabeth Brackley 217–18
    The Concealed Fancies 32, 217–18, 219, 223, 291 n.14
Cavendish, Margaret 129, 272 n.63
Cavendish, William, Duke of Newcastle 217
Cecil, Robert, 1st Earl of Salisbury 98–9, 113, 132
    and anger over Philotas 94, 103

Daniel's letter of apology 136
and Essex circle 95
and Greville 96, 103
and Raleghs 113, 115
Cecil, William, Lord Burghley 52
censorship 28, 44, 130 *see also* 'functional ambiguity'
Cerasano, S. P. 218, 253 n.5
Cesari, Cesare de', *Cleopatra* 11–12
Chamberlain's Men 181–2
Chambers, E. K. 204
Chaney, Edward 271 n.36
Chapman, George 97
Hymnus in Cynthiam 88
Charles I of England 216
Charles V, Holy Roman Emperor 56, 63
Charlesworth, M. P. 291 n.21
Charmion (Daniel) 91, 152, 155
and *Cleopatra* performance 135, 155, 164–6
and similarities to Daniel in Shakespeare 190, 198
Charmion (Garnier–Sidney) 42
Chatsworth House 16
Chaucer, Geoffrey
Legend of Good Women 7, 23
Troilus and Criseyde 7
Children of the Queen's Revels 93, 96, 135, 136, 153
Christian IV, King of Denmark 96, 210
Christie's 107, 110, 111, 112, 116, 269 n.5, 269 n.11, 269 n.13
Churchyard, Thomas 264 n.46
Chute, Anthony 264 n.46

Cicero 65
Cinthio, Giambattista Giraldi 11
civil war in *Antoine* (Garnier) 36–7, 61
in *Discourse* (Mornay) 63
and Protestant anxieties 53, 58, 61, 62, 67, 77, 255 n.29
Civil War English 217–18
Clarke, Danielle 27, 46, 251 n.78
Cleopatra VII, Queen of Egypt 1, 4
in Augustan narrative 1, 5–6, 13, 33, 221
departure from 10, 39, 56, 134
and marked as Other 1, 4
Greek lineage 6, 54
in Plutarch 4, 5–6, 8, 10
age 4, 88
beauty 1, 200
linguistic skills 55, 83
grief after Antony 9–10
suicide 4, 12–13, 23
Cleopatra, representation in the arts
in caricature 22
in decorative objects and jewellery 13–17
portraits 3, 10–11, 18–22, 30–1, 105–29, 131, 135–7, 141–3, 145, 158, 173
Lady Anne Clifford as possible sitter of Cleopatra portrait 106, 120–9, 131, 132, 135–8, 140–3, 154, 173, 219

and lack of plausibility
of Lady Ralegh as
Cleopatra sitter
106–14, 142
statues
Vatican *Cleopatra* statue
8–9, 12, 24, 32, 61, 82,
84, 107, 219
and fountain statue for
Wilton garden 244
tapestries 16–17, 217, 218,
219
Cleopatra, representation in
early modern era 2–3
in dictionaries (sixteenth
century) 22–3, 55
in European tragedies 11–12
and lines of succession in
plays 12
history and myth-making
18–29
pearl story 24–5, 28, 107,
250 n.66
in poetry 9, 11
Cleopatra, representation in
medieval era 6–7, 24
Cleopatra, representation in
literature
affinities with Elizabeth I 25,
26, 27, 29, 46, 53, 54–5,
57, 67, 76, 81–2, 209,
210, 213
ageing 88, 197
beauty 18, 23, 32, 53–4, 57,
166, 191, 199, 220
and disenchantment 60,
89–91, 200
colouring 7, 18, 54, 73, 202,
203, 210, 220
and blushing 73, 101, 210

confusion 81, 83, 90, 100–2,
103, 152, 156, 159, 220
and consequences of
monarchical 81, 156,
166, 164
constancy 13, 39, 46, 59, 99,
132, 134, 195–6
and inconstancy 78, 87,
195, 196
and similarities with
Cordelia in response to
letters 102–3
courage and nobility 8, 13,
18, 39, 45, 48, 146, 192,
196, 211, 220
debt/reckoning imagery
89–90, 198
divided self 74–6, 89, 98
duality of perspectives 13, 39,
70, 79, 178, 188, 192, 227
political readings 26–7, 28,
32, 213–14
elite women's response to
105, 107, 109, 118–19,
134, 139–40, 142–3, 145,
220
eloquence and linguistic skill
54–5, 83–4
as figure of female complaint
31, 85, 87, 212, 221
as figure of resistance in
Royalist plays 32, 214,
218
as figure of resistance to
colonialism in Egyptian
play (Shawqi) 222
as figure of female heroism
67, 87, 105, 119, 130,
134, 139, 142, 145, 152,
167, 218, 220, 223

loss of self 59, 66, 71, 85, 86, 98, 161
motherhood 70, 75, 77, 79–80, 85, 87, 92, 93, 98, 151, 198–9, 220
pathos 59, 68, 70, 73, 80, 83, 91, 219
as positive emblematic figure 2, 223
post-colonial readings 203, 220
post-Shakespeare 214–18
private passion versus public duty 36, 51, 57, 58, 59, 64, 65–6, 74–9, 223
racial identity 2, 6, 7, 8, 33, 54, 73, 146, 201–3
seductiveness 22, 23, 36, 39, 45, 49, 50, 68, 81, 87, 90, 134, 178, 191
suicide 9, 12–13, 15, 23, 33, 69, 90–1, 165, 206
sympathy for 40, 42, 45, 47, 52, 55, 76, 86–7, 103, 106, 143, 174, 219
vacillation 83, 150, 151, 196, 202, 216, 220
virtue 40, 65, 67–8, 85, 101, 102
vulnerability 73, 85, 87, 103, 134, 171, 174, 199
Cleopatra, representation in popular culture 1–2
Clifford, Lady Anne, Countess of Pembroke, Dorset and Montgomery 3, 27, 31, 96, 244
  as sitter of Cleopatra portrait 106, 120–9, 135–8, 140–3, 173, 219
  and close attachment to Daniel 120–3, 133, 136
  and guardian of Daniel's work 122, 136, 139
  and inscription 108, 112–14
  and as deviser 140
  and inheritance dispute 137, 171: James's Award 138, 139–40; pressures and sense of isolation 138, 139
  and masque performance 124, 126–7, 128, 131, 132, 154, 157, 279 n.32: and Berenice costume 127, 128
  and portraits: Great triptych 121, 123–4, 133, 140; Larkin, William, 124; Robert White (engraving) 124, 125
  and Stafford's *Niobe* dedication 132
  and John Donne 133
  and Montaigne's *Essays* 132–3
  and Sidney's *Arcadia* 121–2
Clifford, Francis, 4th Earl of Cumberland 123
Clifford, George, 3rd Earl of Cumberland 86, 120
Clifford, Margaret (née Russell), Countess of Cumberland 86, 120, 121, 124, 136, 138, 271 n.42
Clifford, Rosamond 85, 120
Clinton, Hillary 2
closet drama 29, 31, 69, 70, 74, 110, 118, 148, 173, 179
  as political vehicle 26, 27, 37
  as complex and innovative sub-genre 3, 34, 74, 130

concept of *obscura verba* 30,
    100, 141
  performance (theories) 27,
    29, 129
  performability of Daniel's
    Cleopatra 145–6, 149–54,
    169, 170, 173–4 *see also*
    UCL production
    and Cleopatra portrait as
      record of performance
      27, 31, 110, 118, 129,
      136, 145, 149,
  performance of Daniel's
    Philotas 93–4, 135–6,
    137, 153
  women's drama (research
    performance projects)
    129–30, 273 n.64
Coleridge, Samuel Taylor 185,
  284 n.32
complaint genre *see* female
  complaint
confusion 81, 83, 90, 100–2,
  103, 152, 156, 159, 220
  consequences of monarchical
    81, 156, 166, 164
Conrad, Stephen 270 n.15
Cooper, Thomas, *Thesaurus
  Lingua Romanae et
  Britannicae* 22–3
Cope, Sir Walter 113
Cordelia and similarities to
  Cleopatra (in response to
  letters) 101–2
Corneille, Pierre 290 n.6
Cottegnies, Line 253 n.5, 257
  n.61
Craik, Katherine A. 268 n.95
Crawford, Julie 27, 46, 259 n.78,
  261 n.4

Croft, Pauline 267 n.82
Cuffe, Henry, 'A Poem on the
  Earle of Essex (being in
  disgrace with Queene
  Elizabeth)' 88
Curran, Brian 10, 247 n.27
Curran, Kevin 204, 266 n.68

D'Agostino, Taja 227
D'Anghiera, Pietro Martire 28
Daniel, Samuel
  and influence of Montaigne
    81, 83, 84
  and Lady Anne Clifford 96,
    120–3, 133, 136
  and Mountjoy 93, 94, 97–8,
    100, 135
  and Raleghs 112–13, 114–19
  and revision 71–2, 91–3,
    148, 204
  and sensitivity towards
    situation of elite women
    87, 138, 196–7
Daniel, works
  Brotherton Manuscript, The
    100
  Civil Wars, The 67, 78–9, 94,
    102, 168
  Cleopatra, Tragedie of 3–4,
    11, 12, 13, 27, 30, 31, 32,
    34, 37, 42, 60, 68, 69–73,
    134, 219, 220, 244
    and ageing 88
    and Chorus 70, 73, 78,
      79, 81–2, 153, 155–6,
      163–5, 170, 174
    and collaborative effort
      with Mary Sidney 67,
      68, 69, 70, 71, 82,
      123

and as complaint 82–7,
161–3, 221
and conflict between
public and private
selves 74–9
and confusion 81, 83,
90, 100–2, 103, 152,
156, 159, 220: and
consequences of
monarchical 81, 156,
166, 164
and dedications to Mary
Sidney 70, 83, 205
and disenchantment with
beauty 89–91, 200
and dualism 39, 70, 79,
188, 192
and female heroism 87,
105, 119, 134, 142,
145, 152
and feminist critiques 87,
221
and grace 69, 73, 79, 83,
90–1, 103
and motherhood 70, 75,
80, 87
and nostalgia for
Elizabethan era 95–100
and pathos 70, 73, 80,
83, 91
and performability
149–54, 167, 170,
172–3 *see also* UCL
performance
and as publishing success
74
and topical allusions 71,
72, 75–9, 80, 88, 93,
97, 98, 99–100, 166,
213

and 1607 *Cleopatra* 91–3,
99, 100, 112
Cleopatra and influence on
Dryden 216–17
and influence on
Shakespeare 69, 84,
93, 148, 168, 196–201,
204–5
The Complaint of Rosamond
68, 84–5, 86, 87, 92, 120,
162, 163, 196, 197, 260
n.112
A Defence of Ryme 205, 287
n.97
Delia 70, 71, 87, 92, 163
Funeral Poem 98
Histories 205
Hymen's Triumph 136, 154
*Letter from Octavia to
Marcus Antonius* 12, 86,
138, 200
Musophilus 92
Panegyrike Congratularie
116, 182, 207, 287
n.97
Philotas 72, 91, 93–4, 96–7,
103, 115, 116, 135, 136,
149, 153, 154, 163, 182,
184, 204, 205
and dedications to Prince
Henry 94, 96
and impact on Daniel 72,
91, 93–4, 97, 103
The Prayse of Private Life
271 n.42
The Queenes Arcadia 154,
204, 205
Tethys' Festival 126–7, 136,
154
'To The Reader' 98, 123

Vision of the Twelve Goddesses 131, 153, 158, 159
Dante Alighieri, *Inferno* 6, 244
Danyel, John 72, 158, 162, 265 n.50, 279 n.35, 280 n.45
  Rosa pavan 162–3
  as collaborative effort with Daniel's *Rosamond* 162–3, 280 n.43
Darell, Walter 250 n.57, 287 n.85
Darragi, Rafik 292 n.26
Daunt, Catherine 269 n.5, 269 n.14
Davenant, William 290 n.6
Davidson, Peter 70, 140, 261 n.3
Davies, H. Neville 288 n.102
Davis, Walter R. 259 n.84
Deats, Sara Munson 283 n.28, 284 n.34
decorative objects and jewellery 13–17
Dekker, Thomas
  Lanthorne and Candle-light 203
  The Whore of Babylon 209
Delilah 18, 202
Dent, Leonard and Gerald 111, 270 n.16
Dessen, Alan C. 278 n.27
Dethloff, Diana 269 n.5
Devereux, Lady Dorothy 78
Devereux, Robert, 2nd Earl of Essex 30, 37, 63, 64, 72, 76, 78, 135
  apparent allusions to in Daniel's *Philotas* 72, 94, 97, 115–16 133, 153
  destruction of Greville's tragedy after fall of 25, 37, 78, 103, 183, 184
  and Elizabeth 63, 64, 76, 78, 88, 183–4
  enthusiasm for Roman historians and Tacitus 28, 71, 100, 102
  execution 95
  'Instructions to a Secret Agent in France, circa 1595, Etc.' 102
  secret correspondence with James I 95
deviseship and women 70, 130, 140–1, 148
Dickson, Andrew 284 n.35
dictionaries (sixteenth-century) 22–3
Dido 6, 251 n.70
Dio Cassius 5, 7, 8, 36, 50
Dixon, Mimi Still 87, 265 n.57
Dixwell-Oxenden, Muriel, Lady Capel Cure 110, 142, 269 n.11
Dixwell-Oxenden, Sir Percy 110
Dobson, Michael 205, 208, 267 n.77, 288 n.99
Donne, John, *Biathanatos* 133
Drayton, William, *Matilda* 264 n.46
Dryden, John, *All for Love, or the World Well Lost* 32, 185, 216–17, 290 n.11
  and influence of Daniel 216–17
Dudley, Robert, Earl of Leicester 38, 41, 67
Dudley-Sidney alliance 30, 38, 41, 52

Duggan, Diane 244
Duncan-Jones, Katherine 254 n.24, 260 n.96
Dunne, Derek 276 n.3
Dutton, Richard 186, 284 n.37

Eccles, Mark 264 n.41
Edmond, Sir Thomas 158
Edwards, John Stephen 142, 275 n.105
Egerton, Sir Thomas 95
Eggert, Katherine 26, 178
El Daly, Okasha 247 n.16
Elam, Keir 140, 275 n.98
elite women
   and agency 103, 119, 134, 139, 141, 145
   and responses to Cleopatra 105, 107, 109, 118–19, 134, 139–40, 142–3, 145, 220
   and self-representation 110, 140, 145
   and vulnerable situation 85, 87, 138
Elizabeth I, Queen of England 38, 39, 43, 130, 289 n.1
   and affinities with Cleopatra 25, 26, 27, 29, 46, 53, 54–5, 57, 67, 76, 81–2, 209, 210, 213
   and iconography 25, 53, 88
   and ageing 73–4, 88
   and Anjou Match 38 44, 76
      poem, 'On Monsieur's Departure' 76
   and burden of a female monarch 75–76
   and Essex 63, 64, 76, 78, 88, 183–4
   and motherhood, as nation's mother and lack of motherhood 42, 61, 76, 77, 80
   and mutability 53, 88
   neglect in foreign and domestic affairs 37, 38, 52, 58, 63–4, 65, 72, 76–7, 78, 80, 81
   nostalgia for after death 30, 95–100, 149, 207–209, 211, 212, 214
   and sense of delay (and in death) 78, 88, 95
   Treason Acts 44, 88
Elyot, Thomas, *Bibliotheca Eliotæ Eliotis librarie* 22
Erne, Lukas 155, 182, 185, 186, 278 n.24, 282 n.14
eroticism 7, 9, 24, 191, 194–5, 199, 200
Escolme, Bridget 12–13, 26, 195, 221, 248 n.39, 248 n.40, 286 n.65, 291 n.23
Essex, Earl of *see* Devereux, Robert
Essex circle 65, 78, 94, 95, 103
   and disillusionment with James 95–6
   and nostalgia for Elizabeth 96–7
   and use of Roman history and Tacitus 28, 40, 71, 100–1
   and use of Tacitean aphorisms and sententiae 28, 209, 252 n.81
Eyre, Beth 146, 167, 172, 173, 174, 281 n.62

Farnham, Willard 192, 285 n.54
Favoriti, Agonisto 9, 32, 61, 84, 226, 227
   'Cleopatra in the Vatican Gardens' 236–43
female complaint genre 86, 265 n.52
   Cleopatra as a figure of 31, 85, 87, 212, 221
   and music in *Cleopatra* production 265
   and Daniel experimentation with modes of 85–7, 120
   and English vogue for 84, 120, 262 n.16
female heroism 67, 87, 105, 119, 130, 134, 139, 142, 145, 152, 167, 218, 220
female sovereignty 2, 5, 25, 26, 31, 33, 39, 67, 71, 76, 134, 142, 171, 207, 214 *see* queenship, *see women*
feminine voice 47–8, 68, 86
feminist scholarship 45, 87, 221, 203
Findlay, Alison 29, 129, 130, 134, 160, 252 n.84, 257 n.61, 272 n.63, 273 n.64, 276 n.1, 276 n.4
Fiorentino, Rosso (portrait) 10–11
Fletcher, John 290 n.6
Florio, John 13, 182
   and connection of Daniel 83, 133, 244, 264 n.44
   Montaigne's Essays 13, 133, 182, 204
   Worlde of Workes (preface) 55
Foakes, R. A. 136, 274 n.89
forward protestant cause 27, 30, 38, 40, 45, 52, 56, 57, 63, 64, 72, 76, 77, 78, 81, 95, 99
Foxe, John, *Actes and Monuments of the English Martyrs* 208
Fraunce, Abraham, *The Countess of Pembroke's Ivy Church* 41
Freer, Coburn 257 n.57
Frenée-Hutchins, Samantha 251 n.70, 288 n.112
Frye, Susan 16, 249 n.50
Fulbecke, William 249 n.54
Fulke, William 79, 263 n.34
'functional ambiguity' 28, 44
   see also censorship

Gajda, Alexandra 251 n.74, 268 n.97
Gallagher, Charlotte 146, 147, 155, 162, 167, 168, 172, 173–4, 281 n.62
Garnier, Robert 11, 12, 30, 36, 38
   Cornelie 36–7, 44
   Marc Antoine 11, 12, 29, 35–7, 38–40, 45, 47, 61–2, 81, 82, 222
   Garnier-Sidney Cleopatra 47–58, 67, 89, 133–4, 219, 220, 244
   prefatory poem (Françoise Hubert) 47–8, 219, 257 n.54
   Porcie 36
Garrick, David 185
Gascoigne, George 250 n.57, 287 n.85

Gazzard, Hugh 97, 116, 263 n.27, 286 n.72
gender 29, 33, 40, 85 *see also* women
  and race 2, 3, 4, 6, 7, 8, 26, 33, 146, 201–3
Gentileschi, Artemisia 114
Gheeraerts, Marcus 124, 141, 273 n.69
Gilpin, Bernard 249 n.54
Globe Theatre 157, 158, 277 n.7, 279 n.30
Gloriana (*Faerie Queene*) 26
Goldsworthy, Adrian 222, 292 n.27
Goodenough College 31, 146, 148–9, 166, 167, 170–1, 172, 173, 276 n.1, 276 n.2
Goodman, Evienna 157, 279 n.30
Goodrich, Jaime 43, 227, 255 n.34, 257 n.54
Gouws, John 267 n.84, 269 n.12
Grafton, Antony 257 n.51, 264 n.40
Greene, Robert 249 n.56, 250 n.57, 287 n.85
Greenfield, Peter H. 278 n.26
Greenway, Richard 28
Greg, W. W. 180, 282 n.11, 282 n.15
Greville, Sir Fulke, Lord Brooke 56, 94, 100
  Antony and Cleopatra (destroyed play) 11, 25, 37, 102–3, 183, 213, 219
  'Dedication to Sir Philip Sidney' 56, 96, 99, 102–3, 184
  Letter to an Honorouble Lady 12
Greville, Lady Louisa 110
Greville, Sir Robert 110
Gunpowder Plot, representation of Elizabeth in drama after 208
Gurr, Andrew 284 n.34
Guy, John 79, 254 n.13, 263 n.33, 266 n.74
gypsies 203, 220

Hackett, Helen 29, 77, 146, 252, 37, 263 n.28, 263 n.34, 266 n.74, 272 n.58, 275 n.1, 281 n.56
Hadfield, Andrew 270 n.31
Hall, Kim F. 109, 112, 114, 269 n.9, 287 n.90
Hamer, Mary 26, 246 n.2, 247 n.27
Hammer, Paul J. 259 n.93, 268 n.96, 268 n.97
Hampton Court 131, 154, 158, 159
Hannay, Margaret 27, 41, 44, 45, 130, 253 n.10, 254 n.17, 254 n.24, 256 n.46, 273 n.64, 273 n.68, 276 n.4
Harding, Robert 274 n.73
Hardwick Hall 16, 17, 217
Harington, Sir John 96, 267 n.82
Harington, Lucy, Countess of Bedford 273 n.69
Harington, Lady Mary Rogers 142, 275 n.105
Harvey, Gabriel 46, 55, 57, 65, 258 n.76, 264 n.40
Harvey, Elizabeth D. 86, 257 n.55, 265 n.53
Haskell, Francis 226, 248 n.29
Hearn, Karen 123, 269 n.5, 272 n.51, 272 n.54

Helen of Corinth (*Arcadia*) 26, 46
Helen of Troy 6, 18, 22, 202, 215
Henri of Navarre 52, 62
Henri II, King of France 11, 38
Henri III, King of France 61
Henri IV, King of France 61, 63
Henry Frederick, Prince of Wales 94, 96, 97, 124, 154, 272 n.53
Henslowe, Philip 159, 279 n.38
Herbert, Henry, 2nd Earl of Pembroke 38
Herbert, Mary (Sidney), Countess of Pembroke *see* Sidney, Mary
Herbert, Philip, 4th Earl of Pembroke 115, 124, 244
Herbert, William, 3rd Earl of Pembroke 124, 135, 158
Herbert, William, *England's Sorrow, or, A Farewell to Essex* 209
Heywood, Thomas, *If You Know Not Me, You Know Nobody* 208, 210
Hilliard, Nicholas 25
Hillman, Richard 256 n.47
history
    and classical view of 71
    and use of Roman history (Sidney and Essex circles) 27, 30, 36, 37, 65–7, 70, 71, 73, 223
Hoby, Sir Thomas, *The Courtier* 55, 258 n.76
Hodgson-Wright, Stephanie 129, 272 n.63
Holland, Philemon 202, 285 n.48, 287 n.88
Holt, Mack P. 260 n.96

Hopkins, Lisa 54, 206, 217, 218, 258 n.70, 288 n.101, 291 n.15
Horace 5, 221, 247 n.10, 291 n.20
Hosington, Brenda M. 43, 256 n.37
Howard, Frances, Duchess of Lennox 135, 141, 275 n.103
Howard, Katherine, Countess of Suffolk 159
Hubbard, Margaret 291 n.20
Hubert, Françoise 47–8, 219, 257 n.54
Hughes-Hallett, Lucy 26
Huguenots 35, 38, 44, 46, 52, 62
humanism 12, 65, 67, 132
Hurault, André, Sieur de Maisse 78, 263 n.30, 265 n.61

Isaac, Gaspard (caricature) 22
imagining, danger of 32

Jaggard, Isaac 179, 180
Jaggard, William 180
James I, King of England (and VI of Scotland)
    accession 95, 207
    architectural revisions of Elizabeth's tomb 212
    Basilikon Doron 95–6
    correspondence with 78, 95
    disillusionment with 95, 100, 106, 207–8, 214
    favouritism and court culture 96, 99, 100, 166, 207
    pacifist diplomacy towards Spain and crypto-Catholicism 28, 95, 96, 99–100 207–8, 214

self-identification with Augustus 31, 99, 116, 139, 166, 206–7
union of two crowns 96, 166
Jameson, Anna 221
Jankowski, Theodora A. 251 n.70
Jansen, Sharon L, 251 n.70
Jardine, Lisa 257 n.51, 264 n.40
Jennings, Lucy 166
jewellery, Cleopatra in 14–15
Jodelle, Etienne, *Cléopâtre Captive* 11, 12, 38, 39, 47, 61, 82, 222
Jones, Inigo 124, 127—8, 158, 244, 273 n.72
and Berenice masque design for Lady Anne Clifford 128
Jones, Prudence J. 287 n.82
Jonson, Ben 97, 288 n.103
The Alchemist 202, 287 n.89
Every Man in His Humour 181
Masque of Beauty 126
Masque of Queens 126–7
Sejanus 182
Julius II (Pope) 8, 225, 231
Julius Caesar 4, 7, 22–3, 225, 290 n.6
admired by Sidney 46
allurement and seduction of 22–3

Karim-Cooper, Farah 157, 258 n.72, 278 n.27, 279 n.29, 279 n.31
Kermode, Frank 185, 283 n.31
Kerrigan, John 85, 175, 264 n.46, 265 n.50, 265 n.52

Kewes, Paulina 27, 46, 56, 67, 72, 74, 85, 90, 88–9, 251 n.78, 260 n.109
King's Men 182, 184–5, 207, 210
Kirton, James 136
Knole 31, 131, 133, 136, 139, 142, 281 n.56
staging *Cleopatra* at 31, 149, 170–4, 281 n.56
Kolkovich, Elizabeth Zeman 130, 273 n.66
Krontiris, Tina 256 n.45
Kyd, Thomas 44

Lamb, Mary Ellen 120, 134, 173, 255 n.28, 271 n.40, 274 n.81
Landi, Count Giulio, *La Vita di Cleopatra Reina d'Egitto* 11–12
Langley, Eric 262 n.20, 263 n.25
Lanyer, Aemilia 124
Salve Deus Rex Judaeorum 214–15
Laoutaris, Chris 29, 42, 252 n.86, 255 n.34, 257 n.55, 268 n.95
Larkin, William 126, 273 n.69
Anne Clifford portrait 124, 138
Richard Sackville portrait 126
Lawrence, Jason 227
Leavenworth, Russell E. 86, 204, 261 n.12
Leo X (Pope) 9, 231
Lederer, M., *Bang's Materialien* 155, 278 n.23

letters, dramatic reception of (Cleopatra and Cordelia) 101–2
Levey, Santina 249 n.49
Livy 65
Lloyd, Lodowick 249 n.56
Lodge, Thomas 249 n.56, 264 n.46
Loomba, Ania 252 n.90, 287 n.90
Lucan, *Pharsalia* 5, 215
Lucrece/Lucretia 16, 45, 114, 215
  as good wife 17, 18, 45, 202
  in Shakespeare 197, 248 n.41, 264 n.46
Lumley, Lady Jane, *Iphigenia* 43
  and Rose Theatre Company performance 129
lute, importance of, and music in *Cleopatra* performance 156, 158, 162, 171
Lydgate, John 66, 249 n.56, 260 n.107

McManus, Clare 141, 275 n.102
MacDonald, Joyce Green 54, 258 n.73, 287 n.90
MacLeod, Catherine 109, 269 n.5, 269 n.8
MacMahon, Barbara 217, 218
Macquoid, Percy 111
Machiavelli, Niccolò 65, 100
Maginn, Christopher 267 n.88
Marcus, Leah S. 262 n.23
Marlowe, Christopher
  Doctor Faustus 74, 181
  Hero and Leander 182
  Tamburlaine 49

Marsh, Christopher 279 n.34
Marston, John 97
Martial 24
Martire d'Anghiera, Pietro 252 n.82
Mary Queen of Scots 16, 58, 79, 96, 210, 263 n.34
Mary Tudor, Queen of England 26, 208
masques 124, 126–7, 128, 131–2, 141, 153, 154, 157–8
  and recycling of costumes 131, 273 n.69
  and women and performance 131, 136, 273 n.70, 279 n.32
Massinger, Philip 290 n.6
Matsuoka, Mitsuharu 285 n.57
May, Steven W. 209, 210
May, Thomas, *The Tragedie of Cleopatra Queen of Aegypt* 215–16, 290 n.7
Mengs, Anton Raphael 265 n.63
Michel, Laurence 94, 266 n.72
Miles, Margaret 253 n.91
Montaigne, Michel de 12, 81, 84, 182
  on dangers of certainty 81
  on death and suicide 12–13, 132
  influence on Daniel 81, 83, 84
  influence on Shakespeare 84, 204–5
  and Lady Anne Clifford reading 133
Montreux, Nicolas de, *Cleopatre* 11

Montrose, Louis 251 n.74, 262 n.22
Mornay, Philippe de 35, 46, 61–2, 64
 Excellent discours de la vie et la mort 35, 40, 46, 62–64
  and connection to wife 63
 Of the Truth of the Christian Religion 43
Morris, Helen 209, 288 n.113
Morrison, Mary 11, 12, 39
Mosca, Gianmaria 249 n.47
Mountjoy, Lord *see* Blount, Charles
Mueller, Janel 262 n.23
Munday, Anthony 250 n.57
Munro, Lucy 153, 265 n.51, 277 n.17, 280 n.48
Münster, Sebastian 25
music, use in *Cleopatra* production 157, 158, 162–3 *see also* Rosa; UCL production
Muthukumaran, Rathika 246 n.4

National Portrait Gallery 107, 109, 111, 112
Naunton, Robert 102
Neill, Michael 26, 283 n.27, 285 n.52
Neo-Senecan closet drama *see* closet drama
Neville, Sir Henry 208
New Historicist readings 26, 28, 251 n.74
Nicholls, Mark 113, 270 n.25
Nisbet, R. G. M. 291 n.20
Norbrook, David 28, 95, 215, 266 n.75, 290 n.8

Norgaard, Holger 200, 250 n.62, 252 n.83, 264 n.36, 286 n.79
Norman, Arthur M. Z. 266 n.68
North, Elspeth 155, 171, 172, 173–4, 281 n.62
North, Sir Thomas 8, 69, 177, 187, 190
nostalgia 30, 91, 95–7, 98, 149, 206–9, 211, 212, 214

obscura verba 30, 100, 141
 see also closet drama; Tacitus
Octavia 11–12, 49, 86, 173, 177, 189, 193, 196, 198, 209, 214
 and influence of Daniel on Shakespeare 200–1
Octavius 1, 5, 13, 22, 23 *see also* Augustus
 and affinities with Philip II 46, 56–7
 in Daniel 69, 152, 164, 167, 171
 in Garnier-Sidney 39, 46, 51, 52, 55–6, 57
 in Shakespeare 189, 211–12
Oliver, Isaac 124, 127
Omphale 5, 194, 259 n.88
Orgel, Stephen 273 n.72
Osborne, Francis 166, 280 n.51
Overbury, Sir Thomas 135
Ovid 25, 84, 231, 233

Painter, William 287 n.85
Parr, Katherine 43
pathos 59, 68, 70, 73, 80, 83, 90, 91, 92, 162, 192, 215, 219

patriarchy 29, 121, 137, 139, 172, 173
Patterson, Annabel 28, 44, 252 n.83
Paul III (Pope) 226
Peacham, Henry, *Titus Andronicus* drawing 137, 159, 274 n.90, 279 n.38
pearls 24–5, 28, 107, 250 n.66
Peck, Linda Levy 263 n.31
Pelling, Christopher 221, 282 n.7
Penelope 16, 17, 18, 45, 202
Penny, Nicholas 226, 248 n.29
Pentland, Elizabeth 62, 257 n.49, 260 n.98
Percy, Henry, 9th Earl of Northumberland 78
Pérez, Antonio 28
Petowe, Henry 207
Petrarchan beauty 53–4, 73, 80
Pettegree, Jane 27, 52, 79, 216, 251 n.78, 259 n.86, 259 n.92
Philip II of Spain 26, 28, 46, 56, 57
   and affinities to Augustus 46, 56–7
Philips, Katherine, *Pompey. A Tragedy* 290 n.6
Phillips, James 171, 172
Phillips, James Emerson 263 n.34
Philostratus 58, 60, 99, 100
phoenix 25
Piatt, Wendy 27,
Pistorelli, Celso, *Marc' Antonio e Cleopatra* 11
Pitcher, John 77, 97, 100, 121, 154, 262 n.13, 264 n.45, 266 n.64, 266 n.72, 270 n.22, 271 n.37, 271 n.47, 274 n.89, 279 n.33, 280 n.45, 282 n.17, 286 n.81
Pliny, *Natural History* 24, 25, 285 n.48
Plutarch 7, 36, 94, 221
   Life of Mark Antony
       Antony 188, 189, 190–2, 194
       Cleopatra 4, 5–6, 8, 10: age 4, 88; beauty 1, 200; grief after Antony's 9–10; linguistic skills 55, 83; suicide 23
       and Castiglione poem 9–10
       influences and departures in Garnier-Sidney 36, 49, 50, 83: and in Daniel 68, 83, 88, 93; and in Shakespeare 177, 187–92, 194, 196, 200–1, 212, 284 nn.40–42, 286 n.75
       and translation 8, 67, 190
   Moralia 202
Pointon, Marcia 24 250 n.63
Pollard, A. C 282 n.14
Pollard, Tanya 268 n.95
Ponsonby, William 182, 183
Pope, Alexander 227, 229
Portia 18, 45, 202
portraits 3, 10–11, 18–22, 30–1, 105, 145, 158
   Lady Anne Clifford 125
   possible sitter as Cleopatra 106, 120–9, 131, 132, 135–8, 140–3, 154, 173, 219

Lady Ralegh, Elizabeth
Throckmorton 117
and lack of plausibility
as Cleopatra sitter
106–14, 142
Primaticcio, Francesco 226
Propertius 5, 8
Protestantism 13, 26, 27, 36,
38, 65, 67, 79, 81, 95
cause of international
Protestantism 32, 57, 58,
62
and French Huguenots
38, 44, 46, 52, 62
and St Bartholomew's
Day massacre 61–2,
63
English forward Protestant
cause 27, 30, 38, 40, 45,
52, 56, 57, 63, 64, 72, 76,
77, 78, 81, 95, 99
and civil war and
succession anxieties
30, 38, 53, 53, 58, 61,
62, 67, 76–7, 255 n.29
and view of peace with
Catholic Spain 208–9
Pucci, Giuseppe 291 n.24
Putter, Ad 250 n.65

queenship, ideas of 26, 33 *see
also* female sovereignty
and conflicted response to
26, 223
and female sexuality 37, 59

race and gender 2, 3, 4, 6, 7, 8,
33, 146, 201–3
Radegund (*Faerie Queene*) 194
Rainbow, Edward 274 n.79

Ralegh, Lady Elizabeth (née
Throckmorton) 114–15
appeals 113
portrait 117
and connections with
Anne Clifford 142
see also Clifford as
Cleopatra sitter
inscription 108, 112–14
investigation and
provenance of the
portrait 109–12
lack of plausibility 116,
117
as possible sitter as
Cleopatra 106–9
Ralegh, Sir Walter 109, 142,
portrait 116, 118
and Daniel 114–16
Discoverie of Guiana
112–13
History of the World 115,
271 n.32
*The 21th: and last books of
the Ocean to Scinthia* 88
Tower incarceration 113,
115, 142
Ramsbury 38, 64, 130
Randolph, Thomas 79, 263
n.33
Rankins, William 249 n.56
Rees, Joan 86, 164, 255 n.29,
264 n.38
Renaissance 2, 8, 12, 17, 22, 24,
26, 40, 93, 175, 219
classicism 124, 160
and likeness in portraits
123–4
Revels Office, censorship 44,
130 *see also* censorship

revision, Daniel and culture of
    the Sidney circle 71–2,
    91–3
Reynolds, Graham 275 n.101
Reynolds, Sir Joshua 269 n.7
Rich, Lady Penelope 94, 98, 135
    secret correspondence with
        James I 95
Richardson, Catherine 273 n.69
Robinson, Richard 250 n.57,
    287 n.85
Rodon 150, 155, 164, 165, 170,
    173
Roger, Mary, Lady Harington
    142
Roller, Duane W. 4, 222, 246
    n.6
Roman emperors
    Augustus and affinities with
        Philip II 46, 56–7
    and ambivalence towards
        27, 63, 166, 206–11
    and in Sidney Circle 56,
        63, 284 n.44
    negative accounts of 13, 28
Roman history, importance
    in the Sidney and Essex
    circles 37, 65–7, 73, 223
Roman virtue 65, 100–1
    diminishment in Shakespeare
        211
Roman war machine 169
Romito, Sandra 269 n.5
Rosa (pavan, Danyel) 162–3
    as collaborative effort 162–3,
        280 n.43
Rose, Mary Beth 262 n.23
Rowlandson, Thomas 111
Rowley, Simon, *When You See
    Me, You Know Me* 208

Rowse, A. L. 214, 290 n.3
Royal College of Music 158
Royalist plays, and Cleopatra
    as figure of resistance 32,
    214, 218
Royster, Francesca T. 287 n.90
Russell, Lady Elizabeth 130
Rustcastle, Emma 272 n.63
Rutter, Carol Chillington 287
    n.90
Ruutz-Rees, Caroline 258 n.76
Rylance, Mark 157

Sackville, Edward, 4th Earl of
    Dorset 171, 172
Sackville, Richard, Lord
    Buckhurst, 3rd Earl of
    Dorset 121, 124, 132,
    133, 138, 139, 141, 157,
    171
    and Larkin portrait 126
    and masque performances
        157–8, 279 n.32
    and possession of masque
        stockings 131, 273 n.69
Sackville, Thomas, 1st Earl of
    Dorset 172
Sackville-West, Robert 281 n.56
Salluste Du Bartas, Guillaume
    de, *Divine Weeks and
    Works* 44
Salome 114
Salzman, Paul 271 n.44
Sancroft, Archbishop William
    76
Sanders, Eve Rachelle 51, 60,
    87, 256 n.45, 257 n.54
Savile, Henry 28, 66–7, 252
    n.80
Scarsi, Selene 227

Schafer, Elizabeth 129, 272 n.63
Schanzer, Ernest 193, 204, 285 n.55, 287 n.92
Schiff, Stacy 222, 292 n.27
Schlueter, June 264 n.41
Sedgewick, George 122
Sedley, Sir Charles, *Antony and Cleopatra* 216, 290 n.9
Semiramis 5, 6, 18
Seneca 12–13, 27, 63, 69 *see also* closet drama
sententiae 271 n.42
Seronsy, Cecil C. 266 n.69, 268 n.97
Shakespeare, William, works
   Antony and Cleopatra 1, 2, 3, 24, 25–6, 31–2, 37, 39, 134, 220, 222, 244
     cross-dressing 33, 194
     dominance of Shakespeare's characterization 1–2, 179, 221: and decentring Shakespeare 33–4; part of a continuum of Cleopatras 2, 4, 146, 201–3
     duality of perspectives 178, 188, 210
     experimentation with structure, language and genre 185–6, 187: as court or literary play 185–7
     historical-political context 206–12
     influence of Daniel 84, 93, 148, 168, 196–201, 204–5: and 1607 *Cleopatra* 204–5
     influence of Mary Sidney 192–6, 201
     influence of Plutarch (primary source) 177, 187–192
     nostalgia for Elizabeth and disillusionment with James 206–7, 208, 209, 211, 212
     paradox and variety of Cleopatra 178, 188, 201–3: and race 202–3
     publication history, delay in 179–87
     theatrical challenges, number of locations, speaking parts 178, 185–6
   As You Like It 180, 181, 182
   Hamlet 178, 184
     influence of Daniel's Cleopatra 173
   Henry IV, Part I 183
   Julius Caesar 183–4
   King Lear 177, 178
     virtue in reception of letters, Cordelia and Daniel's Cleopatra 101–2
   Love's Labour Lost 197
   Macbeth 178, 284 n.34
     and Banquo's allusion to Antony 189
   Othello 177
   Pericles 179, 282 n.8
   Rape of Lucrece 197, 248 n.41, 264 n.46
   Richard III 183, 184
   Romeo and Juliet 197
   sonnets 194, 195, 210, 214
   The Tempest 204–5

Shakespeare Institute 149, 170, 278 n.25
Shapiro, James 183, 197, 281 n.2
Shaw, Bernard, *Caesar and Cleopatra* 222, 291 n.25
Shawqi, Ahmed, *Death of Cleopatra (Maṣra' Kiliyūpātra)* 222, 291 n.25, 292 n.26
  and as resistance figure to colonial forces 222
Sidney circle
  and ambivalence to Augustus 56, 63, 284 n.44
  and culture of revision 71–2, 91–3
  and use of history 37, 65–7, 73, 223
Sidney, Sir Henry 40
Sidney, Mary, Countess of Pembroke 3, 26, 83
  Antonius 11, 12, 13, 27, 29–30, 34, 35, 82, 222
  and authorial voice in translation 49–57
  and significance of 37–8
  and collaborative effort with Daniel 67, 68, 69, 70, 71, 82, 123
  and cultural contexts 40–7
  and Garnier-Sidney Cleopatra 47–58, 61, 67, 133–4, 219, 220, 244
  and influence on Shakespeare 192–6, 201
  and metaphor of fire 81
  and political commentary 37–8, 39–40, 44, 53, 55–8, 61, 213
  and private passion versus public duty 36, 51, 57, 58, 59, 64, 65–6
  and sense of regret in 58–61
  and scholarly interest in 45–6
  and virtue 64–8
  A Discourse on Life and Death 35, 40, 43, 61–3, 71
  and Fraunce 41
  and mourning 40–1, 42, 48, 58
  and the Raleghs 114, 115
  Sidney Psalms 43, 45, 92–3
Sidney, Mary Dudley 40
Sidney, Sir Philip 28, 29, 30, 35, 37, 46, 56, 92, 135, 194
  death and memorialization 40–2, 43, 58, 95
  friendship with Philippe de Mornay 35, 61–2
  reading of Tacitus 65, 66, 67, 101
  works
    Arcadia 26, 46, 57, 63, 93, 121, 271 n.43
    Astrophil and Stella 74, 262 n.19
    Defence of Poesy 42, 121, 255 n.29
    Gorboduc 255 n.29
    'A Letter to Queen Elizabeth Touching her Marriage to Monsieur' 38

Sidney, Sir Robert 65, 66, 100, 101
  and reading of Tacitus 65, 66, 67, 100, 101, 260 n.105
Skinner, Quentin 101, 268 n.94
Skretkowicz, Victor 46, 53, 254 n.16, 259 n.88
Smith, Simon 158
Smuts, Malcolm 28, 253 n.9
Spanish Armada 41, 51–2, 57–8, 63, 208, 258 n.63
Spanish imperialism 56–7, 67, 77, 78
Spence, Richard T. 120
Spenser, Edmund
  and Daniel 85, 95,
  and Ralegh 115
  and influence on Shakespeare 193, 209
  and use of allegory 25, 54, 57, 259 n.84
  works
    'Colin Clouts Come Home Againe' 70, 115, 261 n.7, 270 n.31
    Faerie Queene 20, 54, 57, 80, 115, 193, 194, 202, 209–10, 270 n.31
    Mutabilitie Cantos 88
    Prothalamion 95, 266 n.73
    The Shepheards Calendar 57, 259 n.85
Spevack, Martin 183, 193, 197
St Bartholomew's Day massacre 61–2, 63
Stafford, Anthony 131–2, 274 n.73
Stamatakis, Chris 263 n.32, 264 n.46

Stapleton, Thomas 24
Starks, Lisa S. 210, 289 n.118
statues *see* Vatican *Cleopatra* statue
Steppat, Michael 285 n.56
Stevens, Crosby 249 n.48
Stevenson, Jane 70, 140, 261 n.3
Stiff, Emily 165, 173, 174, 281 n.62
Stoicism 12–13, 36, 51, 62, 83, 132, 146, 214
Stoll, Jessica 271 n.42
Straznicky, Marta 26, 29, 129, 252 n.84, 272 n.62, 282 n.17
Streitberger, W. R. 273 n.70, 284 n.37
Strong, Roy 88, 265 n.61, 273 n.72
Stuart, Arbella 159
Stuart, Mary *see* Mary Queen of Scots
Stubbs, John 44
Sudeley Castle 130
Suicide, shifting perspectives 12–13, 132–3
Suzman, Janet 221, 222, 291 n.23

Tacitus 13, 27–8, 55, 61, 65, 100, 101, 223, 288 n.112
  aphorisms 28, 252 n.81
  obscura verba 141, 275 n.100
Talbot, Gilbert, Earl of Shrewsbury 158
Tanner, Marie 259 n.82
tapestries 16–17, 217, 218, 219
Tarn, W. W. 291 n.21
Tassi, Marguerite A. 285 n.48

Telnae, Ann 246 n.4
Thomas, William, *The Historie of Italie* 83, 226, 233, 264 n.40
Tiramani, Jenny 127, 157, 272 n.60, 278 n.27, 278 n.28
Tomlinson, Sophie 131, 273 n.70
tragedies
  Cleopatra in sixteenth century 11–12
  Daniel and language of 83, 205
  performance by child companies136–7
  Renaissance tragedy and complaint in 175
tragic femininity 85, 167 *see also* women and female heroism
translation and women 43–4 *see also* women
Treason Acts 44, 88
Trump, Donald 2
Tsukada, Yuichi 212, 288 n.109
Tuim, Jehan de, *Li hystoire de Julius Cesar* 7
Turberville, George 249 n.52
Tsukada, Yuichi 212, 288 n.109
Tyldesley, Joyce 291 n.21
tyranny 31, 35, 36, 51, 62, 65, 244

UCL production
  staging of Daniel's *Cleopatra* 275 n.1
    actors' response 172–5
    adapting and editing for performance 154–6: costumes 157, 158, 159; lead roles 146; music 157, 158, 162–3, 265 n.50; props 160
    insights gained from performance 161–70: Chorus 153, 15–6, 163–5, 170, 174; *Cleopatra* and idea of complaint 161–3; and *Rosa* pavan 162–3, 265 n.50
    performability 154, 167, 170, 172–3: and implicit performance cues 149, 150–1
    spaces 31, 146, 148–9, 166–7, 170–2
Una (*Faerie Queene*) 26
Union of two crowns 96, 166

Valois, Marguerite de 62
Van Kampen, Clare 157
Vasari, Giorgio 226
Vatican *Cleopatra* statue 8–9, 12, 24, 32, 61, 82, 84, 107, 219, 225–7
ventriloquizing 48, 265 n.53
Virgil, *Aeneid* 5, 13
virtue and *virtù* 65, 100–1, 211
  and confusion as 100–2

Walker, Julia M. 212, 289 n.120, 289 n.123
Walsingham, Lady Audrey 159
Walsingham, Sir Francis 52, 62, 255 n.31
Walter, Harriet 186
Waters, Mike 173, 174, 281 n.62
Waterson, Simon 136, 182, 183, 184

Watkins, John 267 n.77, 267 n.83
Watson, G. 250 n.62
Watson, Nicola J. 208, 267 n.77
Wedderburn, Robert 249 n.56
Weis, René 13, 26, 137, 186, 214, 261 n.11, 274 n.90, 290 n.3
Welbeck Abbey 217, 218
Wells, Stanley 286 n.76
Wentworth, Peter 77, 263 n.29
Whipday, Emma 146, 164, 276 n.5, 281 n.56
White, Micheline 255 n.35
White, Robert (engraving, Lady Anne Clifford) 123–5
Wiggins, Martin 192, 273 n.69, 278 n.25, 279 n.32, 281 n.2, 282 n.11, 282 n.16, 284 n.34
Wilders, John 20, 189, 281 n.1, 284 n.34
Williams, Gweno 129, 272 n.63
Williams, Nigel, *Elizabeth I* (TV series) 279 n.36
Williams, Penry 113, 254 n.13, 270 n.25
Williamson, George 271 n.46
Williamson, Marilyn 7–8, 26
Wilson, J. Dover 204
Wilton House 33, 38, 46, 67, 70, 78, 83, 130, 139, 244
Witherspoon, Alexander M. 257 n.56
women
  as 'devisers' (cultural and literary production) 27, 70, 130, 140
  elite women
    and agency 103, 119, 134, 139, 141, 145
    and responses to Cleopatra 105, 107, 109, 118–19, 134, 139–40, 142–3, 145, 220
    and self-representation 110, 140, 145
    and vulnerable situation 85, 87, 138
  female complaint genre 86, 265 n.52
    and Cleopatra as a figure of 31, 85, 87, 212, 221: and working of music in *Cleopatra* production 265
    and Daniel experimentation with modes of 85–7, 120
    and English vogue for 84, 120
  female heroism 67, 87, 105, 119, 130, 134, 139, 142, 145, 152, 167, 218, 220
  female sovereignty 2, 5, 25, 26, 31, 33, 39, 67, 71, 76, 134, 142, 171, 207, 214
  feminine voice 48, 68, 86
  feminist scholarship 45, 87, 203, 221
  gender 29, 33, 40, 85
    and race 2, 3, 4, 6, 7, 8, 26, 33, 146, 201–3
    and performance 32–3, 105, 146
  tragic femininity 85, 167
    and translation 43–4
Wood, Clive 280 n.41
Woods, Susanne 289 n.2
Worden, Blair 28–9, 64, 71, 95, 254 n.14

Wormald, Jenny 267 n.80, 280 n.50, 288 n.104
Woudhuysen, H. R. 93, 249 n.47, 254 n.15, 254 n.24, 255 n.31, 266 n.65, 266 n.67, 268 n.4, 282 n.11
Wray, Romana 272 n.63
Wriothesley, Henry, 3rd Earl of Southampton 95, 160, 279 n.39
Wroth, Lady Mary 130, 135
Love's Victory staging 273 n.64
Wyke, Maria 4, 246 n.2, 246 n.8
Wynne-Davies, Marion 29, 129, 218, 253 n.5, 255 n.35, 276 n.3

Yedeux, Martial, *The Death of Cleopatra* 15–16

Zenobia 16, 17, 18

www.ingramcontent.com/pod-product-compliance
Lightning Source LLC
Chambersburg PA
CBHW070335240426
43665CB00045B/2009